D1524445

Presidios of Spanish West Florida

Florida Museum of Natural History: Ripley P. Bullen Series

PRESIDIOS OF
SPANISH WEST FLORIDA

JUDITH A. BENSE

University of Florida Press

GAINESVILLE

27 26 25 24 23 22   6 5 4 3 2 1

Library of Congress Cataloging-in-Publication Data
Names: Bense, Judith Ann, author.
Title: Presidios of Spanish West Florida / Judith A. Bense.
Other titles: Ripley P. Bullen series.
Description: Gainesville : University of Florida Press, [2022] | Series: Florida Museum of Natural
History: Ripley P. Bullen series | Includes bibliographical references and index. | Summary: "This
book provides the first comprehensive synthesis of historical and archaeological investigations
conducted at the fortified settlements built by Spain in the Florida panhandle from 1698 to 1763"
— Provided by publisher.
Identifiers: LCCN 2021040784 (print) | LCCN 2021040785 (ebook) | ISBN 9781683402558
(hardback) | ISBN 9781683402770 (pdf)
Subjects: LCSH: Fortification—West Florida—History. | Indians of North America—West Florida—
History. | Spaniards—West Florida—History. | Spaniards—West Florida—Antiquities. | Florida—
History—Spanish colony, 1565–1763. | West Florida—Civilization—Spanish influences. | BISAC:
SOCIAL SCIENCE / Archaeology | SOCIAL SCIENCE / Ethnic Studies / American / Native
American Studies
Classification: LCC F317.W5 B46 2022 (print) | LCC F317.W5 (ebook) | DDC 975.9/01—dc23
LC record available at https://lccn.loc.gov/2021040784
LC ebook record available at https://lccn.loc.gov/2021040785

University of Florida Press
2046 NE Waldo Road
Suite 2100
Gainesville, FL 32609
http://upress.ufl.edu

UF PRESS

UNIVERSITY
OF FLORIDA

This book is dedicated to the people who made it possible, especially the hundreds of University of West Florida archaeology students, staff, and colleagues along with the many loyal volunteers from the Pensacola Archaeological Society. These people worked hard in the long, hot Florida summers, the field and campus labs processing the huge assemblages, and the dusty archives digging out and translating long forgotten documents, plus computerizing all the archaeological information into a database and applying GIS mapping. This book is a testament to their diligence and professionalism in the decades of research on the early Spanish presidios, missions, outposts, and a shipwreck left behind by the Spanish and Native Americans who lived in West Florida in the early eighteenth century.

Contents

Figures

Tables

Appendixes

Supplemental online appendixes are available at
http://doi.org/10.5744/9781683402558-Appendixes.

Preface

In the early sixteenth century, West Florida, specifically Pensacola Bay, was visited by several early Spanish explorers such as Pánfilo de Narváez in 1528 and Francisco Maldonado in 1540–1542. In 1559, Pensacola Bay was selected along with Santa Elena to be one of two new port towns on the two coasts of Spanish Florida. Fifteen hundred people landed in Pensacola and began to build the town of Santa María de Ochuse. Unfortunately, five weeks after landing, a hurricane destroyed the embryonic settlement and almost all their supplies (Worth et al. 2019). This disaster doomed the settlement effort on Pensacola Bay, and it was abandoned in 1561. For the next 133 years, Spanish attention then focused on East Florida while West Florida slipped into oblivion. Several presidios, fortified outposts, and scores of missions were established in East Florida from North Carolina to Miami, but only San Agustín survived.

During the seventeenth century, the English and French grabbed huge parts of Spanish Florida as the Spanish simply could not defend their extensive land claim in eastern North America, and by the end of that century, all that remained of Spanish Florida was little more than the peninsula, with the French and English closing in. This pressure was the cause of the next Spanish occupation of West Florida in 1698, and it is where this book begins. All of a sudden, Pensacola Bay became extremely important to the Spanish, but many changes had taken place since the Luna settlement attempt in 1559–1561: in particular, the Native American population had vanished. During the eighteenth century, Native Americans returned to West Florida either as refugee Christians or hostile British-allied Creeks. Throughout the Presidio Period (1698–1763) there was constant fighting between the English, French, and Spanish in West Florida, turning the region into a war zone with only brief periods of peace.

I have tried to intertwine history and archaeology throughout this book, but there are relatively long technical sections that build the necessary factual basis for the integration, interpretation, and conclusions presented in the latter chapters. For researchers in Spanish history and archaeology, the technical chapters present a summary of a huge archaeological data set and analyses of hundreds of historical documents left behind by the people who lived and survived in the virtual wilderness of Spanish West Florida west of the Apalachicola River between 1698 and 1763. There are eight online appendixes containing a great deal of archaeological data for researchers who wish to see the full suite of data in addition to the summary tables in the text. These appendixes are available at http://doi.org/10.5744/9781683402558-Appendixes.

Most of this book presents a detailed summary of the information gathered from the four presidio communities, a mission village, and a shipwreck. While my colleagues, students, and I have initiated or produced much of the information since 1985, historians have been researching the early Spanish occupation of Pensacola and West Florida long before us, beginning with Woodbury Lowery in 1901 and continuing with many others (for example, Arnade 1959; Faye 1941, 1946a, 1946b; Ford 1939; Griffen 1959; Manucy 1959; Priestley 1928). With the founding of the University of West Florida (UWF) in Pensacola in 1967, colonial historical research increased under the leadership of William Coker, professor of history (Coker 1984, 1996, 1997, 1998a, 1998b; Coker and Childers 1998; Coker and Inglis 1980; Coker and Watson 1986).

Archaeologists have been researching the early Spanish period in West Florida for over half a century, starting with Hale Smith at Florida State University (FSU), who conducted extensive excavations in West Florida at Presidio Isla de Santa Rosa, Punta de Sigüenza on Pensacola Bay in 1964 (Smith 1965) and Presidio San José de Panzacola on St. Joseph Bay in 1965 (no publication). Hale Smith was my department chair while I attended FSU and earned my bachelor's and master's degrees, and he would be astounded that I have followed so closely in his footsteps of research of Spanish West Florida.

Although there had been significant research on the early Spanish period in West Florida, most historians and archaeologists focused on later colonial periods, and the early Spanish period was the least understood. This lack of knowledge was a big part of the intrigue of this mysterious early Spanish occupation in West Florida. Despite the problems of documents written in eighteenth-century Spanish and a 25-year gap in archaeological research in West Florida since Smith's investigations, we started on the quest to answer the big and small questions about what happened and why in the first permanent Spanish occupation of West Florida. From the start, I incorporated historians as full partners to archaeologists, and they searched the archives in Spain, Mexico, and the United States as we located and investigated the material remains of the early eighteenth-century communities. This book is the product of all our research, and my hope is that it brings Spanish West Florida into the sunshine and tells the rest of the story of early Spanish Florida.

Acknowledgments

I have had the good fortune of experiencing a long and very interesting career in archaeology, and this book presents a synthesis of one of the most remarkable endeavors of which I have been a part. I have now reached my "golden years," and pulling together the work of hundreds of people who were part of the discoveries and studies of the once poorly understood early Spanish occupation of West Florida has been a labor of love.

At the very core of the decades of research is the support I have received from the University of West Florida (UWF) administration, and I gratefully acknowledge that it would not have happened without their support. From the time I literally "walked on" to UWF in 1980 to the present day, UWF administrators have supported me and the archaeology program. The latest example of University support is from the UWF Board of Trustees. I had started writing this synthesis in 2006, but in 2008, the Board selected me to be the fifth president of UWF. After having the privilege to serve the University in this capacity for almost nine years, the Board of Trustees provided me with the support to complete this manuscript in my post-presidency years. Their assistance was critical as I re-entered archaeology and prepared this manuscript. I greatly appreciate their faith in me.

Funding was also essential to the research at the presidio and related sites in West Florida. The funds were primarily from several large and small grants from the State of Florida, Department of State, Division of Historical Resources. These grants enabled many large, long-term projects to be conducted over the course of several years, providing an unparalleled sample of the cultural materials and historical documents left behind by the early eighteenth-century residents of Spanish West Florida. The United States Navy funded the initiation of this research endeavor with a Legacy grant, and there has been a great deal of in-kind support from Naval Air Station Pensacola, the National Park Service Gulf Islands National Seashore, the Florida State Parks System, and the City of Pensacola.

It is impossible to acknowledge each and every person who significantly participated in the many projects that have contributed to this project. However,

I will try to point out the key participants who were most critical during the three decades and the many research projects. At the very top of the people to acknowledge are the hundreds of UWF *students* who actually conducted the research as they learned how to do archaeology, how to document an excavation, and how to understand an archaeological site and its transformation from a community of living people into strata, artifacts, and features. They also learned how to decipher historical documents written by and about the people and communities we were studying. The graduate students get a particularly strong acknowledgement as their extra efforts were invaluable. Not only did they learn the next level of conducting historical and archaeological research, but twenty-four conducted their own research for their theses and dissertations, which have added another dimension to the research. These former graduate students and their graduation dates are listed at the end of these acknowledgments, and these scholars are making new contributions to our discipline.

I must also acknowledge the unwavering support of hundreds of volunteers from the Pensacola Archaeological Society who worked thousands of hours alongside the students, faculty, and staff, helping us every step of the way. I thank each and every one of the Society members. I have learned a great deal from working with the volunteers and getting to know them.

Guiding and teaching the students and volunteers were the UWF faculty and staff. When this project started, I was the only archaeological faculty, but others have been added over time, and I thank them. Underwater archaeology Professor John Bratten taught students how to conserve fragile and unstable artifacts, and he along with Professor Greg Cook taught them underwater field techniques of excavating shipwrecks, one of which served Presidio Santa María and sunk here in a 1705 hurricane. Historians were a full partner in all the research projects, and UWF Professors William Coker, Jane Dysart, and John Clune made significant contributions as well as taught all the historical archaeology students the discipline of history. When archaeology Professor John Worth joined the anthropology faculty in 2006, he brought his incredible background in Spanish colonial archaeology and anthropological theory to our study of Spanish West Florida. He focused on the untouched refugee Indian missions that had been allied with the Spanish living at the presidios. His expertise in paleography and ethnohistory added an entirely new dimension of information from the Spanish documents he reads and understands so easily. These faculty members—Bratten, Cook, Coker, Dysart, Clune, and Worth—were an excellent team, and I was very lucky to work with them on the Spanish West Florida research.

There are some key senior staff members who have been indispensable to the myriad of large and small projects conducted on the presidios and missions over the years. Elizabeth Benchley, Director of the Archaeology Institute, has been essential to the support of students and faculty through assistantships and summer salaries. She administered the complex budgets through complex bureaucracies along with Karen Mims, the administrative specialist. Dr. Benchley is also an accomplished archaeologist and has conducted several large presidio projects and served on many thesis committees.

Essential to this or any other integrative synthesis is consistent classification and organization of archaeological artifacts. We are blessed that after teaching high school biology in her first career, Janet Lloyd found archaeology as a second career. Jan earned a degree in anthropology/archaeology at UWF and helped in many presidio research projects in the field, but she found her niche as our laboratory director. She has overseen all the classification, re-classification of older collections, curation, coding, and database of the artifact assemblage of over 94,000 items recovered from the West Florida presidios and missions. One can trust the classifications in this dataset. Organizing and building the database of archaeological provenience and classification information for this synthesis was done by another staff member who must be acknowledged. Jennifer Melcher spent countless hours building the presidio database and then holding my hand as I learned how to use the Access program. In addition, Jennifer generated all the figures for this book and kept her good attitude as I had her edit them many, many times.

It is of great importance that I recognize my editor at the University of Florida Press, Meredith M. Babb, for her encouragement and support of me during the 14 years it took to prepare this manuscript. Meredith understood the "long pause" in its preparation while I served as University President, and when I stepped down in 2017, she supported my completing this manuscript. It took almost four more years and a completely new start, but without her support and encouragement, this book would not exist. Thank you, Meredith Babb.

I must thank the manuscript preparation team, Deborah Mullins, Kyndall Barcomb, and Jennifer Melcher. I am not a strong writer, but Deborah is; she is also a professional archaeologist (and my former graduate student assistant). Her vocabulary is incredible, and she understands how to make my first drafts much, much better. Kyndall comes from the discipline of English, and grammar is her specialty. She had a lot of work to do with copyediting the manuscript, formatting the tables and references, and implementing the press guidelines. Both Deborah and Kyndall have made this book more accurate, readable, and informative. Jennifer handled all the database issues and generated all the figures for this book. After all, a picture is still worth a thousand words.

My final acknowledgment is to my parents, Herbert ("Bud") and Bette

Bense. Although they are long gone, they taught me that hard work always pays off and to finish what I start. Although both died while I was still a young student, they were so happy I was following my dream of being an archaeologist. So am I.

Graduate Student Theses and Dissertations on Spanish West Florida Presidios and Missions

Master's Theses

David Breetzke (1996), Ashley Chapman (1998), Norma Harris (1999), Sandra Johnson (1999), Brenda Swann (2000), James Wilson (2000), James Hunter (2001), Catherine Parker (2001), Marie Pokrant (2001), Michael Renacker (2001), Cynthia Sims now deceased (2001), Carrie Williams (2004), Krista Eschbach (2007), Mary Furlong (2008), Nicholas Laracuente (2008), James Greene (2009), Amanda Roberts (2009), Jennifer Melcher (2011), April Holmes (2012), Patrick Johnson (2012), Morgan Wampler (2012), Danielle Dadiego (2014), Michelle Pigott (2015), Patricia McMahon (2017).

Doctoral Dissertations

Krista Eschbach (2019), Arizona State University, and Patrick Johnson (2018), College of William and Mary.

1

Introduction

This book is a synthesis of a vast body of information produced by historical archaeologists, historians, their students, and the interested public about the Spanish West Florida Presidio Period (1698–1763). East of the Apalachicola River, this early Spanish period of Florida is well understood. Research by archaeologists and graduate students from the University of Florida (UF) and Florida State University (FSU), together with projects carried out by the Florida Division of Historical Resources, the City of St. Augustine, and cultural resource management (CRM) firms, has produced an extensive body of scholarship on seventeenth- and eighteenth-century Spanish East Florida. Their tradition of excellence extends to efforts of interpreting and sharing this knowledge with the public. However, the early colonial Spanish occupation in the Florida panhandle *west* of the Apalachicola River has also been studied by many excellent researchers, but this research is not well known. The main purpose of this book is to pull together the wealth of available information about West Florida in the seventeenth and eighteenth centuries to complete "the rest of the story" of early colonial Spanish Florida.

Before delving into this synthesis of Spanish West Florida, it is important to understand that the historical archaeological research conducted in West Florida was and is a bit different than research elsewhere, owing to the early and continual inclusion of the general public in almost all the endeavors. This inclusion started in the mid-1960s with Hale G. Smith, then chair of the Anthropology Department at FSU, where I was a student between 1963 and 1969 earning my bachelor's and master's degrees. At that time, Smith was one of a handful of historical archaeologists in the country, and he focused on the rich early Spanish legacy of north and west Florida (Smith 1948a, 1948b, 1949, 1994). In the 1950s, Smith, historian Mark Boyd, and archaeologist John Griffin conducted research at the large Apalachee mission of San Luis de Talimali in Tallahassee, and they published their seminal work in 1951 (Boyd et al. 1951). Smith (1948, 1949) also conducted research on other seventeenth-century Spanish missions in north Florida. In early 1964, at the request of Norman Simons, assistant curator of the Pensacola Historical Society museum, Smith viewed a collection of Spanish pottery from a site on Santa Rosa Island near the pass into Pensacola Bay. Smith immediately recognized that the site must be that of the Spanish presidio Isla de Santa Rosa, Punta de Sigüenza that existed there between 1723 and 1756. He conducted extensive excavations there in the summer of 1964 with his students and many members of the Pensacola Historical Society (Smith 1965). Several local and state organizations helped support Smith with housing and funding. The Santa Rosa project marked the beginning of the public's involvement in West Florida historical archaeology. Previously, in 1963, Smith had been asked by the Gulf County Florida Historical Commission and other local interest groups to locate an early Spanish site on the peninsula of St. Joseph Bay near the mouth of the Apalachicola River. Smith found the site of another Spanish presidio, San José de Panzacola, that existed there between 1719 and 1722. In 1965, Smith conducted an eight-week excavation at the San José site with his students and many members of the public, especially members of the Port St. Joe-Gulf County Historical Society. They hoped that the site would be developed for the public as part of a new state park on the peninsula. The park was established, but the site was not developed.

By 1967, the University of West Florida (UWF) was established in Pensacola. One of the special aspects of Pensacola is its long Euro-American history, beginning with the ill-fated Luna settlement in 1559. The public there is well aware of this history, and consequently, history was one of the initial primary academic programs at UWF, and the library special collections section specialized in gathering historical documents and publications about West Florida. In 1980, I started an anthropology-archaeology program at UWF, and within a few years we were conducting research in the Pensacola area. Starting an archaeology program from scratch meant that while we had students to teach and train and wonderful sites close at hand, funding for the myriad of necessary activities to conduct professional archaeology was non-existent. In the city, colonial deposits lie just beneath the asphalt, and at that time, they were being increasingly impacted by growth and development. Like almost all archaeologists of my generation, I had been trained and was experienced in pre-Columbian archaeology, but because of the damage to and significance of the historic archaeological deposits being destroyed in Pensacola, I backed into the historic era. With almost no money, but willing students and local citizens eager to help, I reached out to the general public in the newspaper, asking for help from anyone who was willing. The idea worked, and including the general public has been and still is the secret to our success.

Over the course of the next 40 years, public archaeology in Pensacola became the backbone of our academic program, and it has created a citizenry educated in history and archaeology through hands-on participation, media publicity, public products, and organized assistance by a large local support group, the Pensacola Archaeological Society (PAS). The academic program blossomed into an independent department with a large master's program, a research institute, and a state-wide public archaeology network. UWF historical archaeology includes not only terrestrial historical archaeology but also shipwrecks dating back to the 1559 Luna expedition (Smith 2018). The information from each of the eighteenth-century sites included in this synthesis was produced with members of the public working side by side with our students and faculty in the field, laboratories, computerized databases and mapping, writing, and publications. The following synthesis of the Spanish West Florida Presidio Period (1698–1763) is possible only because of the strong academic and public partnership in Pensacola and West Florida.

Historical Context

Beginning in the early sixteenth century, the Spanish orchestrated several exploratory missions and settlement attempts in Spanish Florida, including Ponce de Leon in 1513 and 1521, Narváez in 1528, and Soto in 1539 (see appendix I, http://doi.org/10.5744/9781683402558-Appendixes). As a result, the Spanish Crown had knowledge of the navigable qualities of Pensacola Bay and the potential of surrounding lands for many years before Tristán de Luna y Arellano led a carefully planned colony of settlers and soldiers to its shores in the year 1559. Aside from establishing Pensacola as a base from which to assist in the protection of treasure ships and conveys (flotas) across the Gulf, Caribbean, and Atlantic seaboard, Luna was also under orders to establish a settlement on Port Royal Sound on the mid-Atlantic coast and to mark a route between the two new settlements, following Soto's previous path through Coosa (Worth 2018a: 2).

Tragically, Pensacola was beset almost immediately by a hurricane that stripped the colonists of food, basic supplies, and most of their ships. What followed was a two-year struggle for survival before Pensacola was abandoned in late 1561. The Luna *entrada* was the costliest in a string of failures to explore and settle Spanish Florida, and in 1561, King Philip announced that Spain no longer had an interest in settling the southeastern part of North America (DePratter and South 1990: 4; Quinn 1979: 200). In addition, the king proclaimed that any future undertakings would concentrate only on the area north of Santa Elena because of its position near the turning point of the silver-laden flotillas bound for Spain (McGrath 2000: 114).

Outside of La Florida, the discovery in the 1540s of vast quantities of gold and silver deposits with large Native populations as a nearby labor source in New Spain and Peru immediately became the beating heart and lifeblood of the

Spanish Empire. Spanish colonial policies in the Americas were doggedly mercantilist, and from the earliest days of colonial expansion in the Caribbean and across North, Central, and South America, these policies were laser focused on exploiting resources and defending the transportation of vast quantities of gold and silver extracted from mines. Toward the end of the seventeenth century, the Spanish king decided that a presidio on Pensacola Bay was necessary to help protect the treasure fleets in the Gulf and Caribbean from piracy as well as to check expansion by the British and French. The Crown now called again upon New Spain to settle and hold the northern Gulf coast of La Florida in order to protect the wealth flowing from more lucrative areas of her empire.

In contrast to riches found elsewhere, the coastal area of Spanish West Florida offered neither mineral wealth nor centers of potential human labor. However, Spanish navigators and cartographers had long praised the area's defensible position along the northern Gulf coast, Pensacola Bay's navigable assets, and even the beauty of the bay and its surrounds. These qualities meant that Pensacola Bay was not forgotten and remained a contender as a suitable location for a military outpost that finally materialized when Presidio Santa María de Galve was established there in 1698.

For two hundred years prior to the establishment of Presidio Santa María, Spain poured human labor, money, and military might into a network of support settlements and garrisoned outposts focused on mining centers and other avenues of resource extraction. As the work of colonization and extraction continued, the Crown struggled to contain European rivals who posed a constant threat to her colonial territories and the vast quantities of gold and silver taken from them. One of those mining regions, the famed Potosí mines of northern Peru, sits high in the Andes (13,300 feet), naturally protected by steep terrain and a trek of almost 500 difficult miles from the coast. In contrast, the Zacatecas silver mines in central New Spain are easily accessible from both the Gulf of Mexico and overland routes from the north. Both the French and British had their eye on the Zacatecas silver mines as part of their expansions in eastern North America, as shown in figure 1.1.

The need to protect the mineral wealth extracted from the vulnerable Zacatecas mines compelled the establishment of a string of presidios across northern New Spain. Maritime presidios were established to police the shipping lanes across the Caribbean Sea, the Gulf of Mexico, and up the Atlantic coast of Florida. From the beginning of Spain's systematic extraction of gold and silver from her colonies via a system of coerced physical labor, the transportation of that wealth to Spain guaranteed that the treasure ships immediately became the target of pirates, especially those sanctioned by the British and French. All treasure extracted from New Spain and Peru was first shipped

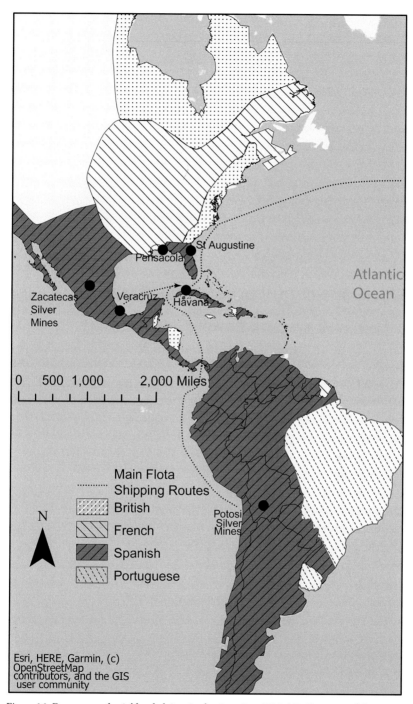

Figure 1.1. European colonial land claims in the Americas 1700 AD. Courtesy of the Archaeology Institute, University of West Florida.

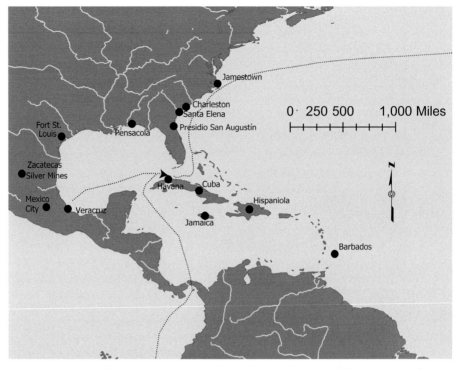

Figure 1.2. Location of some sixteenth- and seventeenth-century colonial settlements in North America and the Caribbean and the flota shipping routes. Courtesy of the Archaeology Institute, University of West Florida.

to Havana, from where flotas of cargo and defense vessels sailed north together up the Atlantic coast to North Carolina before turning east to Spain, as shown in figures 1.1 and 1.2. The routes across the Gulf of Mexico and Caribbean Sea were especially vulnerable to pirates hiding throughout the islands (figure 1.2). The threat of piracy was so serious that by the mid-seventeenth century, the Windward Fleet (*Armada de Barlovento*) was established solely to pursue, capture, or destroy pirates menacing Spanish coastal settlements and treasure ships on their way to Havana (Weddle 1985, 1991: 102).

The Spanish also struggled to protect the flotas sailing along the Atlantic coast, where they rode the Gulf Stream close to shore for 1,000 miles before catching the trade winds to cross the Atlantic. Although they understood that defenses along the east coast were a necessity, the Spanish established and supported settlements on the Atlantic seaboard only after the French secretly built a short-lived fort on Paris Island, South Carolina (Charlesfort) in 1562 and another near Jacksonville, Florida (Fort Caroline) in 1564 (McGrath 2000:

91–115). Sufficiently alarmed, in 1565, the Spanish Crown ordered Pedro Menéndez de Avilés to drive the French from La Florida. Menéndez carried out the king's orders and established three coastal presidios on the Atlantic: San Felipe on the ruins of Charlesfort in South Carolina (DePratter et al. 1996: 8), San Mateo on the ruins of French Fort Caroline in north Florida (Lyon 1996: 44; McGrath 2000: 147), and San Agustín within a thriving Timucuan village in north Florida (Deagan 2009, 2016). In the ensuing 133 years, the Spanish built several forts, missions, and settlements on both coasts of Florida (Lyon 1976) and into the interior west of Santa Elena and San Agustín (Beck et al. 2006, 2016; Bushnell 1994; McEwan 1993). Only Presidio San Agustín survived into the eighteenth century.

During the late sixteenth and seventeenth centuries, a successful Franciscan mission system in the north Florida Apalachee and Timucuan provinces provided Presidio San Agustín with food and labor (Hann 1988; McEwan 1993; Milanich 1999). Administered in San Agustín, the mission system utilized a small number of Spaniards yet controlled a large Native population with adaptable agricultural traditions via a chain of Catholic missions and satellite Native American villages that stretched into the interior of north Florida. In one sense, these now-faithful Native Americans became the king's subjects, who, in the minds of the Iberian elite, owed compensation to the Spanish Crown for their heavenly salvation and enculturation. This presumed debt was paid through labor of all varieties, especially agricultural labor and involuntary rotations on labor crews sent to Presidio San Agustín, and this payment compensated for the fractional Spanish criollo population living in Florida (Bushnell 1996: 66–76; Deagan 1993: 87–102). The late seventeenth century saw the fraying of this mission supply chain and social safety net as San Agustín and the surrounding missions were frequently attacked by British-led Creek, Yamasee, and Westo Indians searching for captives to sell into slavery on the British market (Milanich 1999; Worth 1998).

Presidios were an important part of the colonial defense system of the Spanish Empire. In his overview of the history of Spanish presidios, Jack Williams (2004) states that prior to 1788, a Spanish colonial presidio was a fortified military outpost. In North America, the Crown ordered presidios located in what Russell Skowronek (2002) describes as "protective" rather than "productive" areas. In other words, they were positioned on the contested fringes of the Spanish colonial empire, especially in northern New Spain and Spanish Florida (Skowronek 2002). Two types of presidio systems protected New Spain: terrestrial presidios in the interior of northern New Spain and maritime presidios along the coasts. Between 1688 and 1694, the Spanish established a series of missions in what is now east Texas, but they were short lived (Bruseth et al. 2004: 78; Weddle 1968: 13–15). In 1716, in response to a threat of French invasion on the northeast frontier, the Spanish established another chain of presidios and missions in east Texas and what is now western Louisiana. As J. Williams (2004: 14) details, military discipline at these presidios was lax, and the fortifications themselves were often improperly or under-engineered. Likewise, the presidios of eastern Texas and western Louisiana were occupied by ill-trained militias whose members were poorly supplied, poorly fed, and poorly outfitted; many soldiers lacked even a basic uniform. The presidios in northern New Spain in the eighteenth century were largely self-sufficient, with a garrison of part-time soldiers augmenting their income by ranching, farming, and mining. Gradually, these frontier presidios attracted civilian settlers and became a distinctive kind of military colony, and several developed into current communities and cities (J. Williams 2004: 11). The corruption of presidio commanders was regularly recorded, and officers were often characterized as little more than corrupt storekeepers who profited at the expense of the health and wellbeing of their impoverished soldiers.

By the time Presidio Santa María de Galve was established in Pensacola in 1698, Presidio San Agustín was the lone remaining Spanish outpost on the Atlantic coast. As figure 1.1 shows, the English and French had seized and occupied large swaths of the once vast territory of La Florida; all that remained was the Florida peninsula and a small part of the northeastern Gulf coast. The fact that Spanish Florida was disconnected from New Spain by the French colony of Louisiana was especially vexing for the Spanish as they worked to secure their shipping routes across Caribbean waters from Mexico to Havana and from Havana to Spain. As noted above, it was to these ends that a new coastal presidio on the northern Gulf coast was established on Pensacola Bay in 1698. Together, the West Florida presidio on the northern Gulf coast and Presidio San Agustín on the Atlantic coast shared a two-fold mission: to prevent European rivals from occupying any more of the buffering territory of Spanish Florida and to aid in the protection of Spain's shipping routes.

In contrast to counterparts across northern New Spain, the two remaining Florida presidios at Pensacola and San Agustín were subsidized military installations with formal fortifications and large garrisons of full-time regular soldiers and officers. The shared union of purpose between the two final presidios in Florida invites interesting comparisons which will be explored in detail in chapters 6 and 7 of this synthesis. The presidios differed substantially in both ministerial bureaucracies and community demographics. Presidio San Agustín had its royal orders embedded into the Laws of the Indies. Meanwhile, the Spanish West Florida presidio was under direct control of the viceroy of New Spain and operated by the rules of the Windward Fleet that patrolled the

Gulf and Caribbean (Childers 2004: 27–28). The majority (70%) of the San Agustín Hispanic population were criollo, people of Spanish descent born in the Americas, and *peninsulares*, people born in Spain but residing in her colonies (Deagan 1983: 30–31). In Spanish West Florida, the population began with people of mixed Spanish-Indian-African racial and cultural backgrounds— who Deagan (1973 1983, 2003) identifies as *mestizaje*—who were born in New Spain (Clune 2003: 25; Eschbach 2019: 216, 241). The majority of residents at both presidios were soldiers and laborers, though San Agustín had many civilian settlers, including some from the Canary Islands, Cuba, Hispaniola, and New Spain.

Compounding the woes of La Florida on both coasts, in 1682 René-Robert Cavelier, Sieur de La Salle ventured down the Mississippi River and boldly claimed the entire river drainage for France under the colony of Louisiana. In 1684, he returned and established a small colony, Fort St. Louis, on the northeast Gulf coast of New Spain near modern-day Victoria, Texas. Spain's response to the illegal French settlement was to send out search and destroy parties, though when the Spanish found the site in 1689 it had been destroyed by local Native Americans and abandoned by the French. The Spanish then set out to establish a series of missions between 1688 and 1694 in what is now east Texas, though all were short lived (Bruseth et al. 2004: 78; Weddle 1968: 13–15). Thus, it was the combination of increasingly violent attacks by the British on St. Augustine and the Catholic missions, intrusions by the French along the Gulf coast, and the ongoing security concerns for the Zacatecas silver mines that created the context from which began the story of Spanish West Florida.

Spanish West Florida

Academic research and cultural resource management projects addressing Spanish West Florida during the Presidio Period (1698–1763) have been conducted by the author as well as many archaeologists and historians associated with several universities, government agencies, and private firms. The majority of the resulting data, analyses, and conclusions from these projects is available in books, book chapters, journals, theses, dissertations, and unpublished papers and reports. This book draws on this body of research to provide a detailed summary and synthesis of what is known about the people who lived and survived in the coastal wilderness of Spanish Florida west of the Apalachicola River for 65 years between 1698 and 1763. In addition, this volume points interested readers to the original sources for more detailed information.

This book details how the military community in Spanish West Florida persisted despite almost constant attacks by French and English rivals fighting for control of the southeast and despite Pensacola's isolation on the frontier, some 400 land miles from Presidio San Agustín and 869 nautical miles from Veracruz. For most of the soldiers and civilians who immigrated to West Florida from Veracruz, Mexico City, or other villages and towns in New Spain, Pensacola and West Florida must have felt like the true periphery of civilization. There is no doubt that the presidio community offered hardships enough for everyone, and those hardships were compounded for women, Africans and those of African descent, convict laborers, and the many displaced Native American refugees who passed through or chose to live in satellite mission villages. However, Pensacola's spot at the margins of the Spanish Empire could offer welcome anonymity for some, a chance to work off a debt to society for others, a stable source of income and housing for many, and an economic opportunity for the well-connected, the daring, or the lucky few. Throughout the settlement's existence, Hispanics (*mestizaje*) of every *casta* were sent to Pensacola and survived by hook or crook because they had to, and they did so despite almost constant deprivation of supplies and military support from New Spain and periods of near constant harassment and attack from Spain's European rivals. Their goal was not to build a new society but to secure themselves, their families, and perhaps their fortunes by succeeding within the written and unwritten parameters of a Hispanic frontier military colonial society.

There are at least 23 known locations of occupations in West Florida during the Presidio Period of Spanish West Florida, and they are listed in table 1.1 and shown in figures 1.3 and 1.4. There were seventeen Spanish terrestrial locations and a shipwreck, two French military outposts, and three Indian villages aligned with the British. Several locations were occupied twice for different purposes and by different nationalities. There were ten Spanish military locations: four presidios and six outposts, two of which, St. Joseph Bay and Punta de Sigüenza, were utilized twice at different times. To further complicate matters, there were three refugee communities allied with the Spanish, but two communities had two locations, Apalachee Soledad-Escambe and Yamasee Town-Punta Rasa I. Three short-lived Lower Creek villages were allied at different times with the British and Spanish, and they were located in the upper valleys of the Escambia, Choctawhatchee, and Apalachicola rivers. The French had two military outposts, one on Pensacola Bay and the other on St. Joseph Bay.

After the initial settlement and occupation of Santa María de Galve on the mainland overlooking the entrance to Pensacola Bay, the West Florida presidio was relocated three times. The first move was forced upon the community

Table 1.1. Known settlements in Spanish West Florida, 1698–1763

Type of Settlement	Name	Official Dates	Occupation Dates	Length of Occupation
	Spanish Settlements (18)			
Presidios (4)	Santa María de Galve	1698–1719	1698–1719	21 years
	San Joseph de Panzacola[a]	1719–1723	1719–1722	3 years
	Santa Rosa Punta de Sigüenza[a]	1723–1756	1722–1754	32 years
	San Miguel de Panzacola*	1756–1763	1754–1763	9 years
Outposts (6)	St. Joseph Bay	1700–1703/4 and 1718–1719	[b]	3 or 4 years and 1 year
	Punta de Sigüenza	1703–1704 and 1718–1719	[b]	1 year and 1 year
	San Miguel de Punta Blanca	1741–1756	[b]	15 years
	Santa Rosa	1757–1763	[b]	6 years
Shipwreck (1)	*Nuestra Señora del Rosario y Santiago Apóstol*	1705	[b]	1 year
	Apalachee (4)			
	Perdido River, name unknown	1705–1710(?)	[b]	5 years
	Nuestra Señora de Soledad y San Luis	1718–1741	[b]	23 years
	San Andres	1720–1722(?)	[b]	2 years
Native Refugee Mission Villages (7)	San Joseph de Escambe	1741–1761	[b]	20 years
	Yamasee (2)			
	Yamasee Town	1740–1749	[b]	9 years
	San Antonio de Punta Rasa I	1749–1761	[b]	12 years
	Apalachee and Yamasee (1)			
	San Antonio de Punta Rasa II	1761–1763	[b]	2 years

continued

Table 1.1.—*continued*

| Type of Settlement | Name | British Allied Villages (3) | | |
		Official Dates	Occupation Dates	Length of Occupation
	Los Tobases	1759–1761	[b]	2 years
Lower Creek Villages	Talacayche	1759–1761	[b]	2 years
	Chilacaliche	1715–1763	[b]	48 years

| Type of Settlement | Name | French Settlements (2) | | |
		Official Dates	Occupation Dates	Length of Occupation
	St. Joseph Bay (Fort Crèvocoeur)	1718	[b]	1 year
Outposts (2)	Pensacola Bay (former Santa María)	1719–1722	[b]	3 years

[a] The official and occupation dates did not coincide at these presidios as most of the population was transferred before formal abandonment and official designation of the next presidio.

[b] Occupation dates are the same as official dates.

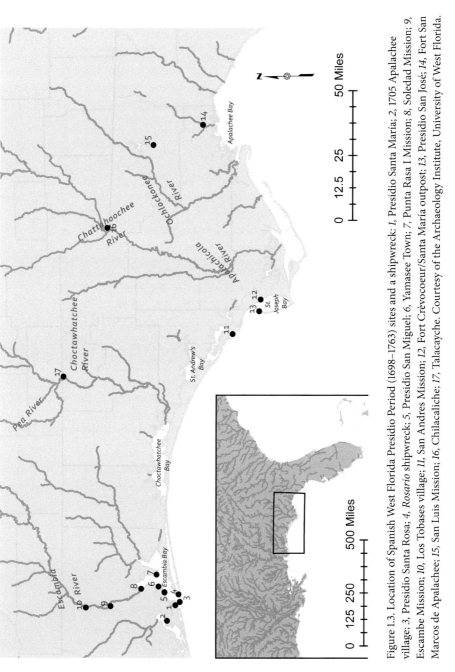

Figure 1.3. Location of Spanish West Florida Presidio Period (1698–1763) sites and a shipwreck: *1*, Presidio Santa Maria; *2*, 1705 Apalachee village; *3*, Presidio Santa Rosa; *4*, *Rosario* shipwreck; *5*, Presidio San Miguel; *6*, Yamasee Town; *7*, Punta Rasa I Mission; *8*, Soledad Mission; *9*, Escambe Mission; *10*, Los Tobases village; *11*, San Andres Mission; *12*, Fort Crèvocoeur/Santa María outpost; *13*, Presidio San José; *14*, Fort San Marcos de Apalachee; *15*, San Luis Mission; *16*, Chilacaliche; *17*, Talacayche. Courtesy of the Archaeology Institute, University of West Florida.

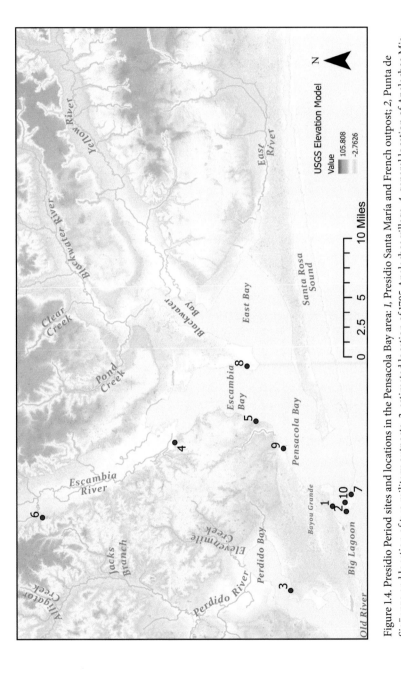

Figure 1.4. Presidio Period sites and locations in the Pensacola Bay area: *1*, Presidio Santa María and French outpost; *2*, Punta de Sigüenza and location of two military outposts; *3*, estimated location of 1705 Apalachee village; *4*, general location of Apalachee Mission Soledad; *5*, Yamasee Town; *6*, Apalachee Mission Escambe; *7*, Presidio Santa Rosa and Santa Rosa outpost; *8*, Yamasee Mission Punta Rasa I; *9*, San Miguel de Punta Blanca outpost, Presidio San Miguel, and Punta Rasa II; *10*, *Rosario* shipwreck. Courtesy of the Archaeology Institute, University of West Florida.

as a result of their defeat and evacuation by French forces in 1719. In 1718, just prior to the French attack on Santa María, the French had covertly intruded into Spanish West Florida and built a fortified outpost 115 miles east of Pensacola at St. Joseph Bay. Though the French quickly left, the Spanish Crown was convinced of the need to better protect the northern Gulf coast of La Florida and ordered the construction of a large presidio, named San José de Panzacola, across the bay from the illegal French outpost. After the French seizure of Pensacola in 1719, the Spanish moved all West Florida operations to Presidio San José, and the newly constructed fortifications became the second location of the Spanish West Florida presidio. Only three years later, in 1722, the Spanish abandoned San José in order to return to Pensacola Bay after a political treaty ended the War of the Quadruple Alliance and returned Pensacola to Spain.

From this point onward in the narrative of the Spanish West Florida presidio community, it should be noted that there is a difference between the dates people arrived and departed from a presidio location and the formal dates of its official establishment and abandonment. For example, much of the population of San José moved back to Pensacola in late 1722, but the official abandonment of Presidio San José and the formal establishment of Presidio Isla de Santa Rosa, Punta de Sigüenza was mid-1723. As shown in table 1.1, there are similar differences at the Santa Rosa and San Miguel presidios. Because the deposition of artifacts and creation of features began when people arrived and ended when they left, in the following archaeological analysis I use the actual occupation dates, not the official records of founding and abandonment.

The third presidio, Santa Rosa, was located on a barrier island near the entrance to Pensacola Bay from the Gulf of Mexico, across from the mainland location of Santa María de Galve. The next and final relocation of the community was caused by a devastating hurricane in 1752 that left Presidio Santa Rosa in ruins. The last Spanish West Florida presidio, christened San Miguel, was relocated to the mainland eight miles from the bay entrance, where it now lies beneath present-day downtown Pensacola.

Following entrenched bureaucratic protocol, each relocation of the West Florida presidio generated scores of government documents, accounts, maps, and letters. Most importantly for archaeologists, the presidio's four relocations produced four separate archaeological sites. The four geographical and sequential chronological divisions of one community over a short 65-year span have provided unprecedented opportunities to identify changes through time in the settlement's demographics, community settlement patterns, military fortification projects, domestic architecture, and material culture of everyday life, among other topics.

In order to present the full range of circumstances and events the West Florida presidio went through, this book consists of two parts. The first is a detailed summary of the archaeological and historical information we discovered at each of the four locations of West Florida's presidio, as well as two mission villages and a wrecked supply ship. Hundreds of documents have been located and studied, and large artifact assemblages were recovered for each archaeological site. The context of the artifact assemblage consists of materials from 545 closed features and sealed midden deposits. The total artifact assemblage consists of 94,501 counted items and 1,285 kg of weighed materials, all of which have been classified using the same system. In addition to the data tables in this volume, there are eight online appendixes with much more detailed data available for researchers to explore and use. The appendixes are available at the University Press of Florida Digital Collections website at http://doi.org/10.5744/9781683402558-Appendixes.

The second section of this book integrates the body of information for comparisons, interpretations, and conclusions. Ultimately, the archaeological information and historical records from the four discrete presidio locations provide the springboard for a narrative of the people, their communities, social organization, and adaptive changes made during the Spanish occupation of West Florida. This was not a typical frontier community of people looking to start a new life in Spanish West Florida. By every measure considered for this study, it is clear that the communities strove to maintain their Hispanic way of life. The maintenance of both physical and cultural boundaries was the purpose of the Spanish colonial presidio. Likewise, in eighteenth-century West Florida, the presidio was established and maintained as a statement of power in the face of Spain's rivals. The settlement was bolstered with a permanent professional military, fortified settlements and outposts, alliances with Native American Catholic mission villages, and ongoing recruitment and conscriptions of Hispanics from New Spain to the frontier.

In sum, this book progresses chronologically through a deep dive into the historical, political, environmental, and material circumstances at each of the four presidio locations before widening the inquiry to include the four presidios in a comparative analysis. The remarkable level of investigative control over time and space for this community is but one beguiling lure for future researchers interested in the archaeology and history of colonial Spanish borderland sites. The topics explored here utilizing the historical and archaeological records of Spanish West Florida lie at the beginning of the anthropological avenues of inquiry possible for further elucidation of human behavior. The author has identified several areas for future research using the available information and hopes that the many years of research integrated in this book will add to the reader's appreciation of the cultural historical processes shaping individual lives and communities at the edge of the Spanish Empire.

2

Return to Pensacola Bay

Presidio Santa María de Galve

With the French and English pushing hard into the southeast, each taking huge portions of Spanish Florida and wanting more, by the end of the seventeenth century all that remained of the original Spanish claim to eastern North America was the Florida peninsula and west to the Apalachicola River. The Spanish had managed to sustain only one settlement, Presidio San Agustín, and a single small, fortified port on the northeast Gulf coast, San Marcos de Apalachee. The mission system was under attack by English slave raiders from the north, and the French had claimed the entire drainage of the Mississippi River for the new Louisiana colony. As shown in figure 2.1, Spanish Florida was hemmed in by land grabs by the French and English who were closing in.

"Rediscovery" of Pensacola Bay and Founding of Presidio Santa María

In 1682, the French had trespassed once again into Spanish Florida 117 years after being driven off the Atlantic coast in 1565. This time, René-Robert Cavelier, Sieur de La Salle, secretly came down the Mississippi River to its mouth at the Gulf of Mexico, where he erected a monument claiming the entire river drainage for France as the colony of Louisiana. This was the first formal claim on the Gulf of Mexico by Europeans other than the Spanish (Weddle 1991: 5–8). Two years later, in 1684, La Salle returned, sailing across the Gulf and intending to go up the Mississippi about 150 miles and establish the capital settlement of the Louisiana colony to protect the river's mouth (Weddle 1991: 12). Leading a fleet of four ships and 300 people to build the new settlement, La Salle missed the river's mouth and landed on the Texas coast near Victoria. There, the French built Fort Saint Louis, and La Salle died searching in vain for the Mississippi; the settlement failed in just a few years (Weddle 1991: 13–25). In 1685, a chance encounter with a La Salle deserter in Santo Domingo alerted the Spanish Court to the covert French intrusion, which the Spanish viewed as a direct threat to their lucrative Zacatecas silver mines in New Spain (Weber 1992: 149).

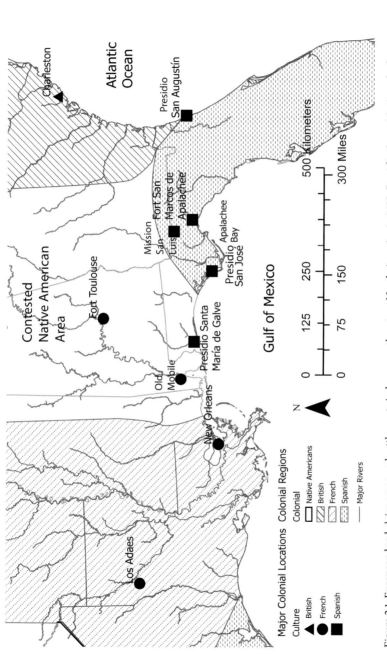

Figure 2.1. European land claim areas and settlements in lower southeastern North America in 1698, Presidio Santa María and other settlements in the region. Courtesy of the Archaeology Institute, University of West Florida.

The Spanish search for Fort Saint Louis began the next year, in 1686, but it was hampered by the Spanish's lack of knowledge of the Gulf coast west of the Apalachicola River. The Spaniards had ignored this portion of the coast since the failed 1559–1561 settlement attempt on Pensacola Bay led by Tristán de Luna y Arellano. They had also forgotten the location of the mouth of the Mississippi River, although Alonso Álvarez de Pineda had discovered it in 1519. In its fervor to thwart French encroachment, the Spanish Crown launched 11 search expeditions, six by land and five by sea, before Alonso de León found the ruins of Fort Saint Louis in 1689 (Bruseth 2014: 34; Weber 1992: 152; Weddle 1968: 14).

The intensive search for French Fort Saint Louis familiarized the Spanish once again with the geography of the northern and western Gulf coast. They "rediscovered" Pensacola Bay and realized the necessity of establishing a Spanish presence in this area of the Gulf coast (Weber 1992: 155–158). The Spaniards first moved to secure the east Texas area in 1688, combining their strategic and religious objectives with a series of three inexpensive missions. However, the Texas Indians rebelled, and the missions failed within a few years (Bruseth et al. 2004: 78; Weddle 1968: 13–15, 19).

During the Spanish search for French Fort Saint Louis, three expeditions entered and explored Pensacola Bay: Juan Enríques Barroto and Antonio Romero in 1686, Admiral Andrés de Pez in 1687, and Juan Jordán de Reina in 1689. Reina was an ensign with the Barroto and Romero expedition and had recorded information in his log about the Indians in the region and described Pensacola Bay as the best he had ever seen (Leonard 1936: 553, 1939: 13–15). While Luna had called the area "Ochuse," Barroto and Romero renamed it "Panzacola" in 1686 after the Panzacola Indians who lived in the area at the time. It is interesting that this expedition went on to Mobile Bay and entered the mouth of the Mississippi. However, the river entrance was choked with dead trees, and neither its significance nor the proximity to the French settlement were understood (Clune 2003: 17; Leonard 1936: 549).

Naval hero Admiral Pez urged the Crown to consider a new presidio on Pensacola Bay before the French or British did so, for the bay had exceptionally deep water and a good harbor. However, the Council of War in Spain called for more research before making a decision and sent Pez and Carlos de Sigüenza y Góngora, Mexico's leading scientist, to lead a group back to Pensacola Bay in 1693 to gather more information (Clune et al. 2003; Leonard 1939). Sigüenza made a map and renamed the bay Bahia de Santa María de Galve. In his report, Sigüenza gave a glowing endorsement for a settlement on the bay, calling it the "finest jewel" possessed by Spain (Leonard 1939: 193–194). Soon after the Pez-Sigüenza survey, the governor of Florida,

Laureano de Torres y Ayala, conducted an expedition to Pensacola Bay by way of Havana to the San Luis de Talimali Apalachee mission and then overland to Mobile Bay. While at Pensacola, Torres confirmed the bay's quality and defensibility, but he also observed the absence of construction-quality stone and the lack of Indian labor (Clune 2003: 19; Coker and Childers 1998: 14; Ford 1939: 21). On this trip, Governor Torres had a chance encounter with British Indian traders north and west of Pensacola Bay. More than the reports of the virtues and potential of Pensacola Bay, it was Torres's description of English interlopers on the doorstep of the Spanish mission provinces of La Florida that finally convinced King Carlos II to support the occupancy of Pensacola (Ford 1939: 20–21; Weber 1992: 156). The next year, in 1694, the Spanish king authorized the occupation of Pensacola, but there was again a bureaucratic delay in action.

It is important to note that in 1686, expedition leader Juan Enríques Barroto reported to his superiors that there were significant timber resources in the Florida panhandle, especially tall, straight pines and cypress for masts and spars. A description of Barroto's findings eventually found the ear of King Charles II (Childers and Cotter 1998: 78). When Pez and Sigüenza mapped Pensacola Bay seven years later, they confirmed the region's forests of tall pines and cypress, especially along the East and Blackwater Rivers. In his report, Sigüenza estimated that these forests could supply stout masts and spars for vessels as large as 600 tons. Pez even had a new main mast made from one of the tall pines while they were in Pensacola Bay (Childers and Cotter 1998: 78; Leonard 1939: 48). In 1694, the king told the viceroy of New Spain to use the forests around Pensacola Bay for masts and spars. While there was a well-established shipbuilding industry in Veracruz, it was reliant on timber imported from South America and northern Europe. The need for a local source of long, straight trees for masts and spars was particularly important (Hunter 2001: 16–17). As James Hunter (2001: 17) describes, by the next year, 1695, Pensacola had "become the locus of a fledgling timber industry designed to supply the Windward Fleet with masts and spars." In 1695, Andrés de Arriola was sent to Pensacola Bay with a crew of 250 men and orders to mark trees and cut poles (Hunter 2001: 34–35; Leonard 1939: 67). In Pensacola, Arriola utilized the forests along the East River, where he cut 86 tall pines. After removing the bark and shaping the trunks, the poles were floated to the ships in the bay and loaded. After much labor, Arriola's crew had also managed to cut 14 huge cypress logs, the size of which made them desirable for use as non-composite mainmasts. The longer, heavier cypress logs proved nearly impossible to move, and when they were finally dragged to the water's edge, a dismayed crew learned that the cypress logs did not float. The cypress logs were left to dry, and a wiser Arriola left for Veracruz with both his desirable cargo of pine poles and important information related to developing a logging industry at Pensacola (Hunter 2001: 37–38).

Meanwhile, in 1696, the English Crown awarded Daniel Coxe, a physician to the English royal family, a huge land grant known as "Carolana," which included all of modern Georgia and extended west to Mexico, infringing on both Spanish Florida and French Louisiana (Clune 2003: 19–20). Two years later, the English governor of South Carolina, Joseph Blake, informed a Spanish visitor to Charleston that he planned to capture Pensacola Bay the following year. This news soon spread to the French Crown, who immediately began preparations to establish a settlement at the mouth of the Mississippi River to protect the Louisiana Colony, which was headed by Pierre Le Moyne, Sieur d'Iberville, and his younger brother Jean-Baptist Le Moyne de Bienville. When the Spanish king learned of the French intentions to settle on the northern Gulf coast, he had finally had enough prompting and ordered the immediate settlement of Pensacola Bay, erroneously thinking that this bay was the d'Iberville brothers' destination (Clune 2003: 20; Coker and Childers 1998: 14; Ford 1939: 29).

Finally, in 1698, the Spanish Crown tasked Arriola and Reina with building a presidio on Pensacola Bay. Reina arrived on November 17 from Cádiz, Spain, with 60 soldiers and two ships and set up camp on the western tip of Santa Rosa Island (Punta de Sigüenza) at the entrance to Pensacola Bay. Arriola arrived from Veracruz four days later with three ships and over 400 men (Clune et al. 2003: 34; Coker and Childers 1998: 16; Ford 1939: 27–28). In addition to establishing a presidio, Arriola was under orders to cut more poles for masts and spars for the Spanish navy and arrange for their transport to Veracruz (Childers and Cotter 1998: 79; Hunter 2001: 40).

Austrian military engineer Jaime Franck was assigned to design and supervise the building of the fort, and he selected the bluffs, named the Barranca de San Tomé, overlooking the entrance to the bay as the site for the new presidio named Santa María de Galve and a new fort named Fort San Carlos de Austria (see figure 1.4). The area along the Barranca de San Tomé selected for the presidio was a level portion of the bluff directly above the bay shore.

Support System for the West Florida Presidio

When Arriola and Reina arrived at Pensacola Bay in 1698, the local Panzacola Indian population seen in the visits to the area in the 1680s was no longer there. The Panzacola seem to have moved to Mobile, claiming they were afraid of the Lower Creeks of southern Georgia who were aligned with the aggressive Creek slave raiders, and as they had recently been at war with the Mobilas, the Panzacolas living on Mobile Bay apparently had either formed an alliance with their former enemies or had been completely subjugated by them (Clune et al. 2003: 28; Coker and Childers 1998: 18; Harris 1999: 47–49). In other words, the Pensacola Bay area was literally uninhabited by Native Americans and remained so for most of Santa María's existence (Worth 2008: 3).

Starting in 1700, presidio officials tried to raise corn and other vegetable crops using convict labor. Unfortunately, the soil was too poor around the settlement, and there was never enough food produced to supply the garrison. House gardens proved to be the most successful source of food, but the quantities were always small. A few livestock were raised during the early years, but as hostilities by English-led Creek armies increased, it became impossible to let the livestock range far from the presidio (Harris 1999: 28–29). The lack of Native-supplied food stuffs and labor, alongside mounting hostilities, resulted in the presidio community of West Florida quickly becoming dependent on supplies from outside sources. A three-part support system was developed to meet the needs of the settlement at Santa María: the Apalachee missions, the *situado,* and trade with the French on Mobile Bay.

At first, an important source of food and supplies for the community at Santa María was the Apalachee Province of the Catholic mission system some 200 miles to the east and its capital at mission San Luis de Talimali at modern-day Tallahassee, Florida. The mission system concentrated the Indian population to focus on the production of food to support both the missions and Presidio San Agustín (see Hann 1988; Hann and McEwan 1998; Milanich 1999). Although their population was diminishing during the late seventeenth century, Apalachees were still the most populous of the remaining Native Peoples in north Florida. The Apalachee mission system had been supporting Presidio San Agustín for decades through an arrangement between the Spanish and Native American chiefs; this arrangement allowed transport of food produced in the Apalachee Province and provided laborers to work there for several months at a time. In addition, mission Indians labored on the large Spanish cattle ranches and farms located across the Apalachee Province (Hann 1988: 139–143). Cattle from these ranches were driven overland to Santa María while other food, supplies, and laborers from the missions were sent by ship to Santa María from the port of San Marcos de Apalachee at the mouth of the St. Marks River. When Santa María was first established, 14.0 percent of the initial supplies came from the Apalachee missions (Clune et al. 2003: 54, 60).

Relationships with the French colonists just to the west on Mobile Bay began in 1700 when the viceroy of New Spain, José Sarmiento y Valladares, required Arriola to search for a reported English settlement on the northern Gulf coast. It was during this expedition that a clandestine French settlement, Fort Maurepas, near present-day Biloxi, Mississippi, became known to the Spanish. Deciding against an attack, Arriola took his expedition of 40 men to visit the settlement and protested the French presence, stating it was a violation of their treaty. However, the demeanor and shabby, hungry appearance of Arriola and his men revealed to the French that food supplies were scarce at Santa María and they were suffering. Arriola later reported that he and his men were treated well by the French (Clune et al. 2003: 60–64; Coker and Childers 1998: 22–24). On their return to Santa María, a violent storm or hurricane struck and wrecked three of the four Spanish ships, forcing them to limp back to Fort Maurepas. The French again received them with great hospitality and gave them both a ship and provisions for Santa María.

On the ground, the relationship between the French in Mobile and the Spanish at Santa María was cordial and mutually beneficial. Trade relationships developed despite French intrusions into the northern Gulf, first with Fort Maurepas (1699) and later with Fort Saint Louis (1702) 27 miles up the Mobile River from the head of Mobile Bay, Alabama (figure 2.1). The official reason behind this amiable attitude was that the new Spanish King Philip V was a descendant of the French King Louis XIV. This familial relationship and alliance between France and Spain alarmed Britain, Austria, and Holland, and they soon joined together to oust Philip from the Spanish throne. Thus began the War of Spanish Succession (1701–1714) (Arnade 1996: 106–107; Falkner 2015).

Good relations between Spain and France helped support their respective colonial settlements on the northern Gulf coast, as they both were poorly supplied by their home countries. Only one shipment every two years arrived from France at Fort Saint Louis (Waselkov 2002: 5), and the Spanish situado was consistent only in its unreliability. In 1700, the alliance between Spain and France allowed French ships to enter Spanish American ports for necessities, which meant that the French at Mobile could purchase supplies at Veracruz (Johnson 1999, 2003: 317). The relationship worked in the following manner: the governor at Santa María would receive food and other supplies on credit from the French at Old Mobile on the condition they would be paid either in silver when the situado finally arrived or with direct reimbursements at Veracruz. Covetous of Spain's silver and desiring of its goodwill, the French at Mobile eagerly came to the aid of the Spanish at Santa María, even when their own supplies were very low (Clune et al. 2003: 61). The French profited from this trading relationship, as most of the food sold to Santa María was produced by local Indian groups living on Mobile Bay. The Native Americans were eager to sell their crops to the French because they were paid with firearms and ammunition, which they could not get from the Spanish. The French used the Spanish silver to purchase supplies for their settlement either at Spanish ports or from French traders arriving in Mobile from the interior rivers of the Southeast (Johnson 2003: 322–325). The Indian-French-Spanish trade, both legal and illegal, was beneficial and essential for all three parties, and it continued with only minor interruption throughout the Presidio Period in West Florida.

Excavations at Fort Saint Louis and the port on Dauphin Island conducted by Gregory Waselkov (1991, 1994, 1999, 2002) and George Shorter (2002) from the University of South Alabama (USA) found archaeological evidence of trade with the Spanish. They recovered 104 Spanish silver coins along with thousands of pieces of Spanish majolica tableware and Spanish olive jars used for storage. These artifacts are tangible results of the vital trade between the Spanish and French along the Gulf and the continued reliance both groups had on Native Americans in the Mobile Bay area for food.

In addition to the legal trade with the French, there was also illicit trade. Early on, the governors and other ranking officials at Santa María began a practice of illegal buying and selling that lasted throughout the 65 years of the Spanish West Florida Presidio Period. Spanish officials privately purchased significant quantities of goods from the French and resold them to the residents of the presidio communities for a profit. The networks of illicit trade that developed between the Spanish and French on the Gulf coast followed a pattern that was prevalent not only throughout Spanish Florida but also across Spain's New World territories. Historical archaeological studies of contraband and alternative economies at Presidio Santa María de Galve and Presidio Santa Rosa are presented by Sandra Johnson (1999, 2003) and Amanda Roberts Thompson (2009, 2012); see Kathleen Deagan (2007) for a detailed analysis of illicit trade from eighteenth-century households in Presidio San Agustín. The Spanish colonial administration was aware of the illegal trading but largely ignored it as they could neither adequately supply their colonial settlements nor patrol their vast coastlines in the Americas.

The reader might question why the Spanish at Pensacola Bay were so dependent on imported food from their French allies next door at Mobile Bay. Why were food shortages a constant problem at Santa María while the French in Mobile had a surplus? The reason is twofold: first, the area surrounding Mobile

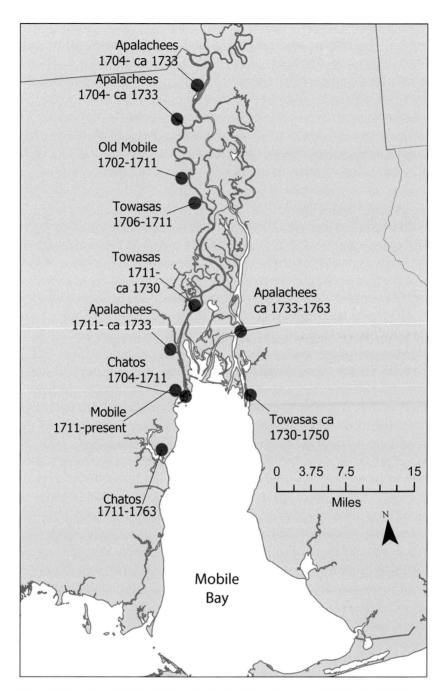

Apalachees
1704- ca 1733

Apalachees
1704- ca 1733

Old Mobile
1702-1711

Towasas
1706-1711

Towasas
1711-
ca 1730

Apalachees
ca 1733-1763

Apalachees
1711- ca 1733

Chatos
1704-1711

Mobile
1711-present

Towasas ca
1730-1750

Chatos
1711-1763

0   3.75   7.5   15

Miles

N

Mobile
Bay

Figure 2.2. Location of "Petites Nations" and colonial settlements on Mobile Bay, AL (after Waselkov and Gums 2000: Figure 5). Courtesy of the Archaeology Institute, University of West Florida.

Bay was very fertile while the area around Santa María was poor. Second, there were multiple Native American groups living and farming the rich soil along Mobile Bay and the river delta (figure 2.2), but there were no Native Peoples residing in the Pensacola Bay area until 1718, with a second group migrating to the area in 1740. The French called the collective of cultural groups living along Mobile Bay "petites nations," and the French colonists there readily acknowledged that the Native Americans were their primary lifeline (Waselkov and Gums 2000: 6). As a general strategy, the French usually located their settlements adjacent to an Indian village or encouraged the relocation of a village close to their settlements. The French and Native American groups immediately began trading partnerships as well, with the French usually trading guns, cloth, personal ornamentation, and tools for food grown or hunted by Native hands.

In sum, the support system for Presidio Santa María de Galve and the following presidio communities in West Florida always depended on imported food and supplies. For the first six years at Santa María, the Apalachee Province mission system and Spanish cattle ranches supplemented the situado. However, the destruction of the mission system in 1704 eliminated that source of support. The situado was always an important part of the support system, and the silver coinage was its most critical element, as it was used to purchase food from the French at Mobile. The newfound alliance between Spain and France through the kinship of their monarchs, Philip V and King Louis XIV, coupled with the poorly supplied French colony on Mobile Bay and their desire for Spanish silver forged a new relationship and lifeline for settlements on both bays that continued for 65 years.

Finding the Remains of Presidio Santa María de Galve

The general area of the Santa María presidio was never lost, as it was located on many historical maps since the time of its inception on the bluff facing the entrance into Pensacola Bay about a mile west of Tartar Point (see figure 1.4). In 1959, historians William Griffen (1959) and Albert Manucy (1959) published articles focused specifically on Presidio Santa María de Galve in conjunction with the 400-year anniversary of Tristán de Luna's 1559 founding of the first Spanish settlement attempt on Pensacola Bay. These articles educated a new generation about the general location of Santa María, its population, and the history of the Spanish colonial community.

As Judith Bense and Harry Wilson (1999: 15–19) describe, the first indication of the specific location of the Santa María archaeological site was in

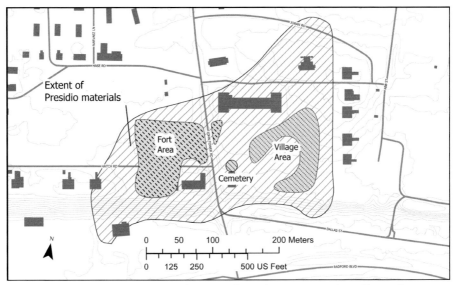

Figure 2.3. Areas of intact archaeological remains of Presidio Santa María fort, village, village cemetery, and site boundary. Courtesy of the Archaeology Institute, University of West Florida.

1979 by Florida State University (FSU) archaeologist Chad Braley. Braley (1979: 36–44) found early eighteenth-century artifacts on Naval Air Station Pensacola (NASP) 1,500 feet east of Fort Barrancas and suggested the area as the possible location of Presidio Santa María. In 1986, a groundskeeper for NASP collected eighteenth-century artifacts in the same area as Braley and contacted us about his find. I and University of West Florida (UWF) archaeology student Thomas Garner recorded the site (8ES1354) with the Florida Master Site Files as the possible location of Fort San Carlos de Austria. Later that same year, a utility trench was excavated through this site area, revealing an early eighteenth-century midden and sub-midden features in the trench profiles containing hundreds of artifacts, and compliance activities were conducted (Neilsen et al. 1992: 3).

In 1994, the commander of NASP requested that Bense locate and study the first permanent settlement in Pensacola as NASP's contribution to the celebration of the settlement's 300th anniversary in 1998. In 1995, Bense and her students, colleagues, and trained volunteers from the Pensacola Archaeological Society (PAS) began four seasons of fieldwork at the site. A big tent was set up for a field lab where scores of volunteers under the direction of a staff lab supervisor rough sorted the artifacts and mapped the shovel tests with diagnostic eighteenth-century Spanish artifacts. In this manner, we confirmed that the site was that of Presidio Santa María de Galve founded in 1698, delineated its boundaries, and identified the fort and village areas based on clear differences in concentration of artifacts, shown in figure 2.3 (Bense and Wilson 1999: 24–29). Having a field laboratory revealed what was being unearthed in real time and enabled us to make strategic adjustments in excavation unit placement and methods. In addition, the volunteers were used as "match" for the state historic preservation grants that sponsored most of the research. Some senior volunteers were experienced in databases and computer-aided design (CAD), which was new at the time in archaeology, and their assistance was invaluable in helping the faculty, staff, and students learn how to use the new technology and programs. The information that the trained volunteers provided in the field was crucial, and they were an important part of the team. The volunteers continued to assist us during the academic year in the laboratory, analyses, and report preparations. This inclusion of the public enriched us all, and because of them, we produced more high-quality information than we ever could have on our own.

One significant finding was that the presidio was *not* located on the highest point of the 30-foot-tall bluff, as one would presume. Historical documents describe the fort location as surrounded by three hills (Clune et al. 2003: 36), which are clearly depicted on a 1713 Spanish map of Presidio Santa María (figure 2.4). Our explanation for the selection of such a low and vulnerable spot for the fort was the pressing need to begin construction as the French and English were known to be on their way to Pensacola Bay. This urgency was coupled with a convenient erosional gully providing the only easy access point to the 30-foot bluff summit for the people, animals, tons of supplies, and cannons. This gully is clearly depicted on the 1719 French Devin map (figure 2.5a), which shows the fort directly adjacent to the gully's head. The actual highest point on the bluff is over 700 feet to the west of the head of the gully; perhaps the time and effort needed to transport everything to that spot could not have been spared. Additionally, locating Fort San Carlos at the head of the gully deterred its use as an access point by Spain's enemies.

The presidio village area was located east of the fort across the erosional gully. In late 1995, construction workers accidentally disturbed nine human burials in the southern village area (Bense and Wilson 2003: 29). As the burials are within 15 feet of the projected cemetery location on the 1699 Franck map (figure 2.6), we concluded that the burials had been interred there. The cemetery and interments are discussed later in this chapter.

Figure 2.4. A 1713 Spanish map of Presidio Santa María showing A, Fort San Carlos; B, the three hills surrounding Santa María; C, Santa Rosa Island; E, proposed canal across Santa Rosa Island. Legend for inset map of Fort San Carlos: A, church; B, hospital; C, warehouse; D, guard post; E, governor's house; F, main gate; G, soldier's barracks; H, cistern (Anonymous 1713).

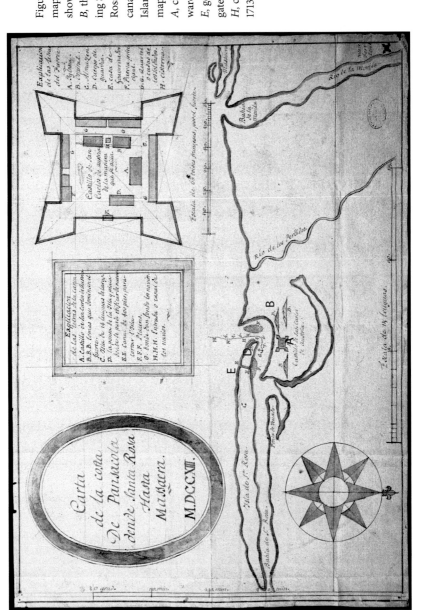

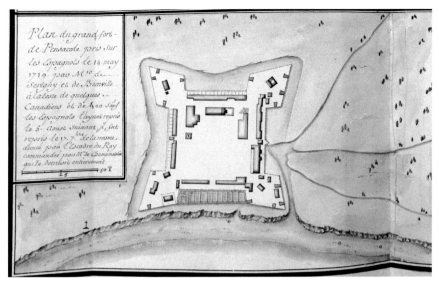

a

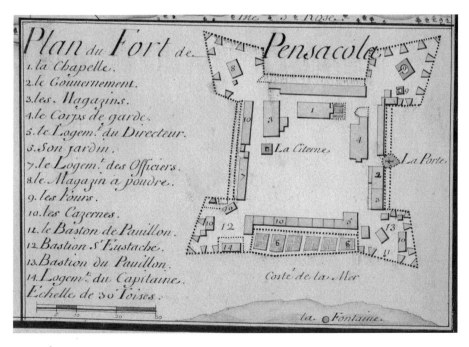

b

Figure 2.5. Two Presidio Santa María maps of Fort San Carlos de Austria by Valentin Devin. *A*, a 1719 map showing erosional gully in bluff leading to main fort gate (Devin 1719). *B*, ca. 1720 map identifying facilities and structures inside Fort San Carlos and translation of legend: *1*, church; *2*, government offices; *3*, warehouses; *4*, guard house; *5*, director; *6*, gardens; *7*, officer's quarters; *8*, powder magazine; *9*, ovens; *10*, quarters; *11*, flagpole; *12*, bastion of St. Eustacious; *13*, flagpole bastion; *14*, captain's house; *15*, cistern (Devin ca. 1720).

Figure 2.6. Map of Presidio Santa María by engineer Jaime Franck, May 1699, showing A, friary; B, church; C, cemetery; D, Captain Juan Jordán de Reina's residential compound; E, note that at least seven more cabins are located here; F, battery that faces the channel; G, guardhouse; H, governor's house; I, powder magazine; J, gate to countryside; K, side gate toward village (Franck 1699).

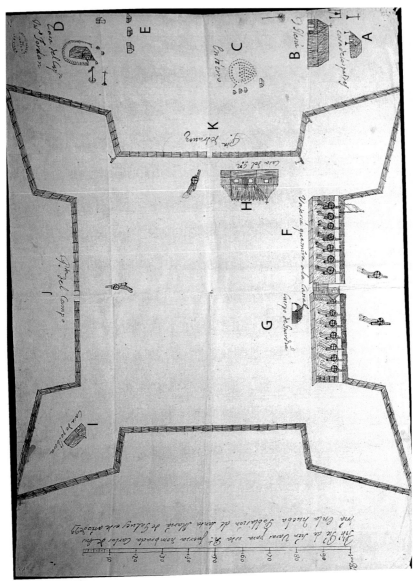

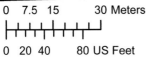

The Early Years, 1698–1707

The People

The original group assembled to set up the Santa María presidio in 1698 consisted of about 460 people (Clune et al. 2003: 32; Ford 1939: 27–28). These people were primarily military men (soldiers and sailors) and convict laborers, but another 28 included 3 priests, 12 carpenters, 6 brick masons, 3 surgeons, and 4 blacksmiths (table 2.1). The soldiers included some semi-voluntary re-enlistments, but the bulk came directly from the slums and jails of Mexico City, Puebla, and Veracruz (Coker and Childers 1998: 16–17). There were also many uncounted people moving in and out of the presidio community, including, women, children, and Indian wage laborers sent from the Apalachee missions to the east. It must be understood that the population figures in table 2.1 are incomplete, at times contradictory, and inconsistent in who was counted, but these figures are what is available to us today. There were large swings in the population at Santa María de Galve as a result of illness, desertion, and the success or failure of recruitment efforts. Population estimates show that Pensacola's first presidio began with about 460 people, dropped by 57 percent within six months, and plummeted to a skeletal crew of 80 by March of 1700 (Eschbach 2019: 217). By 1703, the population was up to 300 with 170 presidio soldiers, 50 convict laborers, and 80 other residents in Pensacola (John Worth, personal communication 2018). Dockworkers also arrived from Veracruz to cut and shape pine trees for ship masts and spars (Childers and Cotter 1998: 77–79; Clune et al. 2003: 32). Sickness, including a yellow fever epidemic in 1702, evacuations of the sick, desertions, and deaths from diseases of malnutrition and hard labor constantly reduced the population. New recruits and convict laborers were continuously sent to Santa María as well as the subsequent locations of the West Florida presidio throughout this period.

With the start of the War of Spanish Succession in 1701, the English and their Native allies increased their attacks on Spanish settlements and missions across north Florida, both to take captives to sell as slaves and to push the Spanish out of Florida. The first major attack was by English-allied Apalachicola warriors on the Timucua mission of Santa Fé in May 1702 (Hann 1988: 233, 249; Hann and McEwan 1998: 165–175). Presidio San Agustín was the next target of British Governor James Moore in November 1702. Fortunately, a fleet from Havana arrived at St. Augustine and drove off the British (Arnade 1959, 1996: 107), but not before they burned down the surrounding town. By mid-1704, the entire area east of Pensacola was in turmoil: all the Apalachees were in revolt, over 2,000 head of cattle had been slaughtered, and over 2,000 Apalachee had surrendered

Table 2.1. Population of Presidio Santa María

Year	Totalᵃ	Soldiers	Convicts	Others	Native Americans
1698	460	389	-	23	-
1699 (February)	260	260	-	-	-
1700 (February)	180	280	-	-	-
1700 (March)	80	-	-	-	-
1703	300	170	50	80	-
1704 (January)	1,100	170	-	130	800
1704 (July)	289	229	-	60	-
1705 (September)	790	200	-	290	300
1705 (October)	530	200	50	80	200
1705 (November)	300	170	50	80	-
1705 (November 7)	318	187	25	31	75
1706	304	187	-	117	-
1707 (November 11)	139	130	9	-	-
1707 (November 17)	359	150	20	-	80
1709 (November)	340	252	-	8	80
1712	500	250	-	-	-
1713	400	212	-	-	80
1719 (March)	800	800	-	-	-
1719 (May)	300	160	-	140	-
1719 (August)	850	850	-	-	-
1719 (November)	1,200	1,200	-	-	-

Sources: Clune et al. (2003); Clune et al. (2006); Coker and Childers (1998); Eschbach (2019); Griffen (1959); John Worth, personal communication 2018.

ᵃ Most totals provided in documents have only partial or no subdivisions.

to the English (Hann 1988: 280). With new threats to the last three missions and no means of defense, the Spanish governor of Florida authorized the abandonment of the Apalachee Province (Hann 1988; Hann and McEwan 1998). The once prosperous Spanish mission system with its three provinces was destroyed along with an important source of food and supplies for Santa María.

Spanish and Indian mission refugees began to arrive at Santa María as early as 1702 following the first English attacks on the missions. The refugee

Spaniards included members of the well-established elite who had extensive control, property, and businesses in the Apalachee Province, especially the large and powerful Florencia family clan. The Florencias were the Spanish "first family" of Apalachee (Hann and McEwan 1998: 54–61, 177–183). Juan Fernández de Florencia had been a deputy governor of the Apalachee Province, and his business maneuverings turned it into a Florencia "fiefdom" during the last quarter of the seventeenth century. He and his extended family established a series of cattle ranches and satellite settlements, and this kin-based network filled most senior administrative posts for the region. The first refugee Florencia family members arrived at Santa María in 1704, having come by ship from San Marcos. Juana Caterina de Florencia, wife of then deputy governor Don Jacinto Roque Pérez, and her children arrived with the wife of her brother Diego de Florencia and their children (Coker and Childers 1988: 31–32; Hann 1988: 280). Soon afterward, their sister-in-law Magdalena de Florencia joined them. As Coker and Childers (1998) describe, the remaining Spanish women and children at San Luis soon arrived by ship at Santa María. This raised the number of refugee Spanish families at the Pensacola presidio to a total of nine, consisting of about 50 people; however, it is not clear how long the majority of the Spanish Apalachee families stayed at Santa María or to where they relocated. We do know that Magdalena de Florencia lived at all four locations of the West Florida presidio, as did her children and grandchildren. Members of the family were evacuated in 1763 after Spanish Florida was transferred to the British (Coker and Childers 1998: 31–32).

Although Indian refugees, including 200 Apalachee families, arrived by the hundreds, the historical documents are stubbornly silent on their exact number and specific ethnic affiliations. It is estimated that 800 Indian and Spanish refugees from Apalachee arrived at Santa María in January 1704, swelling the population to approximately 1,100 people. The Native American refugees were actually a mix of residents of two Apalachee missions—San Luis and Escambé— as well as Christian Chacatos and a few non-Christian Yamasee (Hann 1988: 305; Harris 2003a: 271). Confirming this general composition, Bienville estimated that about 400 Apalachees and 200 Chacatos arrived at Mobile Bay from Pensacola in August 1704 (Higginbotham 1977: 191–193). It is important to note that members of many other Native American ethnic groups arrived as mission refugees at Santa María. Norma Harris (1999, 2003a: 270) relates that the Spanish missions had attracted Indians from many groups in the Southeast, including the Tama, Capara, Amacano, Chine, Yamasee, Ocatose, and Tocobago; they joined the Tabazas, Apalachees, and Chacatos already at Santa María.

John Hann (1988: 264) estimates that "more than 2,000 [of the Native population] were forced into exile." The refugees who arrived at Santa María were both a blessing and a curse. As there was a chronic labor shortage, the influx of hundreds of Apalachees, many of whom were skilled laborers and farmers, was a welcome sight. However, as their number swelled to over 1,000 in 1704, the chronic food shortages at the presidio were substantially exacerbated. The food and supplies the Spanish could provide for the large Indian population were insufficient, as were their promises of protection, and consequently, most of the refugee Indian population left for Mobile within a few weeks.

Soon after most Native American refugees left Santa María, a hurricane hit Pensacola in September 1705, sinking two ships in the vicinity and resulting in the addition of 290 shipwreck survivors to the population of the presidio. Two hundred were from the frigate *Rosario,* a Spanish supply ship, and an additional 90 survivors were from the wreck of a passing French frigate. Santa María's population bounced up to 790 people in September 1705 as the shipwreck survivors were added to the existing 500 residents, including the garrison and Indians working on the fortifications plus 31 female Spanish subjects, most of whom were refugees from Apalachee (Coker and Childers 1998: 34). However, the shipwreck survivors soon left, and the population dropped to about 530 in a few weeks, including 200 soldiers, 200 Indian refugees, 50 convicts, and 80 others (Clune et al. 2003: 32). Two population estimates were made in late 1705 identifying 300 to 318 people at Santa María, consisting of 170 to 187 soldiers, 25 to 50 convicts, 75 Indians, and the 31 women (John Worth, personal communication 2018). In 1706, the population was 304, including 187 soldiers plus another 117 people consisting of 20 refugees from Apalachee, 14 women, 54 Chacato and Apalachee Indians, 26 laborers, and 3 French skilled workers (table 2.1; Coker and Childers 1998: 36). From 1707 to 1719, the population ranged between 139 and 1,200 averaging about 461 to 543 people. The high count of 1,200 soldiers reflects the influx of new troops sent to retake the presidio from the French in 1719. Counts are few for convict laborers, but the numbers we do have range from 9 to 20. Discounting the influx of temporary refugees in 1704 and 1705, there were 80 Indians regularly receiving rations.

Records indicate that Native Americans were living at Presidio Santa María from the earliest years of the settlement, though available records fluctuate and sometimes conflict on the numbers and cultural affiliations of the Native Peoples within the Spanish settlement (Childers and Cotter 1998; Clune et al. 2003; Coker and Childers 1998; Harris 2003a). Indians at Santa María worked for wages and rations as general laborers, and some had honed skills as carpenters and were sought after and valued by the Spanish. Records consistently mention Apalachee craftsmen at Santa María as they had become practiced in Spanish building methods at the missions. These skilled Native carpenters and woodworkers were valued members of the presidio community, where they played a vital role in the building and constant repair of the structures and fortifications at the Pensacola settlement (Coker and Childers 1998: 25–26; Harris 1999: 48, 52; 2003a: 271). Starting in 1705, situado records occasionally document the number of rations for Indians. However, this likely was not the actual number of Indian residents, as some may have lived elsewhere and only worked at the presidio and some had their families with them. In addition, the French sent several groups of Native American paid laborers to assist the Spanish, including Canadian Indians who were experienced woodcutters, hunters, scouts, artillerymen, ship's crews, and escorts (Harris 2003a: 274).

Not unsurprisingly, the historic record for Santa María is not as forthcoming with direct information on the presence of women and families. However, we can piece together a number of minor historical notations with archaeological information to gain a somewhat more comprehensive understanding of the number of women at Santa María as well as the conditions in which they lived (Eschbach 2007, 2019; Harris 1999, 2003a; Holmes 2012; Sims 2001). While their roles within the community were not usually recorded, in 1705, 31 women were noted among the Apalachee and Spanish refugees (Coker and Childers 1998: 36), and 14 women were listed in 1706 who were probably also Spanish refugees from Apalachee. Historians consistently affirm that the Indian mission refugees were primarily in family groups (Hann 1988: 305–306; Hann and McEwan 1998: 170–171). In 1703 and 1704, there were also nine refugee Spanish families with an unknown number of women as well as 200 Apalachee families at Santa María (Coker and Childers 1998: 32). If there was only one woman in each of these families, there could have been at least 209 women with their children at the presidio at that time.

While many refugees moved on to Mobile Bay, some stayed on at the Pensacola presidio. In 1707, there are two mentions of female residents at Santa María. The first record is of an Indigenous woman being captured as she returned from bathing in a nearby bayou, and the second is Governor Moscoso's mention in a letter that four women were on salary (Coker and Childers 1998: 43). The women attached to Spanish military companies and receiving salaries and/or rations were Spanish, not Indian, although there are a few exceptions for women performing specialized tasks at some of the military outposts (John Worth, personal communication 2019). By 1712, there were 25 wives of infantrymen on salary, and in the same year, there were 80 Indian woodcutters, guests, and an unknown number of dependents who were likely wives and children (Coker and Childers 1998: 60; Griffen 1959: 247). Documents also reveal that some soldiers married Indian women and they resided at the presidio (Childers and Cotter 1998: 90). From these brief mentions of women at Santa María, it is safe to assume that families were present at least most of the time because wives, partners, and children accompanied soldiers and Indian male workers also brought their families to Santa María.

While many of the Indians working at Santa María probably lived at the presidio, the first group to return to the Pensacola area were Apalachee refugees who started a village on Perdido Bay in 1705. The officially recognized refugee governor of the Apalachee at San Luis de Talimali, Don Joseph de la Cruz de Cui, arrived at the presidio with 60 men, 60 women, and 80 children. He asked Governor Guzmán to help them establish a new village about 2.5 leagues (eight miles) away on Perdido Bay. Cruz requested agricultural tools, seed corn, and the return of the church ornaments that had been taken to St. Augustine (Childers and Cotter 1998: 89; Coker and Childers 1998: 34; Harris 2003a: 270–271; Worth 2008: 5). The viceroy agreed and instructed officials at Santa María to give the Apalachee leader the seed corn, but they had no tools to give. Within a month, rations for 20 principal men were issued, and the Cruz community is documented to have survived at least until the following September and likely longer (Worth 2008: 5). Little is known about their settlement, but this first Apalachee refugee village was a precursor of things to come.

The Apalachee would form the backbone of the repopulation of Native Americans in the Pensacola Bay area through 1763. During these years, Apalachees moved between Presidio Santa María at Pensacola and Mobile Bay because of economic opportunities, security, and familial and social ties. Almost all the refugee Indians, including the Apalachee, were third generation Catholics who shared cultural and historical bonds. Forced from their homelands and seeking military protection along with religious leadership in the form of Catholic friars, these refugees chose to settle near Spanish and French military installations, began to negotiate their loyalties and futures, and remained valued members of Spanish Florida (see Worth 2008 for the history of the Apalachee and Yamasee missions in the Pensacola area during this time period).

In sum, at Presidio Santa María de Galve the years following the destruction of the missions saw a series of crises. First were the hundreds of refugee Indians and Spaniards fleeing slave raids in the Apalachee Province. Second was an influx of hundreds of shipwreck survivors. Third was a series of seven destructive fires that burned warehouses, churches, barracks, the fort wall, and homes at the presidio and village. Fourth were two hurricanes in 1700 and 1705. The population was composed primarily of military men and convict laborers from the lower castas of Mexico City serving out their terms of enlistment or sentences. Officers were also from New Spain and were rotated through the presidio. Wives and family units were present, but few details are available. The people all expected that their time at Santa María would be limited and they would return home at some point.

The Fort

All the historic maps and descriptions of Fort San Carlos de Austria consistently indicate that it was a Vauban design with a large square interior and rhomboid-shaped bastions on each corner (Duffy 1985; Renacker 2001: 16–30). The interior was 275 feet on each side, and the bastions were 95 by 120 feet, as shown in figure 2.6. The original walls of the bastions and south curtain wall were sand-filled double stockades (terrepleined) supporting a parapet on which cannons were mounted (see Bense and Wilson 1999, 2003; Clune et al. 2003; Renacker 2001: 35; Wilson 2000: 49–50). Documents state that a dry moat surrounding the three landward walls was started immediately, and the excavated sand was used to fill the terrepleined walls (Clune et al. 2003: 46).

Construction of the fort began in late November 1698, and three months later in a February 19, 1699, letter to the viceroy, Franck stated that the fort was enclosed. However, on his May 1699 map (figure 2.6), only the south seawall appears to be terrepleined, and all the walls appear to be made of horizontal planks or logs fastened to posts. Progress on the fort was slow, as Governor Arriola reported the walls were only 2.75 feet high four years later in 1703 (Clune et al. 2003: 46; Renacker 2001: 39–41).

Initially, the fort was used only for defense and security, housing only the most important person (governor), the most dangerous facility (powder magazine), and the guardhouse. A supply warehouse, barracks, church, and a bake oven were reportedly built inside the fort during the first few years, but they are not shown on any historic map (Clune et al. 2003: 49–51). We do know that the first warehouse was 19.2 feet square, 6.9 feet high, constructed of boards, and roofed with shingles. The church and barracks were built by 1702, and they both are described as having board walls attached to a timber frame roofed with palmetto thatch or wood shingles. The powder magazine was placed 9.6 feet underground in the northwest bastion. It was 13.7 by 11 feet in size and made of boards planed on site (Clune et al. 2003: 49–50).

The Village

Historical documents reveal that there were two occupations in the village area east of Fort San Carlos (see Clune et al. 2003; Coker and Childers 1998). The first occupation started with the initial founding of the presidio settlement in 1698 and ended in 1707 when the village was attacked, abandoned, and burned and the population relocated inside the fort. The village was reoccupied in 1715 after peace was again established and continued until surprise French attacks burned the presidio and village to the ground in 1719.

Only two maps depicting the village have been found, both made in 1699,

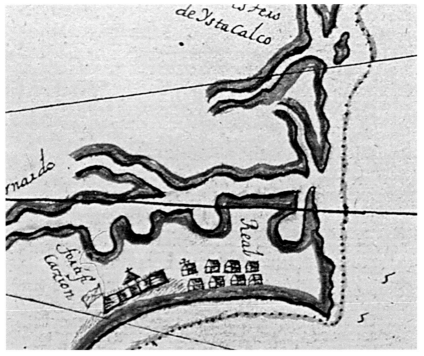

Figure 2.7. Part of the 1698 Presidio Santa María map of the bay of Santa María de Galve by Andrés de Arriola and ordered by the viceroy Count of Moctezuma (Arriola 1698).

and they are very different. The first was by Andrés de Arriola, the governor and commander in chief of the presidio, and engineer Franck. The presidio on the Arriola map is a small part of a large map of the entire Pensacola Bay area based on a survey made between November 1698 and February 1699 (John Worth, personal communication 2019). The resulting map drawn in March 1699 depicts the presidio as a well-designed, fortified, and *completed* community, although in reality, construction had barely begun. Shown in figure 2.7, this portrayal is either a symbolic one or the plan for the future settlement, certainly not the contemporary reality. However, it is a rendering that would have pleased the viceroy and sent a message to Spain's enemies in France and England that the Spanish were well established on Pensacola Bay.

The second map of the village was made by Franck in May of 1699 and appears to be a more realistic, if incomplete, depiction of the village (figure 2.6). It was drawn only six months into the settlement's occupation and three months after the Arriola-Franck survey map was produced. While a copy of this map was available during the UWF 1995–1998 historical archaeological investigations and subsequent research, we now know our copy was not complete and had been modified. Recently, UWF has obtained a new high resolution digital copy of the original map from the Archivo General de Indias in Seville, Spain. The completeness and improved clarity of the new digital version has provided much new detailed information about the early settlement.

Completing an enclosed secure fort was the top construction priority in 1699, and the entire population lived outside the fort in makeshift huts described as having sapling frames with roofs and walls of thatched palmetto fronds (Clune et al. 2003: 37; Coker and Childers 1998: 20). Village and fort structures were soon improved as timbers replaced the sapling framework, boards replaced thatch-covered walls, and shingles or boards replaced thatch roofs. All of the buildings depicted on the May 1699 Franck map appear to have timber frames. Enlarging the structure renderings on the Franck map shows the two-story building over the south gate of the fort already had a shingled roof (figure 2.8). The guardhouse and the church seem to have board roofing, and the lower half of the exterior walls of the governor's house appears to have either horizontal boards that could have been covered with plaster or clay. All other buildings on the May 1699 Franck map are depicted with thatch roofs. The church, the upper half of the exterior of the governor's residence, and the guardhouse had horizontal or vertical plank siding. The exterior walls of all other buildings were either vertical boards or palmetto thatch.

The Early Village on the Franck map depicted two occupation areas separated by a large open space: an area dedicated to religious needs was in the south near the bluff line, and a residential area was in the north. Structures and spaces in the religious area included a church, friary, and cemetery. The friary had a covered entryway or portico, and there was a large, freestanding cross outside the friary about 16 feet east of its entrance (figure 2.8). In addition, there was a large bell suspended from a post and lintel frame between the church and friary. The church had a double-door entryway and a high loft.

A circular cemetery was located about 50 feet north of the church and enclosed with a fence of close-set vertical posts with an opening to the west, facing the fort. Inside the enclosure, Franck drew 37 crosses in seven east-west rows and 17 more crosses close and parallel to the inside of the circular perimeter fence. If the crosses represent individual graves, then there were 54 graves in the cemetery only seven months after landing, which underscores the excessively harsh working and living conditions. A cluster of four small gabled rectangular structures labeled "cabins" were located within 10 feet of the cemetery. Three were in a generally north-south row just west of the cemetery gate while the fourth was larger and separated from the others to the south. The

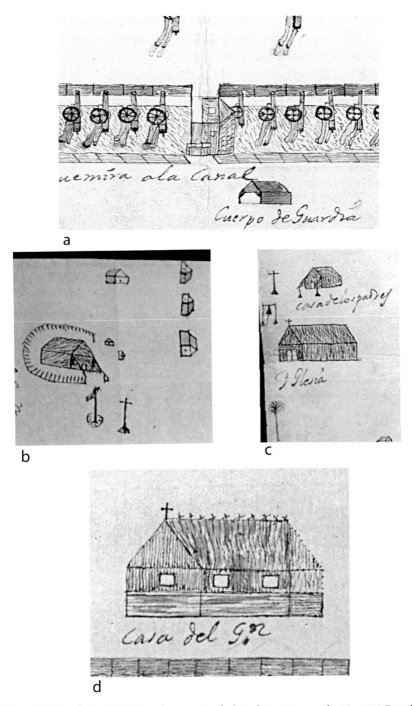

a

b

c

d

Figure 2.8. Presidio Santa María, enlargements of selected structures on the May 1699 Franck map: *a,* structure over gate in seawall; *b,* Captain Juan Jordán de Reina's residential compound; *c,* church and friary in village; *d,* governor's house inside fort (Franck 1699).

close proximity of the cabins to the cemetery likely means that the residents were associated with it, perhaps as workers or caretakers.

The burials disturbed by construction workers in 1995 are thought to have been in this cemetery. UWF archaeologists examined the exposed burials after the foundation trenches were completed. As Bense and Wilson (1999: 50, 2003: 170) explain, nine interments were identified, all in the supine position with no discernible pattern of orientation. Additionally, none were coffin burials, indicating that those laid to rest here were likely buried in shrouds, following Spanish and Catholic custom. Only one grave item, a copper Catholic religious medallion (figure 2.9), was associated with a burial. The bioanthropological field examination identified only one of the nine individuals as possibly Native American, and the others appeared to be European. If the density of graves within the 33-square-foot area enclosed by the construction trenches is representative, then there are likely to be 187 more interments on this small area. It was a crowded cemetery.

Judging from the 1699 Franck map, the northern residential area of the village was within 50 feet of the northeast bastion wall. The largest residence is identified by Franck as that of Captain Juan Jordán de Reina and is partially enclosed by a fence or stockade. Shown in figure 2.8, the house has a gabled roof and covered entryway or portico, similar to the friary. It is about 16.4 by 8 feet in size with a large, freestanding cross and flagpole midway between the residence and the bastion wall. Six small cabins are clustered near the Reina residence (see figure 2.6). Two are very small (about five feet long) gabled rectangular cabins near the entrance with a larger cabin (about 10 feet long) approximately 25 feet to the east. About 33 feet south of the Reina compound is an east-west row of three more of the larger cabins. Despite the accuracy and detail of the 1699 Franck map, there is something missing: the temporary thatch huts described in the documents. There were 260 soldiers at Santa María in February 1699, just a month before Franck made his map of the settlement (Clune et al. 2003: 32), yet there are only eight houses on his map. There had to have been scores of the crude sapling and thatch huts in the village, but they are not included on the Franck map as it depicts only the structures built in the Spanish style.

All areas of the large village were archaeologically investigated (figure 2.10), and scattered throughout were features and a thin, patchy midden. In the central village area, about 200 feet east of the northeast bastion and 150 feet east of the projected location of Captain Reina's residence, the foundations of at least one house and associated refuse features from the Early Village occupation were discovered. As shown in figure 2.11, in the northern end of the excavation unit were four foundation wall sills from at least one

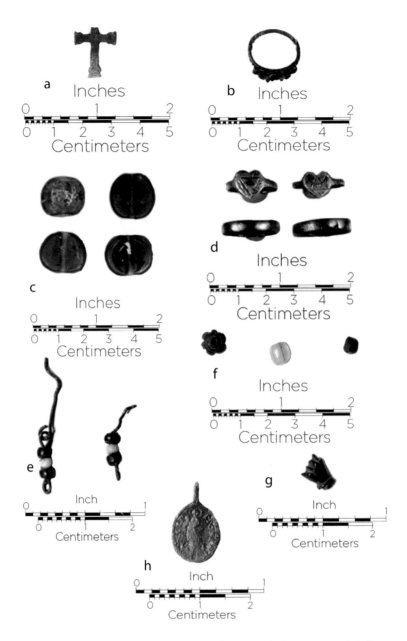

Figure 2.9. Artifacts from Presidio Santa María: *a,* brass crucifix (98N-8094–59); *b,* finger ring (98N-6995–97); *c,* Man-in-the-Moon beads [*top:* (98N-7470–23); *bottom left:* (98N-7691–8); *bottom right:* (98N-8094–73)]; *d,* finger rings [*top:* Jesuit rings; *bottom:* finger ring bands (not cataloged, reburied)]; *e,* glass beaded earrings (95N-1645–66); *f,* personal glass beads (98N-7260–38; 98N-7259–18; 98N-7251–25); *g,* jet higa (98N-6995–97); *h,* religious medallion (ZTR4–2901; at Naval Air Station Pensacola). Courtesy of the Archaeology Institute, University of West Florida.

structure. The foundations of three walls from one structure (Structure 1) are sills from a small square or rectangular building with a post-on-sill framework and large corner posts. Though substantially built, the portion of the structure exposed was narrow, measuring only eight feet wide. The fourth wall trench was parallel to the west wall of Structure 1 and only 2.5 feet west of it. This wall trench was almost identical to the foundation trenches of Structure 1, and because of its close proximity, similarity, and parallel orientation, the fourth wall trench was likely a former wall of Structure 1 or part of a previous, similar building. There was very little cultural material in the foundation trenches, indicating they were probably dug early in the occupation of the village. Structure 1 falls within the size of the small rectangular buildings in the village on the 1699 Franck map. These architectural features showed no signs of burning.

Two refuse pits are associated with Structure 1. The largest pit was within four feet of the residence and was the largest refuse pit encountered anywhere on the site: 13 feet long, almost 6 feet wide, and approximately 2 feet deep. As Marie Pokrant (2001: 55–57) describes, there were at least three depositional episodes of organically stained, artifact-dense soil separated by relatively sterile yellow sand. Interestingly, some sherds from the upper refuse deposit mended with those in the bottom deposit, indicating that the pit was probably filled in a short period of time. The second refuse pit was approximately 20 feet south of the structure and much smaller.

An important aspect of the pottery recovered in the Early Village period features is that 65.1 percent is Native American made. Almost all Native American ceramics are grog tempered (83.1% by weight), followed by some tempered with sand (9.7%) and only a small amount tempered with shell, grit, or grog shell. Grog tempering in West Florida has been clearly associated with missionized Apalachee people. Further analysis may well elucidate the migration of a community of ceramic practice between the female potters from Apalachee who were the producers of household pottery (Pigott 2015: 60–63; Worth 2015: 14–16). As discussed above, Apalachees were the largest ethnic group at Santa María from its beginning to its end. The abundance of their grog-tempered pottery in the Early Village refuse pits associated with the Spanish-style Structure 1 seems to be a strong archaeological reflection of the Apalachee presence at Santa María. Sand-tempered pottery has been found at an early eighteenth-century site on Mobile Bay that is tentatively associated with refugee Chacatos, depicted in figure 2.2 (Waselkov and Gums 2000). The Chacato were a consistent minority at Santa María, and the sand-tempered ceramics in the Early Village refuse pits possibly could have been made by them.

The specific counts and weights of the ceramic types in the Early Village

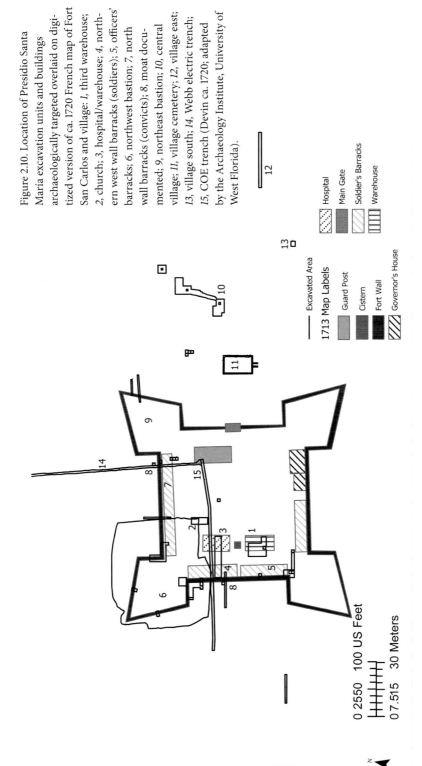

Figure 2.10. Location of Presidio Santa María excavation units and buildings archaeologically targeted overlaid on digitized version of ca. 1720 French map of Fort San Carlos and village: 1, third warehouse; 2, church; 3, hospital/warehouse; 4, northern west wall barracks (soldiers); 5, officers' barracks; 6, northwest bastion; 7, north wall barracks (convicts); 8, moat documented; 9, northeast bastion; 10, central village; 11, village cemetery; 12, village east; 13, village south; 14, Webb electric trench; 15, COE trench (Devin ca.1720; adapted by the Archaeology Institute, University of West Florida).

Hospital
Main Gate
Soldier's Barracks
Warehouse

Excavated Area

1713 Map Labels
Guard Post
Cistern
Fort Wall
Governor's House

0 2550 100 US Feet
0 7.5 15 30 Meters

N

assemblage are presented in appendix II, table II.1. When temper is not considered, of the 417 typable ceramics, the most abundant ceramic types are Grog Tempered Plain (42.7%), Grog Tempered Burnished (18.5%), and Jefferson Check Stamped, *variety* Leon (14.3%). Regardless of ceramic type, 56.4 percent of the surfaces are plain and 21.6 percent are burnished. The remaining sherds have a variety of surface decoration, including incising, check stamping, punctating, and red filming/slipping.

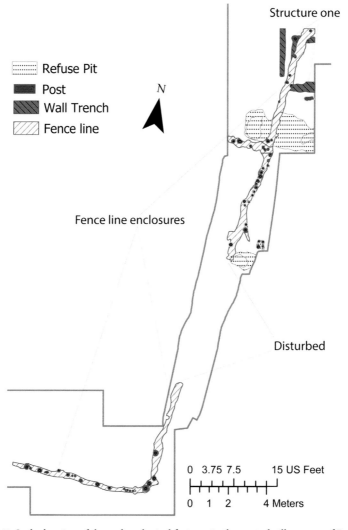

Figure 2.11. Scale drawing of the archaeological features in the central village area of Presidio Santa María. Courtesy of the Archaeology Institute, University of West Florida.

Almost all the Euro-American ceramics recovered from the Early Village refuse pits are in the general classes of Other Coarse Earthenware (80.5%) and Majolica (19.6%). Of the 226 typable sherds, the most abundant by count are Unglazed Olive Jar (25.5%), El Morro (17.5%), and San Luis Polychrome (17.0%). Notable are 16 pieces of Guadalajara Polychrome in the pit adjacent to Structure 1, which is a high count for this relatively rare ceramic type.

Over two-thirds (67.7%) by weight and 85.5 percent by count of this residential assemblage is associated with Kitchen activities. This high proportion is to be expected because the village is where the residents lived and where domestic activities took place for the first nine years of the Santa María occupation. While ceramics dominate the Kitchen items (79.0% by count and 83.6% by weight), the remainder is made of glass, especially wine bottle fragments and a few pieces of case bottles. Architectural materials consist mainly of bricks, ladrillos, mortar, and nails, but there are a few pieces of window glass and hinges from the large pit. This refuse pit also had four pieces of iron necklace chain and eight pieces of writing slate. The southern refuse pit contained two silver half-real coins. One was an almost square Philip V coin minted in Mexico City between 1706 and 1728, and the other was a triangular Charles II coin also minted in Mexico City between 1688 and 1697. All the Arms artifacts are lead shot. Clothing items include four fragments of silver brocade and glass seed beads.

The refuse pits associated with Structure 1 in the village contained well-preserved food remains (Pokrant 2001: 55–56). Mammals included cattle, pig, and white-tailed deer. Fish and oyster remains were also present. Plant remains included olives, mullein (a medicinal herb), corn, persimmon, wild grape, and saw palmetto.

The architectural evidence of Structure 1 indicates it was solidly built in the Spanish style. The presence of rectangular bricks, flat and thin ladrillo tiles, and window glass fragments in the refuse pits indicates internal features such as a brick hearth, perhaps a ladrillo tile floor or roof, and at least one glass window, none of which were produced locally. Also present are personal indicators of high status, such as the silver brocade from an officer's uniform, necklace chain, beaded clothing, and writing slates. The total evidence from this residence points to the probability that the male occupant had relatively high status, perhaps an officer.

Pokrant's (2001) study of the Santa María village revealed that it began to flourish in 1703 as more people arrived and the families of Spanish officers and civilians were introduced. Pokrant also notes that another indication of village growth was a shift in how the village was referred to in the documents. Initially, official records referred to huts and tents in the village, but by 1703 the documents mention houses; an English account of Santa María noted about 40 thatched houses in the village (Pokrant 2001: 29). Apparently, houses in the village were quite close because in 1703, Ynes de Bracamonte y Avila, a widow who lived in the village, complained of overhearing an illicit sexual encounter between two soldiers while passing in front of houses contiguous to hers (Pokrant 2001: 29–30). The documents also mention the presence of gardens in the village for the residents, friars, and officers. Indians and convict laborers watered the gardens and added fertile soil from the nearby spring (Franck 1700).

The Rosario Shipwreck

As mentioned previously in this chapter, two ships wrecked near Presidio Santa María in a 1705 hurricane: a passing French frigate that wrecked off Mobile Point and a Spanish frigate, the *Nuestra Señora del Rosario y Santiago Apóstol*, that was blown onto the north shore of Santa Rosa Island near Punta de Sigüenza in Pensacola Bay. The Spanish frigate was part of a small supply fleet led by Admiral Andrés de Landeche. Santa María was only the first of several stops assigned to the fleet, and it is a good example of how various tasks were combined with support shipments to Spanish colonial settlements. Landeche's tasks included the following (Bratten 2003: 22; Childers and Cotter 1998: 80; Hunter 2001: 48):

- deliver the situado to Santa María
- meet two brigantines bound for the Canary Islands in St. Joseph Bay
- drop off a work crew on Santa Rosa Island to cut trees for masts and spars
- conduct a reconnaissance of the San Luis mission near Tallahassee
- escort to the Bahama Channel the two frigates of his fleet carrying the San Agustín situado and the brigantines bound for the Canary Islands
- return to Santa María on Pensacola Bay to pick up the masts, spars, and carpenters
- return to Veracruz

Admiral Landeche's fleet of three frigates arrived at Presidio Santa María on June 1, 1705, delivering the long-awaited situado after a devastating fire in November 1704 had destroyed the food supplies. Landeche also brought the senior master of ships carpentry for the Windward Fleet, Augustin Antonio, and nine other skilled workmen to prepare the 100 trees Arriola marked the previous year on Santa Rosa Island for masts, spars, and topmasts (Bratten 2003: 22). The carpenters and laborers built a warehouse to store poles near Sigüenza Point along with several houses nearby for shelter (Childers and Cotter 1998: 80).

Landeche returned on September 3 in the *Rosario* to pick up the masts and spars that the carpenter and crew had prepared for transport. He moored off Santa Rosa Island (see figure 1.4) near the warehouse, but the next day a hurricane struck, and despite all the efforts of the crew, the *Rosario* was driven into the shallows, struck the bottom, heeled over, lost the rudder, and broke apart (Hunter 2001: 52). After the crew salvaged what they could, the remaining ship was intentionally broken up and burned to the waterline, presumably to salvage metal fasteners and any other useful metal (Hunter 2001: 53). While no one was killed, 200 members of the ship's crew and woodworkers were stranded for a time at Presidio Santa María, along with 90 shipwreck victims from the passing French vessel. Landeche and his men soon returned to Veracruz on a French vessel, *Précieuse*. In July 1706, another ship, the *El Santo Rey David*, picked up the 60 poles intended to be used for masts, spars, topmasts, and yards and took them to Veracruz (Hunter 2001: 55).

Fortunately, the wreck of the *Rosario* has been located, identified, and studied. The Florida Bureau of Archaeological Research (BAR) first investigated the wreck in 1992 (Spirek et al. 1993). The shipwreck has also been investigated several times by UWF between 1998 and 2002 (Bratten 2003; Hunter 2001; Hunter et al. 2000). A large portion of the hull was exposed during these excavations, and over 1,000 artifacts were recovered. For a detailed discussion of the *Rosario*'s construction and architecture, vessel history, artifact distribution, and assemblage, see Hunter (2001), John Bratten (2003), Morgan Wampler (2012), and Kad Henderson (2020).

As shown in figure 2.12, much of the ship's hull is preserved, including the stem, framing components, hull, ceiling planking, and longitudinal support

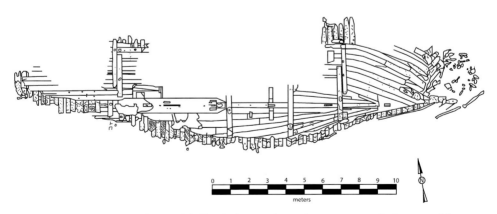

Figure 2.12. *Rosario* shipwreck hull scale drawing (Wampler 2012: Figure 2). Courtesy of the Archaeology Institute, University of West Florida.

timbers such as the keelson and keel (Wampler 2012: 4). The ship was built in Campeche, and its builder extensively utilized mahogany (*Swietenia sp.*) in the hull along with Spanish cedar, which enabled the builder to make immense timbers not possible in Europe at the time. It was an exclusively iron-fastened hull (Bratten 2003: 28–32).

Many organic artifacts were in situ, lying on the inside hull of the ship, and some are shown in figure 2.13. The items include woven matting, 24 wood sheaves for pulleys, 17 straw brooms, a wood quoin for aiming cannons, four pieces of leather shoes, 43 pieces of leather, and a wooden wedge. Half the sheaves were over 10 inches in diameter and stacked in a pile in the bow near preserved lengths of rope, stacked straw brooms, two unused eyebolts, and a wooden box of nails. The spatial arrangement of the sheaves and other rigging

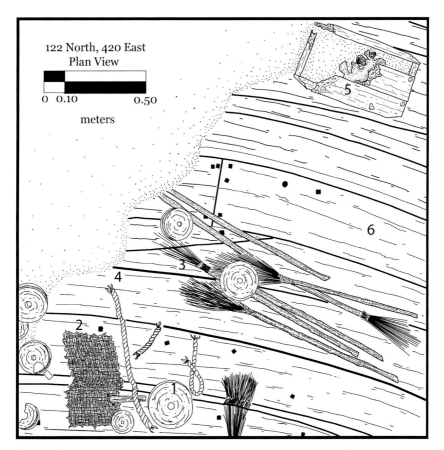

Figure 2.13. *Rosario* shipwreck scale drawing showing *1*, in situ sheaves (pulleys); *2*, woven mat; *3*, straw brooms; *4*, rope; *5*, wooden box of nails; *6*, port side of the bow hull (Hunter 2001: Figure 25). Courtesy of the Archaeology Institute, University of West Florida.

plus repair-related artifacts suggests to Hunter (2001) that they could originally have been in a bowswain's storage locker. Hunter (2001: 131–136) also suggests that while the sheaves could have been used for the ship's largest running rigging, they also could have been used in the pulleys used to pull the extremely heavy pine poles into the ship through temporary ports in the vessel's transom near the waterline.

A variety of other artifacts were recovered. The ceramic assemblage of 412 sherds consists of several coarse earthenware, including Olive Jar and Majolicas such as Puebla and Castillo Polychrome and a few pieces of Mexican Red Painted. The known beginning manufacturing dates of the ceramic types agree well with the 1705 sinking date of the *Rosario*. Personal items recovered from the shipwreck include a razor blade handle, wooden and bone rosary beads, a gaming piece, wooden buttons, a possible leather button, and a finger ring. Wampler's (2012) study of the social identity of the people aboard the *Rosario* provides an interesting insight into the composition of the ship's crew and the shipboard culture on this Spanish warship.

The Violence Begins at Santa María

In early 1707, hostile British-allied Creek Indians began to arrive and camp near Presidio Santa María. By March of that year, the meat supply for the presidio community ran out because 150 hostile Indians camped at the mouth of the Santa Rosa channel posed a deadly threat to any hunting parties (Coker and Childers 1998: 35). Regardless of the dangerous conditions and local struggles for survival, the shipyard of Veracruz servicing the Windward Fleet continued to demand poles for masts and spars from trees found in Pensacola-area forests.

In May 1707, Admiral Landeche again transported carpenters and woodcutters to cut down pines and prepare logs for transport to the Veracruz shipyards. Two months later, presidio Governor Arriola arrived at Santa María on the *David* to pick up the expected shipment of the hewn logs. However, upon arrival Arriola discovered that the carpenters and woodcutters had not been sent out from the presidio (Childers and Cotter 1998: 81; Hunter 2001: 55–56). He reported the reason for the delay was that the entire presidio community was on continual armed alert because an army of nearly 1,200 Creeks together with some Englishmen out of Charleston had surrounded the presidio. The Creeks had burned a nearby Spanish lookout post at the mouth of Bayou Grande, during which 17 Spanish-allied Indians and one Spanish convict were captured. The Indian captives were likely sold as slaves to the Charleston traders. During this same period, the Spanish retaliated when soldiers sent to scout the other side of Bayou Grande found and burned 36 canoes and discovered 60 houses of the British-allied Creek Indians (Coker and Childers 1998: 39).

As Hunter (2001: 56) describes, despite dangerous circumstances and an unhappy crew, Arriola dispatched a logging crew to the East River (Rio Jordan) escorted by an armed contingent of 160 soldiers. Ultimately, Arriola sent a shipment of 62 poles of various sizes as well as 11 anchor stocks to Veracruz in August 1707 (Coker and Childers 1998: 39). That same month, the English and their Native American allies began directly attacking Santa María.

On August 12, 1707, 20 to 30 Creeks invaded the Santa María village and began burning houses while the Spanish and their allied Indians took refuge in the fort. In addition to the loss of shelter, the attack resulted in personal tragedies, as several women and children of the Ocatose Indians living in the village were taken captive and sold into slavery. After this attack, the new friar's house and hospital in the village were dismantled and rebuilt inside the fort.

Four days later, on August 16, a second and more deadly attack on the presidio commenced. Another house in the village was burned, and the remaining unburned houses were used as blinds for the attackers (Coker and Childers 1998: 40–43). The next day, most of the village was looted and burned again. Creek warriors also gathered on the beach at the foot of the bluff and fired on Fort San Carlos. The attack continued for the next 30 hours, killing 12 Apalachee and Chacato residents and wounding many Spanish soldiers (Coker and Childers 1998: 40–43). On the third day, enemy Indians gathered on the hill just west of Fort San Carlos where they raised the British flag and again began shooting at the Spanish; the attacking parties also burned what was left of the village and part of the fort caught fire, though it was extinguished. The enemy then surrounded the fort, attacking and killing those who dared to venture outside the walls.

In the fall of 1707, the village was abandoned and the entire community moved inside Fort San Carlos. Groups of soldiers or civilians who left the fort for water, bathing, washing clothes, gathering wood, and other necessities required heavy military escort and were highly susceptible to attack (Coker and Childers 1998: 40–43). Many residents were killed or maimed on these task groups, even with the armed escorts, and Governor Moscoso pleaded for more arms, cannons, and men. The governor also ordered the clearing of all vegetation and village ruins surrounding Fort San Carlos that might have otherwise provided cover on further attacks. Additional fortification improvements were also made, including the construction of fascine bundles, new or improved sand terrepleined walls for mounting heavy guns, and strengthening of the curtain walls (Coker and Childers 1998: 44).

Summary of Santa María's Early Years, 1698–1707

Presidio Santa María was situated on a bluff overlooking the pass to the Gulf of Mexico at the head of a gulley that provided easy access to the bay shore. Upon the arrival of a military garrison and convict laborers from New Spain numbering about 460 people, construction of a fort immediately began. The fort was a Vauban design with a large square stockade protected by rhomboid-shaped bastions on each corner. The fort was originally designed to defend a naval attack, and the south curtain wall near the bluff facing the bay was a double wall filled with sand (terrepleined), with cannons lining the parapet. The pine logs used in the fort walls quickly decayed and had to be replaced every few years. The adjacent village was east of the fort in a large open area. Archaeological investigations there documented a Spanish-style house and associated refuse pits filled with domestic debris. The materials revealed that the residents had a relatively high status, probably an officer and his wife.

Overall, the early years at Presidio Santa María de Galve were marked by a series of crises, including two waves of refugees, seven destructive fires, two hurricanes, and violent attacks. There was also a chronic and debilitating shortage of food, soldiers, and laborers. This period ended badly because of increasing attacks by English-led Creek allies. The attacks rapidly increased in size and violence so that by the fall of 1707 the village had to be abandoned and was destroyed. Although unbeknownst at the time, the entire population of several hundred people would have to live inside the confines of Fort San Carlos for the next eight long years as Presidio Santa María was surrounded and under siege.

Under Siege, 1707–1715

After the demise and exodus of the indigenous Apalachee and Timucua from the Apalachee Province in 1704, the 400-mile-wide area between Pensacola and St. Augustine was somewhat re-populated by invading Lower Creeks who, in collusion with the English, continued attacks on the Spanish presidios and the villages of their Indian allies. The Spanish had only the two coastal presidios at Pensacola and St. Augustine, as the outpost at San Marcos had been destroyed in 1704 by the British and allied Creeks. The vast region between the presidios had become a war zone.

The Enemy Stays

At Presidio Santa María, the English-led Creek army that arrived in 1707 stayed for the next eight years. They surrounded Fort San Carlos and launched direct attacks and raids, menacing the population (Clune et al. 2003: 31). The English and their allied warrior Indians attacked any party entering or leaving the presidio. Groups of regular soldiers and convict laborers sent outside the fort walls to complete basic survival tasks needed heavy protection at all times; injuries, casualties, and captures were common during these years (Coker and Childers 1998: 42–43). Surrounded by a deadly enemy, the entire presidio community essentially became hostages within their own rundown fort (Clune et al. 2003: 31; Harris 1999; Renacker 2001).

During a lull in direct attacks in the early fall of 1707, the British and their Indian army increased their forces around Fort San Carlos. Groups of Native Americans and Englishmen, including parties on horseback, were seen near the fort (Coker and Childers 1998: 44–46). On November 27, 1707, the English asked for surrender several times, but Interim Governor Moscoso refused. Night attacks then began and were continuous and vicious, and the south wall of the fort on the bluff was constantly fired upon. Out of necessity, Governor Moscoso offered the convict laborers their freedom if they would fight to secure the community. This offer proved fortuitous as two days later Moscoso sent out a military detachment that included these convicts-turned-defenders to secure the barrel wells on the bay beach below the fort. In the fighting that ensued, one of the principal Creek chiefs was killed, causing the entire Indian army to withdraw from the Pensacola area for a time (Coker and Childers 1998: 45–46).

Compounding the general misery, the residents of Presidio Santa María saw their last local source of supplies and support, the French at Mobile, cut completely off during 1709 and 1710. The French were suffering through the worst food shortage of their colony's existence because of a serious drought and an English navy blockade of Port Dauphin at the mouth of Mobile Bay (Coker and Childers 1998: 53). Bienville was forced to send his troops to live in surrounding Indian villages to survive (Higginbotham 1977: 401; Holmes 1967: 49), and in a reversal of fortunes, the French now requested food and basic supplies from the Spanish in Pensacola. Although Santa María was running on fumes in terms of supplies, the Spanish were, nevertheless, indebted to the French for their years of assistance and were obliged to send portions of their own meager stocks to French Mobile (Clune et al. 2003: 63–64; Coker and Childers 1998: 53).

Throughout the eight years of siege, everything seemed to change for the worse in Pensacola. For the Spanish, the only local source of food and supplies from the French in Mobile was becoming, at best, unpredictable, and they could not hunt or garden themselves. By 1709, presidio occupants were left with only the unreliable situado for their survival. Sickness, especially scurvy and beriberi, ravaged the community because of chronic malnutrition.

Life under Fire

Although raids and attacks continued, repair and improvements were made to Fort San Carlos in 1708 and 1709 as the Spanish had little choice but to continue to shore up their only protected space. Coker and Childers (1998: 49) relate that a series of eight two-story huts were constructed for the troops along the curtain walls. Where the curtain walls were repaired, they increased the height by almost two feet. Moscoso ordered the parapets of sand removed from the bastions and curtain walls due to rapid decay of the posts. However, Moscoso died in 1709, and Joseph de Guzmán was named the new governor of Santa María. He disagreed with Moscoso's modification plan for the fort, but apparently the terrepleined bastions and curtain walls had already been removed, except for the northwest bastion, and replaced with single stockade walls (Coker and Childers 1998: 49; Renacker 2001: 47–48).

Ongoing illness plagued the population of the presidio, slowing repairs and new construction projects; deaths were frequent. In November 1709, there was an active workforce of about 340 people including eight salaried women and 80 hired Indian guest laborers and tradesmen. By February of the next year, 70 people had fallen seriously ill. More convict laborers were sent from Veracruz to bolster the presidio, but the constant diet of salted beef and pork along with the lack of fresh produce strained and weakened everyone in the Pensacola community. Scurvy and beriberi were rampant, and the hospital was full to overflowing. It was during this time that the English compounded the misery felt in Pensacola by blockading the mouth of Mobile Bay and cutting off their supplies (Coker and Childers 1998: 53).

One of the reasons for the continual shortage of supplies in Santa María surfaced in 1712 when it was reported that much of the limited space on the situado supply ships out of Veracruz was taken up by merchandise the governor and high-ranking officers had purchased privately. This practice had been conducted since the founding of the presidio. Contraband was brought into Pensacola specifically for the governor's and officers' personal use or to be resold to the presidio soldiers for a large profit (Clune et al. 2003: 66–67). However, as Brenda Swann (2000: 112–113) relates, the sale of illegal goods by officers to regular soldiers provided some of the only suitable day-to-day basics, such as new clothing, or short-lived relative luxuries, such as chocolate and liquor. By 1712, corruption of the governor and colluding officers as well as the exploitation of the soldiers was rampant. The new governor, Don Gregorio de Salinas Varona, even had a personal store and warehouse on Dauphin Island from which he privately supplied the Pensacola garrison to the detriment of the French (Coker and Childers 1998: 59). At this time, Governor Salinas also unilaterally forbade the French to sell any goods to Santa María so he could corner the market for himself. However, by that time, the French were becoming increasingly reluctant to sell goods to the Spanish (Coker and Childers 1998: 61). Apparently comfortable with profiting off the misery and destitution of those beneath him, Governor Salinas even went so far as to flaunt all regulation and charter a French ship at great expense to sail to Veracruz for additional supplies. The viceroy, apparently shocked, refused to pay for the charter, though he did send additional supplies and troops to Pensacola (Coker and Childers 1998: 64).

Enemy assaults were ongoing as both the siege of Fort San Carlos and attacks on task groups outside the walls continued. In 1712, Governor Salinas reported that Fort San Carlos was in such a deteriorated condition that 3,000 stakes in the stockade wall needed to be replaced. Additionally, the supply magazine and gun platforms were falling down, and the newly constructed infantry quarters were already deteriorating. Salinas recommended tearing the troop's barracks down and building two 110-foot-long "sheds" along the walls for their use (Clune et al. 2003: 50). His orders apparently were followed as there are long, narrow, shed-style barracks depicted on the south and west curtain walls on the 1713 map (see figure 2.4). Although the Spanish sent troops outside the fort to drive the encamped enemies back, still they lurked, attacked, and harassed the occupants of Fort San Carlos. As the siege years wore on, more and more armed soldiers were required to protect workers procuring necessary basic supplies outside the fort walls.

Despite the siege conditions at Santa María, General Arriola continued to receive orders to provide more poles for export to Veracruz (Childers and Cotter 1998: 81). However, dangers surrounding the Pensacola presidio made fulfilling the orders an impossibility until 1711 when the felling of timber for masts and spars resumed, but it was extremely dangerous as ambush attacks by the British and their Indian allies continued. As Coker and Childers (1998: 56) relate, in September 1712, a large group of loggers escorted by several officers and 40 soldiers were attacked by three groups of 100 Indians each, and three woodcutters were killed. Soon afterward, another large party of loggers and officers was ambushed, killing three soldiers and the surgeon friar of the hospital. The captain of the group surrendered to the British, and 18 soldiers and five convict laborers were taken captive. Faced with such threats, the timber industry at Santa María effectively ended.

Added to the constant mortal peril at Presidio Santa María was the fact that the community remained underfed and was on half rations throughout most of these years; supply shipments were always late and incomplete. The food, when it finally did arrive, was usually spoiled (Clune et al. 2003: 67; Swann 2000). Things were so desperate within the walls of Fort San Carlos de Austria that a group of convicts and soldiers cut their way out of their quarters, scaled the wall of the fort, and surrendered to the British and Indian forces despite the known brutality and dangers they would be facing (Coker and Childers 1998: 56).

The safety issues preventing the Spanish from leaving their fortified confines meant that Fort San Carlos continued to fall further and further into disrepair. As Coker and Childers (1998: 57, 60) recount, in July 1712, erosion of the bluff had reached both bastions on the south wall (San Francisco and San Carlos), and they had to be repaired. Salinas mentioned the San Francisco bastion would have fallen into the sea if he had not built three large sand cofferdams 110 feet long and 29 feet high, extending from the bluff edge to the rampart. Feeling unjustly ignored by the viceroy, and in increasingly dire straits, in November 1713, Governor Salinas wrote directly to King Ferdinand VI of Spain that hostile Indians armed with 6,000 flintlock muskets surrounded the decrepit Spanish presidio, which continued to fall into the sea (Coker and Childers 1998: 58). Salinas recommended that the presidio be moved from the mainland to Santa Rosa Island at the entrance to the bay, as no observed erosion had occurred there since 1698 and the location had the notable benefit of being protected from surprise raids as there is water on both sides of the narrow island. Comparing the southern wall bastions on Franck's 1699 map (figure 2.6) to those on the 1713 map (figure 2.4), the southeast bastion appears to have been slightly modified, and on both the 1719 and circa 1720 Devin maps (figure 2.5), both southern bastions have been significantly reduced and pulled back from bluff. All the bastions on Devin's 1719 and circa 1720 depictions of the fort (figure 2.5) are different in size, and all their walls appear to be stockaded, not terrepleined. Both maps also show that the area between the southern bastions and curtain wall had been enclosed with a new stockade wall to protect garden plots.

Though the misery continued to compound at Pensacola, big political changes were afoot on an international scale. January of 1713 saw the end of the War of Spanish Succession, an ending that also meant the end of the alliance of France and Spain. The activity of French ships in Spanish colonial waters was once again heavily regulated and discouraged (Coker and Childers 1998: 64). Meanwhile, nothing shifted in the aggressiveness of the English toward the Spanish, and the English-Creek raids continued at Santa María. What did change for the worse at the local level was that Spanish Pensacola's last local supply line with French Mobile was eroding fast, primarily because of the corruption and greed of Governor Salinas and his officers.

The Remains of Fort San Carlos and Six Internal Buildings

The majority of archaeological investigations at the Santa María presidio focused on Fort San Carlos de Austria and six interior buildings and associated activity areas (figure 2.10). Detailed technical results from these investigations are presented in books, edited volumes, journal articles, field reports, and a series of master's theses from students enrolled at UWF and other universities, and many are cited in the discussion below. For more technical archaeological details, readers are pointed to the following publications: Bense (1998, 2003, 2004) and Bense and Wilson (1999, 2003). In addition, calculations and resulting artifact tables are presented in appendix II. The information presented below is a synthesis of the information produced from the archaeological research conducted inside Fort San Carlos.

The Fort

The centerpiece of the Santa María presidio was the Vauban-style Fort San Carlos de Austria. In spite of its nearly constant state of disrepair and the perilous living conditions of its occupants, Santa María de Galve's continued presence on Pensacola Bay was the literal and emblematic key to Spain's hold on West Florida.

Archaeological investigations documented the north and west curtain walls of Fort San Carlos, the northwest and northeast bastions, and the moat along the north curtain wall. Most of the east curtain wall and all of southeast bastion likely have been destroyed by road and housing construction. However, portions of the southwest bastion and south curtain wall should be intact.

As George Renacker (2001: 36) relates, the engineer Franck designed the terrepleined walls and described them in two letters in 1699 as consisting of two rows of one-foot-thick posts set at three- to four-foot intervals. The outer posts leaned inward with horizontal logs fastened to them to deflect cannon shot. The inner wall of vertical posts, logs, and planks acted as a retaining wall to support the sand inside the double wall. In 1706, the terrepleined bastions were repaired and enlarged by Governor Guzmán, and all were armed with cannons placed on the wooden platforms of the parapets (Coker and Childers 1998: 34; Renacker 2001: 42). By 1707, when Indian attacks were on the rise, Guzmán had only half of the northwest bastion terreplein expansion finished. Around 1708, Governor Moscoso removed the terrepleined walls, except for the northwest bastion which contained the powder magazine (Renacker 2001: 48).

As the northwest bastion, named San Antonio, appears to have retained some form of terrepleined walls for its entire existence, it is no surprise that this is where we found the remains of a section of that wall. On the south wall of the northwest bastion, we discovered a 38-foot-long section of the terrepleined wall (figure 2.14), consisting of two parallel linear stains two to four feet apart with large post molds on five-foot centers. The outside linear stain is consistent with a horizontal log that deteriorated in situ, and the interior stain is consistent with Franck's description of the vertical retention wall (Bense 2003:

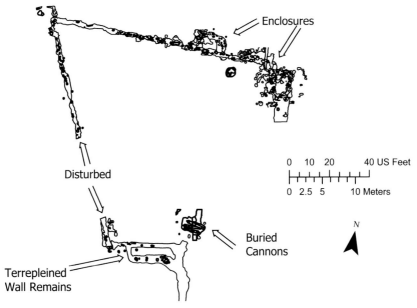

Figure 2.14. Presidio Santa María, scale drawing of the archaeological remains of the northwest bastion and part of the original terrepleined wall of Fort San Carlos. Courtesy of the Archaeology Institute, University of West Florida.

101–103; Renacker 2001: 100–101; Wilson 2000: 49–50). The remains of the entire northwest bastion were covered with two to three feet of sand, which could be from the terrepleined wall.

With the exception of the remnants of the terrepleined wall of the northwest bastion, all fort walls encountered were stockaded. A total of 354 feet of the fort wall was exposed and documented, including five cross sections. The cross sections revealed that posts were raised by setting large poles side by side into long V- or U-shaped construction trenches (figure 2.15). Generally, the inside walls of the construction trenches were vertical while the outer walls had a lower angle to assist in setting the heavy poles upright (Bense and Wilson 2003: 99). The upper sections of the wall posts were charred where heat from the fire that eventually destroyed them penetrated into part of the subsurface portion of the posts within the construction trenches. Below the charred sections of these post features, the posts had decomposed into dark organic stains. There was frequent and clear evidence of post replacement throughout the exposed fort walls. The constant repairs to Fort San Carlos mentioned throughout the historical documents are revealed in the stockade wall of the completely exposed northwest bastion (figure 2.14). The bases of the replacement posts were

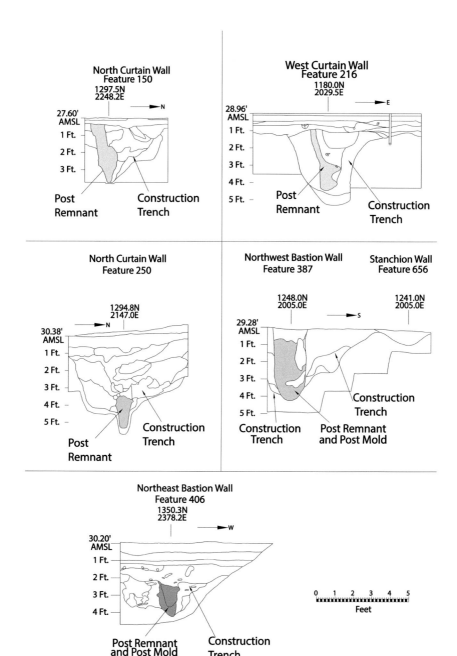

Figure 2.15. Presidio Santa María, scale drawings of cross sections of Fort San Carlos wall trench. Courtesy of the Archaeology Institute, University of West Florida.

consistently shallower than the original posts. While none of the historic maps perfectly matched the actual dimensions of the fort wall as documented via archaeological ground truthing, the shape and size were in very close agreement with Franck's original dimensions.

Artifacts were collected from the wall trench feature in the three cross sections of the north and west curtain walls behind the two barracks and the northwest bastion wall. The three-wall cross sections behind the barracks contained 977 artifacts, but the northwest bastion wall trench feature contained only 18. The area between the back of the barracks and the curtain wall was a very high activity area, and materials from everyday life likely built up against the base of the walls. The high number of artifacts in the curtain wall cross sections behind the barracks was very likely captured in backfill as posts were replaced.

A dry moat was parallel to the fort walls. Historic documents state that the moat was the equivalent of 8.2 feet deep and 16.4 feet wide (Renacker 2001: 48). Arriola reported in 1706 that Franck had attained these dimensions for the moat (Clune et al. 2003: 46). Renacker (2001: 48) and John Clune and colleagues (2003: 46) note that in 1706, the moat was reported to have filled in considerably from slope wash, which effectively lowered the height of the fort walls to the enemy. There is no further mention of the moat by Guzmán or Arriola and in 1718, Governor Matamoros described the fort as a square with four bastions of stakes without a moat (Clune et al. 2003: 46). The moat was documented in two cross sections next to the north and west walls (see figure 2.10), and it was wider and shallower than Franck's original dimensions (Bense and Wilson 2003: 106–107). It measured 23 feet wide at the top, 5 feet wide at the base, and 3.3 feet deep. The inner edge of the moat is about 10 feet from the base of the north fort wall. The sides are sloped about 45 degrees, and the base is relatively flat.

The northwest bastion single stockade wall showed much evidence of replacement posts, and there was little cultural material in the construction trench. Because the powder magazine was located in this bastion, it was literally off limits and, as a result, there was little cultural material there. The two cross sections of the northwest bastion stockade wall included artifacts from its construction (17 whole spikes) and the battles that took place there (two cannon balls and one cannon screw). An unforgettable moment in our excavations came when three complete cannon tubes were discovered buried in a large pit near the south corner of the northwest bastion wall (figure 2.16). The pit was just large enough to hold the three tubes. The touch holes of the cannons were not disabled or "spiked," and the tubes appear to have been operational when buried. Adding to their functional condition, we found part of a linen powder bag inside one cannon tube, indicating it had been fired not long before it was buried. The size of the cannons and cannon balls are well within the range of the 12 eight pounders described in a 1707 inventory of the guns at Fort San Carlos. Based on all these factors, Bense and Wilson (2003: 108) suggest that the three cannon tubes were probably hidden quickly, possibly when the fort was overtaken. Other than the three cannons, the cultural material in the fill of the pit and in the matrix excavated around it was sparse. Almost all of it were pieces of ceramics.

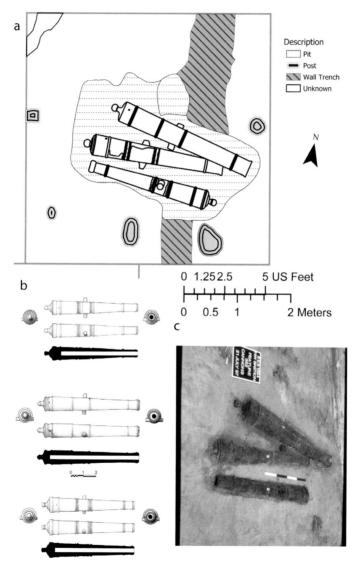

Figure 2.16. Presidio Santa María, image and scale drawing of three cannon tubes in pit inside Fort San Carlos. Courtesy of the Archaeology Institute, University of West Florida.

Officers' Barracks and Activity Area

The circa 1720 Devin map (figure 2.5b) identifies the barracks along the southwest curtain wall as "Officers' Quarters." Excavation units were placed next to the building in the open activity area in the front and back of the building. Fortunately, the remains were preserved under two to three feet of sand placed there in the late nineteenth century in preparation for construction of United States Army officers' houses along the bluff edge that are still there today.

There are three outstanding archaeological aspects of this area of the site: a well-preserved pile of the burned barracks, a multitude of activity features, and compelling evidence supporting the interpretation that the highest status members of the military, the officers, were quartered here. The barracks was built in 1712 as Governor Salinas had recommended (Clune et al. 2003: 50), and the 1713 map of the fort (figure 2.4) documents that they were completed. The barracks was burned to the ground in 1719 along with the entire presidio after French capture. As Bense and Wilson (2003: 109–128) describe in detail, the remains of the burned officers' barracks was covered with a half-foot-thick layer of charred and burned wood. Underneath the charcoal layer were in situ remains of the collapsed framing, walls, and floor of the structure. There were many pieces of burned timbers and boards, some of which were quite large (up to 1.6 feet long). Interestingly, there were identifiable puddle marks on the top of the charcoal layer, indicating that the burned structure sat exposed to weather for a considerable time. The east edge of the burned debris pile was clearly defined against the natural, light brown sand matrix. Throughout the charred deposit were hundreds of fasteners, including 449 whole nails and 27 large spikes, some of which were re-tempered in the fire. These fasteners were often found in concentrations on top of burned boards and floor sills. This burn debris pile contained 41.0 percent of the total fasteners recovered from the entire presidio with a 16:1 ratio of nails to spikes.

Below the burned debris, the subsurface remains of the southwest corner of the barracks building was well protected. The foundation for this barracks consisted of large corner posts with wall sills set in shallow trenches, shown in figure 2.17. The area enclosed by the post and sills contained few artifacts (seven), indicating that the building had a wood floor. Several pieces of burned boards lying on the floor were either part of the flooring or the collapsed walls, or both. There were 14 fasteners including a clinched spike on top of the north-south burned sill. Attached to the outside corner of the barracks were three lines of small posts set about two feet apart in irregular trenches. These lines of posts were likely part of a fenced enclosure similar to that documented at the Spanish house at Mission San Luis (McEwan 1993: Figure 11.8). There were also

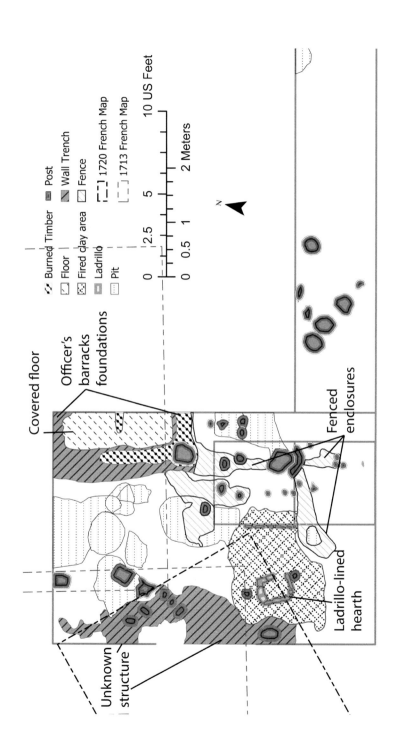

Figure 2.17. Presidio Santa María, scale drawing of features in the Fort San Carlos officers' barracks area. Courtesy of the Archaeology Institute, University of West Florida.

clusters of large posts both east and west of the burned barracks that were likely part of earlier quarters buildings or perhaps sections of the southwest bastion that was redesigned and repaired.

Additional clues about this building are gleaned from the presence and distribution of window glass. A total of 660 pieces of window glass were concentrated in a well-defined 10-foot area just east of the charred debris pile (Bense and Wilson 2003: Figure 4.26). This concentration represents 91.0 percent of all the window glass fragments recovered from the entire site. The tight concentration of the glass pieces strongly indicates that there was a window with glass panes in the east wall of the building that exploded outward during the fire. An additional architectural element of this building was revealed in the recovery of 13 pieces of lead roof sheeting, indicating that at least part of the roof was covered with sheets of lead, probably over the seams of roof boards and the edges of the eaves (Bense and Wilson 2003: 122). This roofing technique is described for the third warehouse, which was only 25 feet east of the officers' barracks.

A clear image of this barracks can be drawn from the architectural information archaeologically recovered in and near the charred debris pile (see Bense and Wilson 2003: 109–128). The building had a post-on-sill foundation with framing timbers spiked to large corner posts. Studs were placed on the sills along with top plates, and wall boards were fastened to the studs with nails. Floorboards were laid on the inside edges of the sills. Windows with glass panes were set in the east wall of the structure. Wood shingles or boards covered the roof and were at least partially sealed with lead sheeting. Taken together, the archaeological evidence for the officers' quarters at Fort San Carlos indicates a comparatively comfortable living situation, or rather, some comforts in the midst of increasing destitution. As discussed below, this living situation contrasts significantly against the basic accommodations for the regular soldiers and laborers residing within the same fort walls.

The open ground area between the rear of the barracks and the fort wall had a labyrinth of refuse pits and a large, open, ladrillo-lined hearth. As shown in figure 2.17, the refuse pits were close together and often intersected, indicating this was an active task space and disposal area. Like the interior of the adjacent barracks, the entire area was covered with the charred debris from the fire that leveled the structure. The material in these refuse pits consisted of a variety of domestic debris, especially from kitchen-related tasks. Continuous use of the ladrillo-lined hearth had hardened a five-by-four-foot area around it. A post adjacent to and behind a large, vertical ladrillo slab apparently used as a windbreak could have been used to suspend food and containers over the fire. There was charcoal and 66 pieces of charred corncobs in the hearth, and 15 charred corncobs were packed in a nearby smudge pit.

A large artifact assemblage was recovered from the officers' barracks and adjacent activity area considering only one corner of the burned structure and the immediate surrounding area was excavated. The assemblage consists of 15,096 counted items and 156.5 kg of weighed material, and it is much larger than the assemblages from any other area investigated inside the fort or the village, making up almost half (45.6%) of the material recovered from inside the fort (table 2.2).

The most abundant material class by count is Ceramics (55.2%, N=8,333), and Building Material is the largest of the weighed materials (34.8%, 45.2 kg), as shown in appendix II, table II.3a. It is better to use count rather than weight in the analysis of Euro-American ceramics as there is a wide weight differential within the Coarse Earthenware and between ceramic wares. Of the ceramics, 56.4 percent are Euro-American and 43.6 percent are Native American (table 2.3; appendix II, table II.3a. Two wares make up 95.0 percent of Euro-American ceramics: Other Coarse Earthenware (73.0%) and Majolica (22.0%), shown in table 2.4. While present, there are only a few pieces of Porcelain, Faience, Redware, and Delft. Of the 3,298 typable Euro-American sherds, the most frequent are Lead Glazed Coarse Earthenware (46.2%), Olive Jar (15.9%), and Unglazed Coarse Earthenware (12.5%). The number and proportions of the Euro-American ceramic types in each ware in the officers' barracks area are presented in appendix II, table II.2. In the Other Coarse Earthenware, 90.5 percent of the sherds are Lead Glazed (56.0%) or Olive Jar (19.3%) fragments, followed by Unglazed (15.2%). All other types of this ware are 4.5 percent or less, but the relatively rare Guadalajara Polychrome (N=122) is abundant and makes up 4.5 percent of the large assemblage of 2,724 typable sherds of Other

Table 2.2. Artifact totals in fort areas and village at Presidio Santa María

Fort Areas and Village	Count	% of Total	% of Fort	Weight (g)	% of Total	% of Fort
Officers' Barracks	15,096	40.7%	45.6%	156,540.2	39.3%	44.0%
Third Warehouse	5,906	15.9%	17.9%	64,135.0	16.1%	18.0%
Soldiers' Barracks	3,420	9.2%	10.3%	45,936.2	11.5%	12.9%
Hospital/Warehouse	4,945	13.3%	15.0%	42,855.0	10.8%	12.0%
North Wall Barracks	1,607	4.3%	4.9%	21,959.6	5.5%	6.2%
NW Bastion	244	0.7%	0.7%	10,911.7	2.7%	3.1%
Church	1,856	5.0%	5.6%	13,361.2	3.4%	3.8%
Village	4,044	10.9%		42,848.2	10.8%	
Totals	37,118			398,547.2		

Table 2.3. Proportions of Euro-American and Native American ceramics in Presidio Santa María site areas

Site Areas	Site Total		Residential Areas Only	
	EA[a]	NA[b]	EA	NA
Officers' Barracks	56.4%	43.6%	56.4%	43.6%
Soldiers' Barracks	55.3%	44.7%	55.3%	44.7%
North Wall Barracks	42.9%	57.1%	42.9%	57.1%
Village	49.3%	50.7%	49.3%	50.7%
Hospital/Warehouse	64.3%	35.7%	-	-
Church	53.6%	46.4%	-	-
Third Warehouse	86.4%	13.6%	-	-
Total count	13,506	8,461	7,263	6,139
Total percentage	61.4%	38.6%	54.2%	45.8%

[a] EA=Euro-American

[b] NA=Native American

Table 2.4. Ceramic wares, classes, and tempers in officers' barracks area inside Fort San Carlos

Euro-American Ceramic Wares and Classes	Count	%	Weight (g)	%
Other Coarse Earthenware	3,438	73.0%	26,936.6	92.4%
Majolica	1,035	22.0%	1,566.1	5.4%
Porcelain	129	2.7%	170.6	0.6%
Faience	65	1.4%	182.5	0.6%
Redware	24	0.5%	178.7	0.6%
Delft	13	0.3%	6.1	[a]
Stoneware	4	0.1%	105.5	0.4%
Totals	4,708		29,146.0	
Native American Ceramic Tempers	**Count**	**%**	**Weight (g)**	**%**
Grog	1,642	45.3%	7,812.4	50.5%
Sand	1,517	41.8%	5,511.3	35.6%
Shell	365	10.1%	1,469.6	9.5%
Grit	58	1.6%	313.9	2.0%
Unspecified	28	0.8%	263.4	1.7%
Grog Shell	15	0.4%	91.9	0.6%
Totals	3,625		15,462.4	

[a] Less than 0.1 percent.

Coarse Earthenware. Guadalajara Polychrome was used almost exclusively by women for cosmetic purposes (Deagan 1987: 44–46). Of the 14 types of Majolica, only four make up almost 75.0 percent: San Luis Polychrome (37.0%), Puebla Polychrome Blue Variant (20.3%), San Agustin Blue on White (10.9%), and Puebla Polychrome Black Lines (10.7%). All typable Porcelain is Chinese, almost all Faience is Seine Polychrome, all Redware is Unglazed, and almost all the Delft is Plain.

Ceramics made by Native Americans are analyzed using weights as there is no significant weight differential between the tempers or ceramic types and the problems of fracturing are bypassed. While there are six temper types (table 2.4; appendix II, table II.4a), 86.1 percent of the sherds are tempered with either grog (50.5%) or sand (35.6%). Shell tempering is present in 9.5 percent of the sherds, and there is only a trace of grit and grog shell tempering. The unspecified temper group makes up 1.7 percent and includes 20 Colonoware sherds and eight clay beads. Regardless of temper type, the most abundant ceramic types are Sand Tempered Plain (27.3%), Grog Tempered Plain (23.3%), and Grog Tempered Burnished (13.9%). Each of the remaining 39 ceramic types makes up 4.8 percent or less. Surfaces of 60.0 percent of Native American ceramics are plain and 20.5 percent are burnished. The remainder have a wide variety of applications: incised, punctated, stamped, roughened, filmed, slipped, and painted.

As the officers' barracks area was a residential one, it is expectable that Kitchen and Architecture materials are most abundant (see appendix II, table II.5a). Three quarters of the counted Kitchen artifacts are ceramics, and 19.8 percent are pieces of glass. Most glass sherds are from wine or case bottles, but there are also pieces of stemmed glass. There were abundant faunal remains. As Catherine Parker (2003: 217) details, 98.0 percent of the faunal remains were from meaty portions of domesticated animals, especially cow and pig, or deer. Other animal foods were fish, sheep or goat, oysters, and other mollusks. Remains of plant food were also abundant in the officers' area of the fort. Corn, faba beans, chickpeas, and field peas were present here as elsewhere in the community. Also present were legumes (beans) and olive and peach pits. With one exception, this is the only area where peaches, persimmons, and passion fruits were found.

As detailed in previous publications (for example, Bense and Wilson 1999: 86–100, 2003: 109–128; Chapman 1998), 75.0 percent of all high-status items recovered from the entire investigation were concentrated in this area. The association of high military/social rank and economic status with specific artifact types is based on known correlations, such as brocade and swords from officers' uniforms as well as expensive luxury items not usually available to those with restricted income or access, especially in such an isolated community. These items include fashionable jewelry, desirable imported ceramics, decorative glassware, and window glass. The officers' barracks area has by far the highest proportions of Arms, Tobacco, Furniture, and Personal items (see appendix II, table II.5a). Almost all the conspicuous or rare items were recovered from the officers' barracks, such as four bone gaming dice; a finger ring with three settings (see figure 2.9); three faceted amber pendants; over 100 personal glass, stone, and clay beads; almost all the silver thread brocade found at the presidio; four buckles, three of brass and one of iron; stemmed drinking glasses; and 660 pieces of window glass. Five silver real cobs were also recovered there, all of which are half reals minted in Mexico City. Three cobs are Philip V and two are Charles II, with manufacturing start dates between 1698 and 1715. See appendix VIII for more information on these and other coins from the presidio communities, Mobile, and Port Dauphin. Additional high-status items are a brass candlestick, candle tool, a brass musket butt plate, shoe buckles, and 45 furniture upholstery tacks. Other reflections of the residents' high status are in their food remains. The officers ate more and better cuts of meat than residents of other areas, especially from domesticated animals and deer plus a variety of fish and shellfish. In addition, the residents ate the only fruit recovered at the presidio.

When considered as a whole, the artifact assemblage recovered from the officers' barracks area produced almost half the material recovered from inside the fort (45.6%). There was no life of ease or luxury at the Santa María presidio, but on a relative scale, the quantity, quality, and diversity of social and economic status indicators strongly support that this was the officers' barracks and activity area. The officers and their companions ranked at the top of this community in terms of their living quarters and access to the most and best of available supplies and materials.

Soldiers' Barracks and Activity Area

As shown in the 1713 Spanish map and the circa 1720 Devin map of the fort (see figures 2.4 and 2.5b), the barracks along the north half of the west curtain wall of Fort San Carlos were labeled "soldiers' barracks." Measuring on each historic map, the barracks, built by Governor Salinas in 1712, were about 90 by 10 feet along the west curtain wall.

In this area of the site, the protective layer of nineteenth-century sand was not present, and the upper portion of the burned debris pile of the barracks had been disturbed by recent plowing and grading. However, the lower half-foot of the debris pile was preserved, and as in the burned officers' barracks, it contained large in situ pieces of burned timbers that overlay undisturbed structural foundations. As shown in figure 2.18, remains of the barracks back wall, front wall, and internal partition walls were documented. For more details about the soldiers' barracks, see Bense and Wilson (1999, 2003: 128–132). The back wall of this barracks was the most substantial of this structure. It had a deep wall trench (1.2 feet deep and 1.0 feet wide) with seven posts about 1.2 feet apart. There were

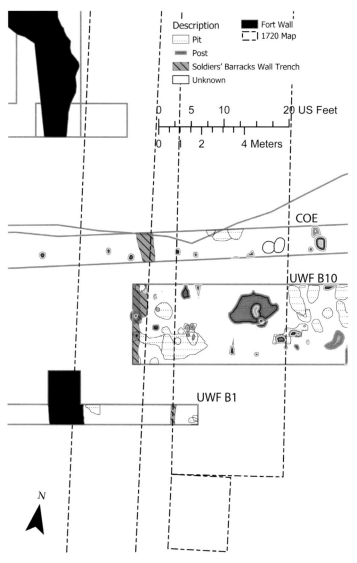

Figure 2.18. Presidio Santa María, scale drawing of features associated with the northwest wall and soldiers' barracks inside Fort San Carlos. Courtesy of the Archaeology Institute, University of West Florida.

also irregularly set replacement posts in or adjacent to the wall trench with bases considerably higher than the original posts. The other three walls had a post-in-ground frame. There were several clusters of posts, indicating frequent replacement. This barracks was eight feet wide, and the floor was dirt and pocked with large subfloor pits probably used for storage. The presence of some plaster and mortar suggests the possibility of finished walls.

There were 33 features associated with the soldiers' barracks. A quick glance at the size of the assemblages inside the fort shows that this artifact assemblage is three to four times smaller than that recovered from the officers' barracks area (see table 2.2). It should be noted, however, that the volume of soil excavated is only a fifth of the amount removed from the officers' barracks area (Bense and Wilson 2003: Table 4.1). As in the officers' barracks, the burned debris pile was rich in artifacts and contained 71.0 percent of the assemblage. When the whole assemblage recovered from the soldiers' barracks is considered (N=3,420, 42.1 kg), ceramics make up about half the counted and weighed materials (see appendix II, table II.3a). The ceramic assemblage consists of 55.3 percent Euro-American and 44.7 percent Native American sherds (see table 2.3), which is almost identical to the proportions in the remains of the officers' barracks. Almost all Euro-American sherds (99.2%) are either Other Coarse Earthenware (73.6%) or Majolica (25.6%), with only eight sherds of other wares (see appendix II, table II.4a). When ceramic ware is *not* considered, of the 1,010 typable sherds, the most abundant types are Unglazed Coarse Earthenware (22.8%), Olive Jar (19.7%), and El Morro (17.1%). The specific counts and weights of the ceramic types in each ware are presented in appendix II, table II.6. Within the Other Coarse Earthenware, Unglazed is most abundant (31.3%), followed by Olive Jar fragments (27.1%) and El Morro (23.6%). Most Majolicas (84.2%) are either San Luis Polychrome (40.9%), Puebla Polychrome Blue Variant (29.8%), or Puebla Blue on White (13.5%).

Almost all of the Native American ceramics (88.7% by weight) are tempered with either grog (59.6%) or sand (29.1%), and only minor amounts of other tempering materials are present (see appendix II, table II.4a). Regardless of temper, the most abundant ceramic types are Grog Tempered Plain (36.0%), Grog Tempered Burnished (21.7%), and Sand Tempered Plain (21.7). Most surfaces (95.4%) are either plain (63.1%) or burnished (32.3%). The surfaces of the remaining few sherds are incised, check stamped, slipped, or punctated. Also, one of the two pieces of Colonoware is from a brimmed plato.

Almost all of the counted artifacts (88.9%) and over half of the weighed materials (61.9%) from the soldiers' barracks are from Kitchen activities, and of the 3,035 counted artifacts in the Kitchen group, all are ceramics except 102 pieces of bottle glass. The artifact assemblage reflects typical residential activities such as illumination (lamp chimney), food preparation and eating (eight manos/metates and remains of deer, cows, pigs, fish, shellfish, corn, and beans), hunting/cutting (glass projectile point/knife and scissors), and writing (slate). Soldiering is reflected in a sword or rapier hilt, shot and sprue, a gunflint, and gunflint fragments. Clothing and personal items include 67 seed beads, straight pins, a piece of brass and copper jewelry, kaolin and earthenware pipes, and two brass buckles.

North Wall Barracks

The third and last barracks investigated inside Fort San Carlos was along the north curtain wall. This barracks is also labeled "soldiers' barracks" on the 1713 map (figure 2.4), and it is drawn but not labeled on the circa 1720 French Devin map (figure 2.5b). This structure was investigated with only two small trenches. The architectural remains of the rear wall of this barracks consisted of small charred posts in an irregular pattern set in a refuse-filled trench. The high amount of refuse in the wall trench reflects repair and replacement after the building was occupied. Posts penetrated the base of the back wall trench up to one foot. Posts from other walls were set directly in the ground, similar to the front and partition walls of the soldiers' barracks. The dirt floor of this structure was not covered. The small size of the posts, along with many replacement posts, indicates that this barracks was the shoddiest of the three studied. The irregular depth and small size of the rear wall posts suggest a much lower quality of building materials for this structure. From this, we deduce that the support poles/posts themselves were of varying lengths and not neatly cut or finished. Because these posts would have had to extend up to the same height in order to support a roof, the irregularity of their lengths probably means that the poles had to be driven down to different depths regardless of the depth of the wall trench. Perhaps they were scrap material left over from other projects. There was a lot of refuse between the north curtain wall and the back wall of the barracks, indicating it was a high activity and refuse disposal area, similar to the rear area of the officers' barracks.

A much smaller portion of this barracks was excavated when compared to the others investigated (5.0% the cubic volume excavated of the officers' quarters and 21.0% of the soldiers' barracks). Fifteen features were associated with this barracks, and the artifact assemblage contains only 1,607 counted items and 22.0 kg of weighed material, which is much less than that recovered from the soldiers' quarters (see table 2.2). Ceramics make up over half of the counted materials (61.7%), and the proportion of Euro-American wares is only 42.9 percent while Native American wares is 57.1 percent (see table 2.3). This assemblage is the only one recovered from a structure inside the fort that has more Native American than Euro-American ceramics. Almost all of the Euro-American ceramics (98.9%) are either Other Coarse Earthenware (55.4%) or Majolica (43.5%), with only four sherds of other wares (see appendix II, table II.4a). Of the 283 typable Euro-American ceramics, Lead Glazed Coarse Earthenware (41.3%), San Luis Polychrome Majolica (19.4%), and Olive Jar (14.8%) are the most abundant. Within the ceramic wares, Lead Glazed Coarse Earthenware (58.5%) and Olive Jar (21.0%) make up over three-quarters of the Other Coarse Earthenware (see appendix II, table II.8). San Luis Polychrome makes up 68.8 percent of the Majolicas, followed by Puebla Polychrome Blue Variant (15.0%). Almost all (94.2% by weight) ceramics made by Native Americans are tempered with either grog (45.0%) or sand (49.2%), with only slight amounts of other tempering agents (see appendix II, table II.4a). Of the 494 typable sherds, Sand Tempered Plain (29.2%), Grog Tempered Plain (21.4%), and Sand Tempered Burnished (15.2%) ceramic types are the most abundant. Surfaces of almost all sherds (87.9%) are either plain (64.3%) or burnished (23.6%), but there are small amounts that are red filmed, complicated stamped, and incised.

The artifacts in the north wall barracks assemblage are mainly associated with the Kitchen (37.9%) and Architecture (43.2%) groups (see appendix II, table II.5a), but there are some interesting aspects of this assemblage. The Activities group is 18.1 percent by weight, which is far higher than any other area inside the fort. The proportion of Activities artifacts is only 1.0 percent in the officers' barracks and 3.9 percent in the soldiers' barracks assemblages. The artifacts that account for most of the weight in the Activities group are an iron pulley and a shovel blade which indicate hard labor activities. The reason these tools were discarded in the north wall barracks may be that they were used there to repair and maintain the flimsy structure. On the other hand, writing materials (slate and ink bottle), a unique glass flask, a pharmaceutical bottle, and a peach pit are unexpected in what is likely the convict laborers' barracks. These items indicate literacy and access to personal and medical materials and fresh fruit. Faunal remains reveal the same suite of animal foods as recovered in the other barracks: deer, cow, pig, fish, and shellfish. Nevertheless, there are two very unusual meats: black bear and land turtles.

The artifact assemblage recovered from the north wall barracks indicated the residents did hard labor, but some were literate and had access to special materials and foods. However, architecture is a strong indicator of social status, and based on this factor, the people quartering in the north wall barracks occupied the lowest ranks of the presidio community. The less-than-superior building materials and slapdash techniques used in the construction of this barracks, together with a meager material assemblage that included the plainest utilitarian goods and the highest number of locally procured Indian ceramics, are all archaeological evidence that the north wall barracks housed residents with the lowest status in the community: the convict laborers.

Barracks Summary

Three barracks were archaeologically investigated inside Fort San Carlos de Austria. All three barracks lined curtain walls of the fort, and each was constructed differently and yielded distinct artifact assemblages. Three lines of evidence show that the barracks along the southern west wall was built for and housed officers: first, it is labeled "Officers' Quarters" on the 1713 map of the fort; second, the building is sturdy and has architectural elements related to personal comfort; and third, it produced the most artifacts of high quality and quantity. Though it would be hard to argue that any structure or building at Presidio Santa María de Galve was luxurious, the southern west wall barracks was the most sturdily constructed and comfortable for residents. The barracks had post-and-sill framing and boasted a solid wood floor, glass windows, and a reinforced roof. These architectural elements must have seemed almost luxurious and enviable by comparison to the other barracks. The artifact assemblage recovered from the officers' barracks was 7 to 41 times larger than that recovered from the other two barracks. By every measure, the artifacts reflect the relatively high social status of the residents.

Archaeological and historical evidence suggests soldiers were quartered in the barracks along the north half of the west wall of the fort. This barracks was not constructed as well as the officers' residence, as the back wall of the barracks was just a series of posts set in a wall trench and the other walls were made of single posts set in the ground. The building appeared to have needed constant repair, as many replacement posts were evident. The interior rooms were small (roughly 8 by 10 feet), and the comforts of windows set with glass and wood floors were not provided for the regular soldiers. The floor of this barracks was dirt and contained pits where soldiers perhaps stored their meager possessions. By comparison, the north wall barracks was a slapdash structure likely built from leftover materials from other projects across the presidio without strict oversight or control for quality or durability. It was a shabby building and undoubtedly uncomfortable for its residents. When compared with the other two barracks, the architectural evidence and artifact assemblage from the north wall barracks indicate that its occupants occupied a precarious niche at the very bottom of the social and economic ladder: the convict laborers.

The artifact assemblages recovered from the three barracks parallel the status associated with the architectural information, but they also provide glimpses into the lives of the people who resided in the barracks. The differences in the proportions of artifact groups from the three barracks raises the following observations and possible interpretations. Kitchen materials are highest by weight in the soldiers' barracks and lowest in the north wall barracks. Three manos/metates were recovered in the officers' barracks, eight in the soldiers' barracks area, but none in the north wall convicts' barracks. This distribution could indicate that the lowest class prepared food for the highest class in their barracks area while the soldiers cooked for themselves. Additionally, the proportions of personal, tobacco, clothing, and furniture items are much higher in the officers' barracks than in the others. It is obvious that the officers were the only ones who could afford such luxuries. Additionally, Activity items are 6 to 18 times higher in the north wall barracks than in the other two. Apparently, the convict laborers did some of their work (activities) at their barracks. The convict laborers also appear to have had access to some unusual foods (peaches and bear meat) and special personal possessions (glass flask), and at least some of them were literate (ink bottle and slate). Evidently, although the residents were probably convicted criminals doing hard labor, some were educated (literate) and clever enough to get high-end food and personal possessions.

The ratio of Euro-American to Native American pottery in the officers' and soldiers' barracks is almost identical, with Euro-American pottery constituting about half (56.0% and 44.0%). In the north wall barracks, however, the ratio is reversed. This difference could indicate the convict laborers had less access to Euro-American wares or perhaps more Native Americans lived there.

History and archaeology have combined to identify who lived in which barracks inside Fort San Carlos. Knowing the rank of the residents in the three separate barracks enabled us to compare the lives of the occupants as revealed in the architecture of their structures and the artifacts each group left behind. Strongly stratified as this community was, their materials reveal how differences in rank and social standing operated on the ground and illuminate several unexpected inconsistencies. Some social rules were flexible on the western frontier of Spanish Florida.

Third Warehouse

Historical records indicate that there were four warehouses at Santa María and, not surprisingly, all were inside Fort San Carlos from the start (Clune et al. 2003: 49). The first warehouse burned along with all the supplies in a January 1699 fire. Two months later a second warehouse was constructed, and historians suggest that if it survived the 1701 fire, then the 1704 fire consumed it along with almost every other building inside the fort (Clune et al. 2003: 49). By October 1705, a third warehouse was constructed. On the 1713 map of Fort San Carlos, a warehouse is listed in the legend as "C" (see figure 2.4);

unfortunately, that letter is *not* on the original map. However, all the buildings in the fort on the map have a letter corresponding with the legend *except* the building directly in front of the officers' quarters. Surely, this building must be the third warehouse and the letter "C" was on the map but was later covered by the insertion of the fort's name at the map's center. Regardless, when the map evidence is combined with the archaeological evidence presented below and in Bense and Wilson (2003: 134–144), we are confident that the third warehouse is the building in front of the officers' barracks on the 1713 map. This warehouse is described in historical documents as a two-story building about 55 by 25 feet in size with a wood floor and a board roof with caulked seams and lead sheeted ends (Clune et al. 2003: 49). Only seven years later, in 1712, Governor Guzmán described this warehouse as being in such a state of disrepair that he recommended it for demolition. As this building is not on either the 1719 or circa 1720 map of the fort, it apparently was demolished sometime after 1713.

The archaeological investigation of the third warehouse revealed a previously unknown cellar pit, six large support posts for the building, support posts of a probable covered entryway, and a cluster of four disposal pits with unique contents just outside the entrance. Both the north edge and steep side of the filled-in cellar pit were clearly delineated against the light tan subsoil in the profile (figure 2.19). The cellar pit fill consisted of many small, multicolored, discontinuous lenses reflective of backfilling with shovels. Another feature of note associated with the warehouse is the largest posthole encountered in the investigation. It was two feet wide and almost three feet deep, shown in figures 2.19 and 2.20. It was located just outside the edge of the cellar, and the post had been removed. This large post very likely was a load-bearing perimeter support post for the large two-story warehouse. Another large support post was identified about 18 feet to the south and was likely a floor/ceiling support for the cellar. There was no evidence of burning in the remains of the warehouse, which supports the contention that it was dismantled as Governor Guzmán had recommended in 1712.

There were four pits of note next to the cellar entryway (figure 2.20), each containing a narrow range of artifacts in very high frequency. Two pits were packed with nearly two pounds (1.3 kilograms) of charred beans and peas. A third was packed with cut cow bones, and a fourth was jammed with broken majolica tableware. The legumes were primarily faba beans, chickpeas (garbanzo beans), and garden peas (Ruhl 2003). The concentration of burned legumes in these two features suggests they were probably from bags of peas and beans burned in the 1704 fire that destroyed the second warehouse. During cleanup after the fire, the charred legumes were probably tossed in the disposal pits in preparation for construction of the third warehouse on the same spot. The faba beans at Presidio

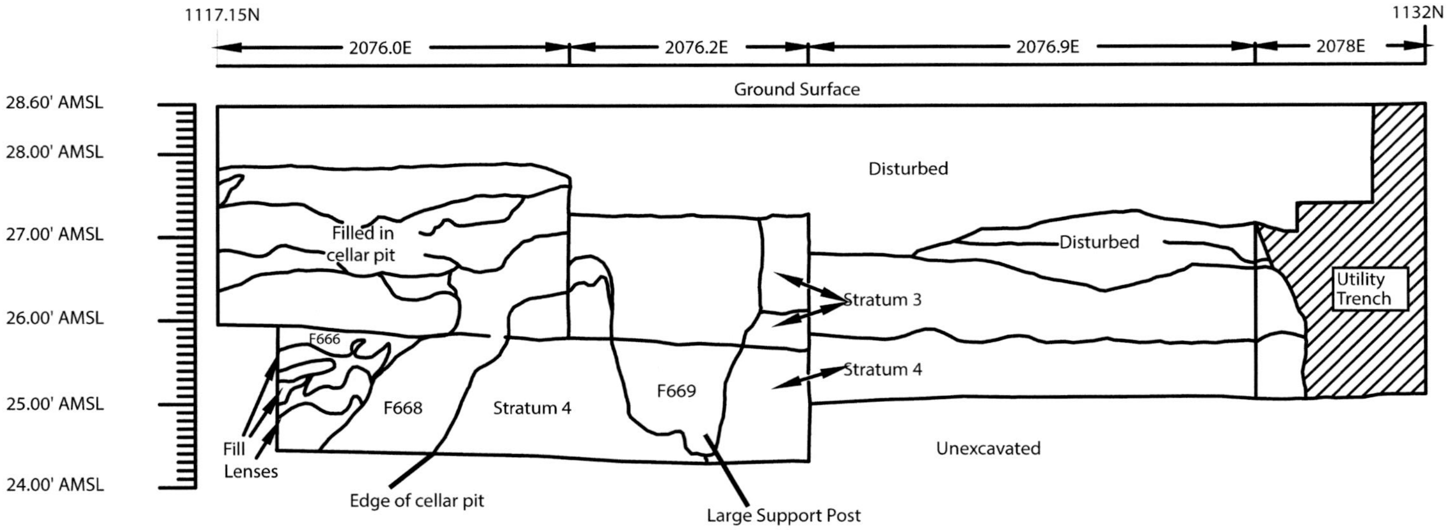

Figure 2.19. Presidio Santa María, third warehouse profile scale drawing showing edge of cellar, cellar pit fill, and support post. Courtesy of the Archaeology Institute, University of West Florida.

Santa María remain the only ones ever recovered from a Hispanic site to date (Ruhl 2003: 251; Donna Ruhl, personal communication 2018).

John Worth, professor and researcher at UWF, has been researching Spanish shipboard rations during the colonial period and has found documentation that faba beans were part of the situado ration shipments to the West Florida presidio (Cook et al. 2016: 77–82). Faba beans and chickpeas along with lentils, pinto beans, and rice were common ingredients in the minestra (vegetable

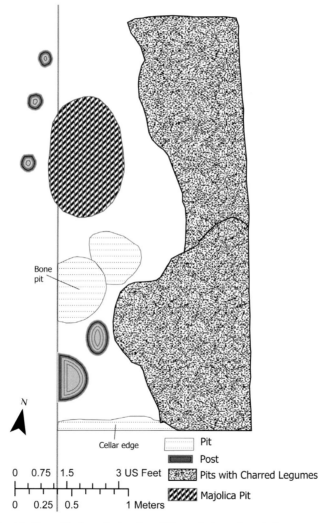

Figure 2.20. Presidio Santa María, scale drawing of disposal pits and postholes near covered entrance of third warehouse. Courtesy of the Archaeology Institute, University of West Florida.

soup) and were the standard shipboard daily rations: six ounces on meatless days and two ounces on meat days. The reason faba beans have been found only at Santa María is twofold. First, the West Florida presidio was classified administratively as a maritime province and, therefore, was sent standard shipboard rations, which included dried vegetables for the minestra. Second, the burning of the second warehouse fortuitously preserved large amounts of the faba beans, which were buried in two large pits. East Florida was not a maritime province in the early eighteenth century and did not receive the components of the minestra. At the missions, Native Americans grew their own vegetables, but not faba beans. Therefore, in the eighteenth century, faba beans were supplied only to the maritime province of West Florida, and the inventory of the situado conveyed to Santa María by the *Rosario* frigate in 1705 documented 106 quintals (5.3 tons) of dried vegetables for the minestra, consisting of equal parts of rice, garbanzo beans, and faba beans (Bratten 2003: 22). Faba beans were also a staple of the French diet and were plentiful in the archaeological remains of the contemporaneous and nearby colonial settlement of Old Mobile (for more detail, see Gremillion 2002). Given the strong trade relations with the French in Mobile, especially in food supplies, the faba beans found at Santa María could have been obtained from either Mobile or the situado from New Spain.

Another disposal pit outside the warehouse entrance contained a large number of animal bones, primarily cow. Historical records frequently describe that spoiled meat was received in the situado shipments (Clune et al. 2003: 67), which could explain the concentration of cow bones from salted beef, a staple food. Report after report includes complaints about the arrival of spoiled food, especially meat, and the inability to hunt due to the hostile forces surrounding the presidio. It must have been a blow to the community to have to throw away the spoiled beef found in these pits.

The fourth disposal pit was small and basin shaped, measuring only 3.5 by 2.5 feet and a foot deep, but packed into it were 2,222 sherds and a handful of other items (Bense and Wilson 2003: 139–142). Of the 2,183 Euro-American ceramics in this feature, 2,075 (95.1%) are Majolica, 103 (4.7%) are Coarse Earthenware, four are Porcelain, and one is Faience. Of the 1,637 typable sherds, 67.8 percent are Puebla Polychrome, 12.4 percent are Abo Polychrome, and 12.1 percent are Pensacola Polychrome. The 203 pieces of Pensacola Polychrome are from a new type of majolica decorated with colorful concentric rings (figure 2.21). This new type was found only in this pit with one additional piece nearby; however, this decoration is still made on majolica in Mexico today. There is a minimum of 54 vessels in this small pit, two thirds of which are platos and a third of which are tazas. Some of the refitted pieces are shown in figure 2.21. None of the majolica sherds in this pit show any evidence of wear,

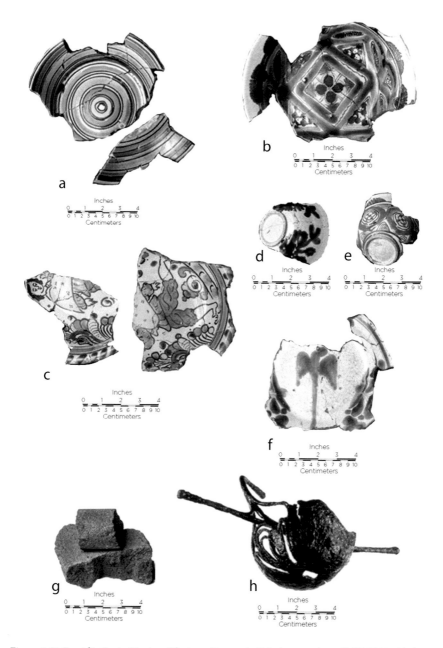

Figure 2.21. Presidio Santa María artifacts: *a,* Pensacola Polychrome platos (98N-7164–61); *b,* Puebla Polychrome plato (98N-7164–84); *c,* Abo Polychrome platos (98N-7164–74); *d,* Puebla Blue on White taza (96N-4850–1); *e,* Puebla Polychrome taza (98N-7163–47); *f,* Puebla Blue on White plato (98N-7330–14); *g,* basalt mano and metate fragments (96N-2823–16); *h,* sword/rapier hilt fragment (98M-8227–1). Courtesy of the Archaeology Institute, University of West Florida.

and our best interpretation of this feature is that the tableware was shipped in a container and broken either in transit or in the warehouse. After breakage, the broken pieces were disposed of in a pit just outside the warehouse entrance. The pit also included a few pieces of Other Coarse Earthenware (97) and Indian-made ceramics (39) along with a variety of other materials that probably were accidentally included in the backfill in this high activity area just outside the entrance and in front of the officers' barracks.

The origin of the cellar fill is not exactly known. Some of the fill was surely from the warehouse and officers' living area, but some could have been brought from elsewhere around the site to fill in the large hole after the warehouse was dismantled. The cellar pit was not completely filled, as on top of the cellar fill was an artifact-rich layer of refuse likely from the officers whose barracks was only 25 feet away. While the actual source(s) of the cellar fill cannot be known, it is considered here to be associated with the warehouse.

When all the materials from the third warehouse are combined, the area contains 18.0 percent of the weighed and 17.9 percent of the counted materials recovered from inside the fort, second only to the nearby officers' barracks (see table 2.2). Euro-American Ceramics (58.0%) and Fauna (19.1%) make up 77.1 percent of the counted items from the warehouse, and three-quarters of the weighed items are either Building Material (42.5%) or Euro-American Ceramics (33.7%), as shown in appendix II, table II.3b. Almost all of the ceramics are Euro-American (86.4%), and only 13.6 percent are Native American (see table 2.3). This high proportion of Euro-American ceramics is undoubtedly due to the 2,183 Euro-American sherds in the majolica disposal pit described above. However, the proportion of Euro-American ceramics is also quite high (70.0%) in the cellar pit fill.

Almost all the Euro-American ceramic wares (99.2%) recovered from the third warehouse are Majolica (71.3%) or Other Coarse Earthenware (27.9). Of the 3,424 sherds from the warehouse, only 24 are from other ceramic wares: Porcelain, Faience, and Stoneware (see appendix II, table II.4b). Of the 2,566 typable sherds, the most abundant ceramic types are Puebla Polychrome Majolica (45.4%), Olive Jar (13.4%), and El Morro (12.2%). As shown in appendix II, table II.9, three types of Majolica predominate: Puebla Polychrome Blue Variant (67.2%), Abo Polychrome (13.6%), and Pensacola Polychrome (11.8%). The Other Coarse Earthenware are mainly Olive Jar (40.5%) and El Morro (33.2%).

Native American ceramics make up only 13.6 percent of the ceramic assemblage found in the warehouse features and cellar fill, and the proportions of tempering agents are primarily grog (53.9%), sand (20.5%), and grog shell (14.2%), as listed in appendix II, table II.4b. This is the largest proportion of grog-shell-tempered ceramics in any of the site areas inside or outside the fort.

Of the 540 typable Native American ceramics, Grog Tempered Plain makes up almost half (43.9%), Sand Tempered Plain makes up 15.6 percent, and all other types are 8.4 percent or less. Over three quarters (76.0%) of the surfaces of Native American ceramics are plain and 12.6 percent are burnished. The few decorated sherds include a wide variety of incising, slipping, painting, and punctating.

Faunal and floral remains in the warehouse assemblage are quite high. Faunal remains are 19.1 percent of the count and 7.2 percent of the weight (see appendix II, table II.3b). Most of the fauna was in the pit near the warehouse entrance that contained almost exclusively cow bones. The total faunal assemblage in the warehouse included a wide range of meat sources, primarily cows, deer, pigs, local fish, turkey, oysters, and scallops. Most of the floral remains, especially faba beans and chickpeas, were contained in the two pits near the warehouse entrance.

Most of the counted assemblage from the warehouse (88.9%) is from Kitchen activities, and of the weighed materials, 83.5 percent are either Kitchen (41.5%) or Architectural (42.0%) items (see appendix II, table II.5b). Ceramics make up most of the Kitchen group by weight (97.5%). Architectural materials are mainly bricks and ladrillos. However, there is also some plaster and window glass, which is unusual for a warehouse; these materials probably came from the officers' barracks only 25 feet away, which had glass windowpanes and plastered walls. The activities represented in the warehouse assemblage are illumination (lamp chimney), food preparation (five mano/metate fragments), writing (slates), and shot production (sprue). The only Arms items are gunflint fragments and shot. Clothing artifacts are brass and iron buckles, 99 glass seed beads, one brass button, and a few straight pins. Personal items include a piece of a Faience drug jar, 11 Guadalajara Polychrome sherds, one jewelry fragment, and a few glass, clay, and stone beads.

In sum, the combination of historical and archaeological information tells us much about the importance and function of this warehouse. We know from the documents that it was a large two-story structure with a cellar and was supported by a perimeter of very large posts along with some large internal posts. It had a wood floor, board roof, and was 55 by 25 feet in size. The unusual disposal pit features just outside the entryway contained large quantities of inedible food remains and a mass of broken tableware, reflecting the types of supplies stored inside. One can almost hear the disappointment of having to lose so much meat and dried peas and beans as well as the anguish over dropping a case of fragile majolica tableware. Both sources of information give us a closer look into the reality of early eighteenth-century life in this presidio on the very edge of Spanish West Florida.

Hospital/Warehouse

Historical documents by officials at Santa María constantly contain complaints about the large number of sick personnel and the problems of caring for them (Clune et al. 2003: 48–49; Coker 1999: 12; Coker and Childers 1998: 21). While there were three formal hospitals at the presidio, the sick were often tended to in makeshift or temporary structures when more bed space was needed, especially during enemy attacks and epidemics such as the yellow fever epidemic of 1702 (Clune et al. 2003: 48). The first hospital was built in 1701 on the bluff outside the fort. It was named Our Lady of Afflictions and administered by the surgeon-friars of San Juan de Dios. This hospital fell into disrepair, and in the spring of 1707 a new and larger hospital was built, presumably in the same location. After the first few days of the English-led raids in the summer of 1707, Governor Moscoso ordered this hospital dismantled and rebuilt inside the fort. Unfortunately, before all the materials could be retrieved, the Indian raiders returned and burned what remained of the hospital along with the rest of the village (Clune et al. 2003: 48; Higginbotham 1977: 308–309). The next and last hospital was built inside the fort and is depicted on the 1713 map (see figure 2.4). Based on measurements on that map, the structure was rectangular and about 30 by 60 feet in size. As Clune and colleagues (2003: 48–49) describe, there is little documentary evidence of the fate of this hospital after 1709 when Governor Salinas reported that it was unserviceable. The same building is identified as a warehouse on the circa 1720 Devin map (see figure 2.5b). It appears that after the third warehouse was dismantled, sometime after 1713, the hospital building was converted to a warehouse.

Many architectural features associated with this building were identified, including posts/postholes, wall trenches, and driplines adjacent to the south and east walls (Bense and Wilson 2003: 143–148). The southern end of this building was exposed. Foundation wall trenches with 12 large perimeter posts outlined a structure that measured 40 feet wide (figure 2.22). The location and size of the structure generally match the location and width of the warehouse identified on both the 1719 and circa 1720 Devin maps. Three small wall trench segments containing 26 small posts marked the southwest corner of the building. These V-shaped wall trenches were narrow, averaging about half a foot wide, with small posts set side by side enclosing what appears to have been an entryway or foyer.

Another noteworthy architectural feature of the hospital/warehouse is a distinctive light brown area with very little cultural material enclosed within the perimeter of the large support posts and surrounded by dark stained soil containing dense artifacts and features. The only feasible explanation for the

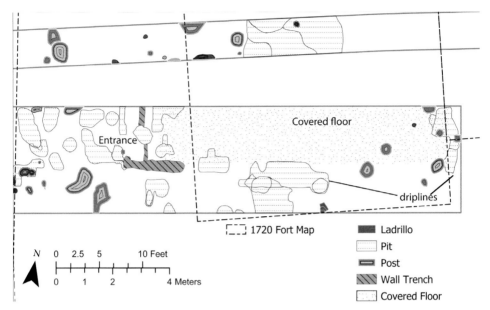

Figure 2.22. Presidio Santa María, scale drawing of hospital/warehouse remains inside Fort San Carlos, associated features, and building projections. Courtesy of the Archaeology Institute, University of West Florida.

sterile interior area of a structure is that it was covered with a solid floor. This area is strikingly similar to the vacant area inside the officers' barracks building (see figure 2.17). It makes sense that the hospital/warehouse would have had a solid floor for cleanliness to keep both patients and supplies off the loose dirt and sand surface. In contrast, the floor of the enclosed entryway was dark and organically stained with abundant artifacts, suggesting it was a dirt floor.

The two partial driplines from the roof of this building were quite different. Along the east wall, seven feet of the dripline was exposed. It was 1 to 1.5 feet wide and contained only clean, gray, coarse washed sand with no organics or fine particles. Along the south wall, the dripline segment was 14 feet long, up to 2 feet wide, and 1.7 feet deep. This dripline feature was also well defined, but the upper portion had half a foot of dense refuse overlying clean, gray, coarse washed sand. Several ladrillos had been stacked on top of the washed sand in the deepest part of the dripline feature, likely to stop further erosion.

The artifact assemblage associated with the hospital-turned-warehouse building includes materials from 53 features (primarily architectural and refuse pits) that were in and near the footprint of the building. Regardless of their original function, most of the architectural features contained refuse. Surprisingly, there were no special disposal pits similar to those outside the entrance to the third warehouse. The refuse pits that were clustered around the entrance to the hospital/warehouse contained materials from general domestic activities associated with the building's function as a hospital, not as a warehouse.

The ceramic assemblage of 3,295 sherds is 64.3 percent Euro-American and 35.7 percent Native American made (see table 2.3). Except for 27 sherds, all the Euro-American ceramic wares are either Other Coarse Earthenware (55.9%) or Majolica (42.9%), as shown in appendix II, table II.4b. Of the 1,613 typable ceramics, the most abundant are El Morro (32.2%), Olive Jar (16.0%), and San Luis Polychrome (15.9%) Within the Other Coarse Earthenware, 90.5 percent are either El Morro (48.2%), Olive Jar (23.9%), or Unglazed (18.4%), detailed in appendix II, table II.10. Also present are 70 pieces of Santa María Stamped and nine pieces of Guadalajara Polychrome. The most popular Majolica tableware are San Luis Polychrome (48.5%), Puebla Polychrome (35.4%), and Puebla Blue on White (8.0%).

Just over half (52.9%) of the Native American ceramics by weight are tempered with grog, 25.4 percent are tempered with sand, and 10.5 percent are tempered with grog shell (see appendix II, table II.4b). Of the 1,161 typable sherds, the most abundant ceramic types by weight are Grog Tempered Plain (32.2%), Sand Tempered Plain (22.0%), and Grog Tempered Burnished (18.3%). Each of the remaining 33 types makes up 6.0 percent or less. Almost two-thirds of the surfaces of Indian-made sherds are plain (64.1%) and over a quarter are burnished (26.5%). The remaining 9.4 percent have surfaces that are incised, stamped, slipped, painted, or punctated.

Most of the cultural material recovered from the hospital/warehouse (87.1%) is from Kitchen activities and includes pieces of ceramic containers and tableware. However, the remaining kitchen artifacts are interesting: pieces of drinking glasses, a glass tumbler, two pharmaceutical bottles, and stemmed glasses. Activities reflected in the assemblage are illumination (lamp chimney pieces and a brass candle tool), food preparation (14 manos/metates), writing (slate fragments), and cloth (two bale seals). Architectural materials are almost all bricks, ladrillos, and mortar, but there are also 11 pieces of window glass and some wall plaster, revealing that the structure had some glass windowpanes and that part of the interior had plastered walls. In addition, there is an iron sword/rapier hilt (see figure 2.21) along with five pieces of silver brocade, an iron needle, brass straight pins, a brass hook-and-eye fastener, and buttons. Personal items include the only jet higa recovered at the site (see figure 2.9), several Guadalajara Polychrome pieces, a brass finger ring, and hardware from a purse or satchel. This assemblage does not even hint at warehouse storage and distribution activities, but it certainly does reflect a mix of people who varied in status, gender, and age. A few items such as bales of cloth and a pharmaceutical bottle can be linked to the hospital function. Also in this assemblage were other special items such as stemmed glassware, drinking glasses, and a brass candle tool. These items usually denote high status, but in this case, they may simply reveal the special care and concern for the sick.

In sum, the building that served first as a hospital and later as a warehouse within Fort San Carlos de Austria was constructed in 1707 partially from the dismantled second hospital originally built in the village. The building served as a hospital at least through 1713, but sometime after that date it was used as a warehouse until 1719 when the French captured and burned Santa María. The building was documented archaeologically to have a framework of large perimeter posts that supported the rafters and roof. It had a solid floor and at least some glass windows. Two dripline segments indicate the building probably had a gabled roof. The artifact assemblage associated with this structure reflects residents of all ages and social ranks. Documents repeatedly state that sickness was rampant, and patients had priority in food and special comfort items that would reflect high status in other contexts. The warehouse function of this structure was not apparent archaeologically, indicating that this function could have been short lived.

The Church

The church was the single most distinguishing characteristic of a Spanish colonial settlement, and this was true at Presidio Santa María where it was always one of the most prominent buildings (Clune et al. 2003: 46). Four churches were built at Santa María, the first two in the village and the last two inside the fort. The first church was built in the village immediately upon arrival, but it burned three months later in the January 1699 fire. The second church in the village was built by May 1699 as depicted on the Franck map (see figures 2.6 and 2.8). Before July 1702, the third church was built inside the fort, but it also burned two years later in the 1704 fire (Clune et al. 2003: 46–47). After using a temporary structure for two years, the fourth and last church was built by January 1706 probably at the same location. This church is described as having an exterior of boards, an interior vault, and stained-glass windows purchased from the French at Mobile. Historians suggest that this church likely had painted images in the interior, as a painter and painting supplies were requested for that purpose from Veracruz (Clune et al. 2003: 47). This church is depicted on the 1713, 1719, and circa 1720 maps of Fort San Carlos (see figures 2.4 and 2.5). The latter two renderings show an addition to the east end, which may have been a convento or an arbor or garden area. Measured on these maps, this church was probably about 30 by 80 feet in size and situated on the north border of the central open plaza area of the fort interior, along with other community-related buildings such as the third warehouse, hospital/warehouse, government house, and guardhouse. The fourth church was in use for 13 years (1706–1719) and was burned by the French when they destroyed Santa María.

The architectural remains of the church documented archaeologically consist of six large posts in postholes, five of which were arranged in two parallel rows on 12-foot centers (figure 2.23). The posts were large (1.0–1.5 feet in diameter) and set up to four feet deep into the earth. One post was offset, likely placed after construction for additional support of the rafters. The bases of four posts were higher than the remaining two posts, indicating that they were replacements. The upper portions of the two posts in the west row were burned. No evidence of any type of floor cover was found, but the ground could have been covered with mats. Architectural materials in the church assemblage also include a pintle, nails, brick fragments, and 23 pieces of window glass, the presence of which adds to the architectural information about the church building.

The dominant aspect of the church is the subfloor cemetery where the crowded remains of a minimum of 25 individuals were discovered between 1.5 and 1.75 feet below the organically stained church floor. There undoubtedly were more interments within the unit, but when human remains were encountered excavation was halted. The burial pits were barely visible in the churned and mottled, tan, sandy matrix. With one exception, the human remains were all at the same depth below the former church floor. Forensic bioanthropologist Nicole Heintzleman (2003) conducted an in-field examination of the human remains and determined the general age of eight people: six young-to-middle age adults, one adolescent, and one child. The gender of only two individuals could be determined: one male and one female. The genetic ancestry of six people was determinable: one European and five non-Native Americans.

The burials were organized in two north-south rows with interments oriented east-west, as shown in figure 2.23 (Bense and Wilson 2003: 150–160). One interment, a young male, was oriented north-south and was much higher than the others; it was one of the last interments in this area. Most burial pits intersected adjacent grave shafts. All intact interments were extended and lying on their backs with arms folded across their chests. There were no traces of any coffins or vaults. The individuals were in all likelihood buried in shrouds, the Spanish tradition of that time. Numerous contemporaneous examples have been documented across Spanish Florida (see Saunders 1996; Shapiro and Vernon 1992; Stojanowski 2005). Eleven brass straight pins recovered in the cemetery were probably used to fasten the shrouds.

Disarticulated human remains were scattered throughout the area investigated, indicating earlier burials had been disturbed in the excavation of new

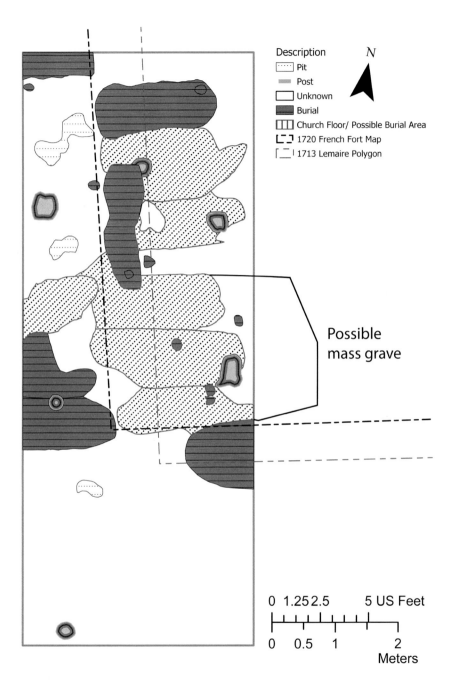

Figure 2.23. Presidio Santa María, scale drawing of archaeological features and graves in the southwest corner of the third church inside Fort San Carlos and two map projections of the church location. Courtesy of the Archaeology Institute, University of West Florida.

graves. Nine disarticulated crania were encountered, and they were usually placed near a body. If the 30-by-80-foot church had the same density of burials as that exposed in the 162-square-foot unit examined, there are at least 280 burials under this church.

Only one burial had directly associated materials, though many items once associated with burials were found in the churned soil above the interments. The single burial with directly associated material was only partially exposed in the northwest corner of the excavation unit. This was a non-Native American person laid to rest wearing four finger rings and clothes decorated with seed beads. The rings were two plain copper bands and two Jesuit rings with heart-shaped faces (see figure 2.9). The Jesuit rings are made of brass with a heart-shaped bezel, and they represent two different styles in Charles Cleland's (1972) classification. One is a Double-M series with superimposed inverted M's, and the other is the L-Heart series with a stylized L, a heart, and radiating spikes representing the nails of Christ's crucifixion (Furlong 2008: 89; Sims 2001). Jesuit rings were distributed by both Jesuit and Franciscan missionaries across North America in the seventeenth century (Deagan 2002: 123), and they have been found primarily on French colonial sites in Michigan (Cleland 1971: 30, 1972; Stone 1974: 125–127). Recently, 1,603 Jesuit rings were recovered from the wreck of La Salle's ship *La Belle* sunk in 1686 in Matagorda Bay, Texas. There are 13 different types of rings in this collection, each with a different icon embossed on a circular bezel (Bruseth 2014: 43; Bruseth et al. 2017). Deagan (2002: 83–84) describes religious finger rings found on Spanish colonial sites and notes that they are different from French Jesuit rings. The French Jesuit finger rings found with the interment at Santa María very likely were distributed by the French priest Father La Maire who served at Santa María between 1710 and 1715.

A total of 1,856 counted artifacts and 13.4 kg of weighed material were recovered from the church floor and subfloor. With the exception of the four in situ finger rings described above and seed beads that appear to be from in situ clothing, the artifacts recovered were in disturbed contexts primarily due to the frequent and intersecting grave excavations that constantly mixed the soil containing cultural material from previous graves. In addition, materials were surely lost during religious activities inside the church. As Bense and Wilson (2003: 156–160) note, the soil matrix is soft sand that is easily churned by grave digging and trampling. Nonetheless, the religious context of the cultural material recovered from under the church floor has retained its integrity (Bense and Wilson 2003: 156).

The first observation of the assemblage is its small size (see table 2.2). It comprises only 5.6 percent of the counted and 3.8 percent of the weighed materials recovered from the fort interior. As listed in appendix II, table II.3c, 70.6

percent of the recovered materials are ceramics, and this ceramic assemblage consists of 53.6 percent Euro-American and 46.4 percent Native American sherds by count. These proportions are almost identical to those from the officers' and soldiers' barracks areas (see table 2.3). Almost all the Euro-American sherds (99.1%) are either Other Coarse Earthenware (57.1%) or Majolica (42.0%), with only six pieces of other wares (see appendix II, table II.4c). The second notable observation is the lack of diversity of ceramic types. Of the 527 typable sherds, the most abundant are El Morro (45.7%), Olive Jar (14.6%), and San Luis Polychrome Majolica (12.5%). There is little diversity in the types of Other Coarse Earthenware as three types make up 97.3 percent: El Morro (65.3%), Olive Jar (20.9%), and Unglazed (11.1%), as shown in appendix II, table II.11. Of the Majolicas, 86.5 percent of the pieces are the following three types: San Luis Polychrome (42.3%), Puebla Polychrome (34.0%), and Puebla Blue on White (10.3%).

Native American ceramics are tempered primarily with grog (67.4% by weight) or sand (23.4%), with a minor amount of shell (4.3%) and grog shell (4.0%) tempering (see appendix II, table II.4c). Of the 606 typable sherds, listed in appendix II, table II.11, the most frequent are Grog Tempered Plain (57.6%), Sand Tempered Plain (20.1%), and Grog Tempered Burnished (6.8%). Only 24.6 percent of the surfaces of the Indian ceramics are plain and 12.0 percent are burnished. The surfaces of 63.4 percent of the typable sherds are decorated with incising, painting, filming, stamping, or punctating. The church assemblage has the highest proportion of surface decoration of Native American ceramics of any site area, which is very likely related to the religious context of the church.

The church/burial assemblage has several interesting and telling elements. First, as listed in appendix II, table II.5c, the proportion of counted clothing items in this assemblage is higher (9.6%) than that of any other area inside the fort and more than twice that of the total fort assemblage (3.7%). Most of the Clothing artifacts (92.0%) are glass seed beads (163), but there are 11 brass straight pins, 3 buttons, and a small piece of cloth. Seed beads are associated with clothing decoration, and Burial 24 had in situ seed beads in the chest area, supporting this association. Therefore, we can assume the seed beads recovered from the churned burial pit fill must be from disturbed graves in which the dead were buried in clothes adorned with beads.

Five artifacts with specific religious meaning in addition to the two Jesuit and two ring bands described above have been studied as part of two UWF master's theses (Furlong 2008; Sims 2001). The artifacts are four Man-in-the-Moon beads and a brass crucifix (see figure 2.9). The Man-in-the-Moon beads are lovely blue disks with the crescent moon and stars painted in gold on each side. One of these beads was in the fill of Burial 20, two were near a pair of disarticulated skulls (Burial 12), and one was from the base of the mottled grave fill in the northeast corner of the excavation unit. These beads have been found throughout the Great Lakes area at French colonial sites dating to the first quarter of the eighteenth century (Smith 2002: 59). As of this writing, they have not been found on any other Spanish colonial site. The only sites in the Southeast at which Man-in-the-Moon beads have been found are French Old Mobile and Port Dauphin (Lorenzini and Karlins 2000–2001: 40; Smith 2002: Plate 2; Waselkov 1999). The brass crucifix recovered near one of the Man-in-the-Moon beads is very similar to a crucifix recovered from French Fort Michilimackinac (for more detail, see Stone 1974). The French religious artifacts along with the Jesuit rings described above were surely due to the presence of the French priest Father La Maire. La Maire served at Santa María during the siege years and likely distributed them to the parishioners at Santa María.

In sum, the fourth church at Fort San Carlos de Austria had a unique construction method at this settlement: large interior poles set on 12-foot centers. Historical records describe the church as having board walls, a vault, and stained-glass windows. The church also had a crowded subfloor cemetery. In the 600 square feet exposed during field investigation, the remains of at least 24 people were recorded. Disarticulated human remains were encountered throughout the cemetery fill. The artifact assemblage from churned soils adjacent to and above burials consisted mainly of materials from graves disturbed during later interments and items worshippers dropped on the church's soft, sandy dirt floor. The unique cultural context of the assemblage provides a glimpse into the personal and religious lives of the presidio residents: Jesuit religious finger rings, special Man-in-the-Moon beads, decorative seed beads from what must have been specifically chosen burial clothing, fragments of glass tumblers, and wine and case bottles.

This church and cemetery were very special places and still are. At the close of the archaeological investigation of the church at Santa María, the church and cemetery were re-consecrated by Father Richard J. Bowles, then priest of historic Basilica of St. Michael the Archangel in Pensacola, Florida. Today, the location of the presidio church and cemetery is identified with signage as part of a walking tour of the site. It is important that the remains of hundreds more people are resting where they were originally buried and are under federal protection administered by NASP.

Summary of the Remains of Fort San Carlos de Austria

Architecture is one of the most revealing features of a community because differences in the quality, size, and features of structures are closely related to the importance of the building and, for residences, the social status and rank of the intended occupants. Differences in the relative importance and function of structures that serve the entire community are also revealed in architectural elements. The fort was the most important construction at the presidio, for it was the only protection for the residents. The walls of soft pine posts were under siege not only from enemy attacks but also from decay and insects. Post replacement in the stockade walls was constant, and the terrepleined walls of the bastions and seawall eventually were torn down and replaced with a single stockade. Only the northwest bastion containing the powder magazine retained the terrepleined wall a bit longer, but it eventually became a single stockade line as well.

Architectural features of the six structures investigated inside Fort San Carlos reflect the status of the occupants and importance to the community. In contrast to the threadbare living conditions of the convicts living in poor quality barracks along the fort's north wall, the officers of the presidio lived in the most secure and comfortable barracks. They resided along the southern west curtain wall, farthest from the dangerous facilities in the northern bastions and nearest to the sea breezes. Their barracks was the most substantially built and had the comfort of a wood floor and windows with glass panes. The officers also had access to and consumed the most valued materials and foods available. Substantially more humble than the officers' accommodations, yet a definite step up from the shoddiness of the convict labor housing, was the northern west wall barracks that housed the regular paid soldiers of the presidio.

The top priority building in the community was the warehouse as it held all the food, arms, and supplies. Appropriately, it had a cellar and was the most substantial building investigated. The hospital/warehouse was next in importance, along with the officers' barracks. All three of these structures had large post-in-ground or post-on-sill framing and solid floors, and two had caulked board roofs. The church with its subfloor cemetery was also very important and had a large, open interior with internal posts as roof supports, board walls, and a dirt floor above the crowded subfloor cemetery. The remaining two barracks were simple by comparison, with walls of posts set in trenches or directly in the ground. Post replacement was evident especially in the barracks designated for convict laborers, which was likely always in a ramshackle state.

The materials left behind in and near the structures inside Fort San Carlos are abundant: 33,704 counted items and 355.7 kg of weighed material (table 2.5). The quantity alone reflects the presence of 300–500 people crowded into the confines of the fort for eight years. As expected, the distribution of the materials inside the fort is uneven, and the amount and kind of materials left behind correlate with the status and rank of the residents of the three barracks and the functions of the public-use buildings (church, warehouse, and hospital). As shown in tables 2.2 and 2.5, almost half (45.6%) of the counted and 44.0 percent of the weighed materials recovered inside the fort were from the officers' barracks and activity area. There was significantly less material associated with the barracks for the soldiers and laborers. The third warehouse provided 18.0 percent of the weighed materials in the fort assemblage, and the unique collection directly relates to the third warehouse's function and demise. The artifact assemblage recovered from the warehouse is composed of concentrations of specific items that were disposed of in separate pits because they were either burned, broken, or spoiled. In addition, while the cellar pit fill had abundant cultural material, the backfill origin could be anywhere in the settlement. Surprisingly, at the hospital/warehouse we found no features or artifact concentrations similar to the special disposal pits at the third warehouse. However, there were architectural similarities such as the large size, covered floor, and covered entrance. There was also a similar concentration of pit features outside the entrance, but they were filled with domestic refuse associated with the building's use as the hospital, not the warehouse. The church/cemetery structure was unique in its construction of interior poles, and, expectedly, the artifact assemblage reflects the special functions of the building as a place of worship and burial.

Valuable information that crosscuts the differences among the separate spaces can be gleaned from pooling all the materials from the fort. For example, as detailed in appendix II, table II.5c, Kitchen materials dominate the counted items in every area inside the fort as well as in the fort assemblage as a whole (79.5%). Kitchen (48.0%) and Architecture (44.2%) materials comprise almost all of the assemblage by weight (92.2%), and these artifact groups are almost

Table 2.5. Material recovered in each area of Fort San Carlos

Fort Areas	Count	%	Weight (g)	%
Officers' Barracks	15,096	45.6%	156,540.2	44.0%
Third Warehouse	5,906	17.9%	64,135.0	18.0%
Soldiers' Barracks	3,420	10.3%	45,936.2	12.9%
Hospital/Warehouse	4,945	15.0%	42,855.0	12.0%
North Wall Barracks	1,607	4.9%	21,959.6	6.2%
Church	1,856	5.6%	13,361.2	3.8%
NW Bastion	244	0.7%	10,911.7	3.1%
Totals	33,704		355,699.0	

equal in proportion. Ceramics comprise 60.3 percent of the counted materials in the total fort assemblage, and 62.8 percent of the sherds are Euro-American while 37.2 percent are Native American (see appendix II, table II.3c). There are several patterns that crosscut internal fort areas. In both European and Indian ceramics, there is a very narrow range of wares and types. Almost all of the counted Euro-American sherds (97.5%) are either Other Coarse Earthenware for cooking and storage (56.1%) or Majolica tableware (41.4%), and all other wares are 1.3 percent or less each (see appendix II, table II.4c). While there are 41 different Euro-American ceramic types, only four make up 77.9 percent of the 9,505 typable sherds: Lead Glazed Coarse Earthenware (19.0%), Olive Jar (17.9%), Puebla Polychrome (17.1%), and El Morro (12.8%). All other Euro-American types are 7.3 percent or less each. In the Native American ceramics, grog tempering is most abundant (54.2%), followed by sand (31.7%), and each other temper is 7.8 percent or less (see appendix II, table II.4c). The same narrow range of types is true for the 60 ceramic types of Native American sherds as only three types make up 69.0 percent: Grog Tempered Plain (29.1%), Grog Tempered Burnished (16.3%), and Sand Tempered Plain (14.6%). The other 57 ceramic types each make up 9.3 percent or less.

Euro-American and Native American ceramics are present in every investigated area of the fort, which reveals that they were a needed commodity throughout the fort. Nonetheless, the proportions vary considerably among the living areas. There appears to be a correlation between the percentage of Euro-American ceramics and the status and rank of the residents. The highest proportion of Euro-American ceramics (56.4%) and lowest proportion of Native American ceramics (43.6%) are in the officers' barracks and living area (see table 2.3). However, in the north wall barracks area for the laborers and convicts, the proportions are reversed: 42.9 percent Euro-American and 57.1 percent Native American. The proportions in the soldiers' barracks are very close to those in the officers' barracks. The proportion of Native American ceramics inside the fort is 37.2 percent, revealing that the Spanish supplied Santa María with only about 62.8 percent of the ceramic containers and tableware necessary to meet their needs.

One would expect the Arms artifact group to be very large considering the fort's use as a military installation with a permanent garrison of over 200 armed soldiers at any one time, the presence of over 20 cannons, and the many battles that took place during these years. Arms-related artifacts were recovered in every area of the fort, and by count, Arms is the second-most abundant group of the total fort assemblage. However, almost all artifacts are small shot (87.3% by count) and pieces of gunflints (12.7%). There are only 10 other arms artifacts, seven of which are associated with cannons: three cannons, three cannon balls, and a cannon screw. Only one firearm part was recovered, a brass butt plate, along with parts of two sword hilts. My explanation for this dearth of arms artifacts inside a fort that was under active siege for eight years is that the Spanish simply kept close track of all cannons, firearms, hand arms, and associated items and took all they could carry, whether serviceable or not, when they exited.

Summary of the Siege Years 1707–1715

The siege years from 1707 to 1715 were the worst of times for everyone at Presidio Santa María de Galve. During these years, the entire community of 300–500 people lived inside Fort San Carlos de Austria, and internally, the fort began to resemble a walled town. Crowded residential structures lined three walls, and large facilities serving the community lined a central open space or plaza. Potentially dangerous facilities such as the bake ovens and powder magazine were isolated within the northern bastions. It is worth noting that the members of the community with the lowest status (convicts/laborers) lived along the north wall nearest the dangerous facilities.

The English and their Indian army of up to 1,200 warriors surrounded and directly attacked Santa María for eight years. Driving the English-led violence was both a desire for Indian slaves to sell to British sugar plantations and a desire to drive the Spanish out of Florida. Tens of thousands of Indians in the interior of the Southeast, including those captured around Santa María were sold to slave traders at Charleston. Attack after attack was waged on the fort, and a relentless guerilla war continued outside its walls. Heavily armed escorts were required for all task groups venturing outside the fort for water, wood, poles for the fort wall, ship masts and spars, and other necessities. Casualties, cruel tortures, and captures were constant.

During the War of Spanish Succession, the French colony in Mobile and Spanish Santa María had an important reciprocal trade relationship. Buying and selling food, arms, and even ships was a crucial lifeline for both communities. As the English did not focus their attacks on the Native American villages around Mobile Bay, the French-allied Indians there were able to provide food for both colonial communities. However, when the formal alliance between France and Spain ended in 1713, relations began to deteriorate between Mobile and Pensacola. In addition, drought, famine, and a two-year English blockade of Mobile Bay hurt the food supply at Santa María.

Historical records state that during these siege years, Indians were living inside the fort at Santa María, but their ethnic identity was rarely recorded. Apalachee and Chacato Indians are mentioned more frequently as carpenters, laborers, and hunters, and the presence of these two ethnic groups is supported by the abundant grog- and sand-tempered Native American ceramics recovered throughout the fort. Additionally, there were casualties recorded in both ethnic groups.

With hundreds of people forced to live inside the fort walls, many new structures had to be built and rebuilt to accommodate the population. Three new military barracks were constructed along two curtain walls, and three new, large public buildings lined an interior open plaza area: a hospital, a warehouse, and a church. New government buildings, a guardhouse, and another warehouse were also constructed along the east wall of the fort. As all the buildings and the fort were made of soft pine, decay and fires were a constant problem. Hurricanes and strong storms also damaged the fort and buildings, and the bay bluff eroded all the way to the fort's southern bastions, which at one point were described as teetering on the bluff edge. Bluff erosion caused the south bastions and curtain wall to be redesigned. Nevertheless, despite this wave of new construction and redesign of the fort walls, the pine logs seemed to be rotting faster than they could be replaced. The demands from the viceroy for more masts and spars hewn from the tall pines around Pensacola Bay continued throughout this period. However, woodcutters continued to be ambushed, killed, and captured, even under heavy guard. As a result, the fledgling timber industry fell into decline.

The archaeological remains of the fort and six internal structures have been summarized in the previous section but suffice it to say here that the architectural and artifactual information recovered from them revealed important information. All elements of the three barracks' architecture and associated materials reflect rank and income. The three special-use structures were all well-built and have different artifact assemblages reflecting their different functions. The northwest bastion protected the powder magazine and contained materials reflecting its restricted and special use.

Peace at Presidio Santa María, 1715–1719

During the last years of Presidio Santa María de Galve, three major events occurred outside of Spanish Florida that directly affected the community on Pensacola Bay: the aftereffects of the end of the War of Spanish Succession, the Yamasee War of 1715–1718, and the beginning of the War of the Quadruple Alliance in 1718. Spain lost the War of Spanish Succession and Britain emerged as the victor, becoming the leading European maritime and commercial power and ending the alliance between Spain and France. These changes caused two serious problems for Santa María. First was uncertainty about their source of vital supplies, especially food, from French Mobile. Second was an increase in attacks on the presidio by British-led Indian groups. However, the Indian slave trade largely ended in 1715 with the rebellion of the Yamasee and other Indian groups in the Yamasee War. This rebellion initiated a mass migration of Native Americans away from the British to Spanish and French colonial territories or interior river valleys where they coalesced into new confederacies. At Presidio Santa María, the result of this rebellion had two good outcomes. Of great importance to the residents was the end of the devastating British-led attacks and the beginning of a time of peace. The second outcome was the migration of Indians away from the British, which began their repopulation in West Florida. Some of the Indian refugees were returning Apalachees and others were Yamasee, their former enemies. Group leaders negotiated terms for relocation in return for military protection and resident friars.

The War of the Quadruple Alliance spelled the end for the presidio at this location. France became an enemy of Spain, and the first action of this war in the colonial Southeast was a surprise attack on Presidio Santa María in 1719 by the French at Mobile, who ultimately burned it to the ground. The entire population was evacuated to Havana and Veracruz, and a small French military unit occupied the site of Santa María for three years. The Spanish retreated to St. Joseph Bay 130 miles east along the coast and built the second West Florida presidio there.

Effect of the Yamasee War on Spanish West Florida

The first effect of the Yamasee War on West Florida was the cessation of the devastating British-led Creek raids on Presidio Santa María and the outpost at San Marcos. Tired of suffering from attacks by British-led Indians, and with the break between the British and Yamasee, Governor Don Gregorio de Salinas Varona saw an opportunity. On April 8, 1715, he sent a letter to the governor of South Carolina informing him that peace now existed between France, Great Britain, and Spain as the treaty settling the War of Spanish Succession was officially signed in February of that year. Salinas requested that the governor of South Carolina stop allowing his English subjects and Indian allies to attack the Spanish in West Florida and, in particular, Pensacola (Coker and Childers 1998: 66–67). This letter never reached the South Carolina governor, as it was sent in the middle of the Creek war against the English. However, the Creeks sent word to the Spanish that they were considering an alliance with them on their own. Though the letter did not change the mind of the English, the Creeks independently rebelled against the English and sought an alliance with the Spanish in both East and West Florida (John Worth, personal communication 2020). At Presidio Santa María, the siege was finally over.

Soon after the raiding stopped, in July 1715, the principal chief of the Upper Creek Tallassee arrived at Santa María with 40 other chiefs and war leaders as a token of their peace and friendship. Governor Salinas gifted the men with gunpowder, ammunition, and clothing (Coker and Childers 1998: 67). Two months later, the principal chiefs of the Tukabatchees and Tallapoosas, part of the Upper Creek Confederacy, visited with 50 chiefs and war leaders plus more than 300 armed warriors. During this visit, they pledged their loyalty and cooperation to Spain (Coker and Childers 1998: 67–70).

It was not until three years later in 1718 that the first Native Americans came to settle in the Pensacola area. Following a diplomatic visit to Mexico City, Apalachee Governor Juan Marcos Fant gathered scattered bands together at the mouth of the Escambia River about 15 miles from Presidio Santa María and established a settlement called Nuestra Señora de la Soledad y San Luis (Worth et al. 2011: 3). Worth and colleagues (2011: 2) note that most of these Apalachee were descended from the refugees from the Spanish missions who had fled north after the English-Creek invasion of their homeland in North Florida. Juan Marcos had gathered approximately 100 refugee Apalachee from French Mobile and Presidio Santa María in addition to other refugees from Creek territory (Worth 2008: 7). New Governor Juan Pedro Matamoros de Ysla promised Apalachee Governor Juan Marcos Fant that he would give them the same rations as before when they were living and working at the presidio, as they had missed the growing season that year and needed food (Harris 2003a: 276). Mission Nuestra Señora de la Soledad y San Luis quickly grew as other Apalachee refugees joined this community. This little-known mission and village community has not yet been relocated.

The following year, 1719, Juan Marcos took some Apalachee Indians from La Soledad and Mobile and established a new settlement 215 miles east of Pensacola near Spanish Fort San Marcos de Apalachee, named Mission San Antonio de la Tama (Harris 2003a: 277; Worth 2008: 7). The Spanish had just constructed a new outpost fort there the year before in an effort to stem encroachment of French forces at St. Joseph Bay near Apalachicola. The new San Marcos fort was built on top of the previous forts at the confluence of the St. Marks and Wakulla Rivers and had access to Apalachee Bay and the Gulf. It was a typical square fort with bastions on each corner facing the cardinal directions. The construction was assisted by Christian Apalachee leader Adrián and a detachment of 70 Spanish soldiers and artillerymen from Santa María (Sappington 2018).

As Worth (2018b: 310–314) details, a group of Yamasee also settled at San Marcos about the same time, establishing the town of Tamasle called Mission San Juan. Both mission villages, Apalachee San Antonio de la Tama and Yamasee San Juan/Tamasle, seem to have existed through the 1720s, but only Tamasle survived through the 1730s and afterward. Worth (2018b) notes that

Yamasee Indians outnumbered the Apalachee who lived in both settlements. A trading store was established at San Marcos, making the port of San Marcos once again a trading spot for Apalachee, Lower Creeks, and Yamasee bringing deerskins to trade for Spanish goods. In addition, Ericha Sappington (2018: 24–25) notes that through this trade the Spanish gathered much useful intelligence about the movements and plans of the British and their Indian war parties in the interior who continued to push south.

The repopulation of West Florida with Apalachee and Yamasee refugee groups after the Yamasee War benefited the Spanish in West Florida. The Apalachee had been well trained in Spanish carpentry at the missions, and they were hired to assist with the continual repairs and reconstruction of the forts and buildings at both Santa María and San Marcos. Once the Indian mission villages were established, they provided two very important new food sources for the Spanish, corn and venison. The Spanish desperately needed these resources because the situado had become even more unreliable and trade with the French was becoming increasingly difficult.

During this time of peace, Governor Matamoros decided to address the issue that cannon fire from Fort San Carlos could not protect the pass into Pensacola Bay. In 1718, he built an outpost with a small fort near the western tip of Santa Rosa Island and pointed guns directly at the pass. It was a redoubt of stakes with sand parapets, three cannons, and a moat. A few grass huts and a chapel with a priest were soon added for the detachment of soldiers stationed there (Coker and Childers 1998: 72).

Late Occupation of the Santa María Village

As peace finally descended on Santa María in 1715 after eight years of siege, the population could once again live outside the walls of Fort San Carlos de Austria, and the former village area was reoccupied. Although historical records directly discussing the presidio village are scarce, we do know that by 1718 some houses had been built directly on or next to the east wall of the fort. As these structures interfered with cannon fire, Governor Matamoros ordered them torn down in the summer of 1718 (Coker and Childers 1998: 71).

Archaeological investigations in the Santa María village exposed and excavated part of a long wall trench complex attributed to the late occupation. The feature consisted of a 90-foot-long section of a wall trench oriented about 25 degrees east of north (see figure 2.11). Two additional wall trenches connect to it at a 90-degree angle. One extended at least 25 feet to the west-northwest, and only about eight feet of the northern connecting wall trench was exposed and excavated. The southern end of the long northeast-southwest wall trench was clearly identified.

As Pokrant (2001: 45–50) describes, the long northeast-southwest wall trench was between 0.5 and 2.0 feet wide, and the abutting wall trenches were narrower. All wall trenches had a V-shaped cross section. A total of 54 post-holes 0.5–2.8 feet deep had been set into the base of the wall trench at irregular intervals often in clusters, probably for repair purposes. Given the exceptional length, shallow depth, and irregular placement of the posts, Pokrant (2001: 45–47) suggests, and I concur, that this wall trench complex is very likely the remains of a fence complex for animal pens or gardens.

The cultural material in the extensive network of fence lines consists of 518 counted items and 7 kg of weighed material. However, the context of the as-semblage is secondary, not primary, as the material in the fence line wall trench backfill is from pre-fence-line construction. The material was on and near the surface when the long, shallow, narrow trenches were excavated and backfilled. Since the fence line network intersected the earlier residential features dis-cussed previously in this chapter, the fence lines were very likely part of the second occupation (1715–1719).

Total Santa María Village

Considering the village as a whole, regardless of internal chronology, materials were scattered in a large area 400 by 500 feet in size. The entire area was shovel tested on a 50-foot grid with tighter spacing in areas of artifact concentra-tions and features. Four areas of artifact concentration were investigated in addition to the village cemetery. The distribution of materials appears to be in an arc bordering a central area with very sparse cultural material (see figure 2.3). Pokrant (2001: 80–82) interprets this pattern as the Spanish village model with a vacant, open central area from which dwellings were organized in a grid pattern oriented to the cardinal directions. The distribution of high-status markers or their absence in the three village areas leads Pokrant to interpret the central area as having the highest status residents and the eastern area as hav-ing the lowest status residents. The southern area may have had middle status residents, but it appears to have been eroded by sheet wash and the materials may not be in situ (Bense and Wilson 2003: 169).

Considering the village area as a whole, 55 features were identified, in-cluding structures, refuse pits, and gardens or animal pens in the central and east areas. However, most features could not be specifically associated with either the early or late occupation. Other features include a smudge pit filled with charred corncobs in the central area. A total of 10 burials were also documented in the village, nine graves in the southern cemetery drawn on the 1699 Franck map (see figure 2.6) and an isolated grave in the north part of the village. The midden in all areas of the village was thin and patchy, reflective of the expansive area occupied and the long interruption between the two occupations.

A total of 4,044 counted items and 42.9 kg of weighed material were recovered from the village, comprising 10.9 percent of the total site assemblage (see table 2.2). The most abundant materials by count are Native American ceramics (27.3%), Euro-American ceramics (26.7%), and glass fragments (16.7%), as presented in table 2.6. By weight, almost all of the artifacts (95.8%) are associated with either the Kitchen (68.6%) or Architecture (27.2%) artifact groups. The ceramic assemblage consists of almost equal proportions of Native American and Euro-American ceramics, 50.7 percent and 49.3 percent respectively (see table 2.3). Of the 1,069 Euro-American ceramics, 68.7 percent are Other Coarse Earthenware and 30.2 percent are Majolica with only 12 sherds of Porcelain, Faience, and Redware (table 2.6). Of the 896 typable Euro-American sherds, the most frequent types are Lead Glazed Coarse Earthenware (29.2%), Olive Jar (23.7%), and San Luis Polychrome Majolica (14.6%). In the Other Coarse Earthenware, Lead Glazed (38.1%), Olive Jar (30.9%), Unglazed (13.5%), and El Morro (11.5%) are most abundant, and the remaining types are each 3.3 percent or less (see appendix II, table II.14). San Luis Polychrome (63.9%) and Puebla Polychrome (28.8%) dominate the Majolicas, with the remaining 15 pieces spread between six other types.

Native American ceramics, shown in table 2.6, are tempered primarily with grog (60.9% by weight) or sand (24.1%), followed by shell (10.7%). The most abundant ceramic types by weight are Grog Tempered Plain (31.8%), Sand Tempered Plain (14.7%), and Grog Tempered Burnished (10.0%). The surfaces of over half (53.4%) are plain and 15.9 percent are burnished. The remaining Native American ceramics are a wide variety of incised, painted, punctated, stamped, and red filmed types (see appendix II, table II.14).

Artifacts associated with Kitchen activities are primarily ceramics (89.6%). As Parker (2003: 220–221) describes, while the variety of the faunal remains in the village is quite low, this area has the highest number of domesticated mammals, as 17 of the 19 individual cows and pigs identified at the site were found in the village. The only bird is a chicken, and there are only three species of fish. Initially, Parker expected that wild mammals (especially deer) would be a major part of the villagers' diet, but just the opposite is true. Perhaps the large fenced enclosures in the village area were for domestic animals and the villagers had easy access to them rather than hunting wild animals. It is interesting that pig bones inside the fort came from all parts of the body, but the only parts of the cow represented in the village are the head, shoulder, lower leg, and feet. This could mean that the more desirable, meatier parts of cows were consumed in the fort and not by the villagers.

Table 2.6. Presidio Santa María Village artifact assemblage

Artifact Classes[a]	Count	%	Weight (g)	%
Ceramics Native American	1,095	27.3%	6,593.0	16.7%
Ceramics Euro-American	1,069	26.7%	11,847.6	30.0%
Glass	672	16.8%	1,343.6	3.4%
Fauna	669	16.7%	4,051.4	10.3%
Metal	421	10.5%	3,865.7	9.8%
Lithics	60	1.5%	679.9	1.7%
Building Material	10	0.2%	7,535.5	19.1%
Flora	7	0.2%	3,533.0	9.0%
Fauna Modified	3	0.1%	0.8	[c]
Flora Modified	3	0.1%	0.4	[c]
Totals	4,009		39,450.8	
Artifact Groups[b]	**Count**	**%**	**Weight (g)**	**%**
Kitchen	3,365	84.2%	23,129.2	68.6%
Architecture	155	3.9%	9,180.0	27.2%
Activities	71	1.8%	1,170.9	3.5%
Arms	248	6.2%	156.4	0.5%
Tobacco	26	0.7%	40.2	0.1%
Clothing	85	2.1%	15.8	[c]
Furniture	4	0.1%	8.8	[c]
Personal	41	1.0%	8.8	[c]
Totals	3,995		33,710.0	
Euro-American Ceramic Wares and Classes	**Count**	**%**	**Weight (g)**	**%**
Other Coarse Earthenware	734	68.7%	10,541.3	89.4%
Majolica	323	30.2%	1,230.5	10.4%
Porcelain	6	0.6%	8.5	0.1%
Faience	4	0.4%	8.7	0.1%
Redware	2	0.2%	2.4	[c]
Totals	1,069		11,791.4	
Native American Ceramic Tempers	**Count**	**%**	**Weight (g)**	**%**
Grog	618	56.4%	4,012.2	60.9%
Sand	342	31.2%	1,592.0	24.1%
Shell	87	7.9%	703.4	10.7%
Grog Shell	18	1.6%	209.5	3.2%
Grit	29	2.6%	73.4	1.1%
Unspecified	1	0.1%	2.5	[c]
Totals	1,095		6,593.0	

[a] No Other
[b] No Unspecified
[c] Less than 0.1 percent.

Glass artifacts make up 21.4 percent of the counted Kitchen group artifacts in the village, and most are from wine and case bottles. However, there is part of one glass condiment bottle. Parts of an iron pot and lid are also present. Architectural materials were primarily bricks and ladrillos (82.0%), but there were 22 pieces of window glass, all associated with Structure 1 in the early central village. Thirty-four pieces of writing slate were also recovered in the village area, and all but three were also associated with Structure 1 in the central village.

Personal items recovered in the village include 23 pieces of Guadalajara Polychrome, two finger rings, a few glass beads and metal parts of necklaces, and a metal ornament. A metal bead spacer could indicate that at least some of the beads are from a rosary. Three pieces of manos/metates were also recovered near Structure 1. Four silver coins were recovered in the village: two half-reals in the refuse pit associated with Structure 1, a third from the southernmost excavation block near the bluff, and the fourth in the northern village area. The two half-reals in the refuse pits of Structure 1 have been identified previously in this chapter. The remaining two coins are identified by James Gazaway in appendix VIII, a one-real Charles II minted in 1699 at Potosí and a half-Charles II minted in Mexico City between 1677 and 1697 (see appendix VIII for more information on these and all other coins).

In sum, the features and cultural material recovered from shovel tests, test units, and excavation blocks east of Fort San Carlos have clearly defined the village area. It was first occupied for nine years (1698–1707), abandoned for eight years (1707–1715), and reoccupied for four more years (1715–1719). As Pokrant (2001) suggests, materials and features are concentrated in specific areas and likely represent residential compounds perhaps organized in a grid pattern around a central vacant plaza. The midden was thin and patchy.

The demographics of the two village communities probably were different. At first, everyone except the governor lived in the village. Barracks were first built inside the fort by 1702, but Clune and colleagues (2003: 49–50) state that they were destroyed in the 1704 fort fire, and soldiers and laborers once again had to live in palmetto huts in the village until 1707 when it was abandoned. When the village was reoccupied in 1715, there were at least three barracks inside the fort for officers, soldiers, and laborers. It is likely that when the village was reoccupied, married soldiers with their families moved there while single men stayed in their barracks, but we do not know that. It was possible to chronologically separate a few significant features in the village based on feature intersection: a Spanish-style structure with two associated refuse pits were in the Early Village, and the large network of fenced enclosures were in the Late Village.

The artifact assemblage from the village was relatively large as it comprised 10.9 percent of all the cultural material recovered from the entire site of Santa María. A notable detail of the village assemblage is its high proportion of Indian-made ceramics (50.7%) compared to the smaller proportion inside the fort (37.2%). An unexpected aspect of the village is the virtual absence of wild animal foods. Perhaps the fenced enclosures documented in the village were for domesticated animals, especially cows and pigs, and provided easy access to them as a food source.

The French Intrusion into St. Joseph Bay

Relations with the French in Mobile began to cool soon after the War of Spanish Succession in 1713 as Governor Salinas began to purchase great quantities of food at Port Dauphin. Coker and Childers (1998: 66) relate that in 1713 the new governor of Mobile, Antoine de la Mothe Cadillac, complained bitterly that the Spanish were buying all the fresh supplies in Mobile with their silver, which in turn drove up the prices locally. The French had very little currency, the governor explained, and when they did manage to get coinage, there was nothing left to buy. A 1713 letter from Father La Maire stationed at Santa María to Louis Phélypeaux, Comte de Pontchartrain in Louisiana, stated that Salinas had disrupted the economy at Mobile by buying all kinds of food and merchandise and storing it in his personal shop and warehouse at Port Dauphin to sell at a profit to the soldiers at the presidio (Coker and Childers 1998: 65–67). In 1715, the Spanish further aggravated the French in Mobile by giving refuge to their deserters, sending them to St. Augustine or New Spain instead of back to Mobile as they had previously done. In 1717, the French placed a partial ban on commerce with the Spanish at Pensacola, harshly enforced with fines, prison, and even house burning for those who sold anything to the Spanish (Coker and Childers 1998: 67–68). By this time, Governor Salinas was growing suspicious of French expansion, and there were rumors that the French intended to take Pensacola (Coker and Childers 1998: 68). Florida Governor Ayala in San Agustín was also worried the British would attack St. Augustine yet again. Spanish Florida was again threatened on both coasts.

Between 1716 and 1718, the French had constructed a new colonial town of New Orleans in addition to two new forts/trading posts, Toulouse (Montgomery, Alabama) and Rosalie (Natchez, Mississippi), on interior rivers. A hurricane hit Mobile Bay in 1718, rendering the port on Dauphin Island unusable. Desperately needing a new port on the northern Gulf, the French Council of the Marine ordered Bienville to set up an alternate port on St. Joseph Bay, about 115 miles east of Pensacola (Faye 1946a: 184–185). In April 1718, Bienville sent his brother Antoine Le Moyne, Sieur de Châteaugué, with 50 men to St. Joseph

Bay where they built a fortified outpost, Fort Crèvocoeur, on the mainland in the woods, hidden from view by the water (Faye 1946a: 185). It is shown on a 1718 Beringer map (Weddle 1991: 209), and French priest Pierre Charlevoix (1923 [1761]: 323) described the fortification as a rectangular stockade with bastions on each corner, terrepleined walls, and five cannons. Inside the fort was a powder magazine, chapel, guard house, and store house.

News of this clandestine intrusion into Spanish Florida soon reached the acting lieutenant governor of Presidio Santa María, Captain Juan Manuel Roldán, who sent out scouts and confirmed the French outpost (Matamoros 1718). Roldán reported this to Governor Matamoros, who sent Roldán back to Fort Crèvocoeur to tell Châteaugué to leave. When Châteaugué refused, Matamoros complained directly to Bienville at Mobile. In July, Bienville presented the Spanish complaints to his Council, and they agreed to abandon St. Joseph Bay (Matamoros 1718). In reality, Bienville knew the Spanish would challenge this fort, and he was eager to get out of St. Joseph Bay as the location was indefensible, had non-productive land, and his soldiers were deserting. After a meeting in June with several hundred Creek principal men and chiefs, the French abandoned Fort Crèvocoeur and tried to burn the fort on their departure, but a rainstorm quickly put the fire out. By August 1718, the French were gone, having stayed there only two months.

On August 6, 1718, Governor Matamoros requested that the commandant of San Marcos send a detachment of 12 men and an officer to hold San José. They immediately repaired the partially burned fort and set up a watch post (Faye 1946a: 187). Meanwhile, the aggressive French intrusion into St. Joseph Bay had grabbed the attention of the Spanish Council of the Indies in Madrid, who considered it a sign that they needed to strengthen their hold on the northern Gulf coast. King Felipe agreed and ordered the viceroy of Mexico to send troops and otherwise strengthen the defenses of the Gulf coast (Faye 1946a: 187). By March 29, 1719, 800 troops from Veracruz arrived at St. Joseph Bay under the command of Don Gregorio de Salinas Varona. Using the repaired former French fort as a temporary base of operations, Salinas immediately began the construction of a large fort named Fort San José de Panzacola on the peninsula (Coker and Childers 1998: 69; Faye 1946a: 187). As had happened so many times before, it was only after a European rival made a move against her Florida territories that the Spanish Crown was willing to devote energy, money, and resources toward securing the northern Gulf coast.

The War of the Quadruple Alliance and the Fall of Santa María

With the end of the War of Spanish Succession in 1713, Spain lost all of her possessions in Italy and the Low Countries in Europe. These lands had been under

Spanish Habsburg control for nearly two centuries, and their loss was a great blow to the country in both practical economic terms and prestige. In 1717, the Spanish began a European campaign to retake the territories of Italy and Sicily and claim the French throne. These aggressions led to Britain, France, Austria, and Holland forming an alliance (the Quadruple Alliance) in August of 1718 and declaring a war against Spain.

In the Louisiana colony, the French immediately began planning attacks on Spanish settlements on the Gulf coast in Florida and Texas. Several frigates were sent from France to Mobile with troops, supplies, and orders for Bienville to occupy Pensacola and make it the new capital of the Louisiana colony and its primary port (Faye 1946b: 305). The French desperately needed a new harbor on the Gulf as Port Dauphin was still closed from a hurricane and Fort Crèvo-coeur on St. Joseph Bay had been abandoned. Bienville quickly received the news of the Quadruple Alliance and declaration of war against Spain when the fleet arrived from France, and he hoped the Spanish in Pensacola had not heard the news. Moving quickly on his orders, Bienville and his two naval officer brothers immediately launched a surprise attack on Presidio Santa María on May 13–15, 1719, with 1,000 men—including 400 Indian allies—several frigates, seven or eight other smaller vessels, and overland troops (Coker and Childers 1998: 73). Just before dawn on May 14, one of the French ships landed a party of 100 men on Santa Rosa Island at the entrance to Pensacola Bay, quickly overwhelmed the Spanish soldiers at the new battery there, and dismantled their cannons. The next morning, four French frigates entered Pensacola Bay and fired broadsides at Fort San Carlos with heavy guns for five hours. Ceasing fire, the French sent word to the Spanish that war had existed between their countries since January 14 of that year and asked the Spanish to surrender. Bienville landed 80 men near Santa María who joined another 100 French soldiers and the large Indian force that had arrived over land from Mobile. Surrounded and outmanned, Matamoros surrendered later that day. This was the first action of the War of the Quadruple Alliance in North America. France had captured Spanish Santa María de Galve, and the settlement was immediately designated the new capital of French Louisiana (Mays 2008; McKay and Scott 1983; Weddle 2002: 94–95).

At the end of May 1719, 300 captured soldiers of the Santa María garrison were sent on two French frigates to Havana. In the meantime, the Spanish had been planning an attack on Charleston from Havana to prevent an attack on Presidio San Agustín. Just as the attacking force was leaving Havana, the Spanish spotted the two incoming French vessels and captured them. To their surprise, they found the 300 Santa María prisoners of war aboard the ships (Coker and Childers 1998: 74–75). The Spanish in Havana were not aware of the declaration of war against them by the Quadruple Alliance. Fearing a French attack on New Spain, the Spanish immediately decided to retake Presidio Santa María instead of Charleston. On July 29, 1719, a force of 850 Spanish soldiers landed at the small outpost on St. Joseph Bay to gather intelligence and develop a plan to retake Pensacola (Coker and Childers 1998: 74–77).

In the interim, the French had begun transitioning from Dauphin Island to Pensacola and were relocating people, ships, and materials. Two ships with 450 enslaved Africans from Guinea bound for French plantations were unloaded at Pensacola, though eventually a majority were sent on to Dauphin Island and assigned throughout the French colony (Coker and Childers 1998: 75). However, some of the enslaved were held at Pensacola to perform the hard labor of fort reconstruction and reinforcement. Other ships from France arrived at Pensacola loaded with troops, slaves, tobacco workers, miners and supplies, but most were sent on to Dauphin Island. By mid-July, Louisiana's new capital of Pensacola hosted about 250 troops, 60 African slaves, 40 officials, and various other laborers.

On August 5, the Spanish returned in force to retake Santa María. Led by Don Alfredo Carrascosa de la Torre, they fired cannons at the fort and two French ships at anchor nearby. The French surrendered the next day. About 350 French troops were captured and Matamoros was restored as governor. Two days later Carrascosa sent the French officers to Havana. The remaining French troops were put on one of the captured French frigates with a Spanish guard and set adrift without sails or a rudder, and their fate is unknown (Coker and Childers 1998: 75–77; Faye 1946b: 307–308; Griffen 1959: 254).

The Spanish found Fort San Carlos in the same condition as they had left it, and Carrascosa added the 150 troops from Havana to bolster its forces (Coker and Childers 1998: 77; Faye 1946b: 309). The French in Mobile immediately learned of the Spanish attack and sent two forces to retake Pensacola on August 8. Sérigny, one of Bienville's two naval officer brothers, took about 100 troops by sea while 30 Frenchmen and 400 Indians went overland and attacked Santa María, but they were repulsed and left. Carrascosa then attacked and defeated a nearby village of 25 Native Americans and 160 of the French African slaves. Carrascosa also sent a force to attack the French at Dauphin Island but found an overwhelming force of about 2,300 Frenchmen and Indians there along with several batteries and a French ship. After conducting a few raids on farming communities, the Spanish left. In the meantime, the Spanish had rebuilt the battery on Sigüenza Point at Pensacola Pass and installed 15 cannons there. Repair of Fort San Carlos continued, and the grounds around the fortification were cleared of any fire hazards (Coker and Childers 1998: 78).

French reinforcements arrived at Dauphin Island in five ships with 250 men on September 1, 1719, and on September 16, Bienville arrived in Pensacola and surrounded Fort San Carlos with siege lines. The next day, French ships entered the bay and began bombarding Fort San Carlos and the Spanish vessels anchored in front of it. Matamoros surrendered that day and French soldiers pillaged the fort. Bienville sent the Spanish officers, sailors, and marines to France and 600 soldiers to Havana. The French then burned Fort San Carlos de Austria, the village, and the battery on Sigüenza Point to the ground. A small detachment of 12 French soldiers remained at the site of the former presidio for the next three years to claim and secure the area for France (Coker and Childers 1998: 79–80).

The burning of Presidio Santa María de Galve was clearly evident in the archaeological remains of Fort San Carlos de Austria and the structures we investigated. As described in previous sections of this chapter, burning was very distinct in all three barracks, the church, hospital/warehouse, and the fort walls. Pieces of charred timbers, boards, rafters, walls, and posts were common. The most well-preserved burned structure was the officers' barracks, where large numbers of nails and spikes lay in the charred debris pile that was at least half a foot thick, and many iron fasteners had been re-tempered in the hot fire. The clearest evidence of the burning of Fort San Carlos de Austria was the charred remains of the stockade wall. In every cross section of the fort wall and the entire 354 feet examined, the wall had been burned. Charring of posts in the stockade wall or structures did not extend to the base of the posts. Instead, the lower portions of the posts were unburned organic stains.

Summary of the Peace Years at Santa María

With the end of the British attacks on Presidio Santa María in mid-1715, four years of peace began. Finally, the population could leave the confines of the fort and begin to rebuild the abandoned village area outside its walls. This period saw formerly hostile Creek Indian groups sending large and frequent delegations to Santa María to receive gifts and supplies for their relocation and allegiance. Eventually, in 1718, one Apalachee group settled at the mouth of the Escambia River and established the village and mission of Nuestra Señora de Soledad.

From 1716 to 1718, the French had rapidly expanded up the river systems into the interior and west along the Gulf coast to St. Joseph Bay. Aware that the French wanted Pensacola the Spanish re-established the San Marcos outpost in 1718, and after causing the French to leave St. Joseph Bay, they began building a new fort on the St. Joseph peninsula in 1719. Under pressure to establish another French port after a 1718 hurricane closed Port Dauphin and as the War of the Quadruple Alliance against Spain had just been declared, France immediately attacked Santa María in May 1719. The Spanish regained their presidio in August but finally lost it again to the French in September of that year. The Spanish presidio, its village, and the newly reconstructed battery on Sigüenza Point were burned to the ground. The burning of Fort San Carlos and all of its buildings left an undeniable archaeological signature across the site, leaving no doubt that the fort and buildings were destroyed by fire.

Archaeological Summary of Presidio Santa María

Four seasons of archaeological investigations at the site of Presidio Santa María identified 243 features and recovered an artifact assemblage of 37,118 counted items and 398.6 kg of weighed material. As shown in table 2.2, 89.2 percent of the material by weight is from inside Fort San Carlos and 10.8 percent is from the village. Ceramics (68.6%) are the most abundant class of materials in the total assemblage by count, while Building Material (30.7%) and Euro-American Ceramics (27.6%) make up 58.3 percent of the weighed materials (table 2.7). Within the total ceramic assemblage of 21,684 pieces, 61.4 percent are Euro-American and 38.6 percent are Native American. However, as shown in table 2.3, the proportions of these two groups of ceramics vary internally within the site. Native American ceramics are in the majority in two areas: the north wall barracks and the village. The area with the highest percentage of Euro-American ceramics is the third warehouse (86.4%), but this percentage is skewed by the 2,183 pieces of broken Euro-American ceramics in a disposal pit just outside the entryway and is reflective of warehouse storage and handling rather than everyday living. When only the four residential areas are considered, the ratio is 54.2 percent Euro-American and 45.8 percent Native American ceramics (see table 2.3). This adjusted ratio excludes the special-use areas—such as the third warehouse, hospital/warehouse, and church—and is more representative of what the residents used in their daily lives. The strong presence of Native American ceramics throughout the residential areas ranges from 43.6 percent to 57.1 percent and reflects that Santa María was supplied only about half the Euro-American ceramics needed to meet its needs, but fortunately, Indian-made ceramics were available.

Almost all of the 13,506 pieces of Euro-American wares (97.6%) are either Other Coarse Earthenware (57.1%) or Majolica (40.5%), as shown in table 2.7. The remaining 324 sherds are Porcelain, Faience, Redware, Stoneware, and Delft, in that order. The distribution of the utilitarian Other Coarse Earthenware and Majolica tableware in the different areas of the site is shown in tables II.4a–c in appendix II. The area with the highest proportion of Majolica tableware is the third warehouse (71.3%), and the area with the second highest proportion

Table 2.7. Total Presidio Santa María artifact assemblage

Euro-American Ceramic Wares and Classes	Count	%	Weight (g)	%
Other Coarse Earthenware	7,716	57.1%	79,382.5	81.6%
Majolica	5,466	40.5%	16,908.6	17.4%
Porcelain	165	1.2%	231.8	0.2%
Faience	87	0.6%	367.2	0.4%
Redware	30	0.2%	195.0	0.2%
Stoneware	27	0.2%	170.4	0.2%
Delft	15	0.1%	7.3	c
Totals	13,506		97,262.8	
Native American Ceramic Tempers	**Count**	**%**	**Weight (g)**	**%**
Grog	4,243	50.6%	22,433.3	55.2%
Sand	3,113	37.2%	12,423.3	30.6%
Shell	672	8.0%	3,374.1	8.3%
Grog Shell	195	2.3%	1,493.4	3.7%
Grit	108	1.3%	540.6	1.3%
Unspecified	47	0.6%	349.2	0.9%
Totals	8,378		40,613.8	
Artifact Classes[a]	**Count**	**%**	**Weight (g)**	**%**
Building Material	314	1.0%	109,711.2	30.7%
Ceramics Euro-American	13,306	42.1%	98,345.8	27.6%
Metal	3,755	11.9%	58,151.3	16.3%
Ceramics Native American	8,378	26.5%	40,613.8	11.4%
Flora	7	c	19,415.4	5.4%
Fauna	-	c	15,537.2	4.4%
Glass	5,355	16.9%	7,744.3	2.2%
Lithics	449	1.4%	6,014.3	1.7%
Flora Modified	44	0.1%	1,276.2	0.4%
Totals	31,608		356,809.5	
Artifact Groups[b]	**Count**	**%**	**Weight (g)**	**%**
Kitchen	24,240	76.9%	158,831.0	49.9%
Architecture	2,065	6.5%	135,659.7	42.6%
Activities	467	1.5%	11,735.1	3.7%
Arms	2,329	7.4%	10,240.6	3.2%
Tobacco	676	2.1%	861.6	0.3%
Personal	385	1.2%	418.3	0.1%
Furniture	75	0.2%	250.6	0.1%
Clothing	1,292	4.1%	241.2	0.1%
Totals	31,529		318,238.1	

[a] No Other
[b] No Unspecified
[c] Less than 0.1 percent.

is the north wall barracks (43.5%). The area with the lowest proportion of Majolica tableware is the officers' barracks (22.0%). However, the officers' barracks had the highest proportion of utilitarian Other Coarse Earthenware (73.0%) for storage and cooking. This distribution of Euro-American ceramics reveals that the proportions and distribution of Other Coarse Earthenware and Majolica are *not* related to status or rank. Personal artifacts, food remains, and quality of architecture are much more revealing of rank and status. These results support Worth's (2018c: 8) recent reevaluation that in ship and military contexts, ceramics were usually held in common and seem unlikely to be good reflections of the social status of individuals or groups. Worth (2018c: 8) further contends that as ceramics were always among the cheapest items listed in inventories, they are somewhat poor reflections of comparative wealth. This contention is supported at Santa María, where we know the status of the residents of three barracks with large and directly associated artifact assemblages.

Using the known rank and status of the occupants of residential structures as a guide, there is one ceramic ware that *does* correlate with high status: porcelain. In the assemblages from the three barracks and associated activity areas, 133 pieces of porcelain were recovered and 129 (96.9%) were from the officers' barracks. There was only one piece in the north wall convict laborers' barracks and three in the soldiers' barracks. The remaining 30 pieces were scattered in the other site areas.

The 10,215 typable Euro-American sherds recovered from Santa María fall into 41 different ceramic types, the most abundant of which are Lead Glazed Coarse Earthenware (20.3%), Olive Jar (18.4%), Puebla Polychrome Majolica (16.3%), and El Morro (12.2%). As detailed in appendix II, table II.15, within the Other Coarse Earthenware, Lead Glazed (30.3%) and Olive Jar (27.5%) make up over half the sherds and are followed by El Morro (18.3%) and Unglazed (16.8%). The 14 additional types make up 2.7 percent or less each. The prevalent types of Majolica are Puebla Polychrome (51.0%), San Luis Polychrome (24.8%), and Abo Polychrome (9.5%). There are 10 additional Majolica types, but at 6.2 percent or less each, their proportions are small. The remaining 129 typable sherds include a few Faience (41), Porcelain (44), Redware (30), Delft (9), and Stoneware (5) sherds.

A total of 8,378 pieces and 40.6 kg of Native American ceramics were recovered from Presidio Santa María. Most are tempered with grog (55.2% by weight) or sand (30.6%), as shown in table 2.7. Other tempering materials are shell (8.3%), grog shell (3.7%), grit (1.3%), and unspecified (0.9%). The proportions of temper types between the fort and village are similar. Almost all the unspecified-tempered sherds are Colonoware. Within the fort and excluding the northwest bastion, the church and soldiers' barracks had the highest percentages of grog tempering. The north wall barracks had the highest proportions of sand tempering, and almost all the Colonoware was in the officers' barracks area. Most of the ceramics tempered with grog shell were in the hospital/warehouse and third warehouse.

Most Native American ceramics were tempered with grog (55.2%) or sand (30.6%) by weight, with low proportions of shell (8.3%) and grog shell (3.7%) temper and only traces of grit and unspecified temper (see table 2.7). Of the 8,351 typable Native American sherds weighing 40.5 kg, the most abundant types in the total Indian ceramic assemblage are Grog Tempered Plain (29.6%), Sand Tempered Plain (22.5%), and Grog Tempered Burnished (15.3%). The remaining 57 ceramic types make up 4.9 percent or less each. Almost two-thirds of the Native American sherds have plain surfaces (65.0%), and 22.9 percent have burnished surfaces. Burnishing is also present on some surfaces decorated with slipping, incising, and punctating. The most abundant ceramic types other than plain or burnished are Mississippi Plain, *variety* Unspecified (3.8%); Pensacola Plain (3.3%); Jefferson Plain (2.4%); Jefferson Check Stamped, *variety* Leon (1.3%); and Mission Red Filmed (1.0%).

Kitchen and Architecture activities generated 92.5 percent of the weighed and 83.4 percent of the counted items in this large artifact assemblage (see table 2.7). Most of the materials are Ceramics (68.6% by count) and Building Material (30.7% by weight). Food remains make up 9.8 percent of the weighed materials. Glass items (16.9% by count) are primarily fragments of bottles (46.0%), but of the 1,632 pieces identifiable to bottle type, there are far more fragments of case bottles (88.9%) than wine bottles (10.2%). There are also pieces of a few other types of glass bottles: pharmaceutical, condiment, flasks, and ink. Twenty-eight percent of the glass fragments are from tumblers, stemmed glasses, and general drinking glasses. Of note, 13 of the 15 stemmed glass fragments were in the officers' barracks, which correlates with the high rank of the residents. There were also fragments of a glass bowl and a decanter in this area. Most of the glass (59.9%) was recovered in the ruins of the officers' barracks and activity area with the remainder relatively evenly distributed in the other site areas, excluding the northwest bastion of the fort. There were only seven metal (iron) Kitchen items, and they include a cap, pot, and knife. The Kitchen group was between 72.5 percent and 88.9 percent of the counted artifacts recovered from each area of the fort and village, excluding the northwest bastion (see appendix II, tables II.5a–c). The village Kitchen assemblage (84.2%) is slightly higher than the fort assemblage (79.5%).

Architectural materials are usually either the highest or a close second of the weighed materials, but the Kitchen group is the heaviest in the soldiers' barracks, hospital/warehouse, and church. When the total weighed assemblage is considered (see table 2.7), there are more Kitchen materials (49.9%) than Architecture materials (42.6%). Expectedly, most of the architectural materials are bricks and ladrillos (79.8%) and iron nails and spikes (12.4%). Of the 725 fragments of window glass, most (91.0%) were in the burned remains of the officers' barracks, but pieces also were recovered from Structure 1 in the village, the hospital/warehouse, the third warehouse, and the church. From this distribution, it can be safely deduced that four buildings inside the fort had some glass windowpanes, as did the Spanish house in the village. The high number of window glass fragments in the officers' barracks indicates that there probably were several windows with glass panes, reflecting the high rank of the residents. Whole spikes (N=79), several re-tempered from fire, were found in all areas of the fort and village. Most (27) were recovered from the burned officers' barracks, but 17 were found in the remains of the burned wall of the northwest bastion, where they must have fastened large posts and timbers together. Eleven spikes were also found in the remains of the church, likely used to fasten the rafters to the internal posts. Some door and shutter hardware were also recovered, including five hinges, a latch, and a pintle.

While 2,329 Arms artifacts were recovered from Santa María, almost all (99.5%) were pieces of shot (87.3%) or gunflint fragments (12.2%). Seven artifacts are directly associated with cannons: three eight-pounder cannons, three cannon balls, and part of a cannon screw used to clean out a cannon tube after firing. Three personal arms artifacts were found: a musket butt plate from the officers' barracks and two sword/rapier hilts, one from the hospital/warehouse and the other from the soldiers' barracks.

Artifacts associated a wide range of activities were found. The 36 mano/metate fragments were recovered in almost every area of the fort and village, but there were more (13) in the hospital/warehouse, probably indicating the preparation of food for the many sick people. Writing slate fragments (46) were recovered from most areas inside the fort, but the majority (34) were from the village and are associated with the Spanish house (Structure 1). Interestingly, while illumination was needed throughout the settlement, almost all (15) of these 18 artifacts were from the warehouse, indicating they were stored there. A fancy brass candle tool was found in the officers' barracks and hospital/warehouse. Seven bale seals that secured rolls of cloth were recovered in the church, hospital/warehouse, officers' barracks, and third warehouse. One of the bale seals is made of brass and the others are lead. Other general activities represented include hunting (shot), fishing (weights and fishhooks), writing (ink bottle and writing slates), labor (shovel and pulley), shot manufacture (sprue), and sewing (needle, thimble, and scissors). Almost all the ochre was found in the officers' barracks area, perhaps a cosmetic for the officers' wives.

Almost all of the Personal artifacts (83.9%) are either pieces of Guadalajara Polychrome (44.4%) or glass beads (39.5%). While these items were found in every area investigated, the officers' barracks contained 62.5 percent of the glass or stone (jet) beads and 71.3 percent of the Guadalajara Polychrome sherds. Other jewelry items in the remains of the officers' barracks include three glass pendants and several silver, copper, and brass jewelry parts. Nine silver coins were recovered from Santa María, five from the officers' barracks and four from the village, including two in a refuse pit associated with the Spanish house. Seven are half-reals and two are one-reals, one from the Spanish house refuse pit and the other from the officers' barracks. All were minted in Mexico City except for one of the one-reals, which was minted in Potosí. There are 30 pieces of jewelry, including a brass crucifix, two Jesuit rings, two brass finger ring bands from the church/cemetery context, and four unique Man-in-the-Moon blue glass beads. Four additional finger rings were recovered: two brass bands from the hospital/warehouse, a copper band from the officers' barracks, and a brass band from the village.

Tobacco pipe fragments were abundant at Santa María: 662 kaolin and 14 coarse earthenware. Over half (59.2%) were found in the officers' barracks. Clothing items provide indicators of officer rank, and just over half of the total clothing items (51.6%) were recovered from their barracks, including brass buckles, silver and brass rivets, one wood and eight metal buttons, a brass thimble, 82 straight pins of brass and iron, and uniform brocade of gold, silver, and brass. Most clothing items (80.9%) are glass seed beads used either as clothing decoration for residents or as gifts for Native Americans. The hospital/warehouse and village also contained silver brocade, reflecting that officers lived in the village and were treated in the hospital. Other clothing items are metal and wood buttons and metal buckles of brass, pewter, and iron. The officers' barracks also had more furniture than any other area as evidenced by 45 of the 74 furniture tacks. The remaining tacks are distributed through the other site areas.

In sum, the two greatest strengths of the artifact assemblage recovered from Presidio Santa María are its large size and the high integrity of its contexts. The artifact assemblage is associated with known areas of the fort, internal structures, the village, and the cemetery. The distribution of cultural material in the large artifact assemblage produced some expected and unexpected results. Unexpectedly, the ceramic assemblages associated with residential structures were not helpful in deducing status, gender, or ethnicity. The quality and scale of the architecture reveal the most about status and rank, as do the food remains and personal, activity, and status-related artifact types such as porcelain, window glass, and stemmed drinking glasses.

Another unexpected result is the dearth of French materials recovered at Santa María despite the well-documented alliance with French Mobile throughout most of its existence. As Johnson (1999, 2003) discusses in detail, archaeological research at Old Mobile revealed that Spanish support was as important to its survival as it was to Santa María's (for extensive reporting on French colonial archaeological excavations in Mobile, see Waselkov 1991, 1994, 1999, 2002). The sale of local, Indian-grown food from Mobile to Santa María provided the French with coinage, which they used to purchase Spanish goods at Spanish ports. The site of Old Mobile has a great deal of Spanish material, especially tin and lead-glazed tableware, olive jars, and 104 Spanish coins (see appendix VIII; Johnson 2003: 325–327). At Santa María, French-made artifacts include Faience and Saintonge ceramics, bale seals, Man-in-the-Moon glass beads, Jesuit finger rings, a catlinite pipe fragment, and gunflints. Our explanation for the sparse artifact evidence of the lifeline of trade between Santa María and Mobile is that the Spanish purchased items that were consumed—particularly food, cloth, and gunpowder—with silver coins, many of which were lost at Mobile and Port Dauphin.

Patterns among personal artifacts, food remains, and architectural construction are distinctive in the residential buildings and activity areas. For example, quality of construction, such as wood vs dirt floors or post-on-sill vs post-in-ground foundations, corresponds directly with the rank and status of the residents. The architectural elements and artifact assemblages from special-use buildings such as the third warehouse, church, and hospital are unique and directly related to their specific functions. Many more research questions can be addressed using the large, well-controlled, and accessible historical and archaeological information recovered from Santa María.

Summary of Presidio Santa María de Galve

Presidio Santa María de Galve was the first location of the Spanish presidio in West Florida and has been the subject of much research. I have drawn on many sources for this synthesis to highlight the cultural context in which Santa María was enmeshed and the historical and tactical reasons behind the Spanish Crown's selection of Pensacola Bay. The rich historical and archaeological information that has been unearthed is but a small fraction of what remains in the archives and on the bluff overlooking the entrance to Pensacola Bay, protected by federal cultural resource laws and regulations.

The Spanish rediscovered Pensacola Bay while searching for the French Fort Saint Louis, which La Salle had built when he trespassed into northern New Spain in 1684. The Spanish realized they needed to protect both the deep entrance into the large Pensacola Bay system and the rich timber resources the Veracruz shipyards sorely needed. Harvesting the tall pines for masts and spars was the Spanish's first use of Pensacola Bay. Later, in 1698, the Spanish established Santa María on a bluff overlooking the entrance to Pensacola Bay. Unfortunately, Native Americans were not in the area when they arrived, nor were they there for most of the presidio's 21-year duration at this location. However, the Spanish brought a steady supply of convicts and conscripts from the slums and prisons of Veracruz and Mexico City to perform the necessary heavy labor. The population was reflective of New Spain: Spanish descendants born there, people of mixed Spanish-Indian-African descent who were classified in the lower castas, and foreigners. Most of the people were in or associated with the military as soldiers, officers, and administrators, along with Indian wage laborers and unpaid convict laborers. Some wives and children of the military and Native American men were present almost from the start, and some Spanish military men had Indian women as partners and wives. The size of the population varied, ranging from a low of 80 soldiers in 1700 to a high of 1,100 people in 1704, with an average of about 400 to 500 people. Native Americans of many ethnicities were recorded at Santa María, but Apalachees and Chacatos were the mainstay of the community, as many were trained carpenters and skilled hunters.

There were three distinct periods in the 21-year duration of Presidio Santa María: the early years (1698–1707), the siege years (1707–1715), and the return of peace (1715–1719). In the early years, construction of the large Vauban-style Fort San Carlos de Austria took place. Everyone lived in a sprawling community east of the fort in frame houses and thatch huts with a religious area and cemetery near the bluff. Initially designed to defend a naval attack, the seawall and bastions were double-walled terrepleins with cannons on the parapets. The curtain walls were a single row palisade designed to defend against land attacks.

For its duration, the presidio was dependent on outside sources for food and supplies. For the first few years, the productive Spanish missions east of the Apalachicola River supplemented the situado from New Spain, which was unreliable and usually late. By 1704, the missions had been destroyed by the English and the mission Indians scattered. About 800 refugee mission Indians and nine Spanish families arrived at Santa María in 1704, most staying only a short while because the Spanish could not support them. More refugees arrived in 1705 as a hurricane had wrecked two ships and about 300 survivors needed assistance. One of the ships, the *Rosario*, that was there during the hurricane to pick up pine masts and spars was wrecked but has been found and investigated. Traces of the original terreplined wall of the northwest bastion of the fort have been documented along with a Spanish-style house and associated refuse pits in the village. In addition, the village cemetery near the early church and friary was documented archaeologically. The French and Spanish established a reciprocal trade, and this alliance became a lifeline of support as both nearby settlements were poorly supplied by their home countries.

An eight-year siege of Santa María began in 1707 when, after destroying the Spanish mission system, the English and their Indian army of up to 1,200 targeted Santa María. They surrounded the presidio, constantly attacking it and ambushing anyone venturing out for necessities. The village was burned in 1707, and the entire population was forced to live inside the fort until 1715. To accommodate the surge in population inside the fort, many new buildings were constructed, including three barracks, warehouses, a hospital, administration buildings, and a church. The fort walls and bastions were also changed from terreplein to a single stockade, and the cannons were redirected to fend off attacks in all directions.

Archaeologically, we were able to locate the remains of six structures inside the fort: three barracks buildings, each housing military men of different ranks and incomes, along with a warehouse, hospital, and the church/cemetery. Hundreds (243) of architectural and refuse features were identified as well as 24 burials in the church subfloor cemetery, nine interments in the village cemetery, and another isolated burial in the village. The artifact assemblage recovered from inside the fort is very large, consisting of 37,118 counted items and 398.6 kg of weighed material. The analysis of the archaeological information inside the fort revealed several important correlations:

- The best correlations of archaeological materials with status are architectural quality, access to good food, special personal and activity items, porcelain, and clothing.
- Euro-American ceramic assemblages, with the exception of Porcelain, *do not* correlate well with the status or wealth of the residents.
- Tempering of Native American ceramics *does* seem to correlate with ethnicity, but surface decoration is almost negligible in all temper types.

The last four years at Santa María were peaceful until the very end. The crushing raiding stopped, the village was reoccupied, and Indians arrived at the fort negotiating peaceful relationships. In 1718, a new mission village of refugee Apalachees was established at the mouth of the Escambia and the repopulation of West Florida began. However, relations with the French in Mobile deteriorated as support from New Spain worsened and the lifeline with the French was broken. Food was a chronic and critical problem, and combined with corrupt and greedy presidio officials, it was the Achilles' heel of Santa María.

During these years, the French were expanding their territory. In search of a new port, the French trespassed into West Florida and built a fort on St. Joseph Bay in 1718, but it was soon abandoned after Spanish complaints. Fearing more French intrusions, in 1719, the Spanish rebuilt the fort at San Marcos and constructed a new presidio on the St. Joseph peninsula. Immediately after the War of the Quadruple Alliance against Spain broke out in Europe in 1719, the French from Mobile, still needing a new port on the northern Gulf, successfully attacked and took Santa María. The Spanish retreated 115 miles to the east to their new position on St. Joseph Bay; however, they did not give up on Pensacola Bay. They would return.

3

Presidio San José de Panzacola

Retreat to St. Joseph Bay

St. Joseph Bay is located about 115 miles east of Pensacola Bay along the Gulf of Mexico (figures 1.3 and 3.1). The "bay" is actually a body of Gulf water enclosed between the mainland and a narrow barrier spit 17 miles long, known as the St. Joseph Peninsula. As there is no inflow of fresh water, the enclosure is not a true bay. St. Joseph and Pensacola Bays are the only deep-water harbors on the northern Gulf coast, with entrances up to 25 feet deep and depths up to 35 feet within the bays.

The Spanish first occupied St. Joseph Bay in 1700 with a 25-man garrison outpost from Presidio Santa María to protect the shipping lane between Fort San Marcos and Santa María on Pensacola Bay (Coker and Childers 1998: 25). A group of 250 missionized Chacato Indians were resettled nearby at the same time to hunt and supply meat to Santa María (Coker and Childers 1998: 25). This outpost was abandoned in 1703 or 1704 as a result of British-led raids that destroyed the Spanish mission system, and the St. Joseph Bay area lay unoccupied for the next 14 years.

The second colonial occupation on St. Joseph Bay was in 1718 by the French, Fort Crèvocoeur (figure 3.1). As detailed in the previous chapter, this outpost of French Mobile lasted only two months. Fearing more French intrusion on the northern Gulf coast, the Spanish occupied the site of the former French outpost, and in March 1719 they sent 800 soldiers there from Mexico City and Veracruz to increase their presence on St. Joseph Bay. The Spanish quickly upgraded the damaged French fort on the mainland, used it for a base of operations, and began construction of a large new fort near the tip of the narrow peninsula at the entrance to St. Joseph Bay. After the French attacked and took the Santa María presidio on Pensacola Bay, the Spanish moved their operations to St. Joseph Bay where they finished construction of the new fort named Presidio San José de Panzacola.

The second Spanish occupation of St. Joseph Bay included the presidio and at least one mission village for the Apalachee, located on St. Andrew Bay and

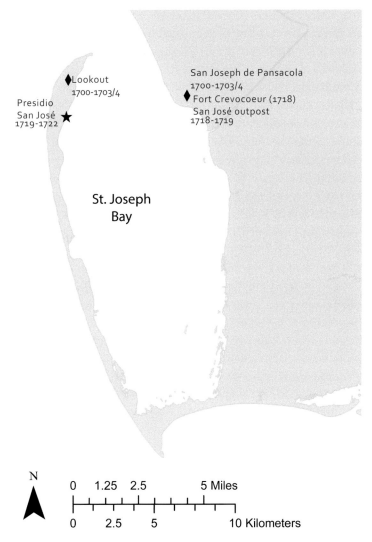

Figure 3.1. Map of colonial sites on St. Joseph Bay. Only Presidio San José is confirmed. Others are estimated locations. Courtesy of the Archaeology Institute, University of West Florida.

named San Andres (figure 1.3; Rivera 1723). Construction of the new presidio fort near the tip of St. Joseph Peninsula began in 1718 under the command of Don Gregorio de Salinas Varona. Wayne Childers (2001: 16) estimates that there were probably 800–1,200 soldiers at the beginning of this presidio with an additional large contingent of wives, children, and servants. Among the troops were many of the soldiers and artillerymen who had been captured at Santa María (Childers 2001: 16). Childers estimates that the fort on the St. Joseph Peninsula was possibly completed by early 1720 based on the documentation of a French fleet of four warships and a storeship that anchored in the roadstead of St. Joseph Bay in March 1720. On seeing the newly completed fort, Commander Chevalier de Saugeon decided to withdraw without attacking (Childers 2001: 17).

The presidio on the St. Joseph Peninsula officially had two names: Presidio of Asturias (after the heir apparent to the Spanish throne) and Presidio San José de Panzacola. While no maps of the fort have been located, a French priest named Pierre Charlevoix shipwrecked in 1722 and visited the San José presidio, and his letter contains the only known description of the presidio to date. He described the fort as built only of earth, lined with palisades, and defended with numerous pieces of artillery (Charlevoix 1923 [1761]: 323). Of the fort's residents, Charlevoix (1923 [1761]: 323–324) noted that most officers had their families there and that the officers' houses were neat and spacious, lining unpaved streets of deep sand. The priest also spent a night at what he described as a fortified country house where the captain of the garrison at San José, Captain Dioniz, resided (Charlevoix 1923 [1761]: 321).

To date, there is only one partial population count for Presidio San José, written in January 1723 when the location was being closed and people were being transferred to the new presidio of Santa Rosa on Pensacola Bay. The document states that 179 soldiers and sailors, 24 forced laborers, and an unknown number of women and children were transferred to the new presidio location (Childers 2001: 29). Childers also notes that an unknown number of Tocobaga and Apalachee Indians went with them.

In sum, historical information about the San José presidio is quite limited, but we know the fort appeared to have had earth walls topped with palisades and bastions armed with several cannons. Construction of the fort began in 1718 and was probably completed in early 1720. It is likely that the population lived inside the fort. By the end of January 1723, almost all the buildings at San José were dismantled, the materials and furnishings moved to Pensacola, and the officers and regular troops reassigned. The rest of the remains of the short-lived San José presidio were abandoned to the white sands of the peninsula it had briefly occupied. The "ruins" of the presidio were still visible both in 1766 when George Gauld conducted a survey of the coast of West Florida (Ware 1982) and 18 years later in 1784 when José de Evia conducted a survey for the Spanish (Holmes 1968).

The archaeological remains of Presidio San José de Panzacola (8GU8) are located near the tip of the St. Joseph Peninsula in what is today the T. H. Stone Memorial St. Joseph Peninsula State Park (figure 3.1). The site has been preserved from development as it has been either federal or state property to date. Professional archaeologists discovered the site in 1964 when a local resident brought it to the attention of Florida State University (FSU) Professor Hale Smith. Smith was one of the few Spanish historical archaeologists in the country at the time and quickly determined it was the site of the Spanish Presidio San José de Panzacola.

In the summer of 1965, with support from the Gulf County Historical Commission and Chamber of Commerce, Smith conducted an excavation with his students and once again included volunteers from the Port St. Joe-Gulf County Historical Society. The field project was covered by the local media, and while Smith did not complete a report of his work at the site, some information of the results can be gleaned from newspaper articles (Darby 1965; Darley 1965; PCNH 1965). Thirty-one years later in 1996, Jennifer Azzarello, then an anthropology graduate student at FSU, located some of the original labeled artifact bags from Smith's excavation at Presidio San José in the FSU collections. She classified the artifacts and information in the collection, wrote a research paper, and gave a presentation at a regional historical conference (Azzarello 1997; Azzarello and Hamlin 1997). Azzarello also relocated the site in the field and made a small surface collection.

In 2001, Elizabeth Benchley and Judith Bense from the University of West Florida (UWF) conducted a survey of the recorded archaeological sites in T. H. Stone Memorial St. Joseph Peninsula State Park. Their research located several local newspaper articles about the 1965 Smith excavation. In the articles, Smith stated he found the outlines of buildings in his excavation units, suggesting the presence of intact archaeological deposits. However, Smith also reported that most of the artifacts were in an area that had been extensively disturbed by US Army bulldozers during the 1960s. In the newspaper articles, Smith estimated the site size as extending 700–800 feet along the shoreline and approximately 100 feet into the interior. In 2012, Julie Saccente, then an anthropology graduate student at the University of South Florida (USF), gained access to a local resident's previously unknown, large, private surface collection from the site of the San José presidio. She also interviewed local residents who had been present during Smith's 1965 fieldwork. The analysis of this collection formed the core of her master's thesis (Saccente 2013) and following publication (Saccente and White 2015).

Benchley and Bense surveyed the site of Presidio San José as part of a Phase I study of the recorded archaeological sites in St. Joseph Peninsula State Park. Fieldwork included a controlled surface survey, shovel tests, a test unit, and a site map. Benchley and Bense (2001) determined that all presidio period cultural material was contained in the disturbed upper four inches of sand and there were no intact archaeological deposits. The disturbances included severe shoreline erosion, repeated inundation and churning by storm surges, and the US Army's aforementioned bulldozing during the 1960s. In 2001, the remaining eighteenth-century material was spread across an area measuring roughly 825 feet along the shore and 450 feet into the interior, as shown in figure 3.2. This area is much larger than the site size Smith estimated in 1965.

Both Azzarello's (1997) and Benchley and Bense's (2001) subsurface investigations found that no intact subsurface midden or features remain at the site of the San José presidio, and the vertical and horizontal integrity of the site has been destroyed. These findings differ from Smith's 1965 statements in the local newspaper articles, which specify that Smith had found outlines of buildings at the site, and information on his artifact bags indicates that artifacts were recovered as deep as three feet below surface. Benchley and Bense (2001: 52–53) suggest that in the 35 years between Smith's fieldwork in 1965 and their fieldwork in 2000, the intact archaeological remains of the presidio had been destroyed by erosion. They base their conclusion on several factors. First, no artifacts were recovered below four inches of the surface, and no midden zone or features were observed. Second, the controlled surface collection revealed eighteenth-century artifacts consistently mixed with flotsam, some of substantial size, including a complete, modern concrete block on the surface at the far western edge of the site, 175 feet from the current shoreline. The flotsam size, weight, abundance, and distribution across a very large area indicate that storm surges and high tides regularly wash over the entire area, removing and redepositing both presidio and modern materials. Third, based on known historic shoreline positions, the shoreline has eroded between 250 and 900 feet inland since 1722. Lastly, the military's bulldozing during the 1960s did significant damage to the site.

Today, the archeological remains of Presidio San José consist of fragments of ceramic containers, ladrillos, bricks, metal, and glass scattered in the surf zone, adjacent mudflat, and the upper few inches of 8.6 acres of land. During severe weather, artifacts are repeatedly tumbled, moved, deposited, and redeposited by water action. Despite the loss of site integrity, all archaeologists who have investigated the site agree that the eighteenth-century artifacts are undoubtedly from Presidio San José.

The artifact assemblage discussed below is a combination of the artifacts Azzarello rediscovered from the 1965 Smith excavation, those Benchley and Bense collected in 2001, and the large private surface collection Saccente described in 2013. The FSU and UWF teams screened excavated soil, and UWF made a controlled surface collection of the entire site area. Because of the

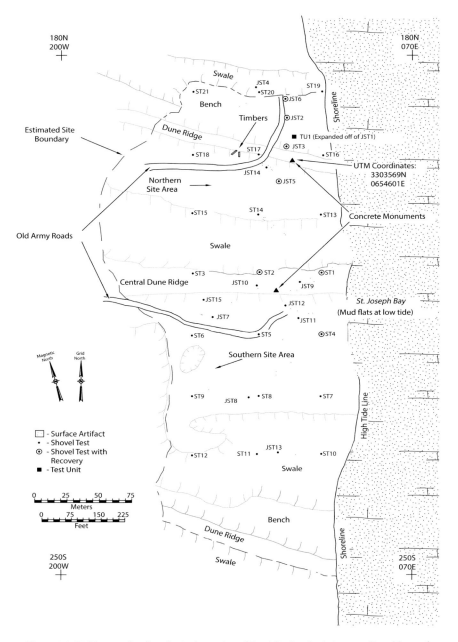

Figure 3.2. Field map of archaeological remains of Presidio San José site area (Benchley and Bense 2001: Figure 12). Courtesy of the Archaeology Institute, University of West Florida.

constant erosion and redeposition processes in action, faunal and floral remains are excluded from this analysis.

The combined artifact assemblage consists of 3,428 artifacts weighing 112.2 kg. The most frequent artifact class is Ceramics (71.7%) and the heaviest is Building Material (57.8%), as listed in table 3.1. Almost all building materials are pieces of ladrillos (85.1%) and oyster shell mortar (14.4%). The ceramic assemblage of 2,528 sherds is 59.7 percent Euro-American and 40.3 percent Native American by count. There are only two Euro-American ceramic classes in this collection: Other Coarse Earthenware (59.6% by count) and Majolica (40.4%), shown in table 3.1. The counts, weights, and proportions of all the typable Euro-American ceramic types and those in each class are presented in appendix III, tables III.1 and III.2. Of the 1,392 typable Euro-American sherds, El Morro is the most abundant (35.6%), followed by Puebla Blue on White Majolica (32.3%) and Olive Jar (18.1%). Of the 811 typable sherds in the Other Coarse Earthenware class, El Morro (61.0%) and Olive Jar (31.1%) are the most abundant. There are also 20 pieces of Guadalajara Polychrome. Over three-quarters of the Majolica is Puebla Blue on White (77.5%), followed by San Luis Polychrome (8.6%) and Plain (7.2%).

Over half of the Native American sherds by weight are tempered with sand (52.7%), and the other frequent tempering agents are grit (26.8%), grog (13.0%), and shell (3.2%), as shown in table 3.1. Very few sherds are tempered with limestone or grog shell. The complete list with quantities of the Native American ceramic types is presented in appendix III, tables III.3 and III.4. The most abundant ceramic types by weight are Grit Tempered Plain (26.4%), Sand Tempered Plain (13.2%), and Chattahoochee Roughened, *variety* Wedowee (12.6%). Over half of the surfaces of Indian-made sherds are plain (61.0% by weight) and 15.7 percent are roughened. The remainder of the surfaces are stamped, incised, burnished, slipped, and fabric impressed. Of note in this assemblage are eight pieces of Colonoware and the strong presence of grog tempering (13.3%), which is characteristic of Apalachee mission pottery.

Almost all the glass by weight is bottle glass (98.6%), either case (57.1%) or wine (38.2%); however, a few pieces of drinking glasses were also recovered. The Metal class has a wide range of artifacts, including seven iron cannon balls, large shot, two pestles, and an axe head. Iron nails are the most frequent metal artifact, but there are also pieces of an iron kettle and a brass pestle. Items made of stone include two mano fragments, two hammerstones, and 13 gunflint spalls.

The Architecture and Kitchen artifact groups make up 94.8 percent of the collection by weight (table 3.1). The Architecture group primarily contains fragments of ladrillos (84.3%) and mortar (14.2%). However, there are also

Table 3.1. Total Presidio San José artifact assemblage

Artifact Classes[a]	Count	%	Weight (g)	%
Building Material	329	9.3%	64,155.3	57.8%
Ceramics Euro-American	1510	42.8%	25,449.2	22.9%
Ceramics Native American	1018	28.9%	9,957.3	9.0%
Metal	423	12.0%	7,560.6	6.8%
Glass	123	3.5%	2,095.0	1.9%
Lithics	22	0.6%	1,721.0	1.6%
Totals	3,425		110,938.4	
Artifact Groups[b]	**Count**	**%**	**Weight (g)**	**%**
Architecture	433	13.4%	64,708.3	59.2%
Kitchen	2,623	81.4%	38,927.1	35.6%
Arms	87	2.7%	3,378.8	3.1%
Activities	27	0.8%	1,963.4	1.8%
Clothing	21	0.7%	112.2	0.1%
Personal	22	0.7%	108.0	0.1%
Tobacco	11	0.3%	39.1	c
Totals	3,224		109,236.9	
Euro-American Ceramic Classes	**Count**	**%**	**Weight (g)**	**%**
Other Coarse Earthenware	900	59.6%	23,104.7	90.9%
Majolica	610	40.4%	2,310.2	9.1%
Totals	1,510		25,414.9	
Native American Ceramic Tempers	**Count**	**%**	**Weight (g)**	**%**
Sand	537	53.2%	5,293.5	52.7%
Grit	209	20.7%	2,691.3	26.8%
Grog	184	18.1%	1,311.1	13.0%
Shell	52	5.1%	322.3	3.2%
Limestone	26	2.6%	162.0	2.5%
Unspecified	8	0.8%	254.0	1.6%
Grog Shell	2	0.2%	13.0	0.1%
Totals	1,018		10,047.2	

[a] No Other
[b] No Unspecified
[c] Less than 0.1 percent.

101 nails, a brass latch, and a roofing tile. Pieces of plaster are also present and indicative of this popular wall covering. Ceramics make up almost the entire Kitchen group. There are also 115 pieces of bottle glass and a fragment of an iron kettle in this group.

The most frequent artifacts in the Arms group are 67 pieces of lead shot. The Arms group also includes seven iron cannon balls and 13 gunflint spalls. The artifacts in the Activities group reflect food processing, including three pieces of manos/metates and a brass pestle. Wood cutting (iron axe head), fishing (10 lead weights), and stone tool working (hammerstone and shatter) activities are also reflected in the assemblage. A few clothing items were recovered, all of which are made of brass: 11 buckles, eight buttons, a hook and eye, and a straight pin. Personal items consist of 20 pieces of Guadalajara Polychrome pottery, a brass pendant, and a piece of silver jewelry. There are also 11 fragments of kaolin tobacco pipes.

Summary of the San José Presidio

The Spanish first occupied St. Joseph Bay in 1700 when an outpost and lookout were established on the mainland to protect supply ships sailing along the coast from the port at San Marcos to Presidio Santa María on Pensacola Bay. The outpost was abandoned in 1703 or 1704 when the mission system was being destroyed by English-led Indian armies from the interior. A clandestine French fortified outpost, Fort Crèvocoeur, was built on the mainland in 1718 but was quickly abandoned under Spanish pressure after a few months. The Spanish occupied and repaired the outpost and immediately began constructing a large fort near the tip of the spit-like peninsula at the entrance to the bay. Construction on the narrow peninsula started in 1719 with the purpose of increasing protection of the Spanish West Florida coast from British and French aggression. However, with the sudden and surprise loss of Presidio Santa María on Pensacola Bay to the French, San José became the new Spanish headquarters and second location of the Spanish West Florida presidio until 1722 when Pensacola was returned to Spain by treaty.

During the three-year duration of Presidio San José, the Spanish assisted in establishing at least one Apalachee mission village, San Andres, on St. Andrew Bay. Although no maps of Fort San José have been located, a letter by a visiting French priest in 1722 described the large fort as being made of earth with palisaded walls and several cannons. The population at first was quite large, including up to 1,200 soldiers plus many women and children.

The archaeological remains of Presidio San José have been investigated four times by professionals from three Florida universities beginning in 1965. Survey and testing by Benchley and Bense (2001) revealed that sometime prior to 2000, the archaeological remains of the presidio lost their integrity as a result of shoreline erosion and storm surges. Today, the surf zone and mudflats just offshore contain thousands of artifacts that are tumbled and deposited over an 8.6-acre area during high tides and storm surges. The surface-collected artifact assemblage is the primary source of the archaeological assemblage.

The combined artifact collections consist of 3,428 artifacts weighing 112.2 kg. Most of the material by weight consists of ladrillo fragments, oyster shell mortar, and ceramics. Euro-American ceramic wares are Coarse Earthenware, and about half of the Native American sherds are tempered with sand, followed by grit, grog, and shell. The assemblage revealed many of the activities of the residents, such as fishing, hunting, construction, and food processing. Personal and clothing items were also present.

It is unfortunate that there are no intact remains of Presidio San José de Panzacola. Yet we do know where it was, and historical records can continue to contribute new information about this community. Although short lived, the second location of the West Florida presidio fulfilled its *raison d'être*: to deter further territorial encroachment from Spain's European adversaries. The abandonment of the San José location marked the end of the Spanish's presence in the Apalachicola delta region during the Presidio Period.

4

Presidio Isla de Santa Rosa, Punta de Sigüenza

Return to Pensacola Bay

The third location selected for the West Florida presidio was geographically very similar to the previous one on the St. Joseph peninsula. Santa Rosa Island is on a long, narrow barrier island near the entrance of the bay. It is 40 miles long, extending from Pensacola to Choctawhatchee Bay (see figures 1.3 and 1.4). Across the narrow, deep entrance is the end of another barrier island, Perdido Key, that extends from Pensacola Pass 16.5 miles west to Orange Beach, Alabama. The location of the presidio was militarily strategic as it enabled defense of the bay entrance and prevented attacks on the mainland; however, it was a very difficult place to live.

Founding of Isla Santa Rosa, Punta de Sigüenza Presidio

Since the late seventeenth century, Pensacola Bay has been considered the best harbor on the northern Gulf coast (Leonard 1939). Its narrow entrance is permanently open and deep enough to accommodate large colonial-era sailing vessels. The bay offered a deep harbor and good anchorages, but unfortunately, it had proved impossible for the Spanish to defend the entrance from the mainland, as evidenced by the two successful naval attacks by the French in 1719. To make matters worse, as at San Agustín, the Pensacola Bay area did not have any natural resources to offset the cost of supporting a presidio, making it yet another expensive liability. However, the Spanish understood that both of their main European rivals, France and Britain, continued to seek control of Florida, and the Crown remained unenthusiastic but resigned to the reality of protecting the northern Gulf coast at Pensacola Bay.

In an effort to protect Pensacola Bay without building and maintaining an expensive presidio, in late 1722, King Philip V promoted the possibility of digging a drainage canal across Santa Rosa Island to lower the water depth over the sandbar at the bay's entrance to make it impossible for armed ships to enter (Clune et al. 2006: 28). This proposal had been made at least a decade before, and the proposed location of the drainage canal is shown on the 1713 French map of Pensacola Bay (see figure 2.4). However, concerned that the drainage canal might prove to be impractical, the king ordered that a fort and settlement be built on Sigüenza Point at the bay entrance. The king also ordered that the remains of the former presidio site of Santa María de Galve be destroyed and the San José location abandoned (Clune et al. 2006: 28; Ford 1939: 127–128).

Alejandro Wauchope, a Scottish colonel in the Windward Fleet, was tasked with reconciling the options the Spanish king had ordered (Clune et al. 2006: 28–31). Wauchope arrived in late November 1722 to accept the formal delivery of Pensacola Bay from the French commander. He and engineer José de Berbegal had brought a group of laborers, convicts, and excavation tools and immediately went to Santa Rosa Island to carry out the king's orders. The feasibility of digging a cross-island drainage canal to lower the water level in Pensacola Bay was soon determined impracticable, but Wauchope also determined that Sigüenza Point was too sandy, too low and swampy, intermittently inundated, treeless, and overall, too exposed to the elements to be a suitable location for the new fort and community. Instead, he selected the first place on the island with a modest stand of pine trees and some protective dunes, about half a mile from Sigüenza Point on the bay shore; he named the new presidio Isla de Santa Rosa, Punta de Sigüenza.

With the selection of the third location of the West Florida presidio determined, the transfer of people and materials from Presidio San José and Veracruz began immediately in December 1722. Captain Pedro Primo de Rivera, the first governor of Presidio Santa Rosa, soon arrived from Veracruz with 70 soldiers. In all, Wauchope settled about 200 people in late 1722 and early 1723. In January 1723, ships arrived with supplies for 200 men (Clune et al. 2006: 38). Some of these soldiers had originally served at Santa María (1698–1719) across Pensacola Bay. Others were native Spanish West Floridians originally from the Apalachee mission province who had lived at Santa María and San José. In early February 1723, Wauchope transported 84 men, women, and children from San José to Veracruz, with an additional 28 people slated to be taken in the near future (Clune et al. 2006: 38). Over time, the population at Santa Rosa fluctuated between about 100 and 400 people.

The Community

Initially, much of the building material used at Santa Rosa came from dismantled structures at San José and new materials brought from Veracruz. Table 4.1 presents the list of buildings, the source of the materials, and dimensions of initial structures at Santa Rosa. John Clune and colleagues (2006: 35) and

William Griffen (1959: 258) describe the new buildings at Santa Rosa, which included two large barracks 40 by 18 feet in size and 8 feet high with cedar bark roofing. The guardhouse was made of cedar boards and was 8 by 10 feet in size and 8 feet high. The powder magazine, also made of cedar boards, was 15 by 10 feet and 5 feet high and covered with cow hides. Other buildings included the commandant's house, paymaster's office, warehouse, 24 small houses for workers, and eight larger houses for senior officers and officials. Surprisingly, the church is not specifically mentioned in the first structures constructed, but it must have been built during this time because Wauchope's 1723 inventory mentions furnishings for the church, and church supplies were received a year later (Eschbach 2007: 97). Ten years later, in 1733, paymaster and quartermaster Benito Buscarons (1731–1733) briefly described 10 structures in his account book, which has recently been discovered and translated by John Worth (table 4.1). In this account book, the church, armory, paymaster's house, and officers' quarters are described as being in a state of disrepair.

The first fort at Santa Rosa was described in 1727 as a small stockade of pine posts with 12 guns, a covered way, a warehouse, and a powder magazine. Initially, it had no bastions or troop quarters (Clune et al. 2006: 34). By 1731–1733,

Table 4.1. Descriptions of buildings at Presidio Santa Rosa in 1723 and 1731–1733

Initial Structures in 1723 at Presidio Santa Rosa[a]		
Building	Materials	Dimensions (LxWxH)[b]
Warehouse	Cedar boards and nails from Veracruz	40x20x20
Powder magazine	Cedar boards and nails from Veracruz; covered in cured cow hides	15x10x5
Paymaster's office	Material from Veracruz	20x9x9
Barracks (2)	Cedar boards and cypress bark roofing from San José; cedar board flooring from Veracruz	40x18x8
Captain's house	Cedar boards from San José; nails from Veracruz	20x10x10
Powder magazine	Cedar boards from San José	10x8x8
Small dwellings (24)	Cedar boards and cypress bark roofing from San José	Unknown

Larger dwellings (8)	Cedar boards and cypress bark roofing from San José	Unknown
Cook oven	Unknown	Unknown
Lookout	Unknown	55.5 feet high

Buildings Observed in 1731–1733[c]		
Building	**Materials**	**Dimensions (LxWxH)[b]**
Fort	Pine stakes with bark; ribbands; half fort new; sea bastion; outside walkways; 2 sentry boxes; house for artillerymen	Unknown
Church	Made of wood; cypress bark roof, wood rotten	41x22x8.2
Armory	Made of wood and boards covered with cypress bark; useless	82x11x11
Food Warehouse	Made of wood; attic; covered with cypress bark; interior and exterior doors with locks	32.9x22x8.2
Paymaster's House	Made of wood and boards; roofed with rotten cypress boards	54.8x16.4
Guard House	Made of boards covered with cypress bark; floor and weapons locker made of boards	32.9x16.4x8.3
New Principal Guard House	Inside the fort; made of wood; lined and roofed with cypress bark; new floor	Unknown
Old Principal Guard House	Outside the fort; made of wood; lined and roofed with cypress bark	Unknown
Officers' Quarters	Small barrack that served as a residence for the officers; useless	Unknown
Private House	House of Sergeant Torres; living room, bedroom, kitchen, and exterior outbuildings; half use-life	32.9x16.4

[a] Data from Childers (2003b: 13–14) and Griffen (1959: 257).
[b] All dimensions in feet.
[c] Data from Buscarons (1731–1733).

the fort was described as a stockade of pine stakes held together with ribbands (long, narrow strips of timber), with a bastion, two sentry boxes, and a house for artillerymen (table 4.1).

Additional information about the first community is contained in a damage assessment report of the November 1752 hurricane, which states that at the founding of the settlement there were three rows of houses parallel to the bay shore. These houses were submerged during the 1752 hurricane and remained inundated for some time afterward (Eschbach 2007: 103; Yberri 1753). A small fort was on the bay shore on the eastern edge of the settlement. All buildings in the first community were described as made of boards with cypress bark roofs. The first structures were barracks, warehouses, and residences, but there was also a church, guardhouse, armory, powder magazine, and cook oven.

In 1734, new Governor Diego de Escobar arrived at Santa Rosa and realized that the only way to protect the entrance to Pensacola Bay was to have a fort directly on Punta de Sigüenza. He immediately built a wooden fort there and stocked it with eight large cannons. However, just after construction was finished, a storm destroyed the fort and the cannons were lost at sea (Clune et al. 2006: 34; Yberri 1753).

In September 1740, a powerful hurricane struck the Santa Rosa presidio, destroying the small fort and burying three cannons in the sand. The community also lost the hospital and church along with half the residents' homes to flooding, and the food warehouse was badly damaged (Eschbach 2007: 98). Immediately following the storm, the new Governor Colonel Gervasio Cruzat y Góngora rebuilt the soldiers' quarters and a new guardhouse out of wood. A new powder magazine was built of stone and brick. One of the few structures to survive the storm was the "King's House," which was used as the paymaster's office during rebuilding and repairs. As the 1740 hurricane destroyed the warehouses on the island containing all the food and supplies for the community, a new and more secure warehouse was built across the bay on the mainland. The warehouse there was protected with a stockade, and a small resident garrison was stationed there for protection. This new outpost was named San Miguel de Punta Blanca (Faye 1941: 162; Worth 2013: 2). Governor Cruzat also built a new fort of adobe, lime, and stone on Punta de Sigüenza to guard the entrance to the bay. Once again, a storm wiped it out that same year (Clune et al. 2006; Eschbach 2007: 99; Yberri 1753).

As of this writing, the only rendering of the Santa Rosa community rebuilt after the 1740 hurricane is Dominic Serres's 1743 panoramic sketch (figure 4.1). How much "artistic license" Serres employed is unknown. Nevertheless, the sketch is informative in the layout of the settlement and the many architectural details it provides.

Figure 4.1. A 1743 Dominic Serres drawing of the Santa Rosa presidio: *1,* fort; *2,* church; *3,* governor's house; *4,* commandant's house; *5,* well and north-south street; *6,* bongo (Roberts and Jefferys 1763).

In 1751 and 1752, Santa Rosa was struck by five hurricanes with more disastrous results. The last hurricane in November 1752 completely submerged the community by storm surge from the Gulf, leaving only a recently built hospital and the King's House standing. While little is known about the 1741–1752 community, the reports of the storms' aftermath reveal some information about it. For example, the second church is described as having a wood framework with supporting pillars mounted on timbers and a subfloor cemetery. The storm collapsed the north and northeast walls of the church, washing away the floor and the subfloor interments (Yberri 1753). The damage to the church was irreparable, so the hospital was converted to a church (Anonymous 1752a). The reports also reveal that the commandant and paymaster had houses that were ruined by the storm (Anonymous 1752b). A third small fort and at least four buildings were built soon after the 1752 storm.

After the November 1752 storm, the Santa Rosa presidio was declared uninhabitable; however, the population remained there for two more years before permission was granted in the summer of 1754 for the married soldiers and their families to relocate to the mainland outpost of San Miguel. The garrison was moved to the new Presidio San Miguel in late 1756, but a small military unit remained at Santa Rosa as it was used as an outpost until the British takeover in 1763.

In sum, the layout of the Santa Rosa community appears to have been linear and parallel to the bay shore with a small fort on the eastern edge of the community to protect it from land attacks by hostile Native Americans in the vicinity. The community originally had at least three streets that paralleled the bay shore, and the 1743 Serres rendering shows a north-south street on the eastern edge of the community. The largest structures were the warehouses, King's House, church, and barracks. All structures were made of wood except the second hospital, second powder magazine, and the King's House, which appear to have been made of brick and stone. The community was badly damaged in a hurricane in 1740, but structures were rebuilt and occupation continued. After a series of three strong storms or hurricanes in 1752, the site was levelled by storm surge and flooding, setting the stage for yet another relocation of the West Florida presidio.

Life on an Island

Placing Presidio Santa Rosa near the tip of Santa Rosa Island and the entrance to the bay may have been defensively strategic, but as described above, the presidio was never safe nor spared from disastrous natural forces. Barrier islands lie between the Gulf and mainland, receiving the full force of wind, rain, and storm surges. These islands are the most vulnerable locations to harsh weather in the entire Pensacola Bay system. Unfortunately, Presidio Santa Rosa suffered nine hurricanes and/or strong tropical storms in its 32 years of existence (table 4.2). The elevation of the presidio on Santa Rosa Island was very low (a maximum of five feet above sea level today). The ground consists of only loose, soft, white/light gray beach sand. The permanent water table is within two to three feet of the surface depending on the tide and rain. Winds are constant off the Gulf and bay. It is a very difficult place to live at any time.

The first hurricane struck almost on the day Wauchope arrived with the first people and materials from San José. One of the ships carrying a load of cypress bark for roofing sunk, killing an officer and two soldiers. A complacency-inducing 12-year lull in strong storms lasted until 1734 when a hurricane or strong storm destroyed the community's attempt to build a fort on Sigüenza Point. Noteworthy here is the term "hurricane" as used in an eighteenth-century context. Today we understand that along the Gulf coast, tropical storms produce strong winds, ferocious waves, tides, and violent thunderstorms lasting anywhere from hours to several days. These storms can erode a shoreline and deposit many inches of rain in a short span of time. In the eighteenth century, these storms felt like hurricanes and were reported as such. The storm of 1734 may have been a violent summer or tropical storm, not a hurricane, as

Table 4.2. Hurricanes and strong storms affecting Presidio Santa Rosa

Date	Type of Storm	Effects
1722	Hurricane/strong storm	Sunk ship carrying bark roofing from San José; 3 military men killed
1734	Tropical storm?	Destroyed fort under construction on Sigüenza Point
1740	Hurricane	Destroyed most of settlement
1741	Tropical storm?	Destroyed brick fort under construction on Sigüenza Point
1751 (August)	Hurricanes	Flooded settlement; damage to many structures
1751 (September)	Hurricane	Flooded settlement; damage to many structures
1752 (August)	Tropical storm?	Flooded settlement; damage to many structures
1752 (October)	Hurricane	Flooded settlement; damage to many structures
1752 (November)	Hurricane	Destroyed entire settlement except three buildings; Gulf wash-over channel cut through settlement; destroyed primary and surrounding dunes

Sources: Childers (2003b: 10–13); Clune (2006: 37); Eschbach (2007: 103).

the only reported destruction was to the fort just constructed on the exposed Sigüenza Point (Clune et al. 2006: 34). But the 1740 storm was surely a hurricane as it destroyed the fort at the presidio along with half the island's residences, the first church, hospital, and warehouse (Urueña 1741).

An additional problem to living on the tip of a narrow barrier island is the lack of useable natural resources. The few small stands of tall pines provided lumber for building material, masts, and spars but were quickly depleted. Because of the scarcity of island resources, all essentials had to be brought to the settlement from elsewhere, including wood for construction, firewood, and food. It was and still is impossible to grow crops or graze animals in the salty, dry, loose island sand.

Severe weather, the inability to securely anchor structures in the loose and sandy soil, and the use of wood and cypress bark as almost the sole building materials caused continuous site-wide reconfigurations of the community. In ideal conditions, the best location to live in a shoreline settlement is near the shore, where breezes are cooling and scatter biting insects, especially mosquitos. This was not the case at Santa Rosa. Erosion of the shoreline occurred during every fall/winter storm and hurricane, which resulted in the flooding damage or destruction of structures nearest the water, as described above. Shoreline erosion, flooding, and strong winds made the shoreline dangerous and forced residents to seek what higher ground existed in the rear of the low-lying location. As will be detailed below, the cyclic repetition of construction-repair-destruction-reconstruction proved to be the overwhelming aspect of the archaeological remains of this settlement. The archaeological record documented the "flip flopping" of initial high status, near-shore residents moving away from the shore and lower status households moving toward it.

The University of West Florida (UWF) archaeological team experienced the same difficulties of island life when investigating the site of Presidio Santa Rosa during the 2002–2004 seasons of fieldwork. There were storms, torrential rains, searing heat, and glare from the bright sun reflecting off the porous, coarse, soft, white sand. In the winter, cold north winds follow the frequent weather fronts. In September 2004, a Category 3 hurricane (Ivan) made a direct hit on Pensacola Bay. Afterward, once again, the primary dunes along the Gulf shore were flattened, and the storm surge cut through the island in several places (figure 4.2). Santa Rosa Island was and continues to be a very harsh place to live.

Figure 4.2. A 2004 aerial photo of a new breach across Santa Rosa Island caused by Hurricane Ivan, showing dune erosion and wash overs near the site of Presidio Santa Rosa (USGS 2016).

Demography

Presidio Santa Rosa was first and foremost a military garrison, and its population was primarily soldiers, officers, administrators, and their dependents. In addition, convicts continued to be sent as laborers, and local missionized Indians were employed as skilled craftsmen, laborers, fishermen, hunters, and trackers of fugitive deserters. The total number of people recorded receiving rations at Santa Rosa fluctuated between 80 and 400 (table 4.3). Military soldiers and officers numbered between 91 and 236, and they were divided into two companies that each included a captain and ensign, two sergeants, up to four corporals, and a drummer (Clune et al. 2006: 38; Holmes 2012: 72; John Worth, personal communication 2020). Other military personnel included master gunners, master surgeons, sailing master, and seamen. Important civilian members of the community included salaried staff positions for tradesmen with particular skills such as carpenters, paymaster, warehouse keeper, and a chief/supervisor of forced laborers (Eschbach 2007: 79–83). Also present throughout the community's existence were Franciscan friars provided from the province of Santa Elena de Florida centered in Havana and San Agustín. These included at least two chaplains, assistant chaplains, and one or two

Table 4.3. Population of Presidio Santa Rosa

Date	Total	Soldiers	Convicts	Others	Indians
1723	203	179	24	-	-
1724	218	136	-	19	-
1725	280	134	-	19	-
1734	116	93	23[b]	-	-
1737	80	-	-	-	-
1740 (March 28)	346	112	59	19	120
1740 (November 18)	276	84	72[b]	-	120
1741	400	150	-	20	150
1743	375	138	-	19	120
1752	180	91	26	-	-
1753 (August 16)	215	102	-	14	-

Sources: Childers (2003a: 27); Clune et al. (2006: 39–41).
[a] Most totals provided in documents have only partial or no subdivisions.
[b] Arrived as a group.

missionaries who received a ration and stipend through the annual situado (Clune et al. 2006: 41; Holmes 2012: 73).

Convicts continued to be conscripted from the jails of Mexico City, Veracruz, and Puebla to labor at the presidio. In this frontier environment, convicts were often offered the opportunity to enlist in the military, usually upon arrival or during a period of crisis or critical need; many men took this opportunity. The change in rank would have had little impact on their social standing in the short term, but the convicts-turned-recruits did receive a salary in addition to rations (Bushnell 1994; Eschbach 2007: 84). Although convict arrival numbers at Santa Rosa were not consistently recorded in available sources, there are nine documented numbers of convicts in the population, including three arrival groups. The recorded number of convicts at Santa Rosa ranged from 24 to 72 (Clune et al. 2006: 40–41). Meanwhile, regular soldiers sent to Pensacola continued to be recruited from Mexico City, Veracruz, and nearby villages in New Spain. The frequent change in status of convicts to soldiers makes it difficult to determine the number of forced laborers at Santa Rosa at any one time.

From the very beginning and throughout the duration of Presidio Santa Rosa, between 12 and 20 women received rations and salaries in the situado (Clune et al. 2006: 41–42; Eschbach 2007: 86–89). The women receiving salaries were usually identified as widows or relatives of the soldiers and officers, and Krista Eschbach (2007: 87–89) has identified 17 of the women by name. At least half had a relatively high economic status within the community and were the primary kinfolk of military officers. The remaining women were married or related to men with positions of lower rank, such as artillerymen or the chief of laborers. There were also several documented marriages and informal concubine relations between soldiers and Indian women at Santa Rosa (Clune et al. 2006: 42; Eschbach 2007: 88–89). Another example of documented women at the Santa Rosa presidio is in 1754, when officials in Veracruz sent 35 young women to Pensacola on a voluntary basis. These women either were the wives of enlisted men or were recorded as having plans to marry upon arrival (Clune et al. 2006: 41).

While no families were officially documented at Santa Rosa before 1741, sporadic mentions of supplies for families, women, and children before that time substantiate their presence. In 1741, six families totaling 77 individuals were supported through funds paid to the heads of households. By 1743, there were 13 families receiving stipends and rations, and by 1752, there were 21 families. A year later there were 32 families, and two additional families with 10 children arrived at Santa Rosa at some point during this same year (Clune et al. 2006: 41). Families in which the husband (and sometimes the wife) earned a steady wage and rations promoted an overall sense of stability to the presidio community and provided a nascent and necessary element to a community hoping to put down roots.

Historians agree that the population was composed of people of mixed ethnicity who adhered, in general, to the Hispanic cultural customs shared across the Spanish colonial empire. Researchers regularly state that the ethnic makeup at Santa Rosa must have been very similar to that documented a few decades earlier in the 1708 census at Presidio Santa María: 41 percent mestizo (Indian and Spanish), 34 percent Spanish (born in Mexico), 21 percent mulatto (African and European) and 4 percent zambo/lobo (Indian and African) (Clune et al. 2003: 25).

Apalachee and Yamasee Indians living in the two mission villages on the mainland regularly interacted with the Spanish presidio community. The number of Indians receiving rations typically numbered 120 but rose higher on occasion (Clune et al. 2006: 42). Indian and African slaves were also present in the presidio community, though their numbers and situations are largely unknown (Clune et al. 2006: 42).

In sum, the Hispanic community at Presidio Santa Rosa reflected the mixed ethnicities seen across New Spain. A recognizable and clear local social hierarchy stood with convicts, forced laborers, slaves, and servants at the bottom. At the top of the social hierarchy and economic positioning were appointed officers born in Spain or New Spain, Spanish civilians, well-placed Creoles, and Spanish Floridians. In the middle of the hierarchy were important staff and administrators, officers from New Spain, followed by tradesmen and soldiers. Importantly, the status of individuals could rise or fall with changes in their positions (for example, convicts to soldiers). As always, a borderland environment offered some people the opportunity to craft a new narrative for themselves and their families and potentially spin that storyline into advantageous opportunities going forward.

Refugee Indian Mission Villages

Though Native Americans seem to have been present in the community as wage laborers, traders, and visitors, there is little mention of their population in the records of Santa Rosa. This lack of documentation is likely due to the changes in Indian settlement patterns and relations with Europeans across the Southeast during the early decades of the eighteenth century. Structural changes in Indian/European relations began in 1702 when the Spanish missions began to be attacked by British-led Indian armies for slaves. As the attacks escalated through 1704, mission Indians lost faith in the Spanish's ability to protect them, and they literally fled Spanish Florida. By 1712, however,

Indian retaliation and resistance had grown against the British in Carolina. The Yamasee and Creek had become disillusioned with the British because the supply of Indian slaves had diminished due to depopulation and British traders threatening enslavement of the Native traders or their family members to satisfy debts. This disillusionment resulted in a rebellion against the British called the Yamasee War and caused a new diaspora of Native Americans from the interior away from the British into Spanish Florida and French Louisiana, where they negotiated political and economic alliances. In West Florida there were seven Indian refugee settlements (table 4.4), three of which have been archaeologically documented: one Apalachee (Escambe), one Yamasee (Punta Rasa I), and one with both of these groups (Punta Rasa II).

In 1718, a group of Apalachee exiles arrived at the Santa María presidio where Apalachee Governor Juan Marcos Fant successfully negotiated with Governor Juan Pedro Matamoros for rations, religious support, and military protection in return for Apalachee allegiance and trade. The Juan Marcos group included Apalachee refugees who had been residing at Santa María and on Mobile Bay as well as former slaves captured by the Creeks (Worth 2008: 7). They located their mission village, Nuestra Señora de la Soledad y San Luis, near the mouth of the Escambia River. Worth suggests that the Soledad mission village was stable during the three-year French occupation of Pensacola Bay.

During the 1720s, British-allied Lower Creeks once again began to attack Spanish-allied Apalachee and Yamasee mission villages around San Agustín

Table 4.4. Native American refugee settlements in Spanish West Florida

Years	Name	Ethnicity	Location
1705–?	Joseph de la Cruz Cui	Apalachee	Perdido Bay
1718–1741	Nuestra Señora de la Soledad y San Luis	Apalachee	Escambia River mouth
1720–1722	San Andres	Apalachee	St. Andrews Bay
1741–1748	Yamasee Town	Yamasee	Escambia Bay west shore
1741–1761	San Joseph de Escambe[a]	Apalachee	Escambia River
1749–1761	San Antonio de Punta Rasa I[a]	Yamasee	Escambia Bay east shore on Garcon Point peninsula
1761–1763	San Antonio de Punta Rasa II[a]	Apalachee and Yamasee	Adjacent to Presidio San Miguel

Sources: Childers (2001); Worth (2018).

[a] Archaeologically documented.

and San Marcos. The brutal proxy raids throughout Spanish Florida were an outcome of a series of ongoing wars fought between the British and Spanish throughout the eighteenth century: the War of the Quadruple Alliance (1718–1720), the Blockade of Porto Bello (1726), the Anglo-Spanish War (1727–1729), the War of Jenkins' Ear (1738–1748), and the French and Indian War (1756–1763). The English under General James Oglethorpe invaded northeast Florida in 1740, capturing two forts on the St. Johns River, attacking and burning San Agustín, and destroying several Yamasee mission settlements nearby. The British siege of San Agustín brought the first refugee Yamasees to Pensacola. As Worth (2018b: 321) states, the siege of San Agustín was a watershed event for all the refugee mission villages there as it reduced the number of refugee villages from eight to four and caused the flight and relocation of many Yamasee to West Florida. In fact, Pensacola and San Marcos became gathering points for refugee Yamasee fleeing British and Creek attacks.

The exact date of the first group of Yamasee refugees from San Agustín to settle on Pensacola Bay is unknown, but in 1741, the Franciscans at Presidio Santa Rosa requested two complete sets of supplies for a "new town of the Chiscas" plus an additional 30 one-time rations for the 30 residents of a new town (Worth 2018b: 322). While the Yamasee are not specifically mentioned, Worth (2018b) suggests that the likely explanation for equipping two churches is that one set of supplies was for a new church in the new Yamasee town while the other was for the newly rebuilt post-hurricane church at Presidio Santa Rosa. The exact location of the first Yamasee settlement is not clear, but in 1750, the presidio commander recorded the Yamasee as living only two leagues from the San Miguel outpost on the west side of Escambia Bay (Worth 2018b: 322). Michelle Pigott (2015: 30) places the settlement in the vicinity of the Gaboronne freshwater wetland on Escambia Bay (see figures 1.3 and 1.4). During the 1740s, more displaced refugee Yamasees joined the East Florida immigrants in Pensacola. In 1747, Yamasee from Lower Creek towns along the lower Chattahoochee joined the Pensacola group, and the settlement became a new aggregation point for refugee Yamasees. Worth (2018b: 322) states that at this point, the Yamasee population became larger than the Apalachee population at Escambe.

The Apalachee mission village of Soledad moved 10 miles up the Escambia River in 1741 and changed the name of their community to San Joseph de Escambe. This is the same year the Spanish established the new fortified warehouse outpost of San Miguel de Punta Blanca on the mainland after the November 1740 hurricane badly damaged the island presidio of Santa Rosa. These three coinciding actions of the Spanish establishing a new outpost on the mainland, the Yamasee establishing a settlement nearby, and the Apalachee moving to a new location 10 miles upriver were no coincidence. The Spanish outpost apparently was too close to the independent Apalachee at Soledad, about 15 miles away by water. By moving 10 miles farther upriver, the Apalachee increased the distance from the San Miguel outpost to about 25 miles by water (Worth 2012: 3–4).

Prior to the Apalachees' move to Escambe in 1741, Upper Creek Tawasa Indians migrated south, primarily to Mobile, but one town called Los Tobases was located on the upper Escambia River about 22 miles from the river's mouth and 10 miles from the Soledad mission (see figures 1.3 and 1.4). This Lower Creek town was occupied at least as late as 1738 but was abandoned soon after Escambe was established. Worth and colleagues (2015: 44) suggest that the new location of the Apalachee Escambe mission only 10 miles downriver was too close for the Tawasas at Los Tobases and caused them to abandon their town site.

In 1749, the Yamasee moved their settlement across Escambia Bay to the southwest shore of the Garcon Point peninsula, where they renamed the settlement San Antonio de Punta Rasa I (see figures 1.3 and 1.4). Worth (2018b: 323) relates that facilitating illicit trade with the Creeks was a major factor in the relocation of both the Apalachee and Yamasee missions in the Pensacola area. The mission villages were positioned precisely on the two trading paths between the Lower Creek Indians and the garrisoned warehouse of San Miguel de Punta Blanca. The missions also served as outguards and information gateways between the Lower Creek Indians (Uchises) and the English provinces. As Worth (2018b: 324) describes, Indians travelling from the east had to pass through Punta Rasa I, and those coming from the north had to pass through Escambe. Punta Rasa I accessed the Lower Creek towns south of Columbus, Georgia, while Escambe was on the main path of the Upper Creek towns near Montgomery, Alabama. These two strategic locations provided the Pensacola missions with access to the widespread British trade system with the Creeks. Officially, the Spanish considered trade between their mission villages and the British-allied Creeks illegal, but they could not enforce it and often benefited from intelligence on British movement and trade in goods and horses. By 1750, these two mission villages had a resident military garrison and were the only Native American communities west of San Marcos in Spanish West Florida (Worth 2018b: 323).

Investigations at Refugee Indian Mission Villages

The sites of both mission villages of San Joseph de Escambe (1741–1761) and San Antonio de Punta Rasa I (1749–1761) have been found and investigated by Worth and his students from UWF. Mission Escambe is the more extensively studied site, as Worth spent six seasons (2009–2015) of archaeological investigations there (Worth et al. 2011; Worth et al. 2012; Worth et al. 2015). Punta Rasa I was investigated for two seasons (2015–2016) by then graduate student Patrick Johnson (2012, 2013, 2018) under Worth's direction.

Mission San Joseph de Escambe

Worth and colleagues (2015: 39) describe the population of Mission San Joseph de Escambe as composed of Christian Apalachees who voluntarily chose to live on the periphery of Spanish colonial territory to exploit trade opportunities with the interior. While the mission village residents regularly went to the Santa Rosa presidio for rations, trade, and to work for wages, their home was Mission Escambe. At this point in their history, the Apalachee had a "creolized identity" (Worth et al. 2012: 4). The Apalachee at Escambe saw themselves more as part of the Spanish colonial "Republic of Indians" rather than as part of the Native Americans living outside European land claims (Bushnell 1994, 1996; Worth 1998). The long association of Apalachee and Spanish colonial cultures is exemplified in the request for a resident friar at Escambe and, after 1750, the inclusion of 4 to 15 resident soldiers. The total population of Escambe ranged from 30 to 50 people plus a Spanish friar and soldiers. From the historical records, Worth and colleagues (2012: 5–6) conclude that the village likely contained fewer than 10 residences, a single church and convento, a cavalry barracks, a warehouse, and a stable. In 1760, a stockade was begun to enclose the core of the settlement (Worth et al. 2012: 5).

While the remains of Mission Escambe were found in an area about 540 by 240 feet in size, the core mission site area measures about 180 by 120 feet (Worth et al. 2015: 175). One of the most outstanding aspects of the site is its preservation, as the core of the settlement was never plowed. In the unplowed portion of the site, 57 feet of the 1760 stockade wall were archaeologically documented (Worth et al. 2015: 102). The palisade wall's construction technique is particularly unique. The north wall has a narrow trench averaging 18 inches wide and one foot deep with two parallel rows of in situ wrought nails at the base. Worth and colleagues (2015: 102) conclude that the palisade wall was built in a series of prefabricated sections with the bases of several side-by-side posts nailed to a flat board. The prefabricated wall section was then set into the trench and packed with dense soil and clay and surrounded by a shallow moat. When the settlement was burned to the ground in 1761, the portion of the stockade below the surface remained. While the posts deteriorated over time, the nails remained in place, spaced at regular intervals of eight and a quarter inches (the eighteenth-century Spanish standard). The east wall trench was wider (ranging from 16 to 30 inches) than the north wall, which leads Worth and colleagues (2015: 102) to posit that it was stronger and taller than the north wall.

Most of the artifacts recovered in the palisade wall trenches were wrought nails, but Indian ceramics, glass, majolica, and burned wood were also included. There are several postholes in this area of the site, some quite large and some showing evidence of replacement. Another important feature is a large, burned clay floor with numerous Indian ceramics and other materials.

An important factor in understanding the artifact assemblage at this mission village is the knowledge that in 1866 a large steam-powered lumber mill named Molino Mills was built adjacent to the core area of the mission site. Molino Mills operated from 1866 to 1885 (Grinnan 2013), and mill-related activities and heavy machinery compressed the soil and fractured mission-period artifacts, especially ceramics. Because of the post-mission fracturing of artifacts from compression, only the weights of artifacts are used in the analysis of the assemblage.

While the archaeological analysis of the investigations of Mission Escambe is incomplete at the time of this writing, it is possible to carve out at least a ceramic assemblage from the Mission Escambe occupation since there was over a century between the two historic occupations (the first ending in 1761 and the second beginning in 1866) and the Euro-American ceramics of both periods are quite distinct. Based on the known differences in ceramics, a mission-period ceramic assemblage was compiled. However, it was not possible to separate other artifacts.

The key characteristic of the Mission Escambe ceramic assemblage is that it is almost all Native American (98.6%). Although Apalachees were working and living at both the Santa Rosa and San Miguel presidios and had easy access to Euro-American ceramics, they apparently did not need or want them as they were fully capable of meeting their own needs for ceramic containers. The large Indian ceramic assemblage (20.8 kg) is detailed in appendix IV, table IV.1. There are 23 different types of temper, but most ceramics (84.5%) are tempered with either sand (37.1%), shell (24.0%), or grog (23.4%). These three tempering agents are reminiscent of both traditional Apalachee ceramics made in their homeland of North Florida and traits acquired during their diaspora. The original group of Apalachees that established the Soledad mission at the mouth of the Escambia River in 1718 was composed of families who had been living in three different areas since 1704—Santa María, Mobile Bay, and the interior—and their tempering agents reflect the areas in which they were refugees. Traditional Apalachee grog tempering predominates at Santa María; sand tempering reflects the Apalachee families that lived with the Creeks for 14 years; and shell tempering reflects those that stayed on Mobile Bay. Worth (2012, 2017) and Johnson (2012, 2018) have documented the relationship between tempering technique and ethnic identity as well as the flexibility of Apalachee potters to incorporate the ceramic surface treatments of other groups as they migrated through the Southeast.

There is a wide variety of surface treatments in the Native American pottery (see appendix IV, table IV.2). The ceramic types reflect the application of new temper mixes and a new typology devised by Worth and Jennifer Melcher (2015). They have defined three new ceramic series, two of which are specific to the eighteenth century in West Florida: Langdon (shell tempered) and Escambia (grog shell tempered). They defined several varieties in these series and added new varieties to the existing historic ceramic series of Lamar, Jefferson, and Ocmulgee Fields (Worth and Melcher 2015: 14–21).

Of the 16.9 kg of typable ceramics, the three most abundant types are Sand Tempered Plain (21.0%), Grog Tempered Plain (13.6%), and Chattahoochee Roughened, *variety* Chattahoochee (9.7%). The remaining 55.7 percent of the ceramics are classified into 149 different ceramic types (see appendix IV, table IV.2). Half the ceramics have plain surfaces (49.3%), but roughening, burnishing, slipping (brown and red), stamping, and incising are also popular. Diversity is a clear characteristic of this assemblage.

The Euro-American ceramic assemblage from Mission Escambe is quite small (289.9 g) and is presented in appendix IV, tables IV.1 and IV.3. Of the 241.0 g of typable ceramics, the most abundant classes are Other Coarse Earthenware (40.3%), Majolica (31.0%), and Stoneware (21.8%). There is a small amount of Redware and only traces of Faience and Delft. The most abundant ceramic types are El Morro (30.1%), Gray Salt Glazed Stoneware (21.9%), Olive Jar (9.2%), and Plain Majolica (8.6%). Most of the Other Coarse Earthenware are either El Morro (70.2%) or Glazed Olive Jar (25.9%). Majolica types are more diverse with 40.6 percent Plain, 36.3 percent Puebla Blue on White, and 11.9 percent Abo Polychrome. Stoneware is 97.7 percent Grey Salt Glazed, and most of the Redware is unglazed (68.2%).

The historical and archaeological investigation conducted by Worth and his students and colleagues has provided the first glimpse into an Apalachee refugee mission village in West Florida. With only a trace of Euro-American material, the ceramic assemblage from Mission Escambe is an excellent sample of eighteenth-century refugee mission Apalachees. The tempering agents used in the pottery reflect their traditions and their story as displaced but adaptive immigrants in the early eighteenth century. The ceramics also reveal the attempts of this group of Apalachee families to hold on to some of the material traditions from their past despite being displaced from their homeland for two generations.

Mission San Antonio de Punta Rasa I

There is little information about the first Yamasee settlement in the Pensacola area, occupied between 1741 and 1748. The documents mention the settlement was five miles from the outpost of San Miguel de Punta Blanca, which Pigott (2015: Figure 4) places on the west shore of Escambia Bay in the vicinity of the Gaberonne wetland (see figure 1.4).

Under the direction of Worth and Johnson, the site of the Yamasee mission village of Punta Rasa I was located and investigated (Johnson 2012). Johnson (2018) later continued his focus on the Punta Rasa I mission village for his dissertation research, concentrating on questions of interaction and cultural identity among the Yamasee living at Punta Rasa I as well as the evolution of Yamasee culture through time. Using historical documents and maps, Worth and Johnson targeted the southwestern tip of Garcon Point on the eastern shore of Escambia Bay as the probable area of the Punta Rasa I mission (figure 1.4; Johnson 2018: 178–184). While fieldwork yielded an artifact assemblage confirming the site of Punta Rasa I, no intact features were documented because deep plowing had mixed the colonial midden with earlier prehistoric Archaic and later historic components. However, as the Punta Rasa I mission village was the only colonial-period occupation of the site, Johnson (2018) confidently associates all the Indian-made ceramics as those made by the Yamasee living at the Punta Rasa I mission village.

The assemblage of Native American ceramics consists of 773 sherds weighing 1.6 kg (see appendix IV, table IV.4; Johnson 2012, 2018). There are 11 temper types, but 78.4 percent of the sherds are tempered with sand (34.9%), grit (22.2%), and shell (21.3%). Grog (8.8%) and grog shell (6.3%) tempers were also used. Of the 773 typable sherds, the most abundant ceramic types by weight are Sand Tempered Plain (22.3%), Grit Tempered Plain (14.4%), San Marcos Stamped (9.5%), and Grog Tempered Plain (7.3%). San Marcos Stamped is grit tempered and thus far has been recovered in the Pensacola Bay area only from Mission Escambe, Mission Punta Rasa I, and Presidio Santa Rosa. Over half of the surfaces of the Native American ceramics are plain (58.0%) and only 3.0 percent are burnished. Plain is the most dominant surface treatment in all temper groups with the exception of the shell-tempered group, where one heavy sherd of Fatherland Incised, *variety* Bayou Goula skews the weight. There is a wide diversity in the ceramics, which is reflective of the migration experiences and places-made-home by the Yamasee in the seventeenth and eighteenth centuries. Johnson (2018: 184–204) presents a detailed analysis of the Native American assemblage from Punta Rasa I, relating the origin of the variety of ceramic types and tempers and comparing the assemblage from Presidio Santa Rosa to that of Mission Escambe.

Recovered from Mission Punta Rasa I were only 57 Euro-American sherds (90.4 g) with manufacturing dates contemporary with the mission occupation (see appendix IV). Majolicas make up just over half (54.3%) of the 46 typable sherds (see appendix IV, table IV.5). Plain Majolica (32.6%) and Plain Faience (10.9%) are the most abundant types by count. Also present are Other Coarse Earthenware (13.0%), Stoneware (13.0%), and one piece of Delft Blue on White.

Mission Punta Rasa I ended with deadly violence. Rising Creek tensions in the area escalated with accusations of trade abuses from the Spanish. Tensions reached a climax in early 1761 when three Alabama Creek men—who had legitimate grievances over how the Spanish mistreated and defrauded them in a trade transaction—attacked and killed three Spanish soldiers, a soldier's pregnant wife, and a five-year-old female child at Punta Rasa I (Worth 2018b: 327). Two months later, a group of Alabama Creeks seeking further revenge returned to the area and attacked Mission Escambe. Following these two attacks on the missions, the Apalachee and Yamasee communities were compelled to retreat toward the safety of the San Miguel presidio. Punta Rasa I was eventually burned, as was Escambe. Worth (2018b: 328) describes the area around San Miguel as a "war zone" during this time as there were at least seven more attacks by the English-led Creeks between April 23 and July 26, 1761, resulting in 11 deaths, many wounded, and one Spanish soldier captured. The casualties were not only Spanish but also Apalachee and Yamasee. In addition to destroying the two Indian mission villages, the Creek raiders destroyed even the most distant of the satellite ranches in Spanish Northwest Florida. The 1760–1761 Indian War stopped all economic activities outside the confines of the stockade of Fort San Miguel.

Investigating the Site of Presidio Santa Rosa

The site of the Santa Rosa presidio was discovered in 1961 by G. Norman Simons, then the assistant curator of the Pensacola Historical Society. Simons collected eighteenth-century Spanish and Native American ceramics from the surface of the site located on Santa Rosa Island about two miles from its western tip on Pensacola Bay (Smith 1965: x). The site has always been in government hands, and at the time of discovery, it was in Fort Pickens State Park. Today it is within the National Park Service Gulf Islands National Seashore. Soon after his discovery of the site, Simons contacted Professor Hale Smith, then the chair of the Department of Anthropology at Florida State University (FSU) and one of the few historical archaeologists in the United States at that time.

Smith visited the site in 1964 and viewed the material Simons had collected, and he identified the site as the third location of the West Florida presidio, Isla de Santa Rosa, Punta de Sigüenza (8ES22). That summer, Smith conducted the first excavations at Presidio Santa Rosa with his students who were taking a summer course in archaeological field methods. He was assisted in the field by many members of the Pensacola Historical Society including William Lazarus, who made a map to scale of the site, trenches, and landmarks, and Leora Sutton, the avocational archaeologist for the Society. Smith's excavations were quite extensive, including 12 trenches that exposed 17 features and the remains of several structures (figure 4.3). A large assemblage of 28,462 artifacts was recovered from the 1964 investigation, and Smith and his students wrote a short report of the results (Smith 1965).

After FSU's 1964 excavations, the site was professionally observed only twice in the following 38 years. In 1973, Louis Tesar, then a field investigator with FSU, conducted a survey of the Gulf Islands National Seashore and relocated the site of the Santa Rosa Presidio. He made a surface collection, a site map, and documented several disturbances to the site that had occurred in the intervening nine years since Smith's investigation. Two major impacts to the site were up to 20 feet of dredge spoil deposited over the northern area of the site and a 15-foot-wide mosquito control drainage ditch excavated through the entire northern site along the southern edge of the dredge spoil pile (Tesar 1973: 107–111). In 1985, Judith Bense and students from UWF revisited the site, confirmed Tesar's observations of the disturbances to the site, and made a small surface collection (Bense 1985a).

In 2002, Bense and UWF returned to the site of the Santa Rosa presidio and conducted three summer seasons of investigations with UWF archaeological field school students and staff along with many members of the Pensacola Archaeological Society. A large field lab was set up on site under a tent, and trained volunteers were under the close supervision of the staff laboratory director, Jan Lloyd. The volunteers rough sorted the cultural material from screening, providing real time information of the materials being recovered and enabling strategic field decisions. In the fall and spring semesters, the trained volunteers continued their assistance with artifact processing, cataloging, and documentation so that at the beginning of each field season we had up to date information on which to base our strategy and decisions. Once again, the general public made critical contributions to the research project. We also shared our findings with the general public through many presentations, civic talks, and the media as we pursued clues about what had happened at the island presidio of Santa Rosa. Historians were also sent to the Spanish and Mexican archives to ferret out information about the presidio contained in primary documents.

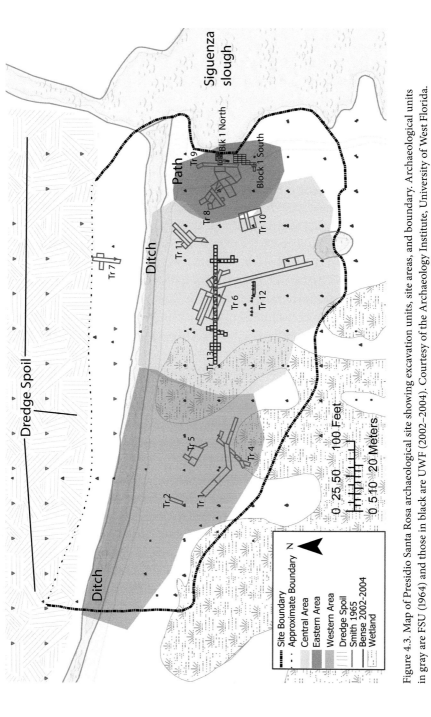

Figure 4.3. Map of Presidio Santa Rosa archaeological site showing excavation units, site areas, and boundary. Archaeological units in gray are FSU (1964) and those in black are UWF (2002–2004). Courtesy of the Archaeology Institute, University of West Florida.

UWF personnel made a concerted effort to locate and borrow as many artifacts and as much documentation from the 1964 FSU excavation as possible to include in our research, but we were only partially successful. Much of the original documentation (photographs, field drawings, and notes) is curated at the Southeastern Archaeological Center (SEAC) of the National Park Service in Tallahassee, and these resources were included in the UWF research. The artifacts were more difficult to locate as the collection had been split between several facilities and institutions. Only 18.1 percent of the artifacts were located and included in the UWF research. Unfortunately, 81.9 percent of the artifacts from FSU's 1964 excavations are missing.

The UWF leadership team prepared reports of each field season as well as a final report (Bense 2002; Harris 2003b, 2004a, b; Harris and Eschbach 2006). Five UWF graduate students included information from Santa Rosa in their master's theses on the following topics: socioeconomics (Eschbach 2007), religion and ideology (Furlong 2008), demographics (Holmes 2012), economics (Roberts 2009), and architecture (Greene 2009). Eschbach (2019) included a great deal of information about the Santa Rosa presidio in her doctoral dissertation. Reports of the historical research conducted for the UWF investigation at Santa Rosa include R. Wayne Childers (2003a, b, c) and Clune and colleagues (2006).

The Archaeological Site

There has not been any significant occupation of the site area since the Santa Rosa presidio community left between 1754 and 1756. However, there have been two detrimental impacts to the site: shoreline erosion and ditching. Shoreline erosion was stopped in 1959 with the deposition of dredge spoil over the shoreline and northern portion of the remaining site (figure 4.3). United States Geological Survey (USGS) maps show that the shoreline eroded about 270 feet between 1940 and March 1959, as shown in figure 4.4. Both FSU and UWF investigations documented midden and features buried under the pile of sand. Based on these findings and the tree vegetation on the southern part of the dredge sand, I estimate that the dredge spoil covers at least 2.2 acres of the archaeological remains of the Santa Rosa presidio. The open site area south of the dredge sand and ditch with intact features and midden encompasses an area of about 2.1 acres. Comparing the historic shorelines of 1940 and 1959 before the dredge sand was deposited, the open site area appears to be in the rear of the eastern portion of the settlement, specifically at the end of the north-south street shown in the 1743 Serres drawing of the presidio (figure 4.1).

The site area today consists of deep, dry, loose, white/light gray, coarse sand. As figure 4.5 shows, the terrain is flat and low (five feet or less above mean sea

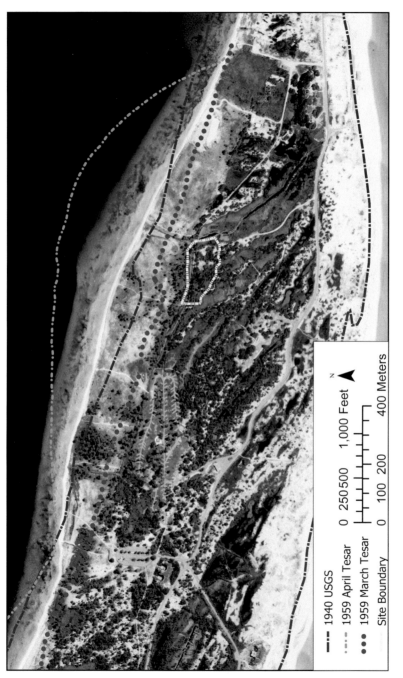

Figure 4.4. Presidio Santa Rosa, historic shorelines of Pensacola Bay overlaid on aerial photograph of site area. (Photograph by USDA 2018; adapted by the Archaeology Institute, University of West Florida).

Legend:
- 1940 USGS
- 1959 April Tesar
- 1959 March Tesar
- Site Boundary

N

0 250 500   1,000 Feet

0   100 200   400 Meters

level) with sparse ground cover and clusters of trees, shrubs, and palmettos. This deep sandy environment greatly affected artifact deposition during the presidio occupation in two ways. First, at least eight strong storms and hurricanes struck the community, flooding, damaging, and destroying structures and scattering their contents (see table 4.2). The materials torn from homes, churches, barracks, and warehouses were quickly buried in the sand, resulting in a far greater number and different array of items than those usually lost or discarded at the other two presidio locations on Pensacola Bay. Secondly, the dry, soft, deep sand throughout the settlement is easily churned by foot traffic to a depth of a foot or more. With at least a minimum of 80 and a maximum of 400 people in the settlement for 29 years, the churned, loose sand became an artifact trap into which any dropped or mislaid items quickly disappeared. Because of the many destructive storms and easily churned, soft sand, the artifact assemblage left behind from Santa Rosa is quite large and unusual. Both the FSU and UWF archaeological investigations encountered a maze of architectural features—especially building foundations, wall sills, wall trenches, and posts in the central and eastern areas of the site—and over 67,000 artifacts.

Figure 4.5. Presidio Santa Rosa archaeological site area in 2002. Courtesy of the Archaeology Institute, University of West Florida.

The Archaeological Assemblage

The artifact assemblage analyzed here is a combination of what UWF recovered and part of what FSU recovered. We were able to locate and borrow only 18.1 percent (5,136 artifacts) of the FSU assemblage, but the provenience was determinable for only 40 percent of the FSU artifacts. The remaining FSU artifacts were included in the general assemblage without specific provenience. The combined artifact assemblage from Presidio Santa Rosa consists of 43,898 counted items and 369.6 kg of weighed material. However, when the 23,326 missing artifacts from the 1964 investigations are included, an incredible total of 67,225 counted artifacts have been collected from the site, which is 1.3 times that collected from the three other presidio sites *combined*.

When the combined artifact assemblage is organized by material class, Ceramics make up 68.2 percent of the counted and 36.7 percent of the weighed materials (table 4.5). In the ceramic assemblage of 29,896 sherds, 66.1 percent are Euro-American and 33.9 percent are Native American. Metal and Glass are the next most frequent classes by count, but Building Material far outweighs them. Faunal remains are the third-heaviest class (44.2 kg) and make up 12.0 percent of the assemblage. There are very little plant remains, worked bone, and wood.

As table 4.6 shows, most of the Euro-American ceramic classes are either Other Coarse Earthenware (48.4% by count) or Majolica (43.4%). The remainder consists of small amounts of Delft (3.1%) and Faience (2.4%) along with traces of Redware, Porcelain, Stoneware, Earthenware, and Greyware. Quantification of the ceramic types in the wares and classes is presented in appendix V, tables V.1 and V.2. There are 63 ceramic types in the 15,977 typable sherds, but two-thirds (66.5%) are either El Morro (44.9%) or Puebla Blue on White Majolica (21.6%), as shown in appendix V, table V.2. The remaining third of the Euro-American ceramics is distributed between 61 ceramic types, led by Abo Polychrome Majolica (4.4%), Lead Glazed Coarse Earthenware (3.1%), and San Luis Polychrome (2.9%). Within the ceramic class of Other Coarse Earthenware, 80.7 percent of the 8,950 sherds are El Morro, and the remaining 19 types are 5.6 percent or less (see appendix V, table V.1). Lead Glazed, Olive Jar, Guadalajara Polychrome, and Mexican Red Painted are the most abundant types. There are 17 types of Majolica in the 5,484 sherds, but 84.6 percent are either Puebla Blue on White (63.4%), Abo Polychrome (12.8%), or San Luis Polychrome (8.4%). Almost all (92.3%) of the 610 Delft sherds are either Blue on White (56.9%) or Plain (36.2%). Almost half of the 465 typable Faience sherds are Plain (49.2%), and the remaining half is more diverse, led by Provence Blue on White (17.2%) and Blue on White (11.6%). Redware is almost

Table 4.5. Total Presidio Santa Rosa artifact assemblage

Artifact Classes[a]	Count	%	Weight (g)	%
Building Material	1,248	2.8%	105,434.5	28.5%
Ceramics Euro-American	19,777	45.1%	89,654.7	24.3%
Metal	6,530	14.9%	50,296.7	13.6%
Ceramics Native American	10,119	23.1%	45,994.7	12.4%
Fauna	60	0.1%	44,206.1	12.0%
Lithics	1,273	2.9%	22,630.7	6.1%
Glass	4,854	11.1%	10,940.5	3.0%
Flora	8	c	336.3	0.1%
Fauna Modified	14	c	68.9	c
Flora Modified	15	c	1.1	c
Totals	43,898		369,564.2	
Artifact Groups[b]	Count	%	Weight (g)	%
Kitchen	33,588	76.6%	177,396.4	50.1%
Architecture	5,661	12.9%	156,838.4	44.3%
Activities	797	1.8%	14,414.6	4.1%
Arms	2,034	4.6%	2,989.7	0.8%
Personal	441	1.0%	864.6	0.2%
Tobacco	607	1.4%	835.1	0.2%
Clothing	666	1.5%	420.1	0.1%
Furniture	73	0.2%	54.6	c
Totals	43,867		353,813.5	

[a] No Other
[b] No Unspecified
[c] Less than 0.1 percent.

all Glazed (87.5%), and most of the Porcelains are either Hand Painted Over Glaze (55.2%) or Chinese (37.3%). There are seven types of Stoneware, and 36.1 percent are Salt Glazed and 27.8 percent are Rhenish. All the Earthenware is Mexican Indian (made in Mexico by Indians), and one is stamped around the shoulder with a Spanish seal (see appendix V, table V.1).

The Native American ceramic assemblage is large, consisting of 10,119 counted sherds weighing 46.0 kg. There are 16 temper types (table 4.6), but most sherds (84.4% by weight) have one of three additives: grog (30.3%), shell (28.1%), or sand (26.0%). The other 13 tempers each make up 5.7 percent or less. There are eight combination tempers, the most frequent being grog shell and grit grog. While there is a wide diversity of Native pottery types (see appendix

Table 4.6. Euro-American ceramic wares and classes and Native American ceramic tempers from Presidio Santa Rosa

Euro-American Ceramic Wares and Classes	Count	%	Weight (g)	%
Other Coarse Earthenware	9,570	48.4%	62,510.4	69.7%
Majolica	8,580	43.4%	20,498.3	22.9%
Delft	612	3.1%	1,721.8	1.9%
Faience	467	2.4%	1,920.3	2.1%
Redware	265	1.3%	1,560.6	1.7%
Porcelain	205	1.0%	592.4	0.7%
Stoneware	45	0.2%	533.2	0.6%
Earthenware	31	0.2%	293.6	0.3%
Greyware	2	a	2.8	a
Totals	19,777		89,633.4	
Native American Ceramic Tempers	**Count**	**%**	**Weight (g)**	**%**
Grog	2,360	23.3%	13,947.4	30.3%
Shell	2,169	21.4%	12,911.5	28.1%
Sand	4,311	42.6%	11,950.9	26.0%
Grit	648	6.4%	2,612.5	5.7%
Grog Shell	355	3.5%	2,038.6	4.4%
Grit Grog	122	1.2%	1,004.9	2.2%
Unspecified	68	0.7%	975.1	2.1%
Sponge spicules	9	0.1%	115.0	0.3%
Grog Mica	17	0.2%	97.8	0.2%
Mica Shell	19	0.2%	89.7	0.2%
Grit Shell	21	0.2%	84.7	0.2%
Limestone	7	0.1%	61.4	0.1%
Grit Mica	8	0.1%	58.4	0.1%
Grit Grog Shell	2	a	23.0	0.1%
Charcoal Grog	2	a	12.0	a
Mica	1	a	11.8	a
Totals	10,119		45,994.8	

[a] Less than 0.1 percent.

V, table V.3), Grog Tempered Plain (21.9%) and Sand Tempered Indeterminate Plain (20.6%) are the most abundant types. The remaining 57.5 percent divide into 107 types, each making up 4.6 percent or less of the assemblage. The surfaces of almost two-thirds (62.1%) of the Native American sherds in a wide variety of tempers are plain. Almost all surface decorations are present on several temper types and include roughening (12.0%), a variety of stamping (6.8%), and slipping (3.2%). Smaller proportions of the surfaces are painted (red and black), impressed (net and cord), incised, and punctated. Smith (1965) also reported 50 pieces of the Aztec IV ceramic type, but they have not been located.

The diversity in Indian-made ceramics is certainly related to the documented presence of several different Native groups at the Santa Rosa presidio (Harris 2007; Harris and Eschbach 2006: 216–218). In addition, the presidio was a regional trading center that drew Indians from throughout the region. There were also resident Natives at Santa Rosa, such as the wives and children of soldiers and workers who received rations. In addition, Norma Harris (2007) and Worth (2017) detail how the eighteenth-century Native peoples were on the move in flexible and fluid groups that split and reformed as they migrated through the Southeast, developing political alliances with different European nations and Indian ethnicities in order to survive as independently as possible. Spanish officials recorded the names of some of the Indian groups who participated in the Santa Rosa community, including the Apalachees, Yamasees, and Tocobagos (Harris and Eschbach 2006: 216–217). Harris and Eschbach (2006) also note that many of the Native American ceramic types, such as the Jefferson and Lamar series, originated in the Apalachee region and that some of the decorations, such as Chattahoochee and Walnut Roughened, were common to Lower Creek groups.

Worth's (2017) detailed analysis of the migrations and combinations of Native peoples in the historic period and consequent changes in pottery manufacture and decoration cautions the direct association of ceramic traits with ethnicity. It is also important to remember that Native American ceramic containers were needed and purchased by the large Hispanic community at Santa Rosa. In addition to the 10,119 pieces of Native American containers, 68 pieces of Colonoware were recovered from Santa Rosa from bowls, platos, small bowls, jars, cups, and a candlestick.

Another factor that contributed to the Native American ceramic assemblage is that at least some of the food traded and sold to the Hispanic community at the presidio, such as corn, beans, and meat, must have been transported in Native American pottery containers. However, more research is needed to accurately interpret the Native American ceramics at this poorly supplied coastal Spanish presidio with direct and indirect trading connections with many other Indian groups. Factors that must be understood and reconciled include historical documents, Indian ceramic manufacturing practices, supply needs of the 80–400 person community, trading relations between coastal and interior Indian groups, and the fluidity of historical identity and practices of nearby Native peoples.

Second only to ceramics by both count and weight, Metal is the most diverse class of materials in the Santa Rosa assemblage, consisting of 6,530 counted items and 50.3 kg of weighed material (see table 4.5). Nails and spikes make up 76.1 percent of the weighed and two-thirds of the counted items. Their abundance reflects the plethora of wooden structures built, destroyed, repaired, and rebuilt at this island presidio. There are 99 different metal artifact types in this large artifact class. Some of the unusual items are tools, hand weapons, firearms, gun parts, keys, pieces of jewelry, clothing, compasses, religious pendants, and coins. There is also a small copper bowl about two by four inches in size (figure 4.6). These items are detailed further in the next section.

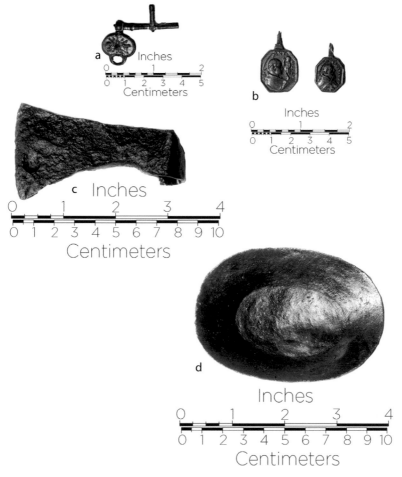

Figure 4.6. Artifacts from Presidio Santa Rosa: *a,* brass music box key (64B-0001–032); *b,* brass religious medallions [*left:* St. Anthony of Padua (64B-0001–048); *right:* St. John of Matha/St. Felix de Valois (64B-0001–27)]; *c,* iron trade axe (64B-0001–084); *d,* copper bowl (64B-0001–001). Courtesy of the Archaeology Institute, University of West Florida.

Glass fragments are also abundant in the Santa Rosa assemblage, making up 11.1 percent of the counted artifacts (see table 4.5). Most of the glass pieces (81.8% by weight) are from bottles, 38.2 percent of which are from wine bottles and 30.6 percent are from case bottles. Pieces of drinking glasses (tumblers, stemmed and footed) are next most frequent. There are several glass jewelry items, such as 78 beads, two pendants, a finger ring setting, and two pieces of a mirror. Glass tableware includes part of a pitcher and a dish. There is also part of a glass jar and a bottle stopper. The architectural glass consists of few pieces of stained glass and window glass.

Stone artifacts are also abundant, making up 1,273 of the counted artifacts and 22.6 kg of the weighed material. Three-quarters of the counted items are gunflint flakes, fragments, and spalls. The other quarter of the counted stone artifacts includes a wide variety of items: 13 basalt manos and two mano/ metate whetstones, a paint palette geode, a projectile point/knife of obsidian, a steatite pipe, fragments of a steatite vessel, many pieces of ochre for pigment, and beads of jet and amber. Smith (1965: Table II) also reported one piece of an "Alabaster Plate."

Catherine Parker (2006) examined the faunal remains from Santa Rosa and identified domestic animals, deer, and bony fish. She determined that fish contributed the greatest number of individuals (MNI), and 26 of the individuals identified are primarily estuarine species found in the Pensacola Bay system year round, such as sheepshead, catfish, and several members of the drum family (Parker 2006: 201–202). Mammals identified include cattle, pig, and white-tailed deer. There are also four pieces of chicken and two types of turtles. Domestic animals provided 53.0 percent of the total biomass, followed by deer (30.0%) and bony fish (14.0%). Meat processing was evident in butchering marks, hack marks, sawing, and spiral fracturing. Parker (2006: 210) concludes that the residents of Santa Rosa followed a traditional Spanish/European diet based primarily on the meat of domesticated animals and supplemented with acceptable and available wild species. Traditionally, it was understood that the official rations were not to be the sole source of food for the presidio community and that local fresh foods were to be obtained. There are records from Santa Rosa that reveal trade with the French settlements of Mobile and New Orleans for food and other supplies. For example, in 1734, the Spanish purchased from the French 5,600 pounds of flour, 63.5 tons of shelled maize, 6,400 pounds of rice, 1,600 pounds of frijoles, 4.5 tons of fresh beef, 4.5 tons of dried vegetables, 11 hogs, 50 pounds of candles, 100 tanned deer skins, a cask of aguardiente, a barrel of white wine, and 100 pounds of bear fat (Buscarons 1731–1733). The situado also included money to buy chickens to provide meat and eggs for the sick.

When the artifact assemblage is organized into artifact groups, by both weight and count, almost all artifacts are from Kitchen or Architecture activities (see table 4.5). Most of the 33,588 artifacts in the Kitchen group are ceramics (86.6% by count and 91.5% by weight). While there are only 43 metal kitchen artifacts, over two-thirds (68.0%) are eating utensils, including 19 knives, three forks, five spoons, and two other utensils. A cleaver and parts of pots, pans, and cups are some of the other metal kitchen artifacts. There are 4,428 pieces of kitchen glass, making up 13.2 percent of the Kitchen group by count and 6.1 percent by weight. Almost half (45.9%) of the kitchen glass is from wine or case bottles, and there are also four bottle stoppers. Drinking glass fragments make up 3.9 percent and are parts of tumblers, stemmed glasses, and a footed tumbler. Glass tableware pieces include a dish, a pitcher, and two jars. While there are 17 different colors of glass, 80.2 percent by weight are a shade of green, especially olive green. Smith (1965: Table III) also lists pieces of enameled and etched glass.

Bricks, ladrillos, tiles, nails, and spikes make up most of the Architecture artifacts by weight (84.1%). Tile fragments (93.6 kg) make up most of the weighed artifacts, followed by fragments of bricks (27.3 kg) and ladrillos (18.6 kg). The abundance of fired clay building material is likely due to the brick kiln established in 1740 on the mainland near the outpost of San Miguel (Worth 2013: 2).

It is surprising how much metal has survived over two and a half centuries in the salty, coarse, sandy environment of this barrier island site. Almost 8,000 nails and spikes were recovered; UWF found 4,330 and Smith (1965: Table III) reported 3,604 more. The 1743 Serres sketch of the settlement (figure 4.1) depicts structures with sides and roofs covered with boards fastened to a timber framework. This building method requires hundreds of nails per structure, and it is expected that nails would be abundant in the archaeological remains. Other metal architectural materials include 26 hinges, two latches, and pintles. There is also some window glass, stained glass, and plaster pieces, some of which were painted. The relatively low numbers of bricks, tiles, and ladrillos likely indicate that these materials were usually used for specific structural features such as hearths, chimneys, and floors. The available historical information of the structures at Santa Rosa (see table 4.1) corroborates this interpretation. Smith (1965: 29) found the intact base of a possible hearth with three bricks in situ in his Trench 6. Only three buildings at Santa Rosa are known to have been made of brick and stone: the second hospital, the King's House, and the second powder magazine (Anonymous 1752c; Urueña 1741).

The 797 artifacts in the Activities group make up only 1.8 percent of the counted assemblage, but they reflect a wide range of tasks and recreation.

Almost two-thirds (61.0%) are made of metal and almost all the rest are stone (36.2%). Stone was used primarily for abrading activities represented by artifacts such as manos, manos/metates, abraders, and whetstones; there is also ocher for pigment and six stone weights. Metal items include pieces of containers (33.1%) and reflect tasks such as illumination (12 ceramic and two brass candlesticks), sewing (six scissors of brass and iron), navigation (two brass compasses), fire starting (three strike-a-lights), wood working (axe), and fishing (weights). Other interesting items include three mouth harps and an eyeglass frame. There are also pieces of horse tack, paint palette geode, lead sprue, pewter handles, rings, chain, three brass bells, and nine lead bale seals.

The Personal artifact group of only 441 items is quite revealing though small. Half of the artifacts are pieces of Guadalajara Polychrome, a ceramic made of special clay and usually fashioned into bowls, but there are also pieces of platos, cups, lebrillos (flat base bowls), tazas, a vacinilla (large handled cup), and three figurines made from this clay. Almost a quarter of the personal items are beads (101): 78 are glass, 15 are jet, one is amber, and seven are metal (five gold, one brass, and one iron). The most frequent colors of the glass beads are dark green, light green, blue, and clear. For greater detail about the personal items, see Mary Furlong (2008) and April Holmes (2012).

A total of 16 coins were recovered from Presidio Santa Rosa; UWF recovered six and FSU recovered ten, only two of which could be located for this study. James Gazaway has examined the six UWF cobs that are described in detail in appendix VIII. Five of the cobs were minted in Mexico City and one was minted in Potosí. Five cobs had dates of 1718, 1731 (2), 1732, and 1715–1727. The two coins located from the FSU assemblage are French copper 9-deniers with dates of 1721 and 1722. Smith's (1965: 59–60) report lists the 10 coins he recovered: four French coppers (one sou each; 1721–1722), one French copper Louis XV liard, five silver cobs (one 1737 and four prior to 1731), and four copper maravedis (1532–1557). The French coins clearly reflect trade with the French. The four copper maravedies coins are very early and were produced at the Santo Domingo mint between 1542 and 1555.

Additional personal artifacts include three iron keys recovered by UWF, 10 keys collected by FSU (Smith 1965: 131), and a rare brass music box key (see figure 4.6). There are 26 pieces of jewelry, most of which are parts of necklace chain, but a glass setting and nine pendants made of gold, silver, brass, and glass are also included. Smith also recovered a brass finger ring with settings and two metal pendants with three and four faceted settings. Other personal items include two saint medals (see figure 4.6), part of a mirror, a wooden toothbrush, and a writing nib.

A wide variety of Arms artifacts were recovered in both investigations. Of the 2,034 items, almost all (98.4%) were shot and pieces of gunflints. However, there are 32 pieces of firearms and hand weapons. Hand weapons include two bayonets, three scabbard tips (brass, iron, and steel), an iron sword blade, and a brass sword hand guard. Gun parts include two triggers (brass and iron), two trigger guards (iron and lead), an iron gun cock, two escutcheon plates (brass and iron), iron flintlock, iron frizzen, four ferrules (two brass and two iron), and a brass barrel band. In the missing FSU artifacts, Smith reported a brass dagger handle (1965: Plate 31), three flintlock strikers, two gun rests, and two butt plates.

The Tobacco group has 607 tobacco pipe fragments, including 517 made of kaolin, 87 of coarse earthenware, and three of stone (steatite and gneiss). Fifty-three percent of the kaolin pipe fragments are pipe bowls. Some of the coarse earthenware pipes have a fine, orange clay body.

The Clothing group has 119 buckles made of brass and iron for belts, clothing, shoes, and unspecified attire. Smith (1965: 130–132) reported 29 more buckles in the missing FSU collection. Almost all buttons (62) are made of metal (lead, pewter, iron, and brass), but one is wooden. Smith (1965: 130–132) accounted for an additional 30 buttons, including a cloth and a collar button. There is a surprising number of cuff links (22) and all but one are made of brass. Decorative elements of clothing are almost all glass seed beads (955), but there are three aglets (two brass and one silver).

The Furniture group includes six escutcheon plates (brass, copper, and iron), one hook and eye, and 66 furniture tacks (most are made of iron, but 10 are made of brass and one is copper). Smith (1965: 130–132) reported three chest handles, two chest corner braces, and a chest knob, though these are among the missing artifacts.

There are a combined 951 high status artifact markers from the UWF and FSU artifact assemblages (table 4.7). While Smith's (1965: 130–132) artifact table does not include many of the high-status artifact types recognized today, such as window glass or glass finishes, 290 items could be gleaned from his report. One such item is what Smith called metal "braid" (1965: Plate 12). It was found in two "clumps," and the material is described as thin, metal, silver foil strands that had been wrapped around a center thread. Four strands are weaved together and then braided or plaited. Smith (1965: 71) suggests the braid was probably a decorative element on the recoil pad of a pistol, but it could also be from an officer's uniform.

Small clay figurines are a very unusual and understudied type of artifact from Santa Rosa. UWF recovered 137 ceramic figurine fragments, and Smith recovered 11 (10 ceramic and one ivory). Smith (1972) conducted a study of the ceramic figurines FSU recovered in 1964 in addition to two figurines

Table 4.7. High status artifact markers from Presidio Santa Rosa

Artifacts	UWF[a]	FSU[b]
Porcelain	205	207
Guadalajara Polychrome	226	-
Glass	-	-
Window	27	-
Stained	1	-
Embossed	14	-
Enameled	20	36
Engraved	60	-
Etched	-	18
Dish	1	-
Tumblers	14	-
Tumblers enameled	1	-
Tumblers engraved	5	-
Painted	2	-
Press molded	7	-
Silvered	1	-
Pitcher	1	-
Goblet stem	-	9
Silver Brocade/Braid	7	many[c]
Cuff Links	22	-
Keys	3	10
Coins	6	-
Nib	1	-
Alabaster Plate Fragment	-	1
Candlesticks	8	-
Insignia	1	-
Jewelry	-	-
Glass unidentified jewelry	7	-
Glass pendants	2	-
Glass setting	1	-
Metal unidentified jewelry	4	-
Metal hook	2	-
Metal jewelry part	2	-
Metal finger ring	1	5
Metal necklace chain	2	-
Furniture escutcheon plates	7	4
Totals	661	290

[a] Collected by the University of West Florida.
[b] Collected by Florida State University.
[c] Artifact image of material called "braid" appears to be a "pile" of silver brocade (Smith 1965: Plate 12).

from a Florida shipwreck and a cave in Mexico. Furlong (2008: 56–65) analyzed 68 figurine fragments greater than 10 mm in length or width from Santa Rosa, from both the UWF and FSU excavations. Some of these figurine fragments are shown in figure 4.7. Twenty are human form, six are various animal forms, and the remainder are indeterminate. Two of the figurines are

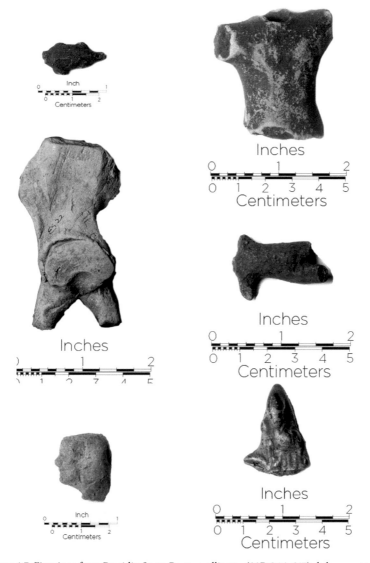

Figure 4.7. Figurines from Presidio Santa Rosa: *a,* alligator (03P-946–017); *b,* human torso (03P-0718–008); *c,* man on a horse (64B-0001–060); *d,* human torso (04P-1416–006); *e,* human head (04P-1024–012); *f,* priest with mitre rim effigy from Guadalajara Polychrome vessel (04P-1489–012). Courtesy of the Archaeology Institute, University of West Florida.

made of Guadalajara clay, one of porcelain, two of red-painted coarse earthenware, and 73 of plain coarse earthenware.

All but one of the ceramic figurines was made by hand molding, and the one exception was made in a hollow mold. The sole ivory figurine (not relocated) is an effigy of a dog sitting on its hind legs with a suspension loop (Smith 1965: Plate 23). Of the 20 human figurines (figure 4.7), one is almost complete and clothing is depicted with incised lines. Interestingly, Smith (1972: 54) notes that religious figures often have costumes of an earlier period. Smith (1965: Plate 23, 1972: 54) recovered the head of a female figurine wearing a "wimple" hat, which is still worn by nuns. Of the figurines for which gender can be determined, only one figurine is female. Figure 4.7 shows a figurine with the upper half of a human effigy wearing a robe and pointed hat and holding a large staff. This figurine was broken off the rim of a Guadalajara Polychrome vessel that Furlong (2008: 59) interprets as a representation of a Catholic clergyman wearing a mitre. There is also a figurine of a horse and rider. Animal figurines include four mammals and one reptile (alligator); three are made of coarse earthenware, one of Guadalajara Polychrome, and one of ivory.

In sum, the artifact assemblage recovered from the site of the Santa Rosa presidio in the FSU and UWF archaeological investigations is very large, containing at least 67,362 items. However, as only 18.1 percent of the artifacts FSU collected could be located, the combined assemblage analyzed here consists of 43,898 counted artifacts and 369.6 kg of weighed material. Most of the counted assemblage is ceramic sherds, of which 66.2 percent are Euro-American and 33.8 percent are Native American. While there is a wide range of ceramic types, a limited number predominate. Almost all artifacts are associated with Kitchen or Architecture activities, but the contents of the smaller and less abundant groups and classes contain many unique and rare items that make this assemblage unusual. The deep, soft sand on which the presidio community was built and the frequent destruction of homes by strong storms resulted in the scattering and trapping of many artifacts that are rarely lost or recovered in archaeological investigations, such as jewelry, coins, small figurines, and rare keys. Almost 1,000 high status items were recovered, and almost all are small in size and low in proportion in the assemblage. However, because of the assemblage's large size, the number of the high status items is quite large.

Spatial Analysis

Central Site Area

At three to four feet above sea level, the northern portion of the site's central area is one of the highest portions of the site today (see figure 4.3). As Harris and Eschbach (2006: 179–184) detail, excavations in the western part of the central area revealed a series of stratified occupation deposits, the first of which was a debris pile from a burned structure that overlaid a large wall trench with irregularly set posts. The pile contained abundant charcoal, nails, bricks, and tile fragments, primarily Kitchen-related artifacts. After the structure burned, a deposit of storm surge sand covered the burned debris pile.

An artifact-rich midden developed on top of the storm surge sand deposit that included 24 pieces of window glass and other architectural materials, barrel band fragments, a basalt abrader, many Kitchen-related materials, glass beads, brass pins, and furniture tacks. Harris and Eschbach (2006: 188) suspect that this midden is from large structures documented about 20 feet to the east. Finally, the area was used for trash disposal after either the construction or demolition of nearby structures (Harris and Eschbach 2006: 192). While most of the artifacts are a mixture of Kitchen and Architecture items, there is an exceptional number of Metal artifacts, including brass and iron hardware rings, pieces of an iron container, horse tack, and copper wire. The *terminus post quem* (TPQ) ceramic date of the upper trash deposit is 1750 based on a piece of Aranama Polychrome Majolica, two pieces of Brittany Blue Faience, 45 pieces of case bottle, and five sherds of Rouen Faience. The refuse layer in this feature contains the few high status items (13) in this complex, including window glass, stemware, a gold bead, porcelain, and Guadalajara Polychrome. The artifact TPQ date suggests that the refuse deposit is associated with the rebuilding of the community after the 1740 hurricane damage. The storm surge deposit was likely from that hurricane. The buried, burned structure below the storm surge layer has a TPQ date corresponding with the initial Santa Rosa community, 1723–1740.

Only 20 feet to the east, the archaeological remains were significantly different. There had once been a large and complex series of buildings in this area, which provides a good example of the clusters of intersecting and parallel wall trenches at this site (figures 4.8 and 4.9). Two close and parallel corner wall sections (Features 40 and 60) are set in narrow trenches with irregularly set posts, some penetrating the base of the wall trenches. The two corner wall segments are almost identical and likely were parts of a structure that was either completely or partly rebuilt. There were few artifacts in these two nested corner wall sections, and the TPQ of both walls is early (1722), indicating they were part of the first settlement.

Adjacent to the west of the corner sections was a 28-foot-long section of a wall trench from a large structure that showed evidence of demolition (Feature 62). Harris and Eschbach (2006: 171) state that the Feature 62 structure is the most well-constructed building documented in the UWF investigations.

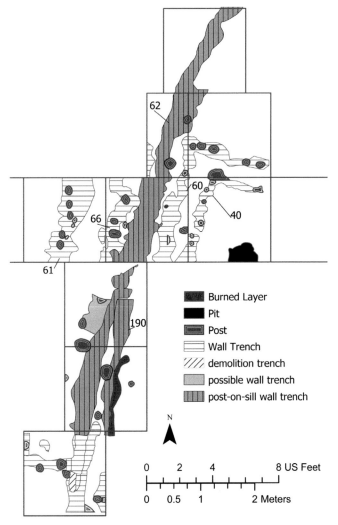

Figure 4.8. Scale drawing of Presidio Santa Rosa architectural remains in west central site area showing wall trenches indicating building and rebuilding of structures. Courtesy of the Archaeology Institute, University of West Florida.

There were also several other wall sections that paralleled and intersected the long Feature 62 wall, probably from its repair or rebuilding. The Feature 62 wall trench was post-on-sill, but the others in this complex, such as Feature 61, were post-in-trench. All structures in this complex are oriented 10 to 15 degrees east of north, probably parallel and perpendicular to the shoreline of the bay at the time, as was the Spanish tradition (Harris and Eschbach 2006: 171). From the TPQ dates and feature intersection sequence, the Feature 62 wall

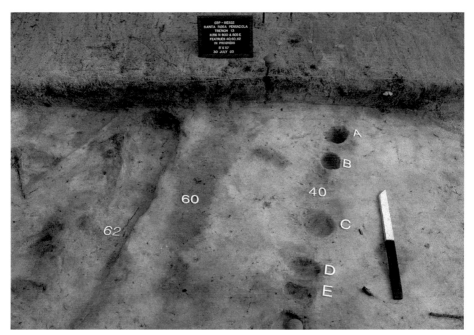

Figure 4.9. Portion of Presidio Santa Rosa structure wall trenches in west central site area. Courtesy of the Archaeology Institute, University of West Florida.

trench is post-1740 and contained window glass. Harris and Eschbach (2006: 171) suspect that the large building Feature 62 represents might have been disassembled and the materials used to build another structure, represented by the wall trench Feature 190 that intersects it. The westernmost wall segment (Feature 61) has a TPQ date of post-1750 and was probably standing when the 1752 hurricane hit the settlement. This short, 5-foot wall segment contained a surprising amount of material suggesting it could have been a high-status residence: window glass, porcelain, and Guadalajara Polychrome.

A midden layer covered all the architectural features described above and had the highest density of artifacts on the site, including many high-status items such as window glass, jewelry, furniture hardware, and bricks (Harris and Eschbach 2006: 175). Other artifacts included many clothing and personal items. These clues have led us to infer that the large structure represented by the Feature 62 wall trench could have been a large home of a high-status individual or perhaps a public building.

The combined assemblage from the two clusters of features and midden in the west central site area is quite large, making up 27.3 percent of the counted artifacts (11,999) and 22.9 percent of the weighed material (84.6 kg) recovered from the Santa Rosa site. Faunal remains are especially high in this area, making up 26.8 percent of the weighed material (see appendix V, table V.5). Most artifacts are from either Kitchen or Architecture activities (95.0%). Seventy percent of the ceramics are Euro-American, which is above the site average of 66.1 percent. By count, Euro-American ceramics are primarily Other Coarse Earthenware (47.4%) or Majolica (37.9%), and Delft, Faience, and Porcelain make up 14.7 percent. There are numerous high-status markers such as 61 pieces of porcelain, 16 pieces of stemmed glassware, a brass sword hand guard, five cuff links, brocade, a furniture escutcheon plate, jewelry, keys, and two pendants. These expensive and rare items indicate that at least for a time, probably after the 1740–1742 rebuild, this was a high-status residential and activity area likely for officers. As this area was hundreds of feet from the bay shoreline at the time, it supports the argument that high-status residents lived away from the dangerous shoreline area to the rear of the site for safety.

In the middle of the central site area, Smith excavated a large unit (Trench 6). UWF documented both the west and east edges of this unit, enabling accurate placement on the site grid (see figure 4.3). Smith found a plethora of architectural features in this unit, including many long wall trenches, four refuse pits, a fire pit, and a hearth. Photographs of this unit depict sections of what Smith (1965: Figures 4, 5, 6) describes as the lower portion of wall trenches or timber sills about a foot wide. One large structure appears to have at least five small interior rooms, but the interior wall features could be from internal sills holding up the floor of a large room. Although Smith did not determine the shape or size of this building, it was clearly very large. The hearth feature was inside this structure. A second structure was identified in the northern section of Trench 6, which is described as smaller than the previous structure, and it had wall sills, post holes, and an internal smudge pit of charred corn cobs. Smith (1965: Figure 3) found four refuse pits in the very northern part of Trench 6, and photographs reveal the following unusual artifacts in situ: an iron trade axe head (figure 4.6), two large manos, an iron knife blade, a glass goblet fragment, and a large roofing tile. Another feature in the northern unit of Trench 6, called a "fire pit," contained a second trade axe head and abundant artifacts (Smith 1965: 29).

In the artifact table of his short report, Smith (1965: Table III) lists 16,484 artifacts recovered from Trench 6, which is 57.9 percent of his total assemblage. There were 185 high status items recovered in Trench 6, including six coins; stemmed, enameled, and painted glassware (N=43); cutlery (N=8); 122 pieces of porcelain; an alabaster plate fragment; a bayonet; a bronze dagger handle; six keys, one of which is a music box key; and furniture hardware.

The size of the structures and the abundance and variety of artifacts, many reflecting high status, are strong indicators that this was a high-status area with large homes.

UWF Trench 13 East is adjacent to Smith's Trench 6 and revealed the same mix of wall segments from large structures, a few refuse pits, extremely high numbers of artifacts, and an unusually high number of personal and high-status markers. The evidence from both investigations strongly supports the interpretation that there were several large homes in this area with high-status residents and families.

About 10 feet east of Trench 6 was yet another complex of large structures, postholes, and a trash pit. Thirty-one feet of a wall trench from a very large building oriented due north-south was exposed. There were also two adjacent wall sections parallel and perpendicular to the long wall. The orientation of these structures is unique on this site as all other structures with discernable orientations were 10 to 15 degrees east of north. The foundations were post-on-sill with a few scattered post molds. Midden was present on both sides of the long wall and was lighter in color on one side (east) and darker on the other side. Harris and Eschbach (2006: 163) suggest the lighter area had probably been covered with a floor and the darker midden was outside the structure.

The artifact assemblage associated with the north-south structures is quite different than that recovered from the other areas of the site. Most unusual are 48 fragments of small ceramic figurines of humans and animals (Furlong 2008: 125). In addition, Holmes's (2012) analysis revealed that half of all female gender-related items are associated with these buildings. Other unusual items include six ceramic and two brass candlestick holders and 25.0 percent of the olive jar pieces recovered from the site. Olive jars had declined in general use by the mid-eighteenth century, but the church continued to use them to store wine and oils. Based on the size, unique orientation of the buildings to the cardinal directions, and the special associated artifacts—figurines, candlestick holders, and olive jars—Harris and Eschbach (2006: 224–225) interpret the structures represented by the north-south wall trenches as the remains of at least two churches.

The TPQ date of the longest church wall trench is 1750, indicating it was built after the 1740 hurricane. The north-south wall trench under the covered floor of the last church has a TPQ date of 1722 and is interpreted to be the remains of a previous church building, possibly the original church at the settlement.

The number of artifacts recovered in the church area (4,922 by count and 49.8 kg by weight) is relatively low compared to the number recovered in the other documented structures in the community (see appendix V, table V.6).

The likely reason for this low number of artifacts is the presence of the solid floors of the last church that once covered most of the area excavated. There are only 19 high status markers in the church assemblage. The assemblage has a high percentage of Euro-American ceramics (74.5%), which is higher than the site average of 66.1 percent. This high proportion could reflect the presence and activities of the resident friars. The proportions of Euro-American ceramic classes in the church area are similar to those of the total assemblage: almost all (94.0%) are Other Coarse Earthenware (60.7%) and Majolica (33.3%), as detailed in appendix V, table V.6. All other ceramic classes make up 2.3 percent or less each. More than half of the Native American ceramics by weight are tempered with shell (57.1%), followed by grog (16.3%) and sand (16.2%). These temper proportions differ from the site averages in which shell, grog, and sand are present in relatively equal proportions. Just as they do in other areas of the site, the Kitchen and Architecture artifact groups dominate the counted and weighed materials (91.6% and 94.3%, respectively). As described above, there are many unusual artifact types in the church area: abundant pieces of figurines, candlesticks, a high number of Guadalajara Polychrome sherds (N=37), and jewelry such as beads, pendants, and ornaments. Another unusual aspect of the church assemblage is the presence of five pipes: two stone (gneiss and steatite) and three ceramic.

Smith excavated two more large units to the east in this area of the site, Trenches 10 and 11 (see figure 4.3), but surprisingly, they contained very few features or artifacts. Trench 11 had one 40-foot-long wall section oriented northwest-southeast (Smith 1965: Figure 16) and one refuse pit. In Trench 10 there was only one refuse pit. Smith (1965: Table III) lists 1,615 artifacts from Trench 11 and only 16 from Trench 10. Compared with the abundant features and artifacts in the units just to the west, the area with these two trenches is unusually sparse.

Smith found the remains of one complete structure at the very end of the long, narrow trench extending southwest from the Trench 6 unit on the southern edge of the central site area (see figure 4.3). The structure is small (about 10 by 9 feet in size) and has the distinction of being the only complete structure identified and excavated at Presidio Santa Rosa. Unfortunately, the artifact assemblage associated with this structure is not known.

In sum, the central site area was characterized by clusters of the remains of many large structures and dense residential cultural material. In the eastern area were the remains of two churches that were built and rebuilt on the same spot. There were very few features and sparse cultural material just 20 to 30 feet east of the churches. Perhaps Trenches 10 and 11 were located in the open north-south street pictured in the 1743 Serres sketch of the community (figure 4.1).

Eastern Site Area

The eastern edge of the open site area is adjacent to Sigüenza Slough (see figure 4.3) and was investigated by both UWF and FSU. UWF excavated a large block unit in this area, designated Block 1 North and South. Block 1 North intersected FSU Trench 9, enabling accurate positioning of FSU Trenches 8 and 9. There was a distinct charcoal-rich deposit about a half-foot thick throughout Block 1 (figure 4.10). In the northern unit, there were three intersecting wall trenches representing at least two structures. Two wall sections were post-in-trench construction and one was post-on-sill (Harris and Eschbach 2006: 141–147). Ceramics in two of the wall trench segments have TPQ dates corresponding to the first community in 1722–1740.

Block 1 South (figure 4.11) revealed several wall trenches from at least five

Figure 4.10. Portion of Block 1 South showing wall trench features from building and rebuilding of structures in northern part of eastern Presidio Santa Rosa site area. Note charcoal layer on former surface and intersecting wall trenches of several rebuildings as identified by corners. Courtesy of the Archaeology Institute, University of West Florida.

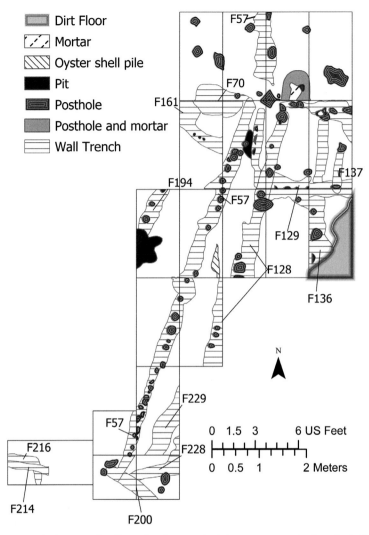

Figure 4.11. Scale drawing of wall trenches from multiple large structures built and rebuilt in southern part of eastern Presidio Santa Rosa site area. Courtesy of the Archaeology Institute, University of West Florida.

buildings, two of which were small rectangular structures (Harris and Eschbach 2006: 157). A sequence of three buildings can be seen in figure 4.10, which shows only a portion of Block 1 South. The earliest building is represented by Feature 136 and was apparently demolished and replaced with a new small structure, Feature 129. This second structure was demolished, and a third, much larger structure was then erected there, represented by a 31-foot section of a wall trench (Feature 128) that included the building's northwest corner. The ceramic TPQ of the Feature 128 foundation is 1722, indicating that it and the previous two structures were part of the first community. The construction method for each of the three foundations was a narrow post-in-trench with posts set irregularly.

A second large building constructed adjacent to the large Feature 128 building was identified by a 41-foot-long section of the foundation wall trench (Feature 57) that has a TPQ date of 1750 and includes the building's southeast corner. There was a gap near the southeast corner of the Feature 57 structure that may have been a doorway. The 130-degree angle of this building's southern corner led Harris and Eschbach (2006: 150) to suggest that it may have been octagonal shaped, similar to the one in the 1743 Serres drawing (figure 4.1). The fire that produced the charcoal debris layer covering all of Block 1 either resulted from both buildings (Features 128 and 57) burning at once or, more likely, only the youngest building (Feature 57) burning because it was the only one standing at the time. There was very little cultural material in the charcoal debris layer, indicating that the fire occurred just before the 1752 hurricane destroyed the settlement and led to its abandonment. Otherwise, the debris probably would have been cleared away and a new structure built on this valuable elevated ridge.

The adjacent FSU Trenches 8 and 9 also revealed a mosaic of wall trenches that appear to be the remains of two additional large buildings. Unfortunately, Smith did not address the details of the wall trenches or interpret the structures, but from photographs in his report and slides of the fieldwork, they were long, shallow, dark stains probably from decomposed timber sills laid in shallow trenches (Smith 1965: Plates 7, 8, 9, Figure 16). Smith (1965: 31) describes the wall features only as wall trenches and/or fallen beams. One wall trench must have been from a large structure about 30 by 15 feet in size as measured in the photographs, with at least two internal rooms or floor sills. The second building Smith exposed in Trenches 8 and 9 was also large, as a 34-foot section of one wall trench/sill was exposed.

Smith found two additional features in the Trenches 8 and 9 complex. One was a large pile of "construction rubble" about eight feet in diameter (Smith 1965: 31) containing oyster shells, mortar, tiles, and dense, compact charcoal, which Smith suggests could have been debris from making oyster shell mortar. The second was a smudge pit filled with charred corncobs located near the large structures. UWF identified a large, deep pit extending to the permanent water table in this area. The pit is in a low spot on the modern ground surface and the water table is close to the surface. Harris and Eschbach (2006: 163) suggest that this feature was probably a well.

The artifact assemblage recovered from the eastern site area is large, comprising 39.2 percent of the counted (17,189) and 28.7 percent of the weighed (106 kg) material recovered from the settlement. Surprisingly, Smith (1965: Table III) recovered only 3,824 artifacts from Trenches 8 and 9. Only a few feet away, UWF Block 1 contained 4.5 times the number of artifacts that the FSU units did, which is curious as Smith screened all excavated soil. Two factors can explain the very different features and artifact densities in adjacent excavation units. First, Smith's Trenches 8 and 9 are below the ridge that borders Sigüenza Marsh, which was an undesirable place to build. Second, the UWF excavation block was placed on top of that ridge, which was a very desirable place to build as evidenced by the many remnants of buildings. A careful examination of the wide north-south street on the eastern edge of the community, shown in the enlargement of the Serres sketch (figure 4.12), has many buildings along both sides. FSU trenches 8–11 with few features and artifacts likely were within the wide open street, while UWF Block 1 North and South were on the ridge on the east side of the street where structures were side by side.

The artifact assemblage and abundance of architectural features recovered from the UWF Block 1 on top of the ridge reflects this area's intense occupation. The artifact assemblage is presented in appendix V, table V.7. Metal artifacts make up 27.3 percent of the artifact classes by weight. This artifact class contains over a thousand nails and spike fasteners (N=1,030) used in the many buildings that once were present. Most of the metal artifacts are fasteners (89.9% by weight). When artifact groups are considered, almost all artifacts are related to the Architecture and Kitchen groups by both weight and count. Fasteners make up almost half (45.8%) of the Architecture group by weight, followed by oyster shell mortar (14.6%), handmade bricks (10.8%), and ladrillos (8.4%). There are also nine hinges, a latch, and wall finishes of plaster and daub. Within the Kitchen Group, 91.2 percent of the artifacts are ceramics by count. Of note are 33 pieces of rare Colonoware. Glass items make up 8.7 percent of the Kitchen materials with 91.0 percent of the typable glass fragments from bottles and the remainder from tumblers and stemmed drinking glasses. In addition to a cleaver, three cups, and a pot, the assemblage includes six metal cutlery items: four knives, a fork, and a spoon. Items in the assemblage's Activities group include two lead cloth bale seals, a brass compass, horse tack, a strike-a-light, 41 abraders, and 152 pieces of iron containers. Two sword scabbard tips are present, as are several parts of firearms, such as a flintlock, two gun cocks, and a lock plate. Glass beads (152) account for most of the jewelry, but there are also pieces of gold and brass jewelry parts and two pendants, one gold and one silver. Most of the 271 Clothing items are fasteners: 90 buckles (84 iron and 6 brass), 59 straight pins of brass and iron, seven brass cuff links,

Figure 4.12. Close-up of buildings along the north-south street in 1743 Serres sketch of Santa Rosa presidio. Arrow shows estimated area of excavation units with architectural remains of several large buildings. (Roberts and Jefferys 1763; adapted by the Archaeology Institute, University of West Florida).

and 16 buttons of brass, pewter, and iron. A silver aglet and five pieces of silver brocade are also part of the Clothing group. The Furniture group includes 25 tacks and a hook and eye.

In general, the large and varied assemblage recovered from the features and midden on the eastern ridge next to Sigüenza Marsh reflects intense occupation and construction and reconstruction of both large and small wooden residences. The abundance, wide range, and high quantity of artifacts in each artifact group reflect the daily life of the many families, some of high status, who lived in these houses on the ridge bordering Sigüenza Slough and the north-south street for over three decades.

Western Site Area

As shown in figure 4.3, FSU and UWF investigated the western part of the site with a cluster of five trenches (FSU) and a series of 34 smaller units (UWF). FSU did not encounter any architectural features in their five large trenches in the southern part of this site area (Smith 1965). As Harris and Eschbach (2006: 120–139) detail, UWF documented 14 features in this site area: sections of five wall trench segments, seven postholes, one pit, and an ash deposit. Two ditch profiles were extended and revealed three parallel sections of post-in-trench walls within half a foot of each other and covered by a layer of sand. The closeness and repetition of the wall trenches suggest that they very likely represent one original building and two replacement walls probably constructed after storms (Harris and Eschbach 2006: 132–133). An ash layer from hearth cleanings and a refuse pit indicate the last use of this area of the site. The artifacts recovered from the two occupations suggest that the first residents enjoyed a more comfortable socioeconomic status than the later inhabitants did (Harris and Eschbach 2006: 133). The TPQ dates of the features imply that the western site area was primarily occupied before the 1740 hurricane destruction.

The investigation of the mosquito control ditch profiles revealed that a dark, continuous midden with features was buried beneath a 1.0- to 1.5-foot deposit of gray dredged sand stretching 600 feet west from Sigüenza Slough (see figure 4.3). The midden exposed in the ditch profiles was thicker and contained more features than the nearby excavation units just to the south, indicating that this area of the presidio settlement was the very rear edge of the community. As Harris and Eschbach (2006: 133) describe, the highest density of artifacts was recovered from the western end of the ditch and decreased to the east. Smith (1965: Figure 4) also discovered a layer of black organic shell midden in Trench 5 buried under almost a foot of gray sand 75 feet south of the ditch. Two factors support the early occupation and abandonment of the western site area. First, a thick layer of gray storm surge sand covers this area of the site, and second, only four sherds out of a total of 1,247, all from ditch profiles, have a post-1740 TPQ date. The storm surge layer is very likely from the 1740 hurricane, and the paucity of post-1740 ceramics indicates most of this area was not reoccupied. The present-day ditch appears to be very near the southern limit of the pre-1740 reoccupation, and this part of the open site area was occupied very lightly after 1740.

Cultural material was present in some quantity in the featureless area south of the ditch; Smith (1965: Table III) recovered 5,677 artifacts from five large trenches, and UWF recovered 1,885 counted items and 13.7 kg of weighed material (see appendix V, table V.8). Most of the cultural material (81.0%) UWF recovered was from the midden exposed in the ditch profiles and extensions along the south wall. Most of the assemblage is either Building Material (35.6%) or pieces of ceramic containers (40.5% by weight). Kitchen and Architectural items are the most abundant by both count (92.3%) and weight (93.8%). Of the 1,247 total ceramic sherds, 62.4 percent are Euro-American and 37.6 percent are Native American, which are the same proportions as the total site artifact assemblage. Majolica is the most abundant ceramic class by count (50.7%) but is closely followed by Other Coarse Earthenware (42.7%). Delft, Faience, Redware, and Earthenware combined make up only 6.6 percent of the Euro-American ceramics. Of the 615 typable Euro-American ceramics, the most frequent are El Morro (39.2%), Puebla Blue on White Majolica (21.8%), and Lead Glazed Coarse Earthenware (7.6%). Almost three-quarters of the Other Coarse Earthenware are El Morro (74.2%), followed by Lead Glazed (14.2%) and Mexican Red Painted (3.2%).

The most frequent tempers used in the Native American ceramics by weight are shell (35.5%), sand (24.7%), and grog (24.3%). Ten other tempers are detailed in appendix V, table V.8. Of the 1.7 kg of typable Native American ceramics, the most abundant ceramic types are Walnut Roughened, *variety* McKee Island (18.9%), Sand Tempered Plain (17.7%), and Grog Tempered Plain (17.3%). Over half of the Indian-made ceramics are plain (52.2%) and 24.3 percent have roughened surfaces. The remainder are decorated by burnishing, slipping, painting, incising, and stamping. Other artifacts of note in the small assemblage recovered from the western site area include a silver Charles II half-real cob minted between 1668 and 1669, a lead bale seal, sword blade, a brass and iron button, and a gold bead.

In sum, the western part of the open site area appears to be the very rear margin of the archaeological remains of the Santa Rosa presidio community. Residential features extend only a few feet south of the mosquito control ditch. Cultural material was scattered south of the ditch to the bordering wetlands, but there are no occupational features. This area of the site shows clear evidence of a sudden storm surge that buried settlement debris with sands deposited from the 1740 hurricane. This part of the site area was not occupied after this storm.

Summary of Archaeological Investigations

Information produced from two intensive historical archaeological investigations of the site of the Santa Rosa presidio have produced a great deal of information about this community and its residents. We now know that shoreline erosion has removed most of the archaeological remains of the settlement, leaving about 4.3 acres relatively intact. The northern half of the remaining site (about 2.2 acres) is covered with up to 30 feet of sand dredged from the nearby ship channel. The southern half of the site is open and remarkably preserved.

Based on the distribution of artifacts and features, we have determined that the primary archaeological remains of the community not covered by dredge sand is the southern portion of the settlement on both sides of the north-south street and structures on the very southern edge of the settlement, shown in the 1743 Serres sketch. The dominant and most abundant archaeological features are building foundations—especially wall trenches, posts, and wall sills—from structures that were clustered on the highest areas of the site. Only one building was identifiable, the church, and it seems to have been built twice on the same spot. In the clusters of building foundations, feature intersection, ceramic TPQ dating, and stratigraphy made it possible to identify structures and refuse strata that were present before and after the destructive 1740 hurricane.

The unusual environment of the site directly contributed to the plethora of architectural remains and the particularly large artifact assemblage. The barrier island on which the presidio was located has loose, coarse sand, and the structures were battered by eight harsh storms and hurricanes in 29 years. These factors necessitated constant repair and rebuilding. The artifact assemblage resulting from this dynamic environment is especially unusual in its large size and many personal items and small arms that are rarely lost or found. The soft, coarse sand churned by hundreds of people on a daily basis was literally an artifact trap. In addition, the constant strong storms and destructive hurricanes scattered and buried most of the community's possessions, which could not be recovered.

Summary of Presidio Santa Rosa

At the end of the War of the Quadruple Alliance in 1722, Pensacola was returned to Spain. However, establishing and supporting another presidio on the northern Gulf coast was not King Philip V's first choice, as it was very expensive to support and it produced little to no revenue. On the other hand, he did not want either Pensacola Bay or St. Joseph Bay to fall into enemy hands. The first option was to try to lower Pensacola Bay with a drainage canal so warships could not enter, eliminating the need for a defensive presidio. As this was not possible, the second option was to abandon the presidio on St. Joseph Bay and establish a new one on Santa Rosa Island on Sigüenza Point at the pass into Pensacola Bay. Unfortunately, neither option was possible and a site was chosen for the third location of the West Florida presidio: then about half a mile from Sigüenza Point on the bay shore in the first stand of trees with protective dunes.

Presidio San José was dismantled, except for the church, and the first structures at Santa Rosa were built using salvaged building materials transported from San José along with additional materials brought from Veracruz. Most of the people from San José were also transferred to Santa Rosa, and others were sent from Veracruz. As the new presidio was protected by water on three sides, a small fort on the eastern perimeter of the community sufficed to defend against a land attack. The fort was a stockade with cannons enclosing only a warehouse, powder magazine, and a covered way. The buildings at Santa Rosa were made of wood, usually cedar imported from Veracruz and local cypress bark for roofing and siding. The layout of the settlement was linear, with several streets parallel to the bay shore. The 1743 Serres drawing depicts one street perpendicular to the shore lined with large, two-story, wooden buildings.

Throughout its existence, the Santa Rosa community suffered from raids and attacks by British-allied Creeks on both the community and working parties outside it. Natural forces also wreaked havoc on Santa Rosa as the barrier island received the full force of wind, rain, and storm surges of at least eight strong storms or hurricanes. In addition, the island is composed of coarse unconsolidated sand with very little vegetation and few useable natural resources.

The demographic composition of the community of Presidio Santa Rosa reflected the mixed ethnicities of New Spain. The clearest social ranks in the community were the convicts/laborers on the bottom and Spaniards born in New Spain at the top. In between were soldiers, staff, craftsmen, and officers; however, the status of individuals could rise or fall with their positions, as happened with convicts-turned-soldiers. A distinguishing difference between the Santa Rosa community and that of the previous presidio locations was the consistent and increasing presence of women and families after 1741, growing to a high of 34 military families in 1753. Families with the husband and sometimes the wife earning a steady wage and rations built an increasingly more balanced colonial community. Children were born here, and extended families began to develop and call Spanish West Florida home. The presidio was developing into a colonial town from the original frontier border military garrison.

During the occupation of Santa Rosa, there were Apalachee and Yamasee mission villages on the mainland, and these Natives traded, worked, visited, and received rations at the presidio. The refugee Apalachees who arrived in 1718 and settled the Soledad Mission at the mouth of the Escambia River had stayed during the three years of French occupation and continued to reside in the Pensacola area during the duration of the Santa Rosa presidio, although in 1741 they moved their village 12 miles upriver and changed its name to San José de Escambe. In 1740, Yamasee refugees from the British siege of San Agustín arrived in Pensacola and settled on the west side of Escambia Bay near the new outpost of San Miguel. In 1749, they moved across Escambia Bay on the southwest shore of Garcon Point and started the mission of San Antonio de Punta Rasa I. In 1738, Upper Creeks had a short-lived settlement on the Escambia River, upriver from the Soledad and Escambe Apalachee mission villages.

Two of the refugee mission locations in the Pensacola Bay area have been found and studied: San Joseph de Escambe (1740–1761, Apalachee) and San Antonio de Punta Rasa I (1749–1761, Yamasee). Worth (2008; Worth et al. 2012) has intensively studied Escambe, and for most of its existence, the mission was a small village of about 10 families, a missionary, and a few resident soldiers. As Creek attacks once again plagued West Florida in the 1750s, the mission was fortified with a small stockade and a cavalry unit. The archaeological assemblage is almost completely made up of Native American ceramics and reflects the Native peoples' diaspora after the English destroyed the missions in 1702–1704.

The site of the Santa Rosa presidio has undergone two archaeological investigations, one by FSU in 1964 and another by UWF in 2002–2004. Both efforts revealed remarkably similar features and large artifact assemblages with an unusually wide variety of artifacts. The archaeological remains of Santa Rosa reflect the low-lying settlement's continual battering by storms and hurricanes. Both investigations revealed clusters of architectural features in the central and eastern site areas that clearly reflect frequent building, repair, demolition, and rebuilding. While the foundation of only one complete, small structure was uncovered, the partial footprints of many large buildings were documented. Most large buildings were framed with posts set irregularly in shallow trenches or on large timber sills. The buildings appeared to be residential except for the church, which was unique in its orientation to the cardinal directions and its special associated artifacts such as brass candlestick holders, figurines, olive jars, and female-related artifacts. Below this structure was a wall of an earlier church also oriented to the cardinal directions.

After the 1740 hurricane damage, a fortified warehouse and kiln were built on the mainland. While many bricks and fragments were recovered in both investigations of the island settlement, they appear to have been used for features such as flooring or hearths within the wooden buildings. As mentioned previously, only three of the scores of buildings are documented to have used bricks in construction. Few features other than architectural ones were discovered, including only 10 refuse pits, a few piles of refuse and construction debris, plus two large pit-like features extending into the permanent water table that likely were sump wells.

The central and eastern site areas contained most of the artifacts lost in the loose, sandy matrix of the settlement. Ceramics dominate the artifact assemblage by both count and weight, and ceramic building materials such as bricks, tiles, and ladrillos make up over a quarter of the weighed material. The ceramic assemblage is 66.1 percent Euro-American and 33.9 percent Native American. The assemblage contains large numbers of unusual personal items, small firearms, small ceramic figurines, and jewelry items that are rarely recovered.

In the end, the harsh weather and living conditions at the island settlement could not be endured. The 1752 hurricane completely destroyed the community and there was simply no safe place to live. By 1754, married soldiers and their families moved to the mainland outpost, and in 1756 the garrison moved to San Miguel, which was officially designated as the fourth presidio location that same year. A small military unit remained on the island at the former presidio location to protect the entrance of the bay until 1763.

5

Presidio San Miguel de Panzacola, 1756–1763

The complete transition from the island location of the presidio across Pensacola Bay to the mainland took 16 years and was driven by direct strikes by devastating hurricanes in 1740 and 1752. The transition to the mainland started immediately after the 1740 hurricane with the construction of a fortified warehouse outpost on the mainland. Twelve years later, in November 1752, the fifth hurricane in two years destroyed the Santa Rosa community and made the location impossible to be used for the presidio. In 1754, married soldiers and their families were granted permission to move from Santa Rosa Island across the bay to the mainland at the San Miguel outpost, and construction of housing and major facilities began. By 1756, the transition from the island and the mainland was complete, and Presidio San Miguel de Panzacola was officially established.

Transitions

Rebuilding efforts at Santa Rosa after the 1740 hurricane coincided with marked changes in the larger economic systems and policies governing the Spanish colonies. The Spanish Crown admitted it could no longer support or control its frontier settlements, and annual support through the situado was decreased to all of Spain's colonies. To compensate for the reduction in government support, local economic development and self-sufficiency began to be promoted where it had once been intentionally hindered (Brading 2008; Kuethe and Andrien 2014; McMahon 2017: 31).

Economic policy shifts began with the Bourbon Reforms at the start of the eighteenth century and gradually affected peripheral borderland settlements such as Spanish West Florida (Kuethe and Andrien 2014: 4–5). At the local level, the most visible result of the policy changes was a shift in demographics and private enterprise. The Spanish tried to model their colonies after the productive and profitable colonial systems of Britain and France (Brading 2008). After 1740, the demographic composition of the population at the West Florida presidio began to include different types of people, especially civilian settlers and more soldiers with families. As the transition from Santa Rosa Island to the mainland neared completion between 1754 and 1756, immigration to Pensacola from New Spain was encouraged through the issuance of private land grants around Pensacola Bay for homesteads and support for commercial businesses in ranching and brick manufacturing (Worth 2013: 1–2, 5). Importantly, the establishment of a new cavalry unit for the San Miguel presidio bolstered the safety of the developing civilian community and its surrounding network of industries. Newly approved private maritime trade and supply routes for ports throughout the Gulf of Mexico also encouraged civilian immigration and merchant traders.

The first indication of the shift to a more balanced colonial community occurred in 1741 when the heads of six family households (either husbands or wives) were designated to receive government support (Clune et al. 2006: 41). While women and children were part of the original population transferred from San José to Santa Rosa in 1722–1723 and there had been some mentions of supplies for families there, after 1741, the number of families and unmarried women in Spanish West Florida steadily increased (Clune et al. 2006: 41).

Krista Eschbach's (2019: 225) recent research found that the six families receiving rations in 1740 totaled 77 individuals. In addition, the heads of one of the families, Juan Ygnacio de Soliz y Carcamo and Doña Magdalena Garcia, had previously served at San José, where they had two children. This family, along with the families of their now-adult children, lived at Santa Rosa in 1741 and are examples of the beginning of long-term family continuity in Spanish West Florida. In 1741, Gervasio Cruzat y Góngora arrived with 6 families, which included 65 children. By 1743, the number of families had increased to 13, and 9 years later, in 1752, that number had risen to 21. By 1753, the number of families stood at 32 (Clune et al. 2006: 41). Outside the accounts of situado support for these families, historical records also document marriages between Spanish soldiers and Native American or Spanish women, as well as unmarried domestic partnerships between Native American women and presidio soldiers at Santa Rosa (Clune et al. 2006: 42). In 1753, officials in New Spain sent two families that included at least ten children to the Pensacola settlement (Childers 2003a: 20). In 1754, officials in Veracruz sent 35 young women to Presidio Santa Rosa as voluntary settlers. These women were the wives of enlisted men or had plans to marry upon arrival (Clune et al. 2006: 41).

From the outset, the San Miguel presidio community was significantly different from its three predecessors. For the first time in Spanish West Florida, Pensacola's protective position on the edge of an empire was paired with Crown policy and investment toward the presidio's development into a productive and self-sustaining settlement. The community at Pensacola now had a different purpose than simply holding the western border of Spanish Florida with a military garrison of rotating military and convict laborers supported by the situado; it was to be a productive, self-supporting colony. Spanish authorities now specifically selected married soldiers with families to serve at San Miguel, recruited civilian families from New Spain with incentives of land for farmers and ranchers, and offered free land to military families willing to stay in Pensacola after their terms of service. Moreover, the increased military presence provided increased security for merchants and tradespeople. The fort and garrison now had a dual purpose: to protect Pensacola's expanding civilian community, as well as the two nearby Indian mission villages, and to hold the western border of Spanish Florida against English and French aggression. Spanish West Florida was being intentionally transitioned to a more diverse and developing colonial community during the 1750s and 1760s. Unfortunately, this process was abruptly cut short in 1763 by the cession of Spanish Florida to Britain at the end of the French and Indian War.

Previous Research

Unlike the previous West Florida presidio locations, the San Miguel presidio was not forgotten because it developed into modern-day Pensacola, and the work of early colonial historians regularly researched aspects of San Miguel (for example, Arnade 1959; Faye 1941, 1946a, 1946b; Griffen 1959; Manucy 1959). This historical research established timelines for each of the Pensacola presidio locations, provided general descriptions of their fortifications and settlements based on archival records and maps, and included a general overview of the political and economic contexts for West Florida during the early eighteenth century. With the founding of the University of West Florida (UWF) in 1967, research into local colonial history was amplified by history professor William Coker, whose research centered on regional conditions during the colonial periods in West Florida. In addition to researching various aspects of the San Miguel presidio, Coker also included the Santa Rosa (Coker 1975) and Santa María (Coker 1978) presidio communities in his studies of the financial history and censuses of the Pensacola presidio settlements (Coker 1979; Coker and Inglis 1980).

Public interest in downtown Pensacola's colonial era archaeological record began following the large excavation in 1964 at the Presidio Santa Rosa site led by Hale Smith of Florida State University (FSU). This was the first archaeological excavation in the Pensacola area and it was initiated by the Pensacola Historical Society (PHS), whose members participated in the project in large numbers. The PHS members' experience in archaeology at Santa Rosa generated a great deal of interest in historical archaeology digs, so in addition to running a local history museum, the society took up archaeological excavations in downtown Pensacola under the leadership of its avocational archaeologist Leora Sutton and her then-teenage son William Sutton. Smith and several of his graduate students provided guidance to Sutton and the PHS archaeology projects, and in turn they were supported by the organization and other local historic interest groups. Then-graduate students Nancy Connelly and David White wrote two brief reports of the excavations (Connelly and White 1968a, 1968b). Most of the PHS digs targeted post–San Miguel presidio colonial deposits in downtown Pensacola, especially the remains of the British occupation (1763–1781) including the fort, hospital, and a well. L. Sutton wrote numerous brief field reports and public booklets about the excavations that were published locally (for example, Sutton 1964, 1976). These archaeological activities were driven by the PHS members for over a decade, and this version of public archaeology continued into the early 1970s. Professional archaeologists also conducted a few investigations in downtown Pensacola during the 1970s (for example, Baker 1975; Long 1976; Shaeffer 1971).

Contemporaneous with my establishing the archaeology program at UWF in 1980, there was a burst of urban construction activity across Pensacola's colonial historic area by the local government, and these projects were impacting archaeological deposits from all historic periods. This damage to the pristine colonial archaeological remains was the root cause of my involvement in historical archaeology because there were simply no other archaeologists in the area. I was the first and only resident archaeologist in the region and simply could not let the damage continue, so I resolved to at least try to find a solution. The first step was to organize a local interest/action citizens group, the Pensacola Archaeological Society (PAS), and we approached the City to develop an official archaeological policy that protects sites on City-owned property and rights-of-way. This policy was to be a local version of Section 106 of the National Historic Preservation Act, and since 1985, the archaeological review policy has been implemented on City property and rights-of-way. Following the City's example, Escambia County also adopted a similar archaeological review policy. The PAS has become the engine of public archaeology in the region. It is a large and active support and action group of members of the community who assist in almost all aspects of every archeological project. There is a Pensacola City Archaeologist who makes sure that the departments within the administration are aware of the archaeological policy and ensures compliance with federal and state regulations as well as private developments. In addition, we began and continue to devise incentives for private development without compliance responsibilities and provide products such as good publicity, public exhibits, public products, media attention, and signage for the public. UWF and Pensacola's public archaeology program was developed in downtown Pensacola and continues to this writing. We have won local, state, and federal awards for our efforts in public archaeology, and in 2008 the Florida Public Archaeology Network (FPAN) developed out of the local grassroots organization. It is a statewide organization of regional public archaeology centers with headquarters at UWF. The interested and educated public provides the vigilance and dedication needed to meet the changing threats to our buried significant archaeological remains throughout Florida.

As the urban renewal program ended and construction projects in downtown Pensacola slowed in the mid-1990s, I integrated the archaeological and historical information generated from seventeen projects into a book, *Archaeology of Colonial Pensacola* (Bense 1999), which is a synthesis and guide to the many detailed technical reports. At that time, I also took a broader look at the bigger picture of the colonial occupation of West Florida, looking for the largest gaps in our understanding of colonial people and cultural landscapes. I immediately realized that the early Spanish Period (1698–1763) was the least understood and studied period, and after discussing it with PAS members, I realized we all were very curious about this early Spanish occupation and decided to turn our focus to it. The first target was the first presidio, Santa María de Galve (1698–1719), located generally on the mainland bluff overlooking the entrance of Pensacola Bay. As summarized in chapter 2, we conducted investigations there for four seasons in 1995–1998 (Bense 2003). Immediately afterward, we investigated the second and third presidio locations (chapters 3 and 4).

UWF archaeologist Elizabeth Benchley and her students, with the strong support of the PAS, led a series of research projects between 2000 and 2007 targeting the communities of people and associated structures both inside and outside the fort of the fourth presidio, San Miguel, underlying downtown Pensacola (Benchley 2007a, 2007b; Benchley et al. 2007; McMahon 2017; C. Williams 2004). Some of the early projects in downtown Pensacola had encountered San Miguel deposits (Bense 1991a, 1999; Joy 1988, 1989a), and these contexts have been reprocessed and reclassified in the UWF laboratory and are used in this synthesis. In addition, a salvage project that encountered a San Miguel residential lot just east of the fort is included in this analysis (Melcher 2015). At this writing, archaeological compliance for extensive underground electric lines in downtown Pensacola is being led by Benchley, and it is encountering in situ remains from all historic periods. Some material recovered in the utility monitoring project from the Presidio San Miguel occupation is included in the analysis below.

Unlike the sites of the previous presidios, the remains of San Miguel pose several unique issues for archaeological research. First, the deposits lie beneath the heart of the modern city of Pensacola (figure 5.1). As a result, the subsequent two and a half centuries of occupation have buried and impacted the material remains of San Miguel. In contrast, the presidio sites of Santa Maria, San José, and Santa Rosa are essentially single component sites lying in relatively protected areas on government property. Second, the main occupation of the San Miguel presidio was only nine years at most (1754–1763). Another unique aspect of Presidio San Miguel is that the remains have been excavated in bits and pieces rather than as the focus of a major archaeological campaign such as those conducted at Santa María and Santa Rosa. Intact and undisturbed remains for the San Miguel presidio have been difficult to identify, isolate, and separate from the ensuing dense archaeological deposition in downtown Pensacola. Notwithstanding these drawbacks, there are excellent historic maps of the Presidio San Miguel community, accurate anchor points connecting those maps to the present environment, and an increasingly accurate archaeological grid for the entire downtown area, enabling good provenience despite the clutter and obstructions of the modern city. Below, I knit together the disparate archaeological pieces of the San Miguel community and offer an updated portrait of the community at the fourth and last location of the West Florida presidio

The Early Years: San Miguel de Punta Blanca, 1740–1756

Immediately following Presidio Santa Rosa's 1740 destruction by a hurricane, Acting Governor Nicholás Ximénez de Florencia, on his own initiative, had a large warehouse constructed on the mainland side of Pensacola Bay to hold munitions, food, and other supplies for safekeeping and protection from storms (Worth 2013: 2). The warehouse and several bark-roofed cabins were protected with a surrounding stockade, and there were other cabins nearby on the bay beach ridge for a small detachment of six infantry troops and a corporal who were routinely garrisoned there (Faye 1941: 162; Worth 2013: 3–4). The newly constructed and fortified warehouse outpost was named San Miguel de Punta Blanca.

A year after the fortified warehouse was built, newly appointed Governor Gervasio Cruzat y Góngora confirmed the need for the warehouse and ordered the construction of a kiln nearby to supply bricks for a new masonry fort to be located on Punta de Sigüenza on the western tip of Santa Rosa Island at the entrance to Pensacola Bay (Worth 2013: 2–3). In 1742, another newly appointed governor, Juan de Yarza y Ascona, responded to yet more storm damage at

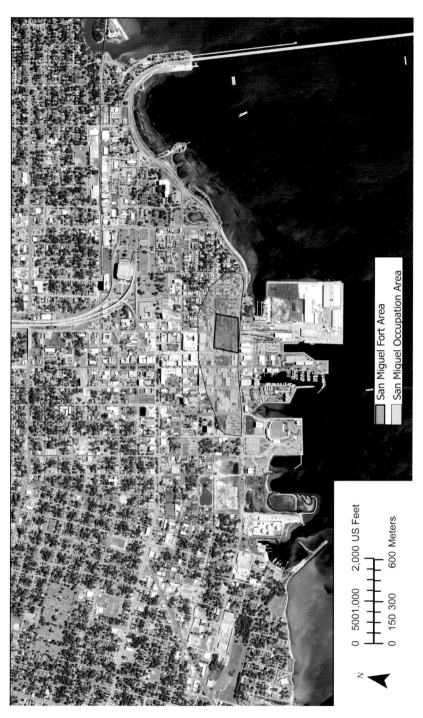

Figure 5.1. Aerial image of modern-day downtown Pensacola showing general boundary of San Miguel community and Fort San Miguel. (Photograph by Esri 2019; adapted by the Archaeology Institute, University of West Florida).

the island presidio by relocating all of the women, children, and necessary food and supplies to the mainland outpost near the warehouse and guards. The families were sheltered in thatch structures with the understanding that the move was temporary (and it was) while the presidio on the island was rebuilt. However, the guarded warehouse, guardhouse, and kiln at San Miguel became fixed features of the landscape over the next decade. John Worth (2013: 2) also notes that in 1741 the annual situado was increased to cover the wages for construction work on the mainland.

Worth's (2013: 4) archival research hints that there may have been other buildings constructed at San Miguel for soldiers during this time, likely inside the stockade around the warehouse. The kiln operated continuously during this period, supplying building materials not only to construct an ill-fated masonry fort at the pass but also for repairs and new construction at the struggling island community. Worth (2013: 3–4) and R. Wayne Childers and colleagues (2007: 28) note that the stockade and warehouse at the Punta Blanca outpost were still standing in 1753, but the stockade enclosure had to be removed as a result of wood rot. As discussed later in this chapter, the warehouse was still standing a decade later and was depicted on official maps made when San Miguel was transferred to the British in 1763.

In sum, historical documents identify several early structures at the mainland outpost of San Miguel de Punta Blanca built to serve the needs of Presidio Santa Rosa. The largest was the warehouse enclosed by a wooden stockade and protected with a manned guardhouse. A kiln was constructed on the mainland near the outpost to supply the constant rebuilding efforts at the Santa Rosa presidio. After a series of storms further damaged Presidio Santa Rosa in 1742, women and children were temporarily moved from the island to the mainland and accommodated in thatch houses during reconstruction. At least one of these early structures, the warehouse, remained in use through the remaining years of Spanish control of West Florida.

Final Move to the Mainland

Despite the complete destruction of the Santa Rosa presidio on the island in November 1752 and Governor Florencia's recommendation for the immediate relocation of the island community to the mainland, the transition was plagued with delays for over four years. A formal junta in Mexico City did not review Governor Florencia's November 1752 report recommending the presidio's relocation to the mainland until September 1753, though when the junta did convene, it made a series of decisions that greatly impacted the trajectory of Spanish Pensacola. The junta ordered an engineer to go to Pensacola to review the storm damage at Santa Rosa and prepare a report and map with options regarding the presidio's repair or relocation. The current military regiment at Santa Rosa was to be bolstered with 160 additional soldiers, with a preference for those with families and agricultural or trade skills. Also encouraged to go to Santa Rosa were single women of marriageable age and civilians who would be granted property in return for their permanent settlement and development of those properties. Lastly, the church, fort, and other structures on Santa Rosa Island were to be repaired, refurnished, or replaced, as necessary. Soldiers were to be moved from Santa Rosa to San Miguel, leaving only six to eight men garrisoned at the former island presidio (Worth 2013: 6).

In December 1753, engineer Phelipe Feringan Cortés arrived along with a new commandant, Santiago Benito Eraso, and 150 new recruits. However, Worth (2013: 6) details that the main population still remained on the island as late as the next summer when a strong storm in June 1754 flooded the Santa Rosa presidio yet again. This storm finally prompted Eraso to send 54 forced laborers and a squad leader to San Miguel to repair the existing warehouse on the mainland, begin construction on lodging for the troops, and erect a chapel for the Franciscans. He also allowed families who wished to move to the mainland and build houses to do so. A friar was assigned to the newly constructed chapel, and a school was started later that year (Worth 2013: 8).

From June of 1754 through 1755, many new structures were built at San Miguel, including the church with a sacristy, two open sheds as barracks for the troops, a hospital, a second warehouse, a powder magazine, the commandant's residence, a new guard house, ovens, mess huts, a shed for the forced laborers, and many "little houses" for the soldiers (Worth 2013: 8). In 1755, Commandant Eraso noted that most of the population had moved to San Miguel. However, the military headquarters was still on Santa Rosa Island along with the garrison of single soldiers and officers. Another viceregal junta convened in July 1756 and officially established the new presidio location on the mainland, formally designated as Presidio San Miguel de Panzacola. Plans for new fortifications were funded, as were funds for a new cavalry company. Additionally, one hundred single women volunteers were authorized to go to San Miguel along with 200 more forced laborers, armaments, and a variety of supplies (Worth 2013: 10).

Insight into the 1752–1756 developments on the mainland can be found on the 1756 López de la Camara Alta map of the Pensacola Bay area, which was produced from maps and notes in engineer Feringan's report to the viceroy. The map, a portion of which is shown in figure 5.2, shows San Miguel labelled as a village for the garrison with 11 buildings in a rectangular arrangement. The map also depicts the outpost on Santa Rosa Island at the site of the former presidio, including a fort and four buildings presumably for the military

headquarters, single soldiers, and officers. For the first time, we can see development outside the fort. For example, there are four outlying haciendas, the
Yamasee mission village of Punta Rasa I, the kiln, and locations of oyster beds
where lime could be produced. From this map, its legend, and the documentary information pointed out above, the following implications can be drawn
about the Spanish expansion around Pensacola Bay between 1752 and 1756:

- Presidio Santa Rosa on the barrier island continued to be occupied
  and served as military headquarters until 1756.
- On the mainland, between 1752 and 1756 San Miguel was greatly expanded, growing from just a fortified warehouse and guarded outpost
  to a large community with public buildings, residences, and a sizeable
  population of families and forced laborers.
- There were three haciendas in the countryside owned by resident presidio officers: Don Luis Joseph de Ullate, Don Diego Casimiro Ximénez, and Don Pedro Amoscotigui y Bermudo.
- Private enterprises (cattle ranches, kilns, fisheries, and lime production) were underway.
- Resources for future development were mapped, including fresh water
  sources, clay beds for ceramics and bricks, and oyster beds for lime.

Despite these important developments in establishing a self-sustaining colony on Pensacola Bay, an important element was missing on the mainland in
1756: a fort to protect the community. However, in late summer of 1757, word
arrived from Mobile that English-allied Upper Creeks were about to attack
Pensacola, and the ongoing absence of a protective wall around the San Miguel
community was swiftly corrected. As Worth (2013: 11–12) relates, within only
two days, brush was cleared to the distance of a musket shot around the San
Miguel village. Engineer Feringan marked out on the ground the outline of a
stockade with four triangular-shaped demibastions set to enclose most existing
community structures. Stacks of poles began to arrive, and in less than 12 days
the north and east curtain walls were in place, with the rest of the stockade
finished promptly thereafter (Worth 2013: 11). Quite suddenly, after years of
bureaucratic deferment, the San Miguel de Panzacola presidio was a reality.

Fort San Miguel

The first image of Fort San Miguel is on a large map of the Pensacola Bay system by Joseph Porlier (1761) and shows a fort with four bastions at San Miguel.
However, the transfer of Florida to the British generated a series of detailed
maps of Fort San Miguel and internal buildings from 1763 to 1765. Two Spanish
maps of Fort San Miguel made in 1763 are particularly informative: a sketch

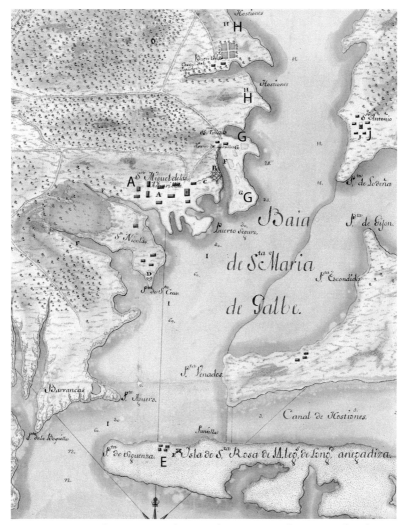

Figure 5.2. Portion of 1756 Camara Alta map of Lower Pensacola Bay area identifying *A*, San Miguel village; *E*, Santa Rosa outpost; *G*, clay deposits; *H*, locations for making lime; *J*, Yamasee mission village of San Antonio de Punta Rasa I (López 1756; adapted by the Archaeology Institute, University of West Florida).

map by Commandant Diego Ortíz Parrilla and the official transfer map by Ortíz and engineer Feringan. Both maps include almost all the same buildings, but they have different and informative legends that I have combined in figure 5.3. Another informative map was made by British engineer Archibald Robertson in 1763 shortly after the British takeover, and it depicts several cross sections of the walls of Spanish-built Fort San Miguel (figure 5.4). Lastly, in

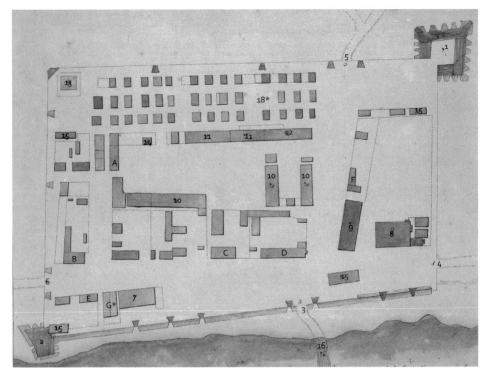

Figure 5.3. Presidio Santa Rosa, 1763 official transfer map of Fort San Miguel with added information from a 1763 sketch map by Ortíz and Feringan: *1*, bastion of Rosario; *2*, bastion of San Francisco; *3–6*, gates; *7*, royal chapel; *8*, houses of the governor; *9*, old warehouse; *10*, barracks for the troops; *11*, gallery for forced laborers; *12*, hospital; *13*, warehouse for gunpowder; *14*, weapons locker; *15*, guard houses; *16*, pier; *17*, houses of officers and residents; *18*, barracks for married soldiers; *A*, house of Pedro Bermudo; *B*, house of Captain of Cavalry, Ullate; *C*, house of commandant; *D*, King's House; *E*, house of paymaster; *F*, stables; *G*, friary (Ortíz and Feringan 1763a, 1763b).

1765, town plan engineer Elias Durnford platted the new town of British Pen-sacola, and in doing so, he identified the Spanish-built homes and structures, shown in figure 5.5.

The most obvious feature of Fort San Miguel is its lack of symmetry, which is undoubtedly directly related to the hurried construction under threat of at-tack and the presence of at least 87 structures prior to fort construction. A close look at the 1763 map by Ortíz and Feringan (figure 5.3) reveals that the curtain walls do not form a square or rectangle, but an irregular polygon. Each wall length and corner angle of the fort is different.

The north, east, and west curtain walls are a single line of posts set in the ground, and the southern seawall and bastions are terrepleined with two rows of posts filled with sand. The cross sections of the fort walls on the 1763

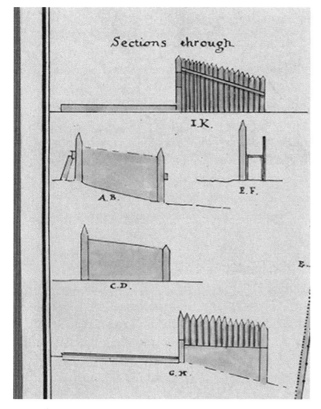

Figure 5.4. Presidio San Miguel, cross sections of portions of the Fort San Miguel walls: A–B, terrepleined seawall; I–K, northeast bastion fortified cannon opening in wall and cannon platform; E–F, curtain wall with fighting deck; C–D, terrepleined northeast bastion wall; G–H, fortified cannon opening in seawall and cannon platform (Robertson 1763).

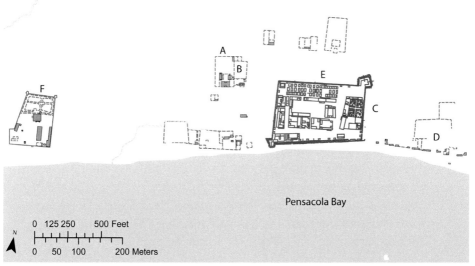

Figure 5.5. Presidio San Miguel, 1765 Durnford Town Plan map showing Spanish buildings and areas of archaeological investigations outside Fort San Miguel identified: A, Ricardos house lot; B, small house lot; C, Old Christ Church residential area; D, Mission Punta Rasa II; E, Fort San Miguel; F, estate of engineer Phelipe Feringan Cortés. (Digitized and enhanced portions of Durnford 1765).

Robertson map (figure 5.4) reveal details of the curtain walls and terrepleined seawall and bastions. The Ortíz-Feringan map shows seven cannon emplacements and openings in the seawall for artillery. The 1763 Robertson map shows a cross section of a cannon emplacement in the seawall and bastion (figure 5.4), revealing that the cannons were on low platforms on the ground, slightly elevated at the rear. The cross section also shows that the openings in the seawall through which the cannons fired were lined/reinforced with posts to contain the earth fill. On the east end of the seawall on the Ortíz-Feringan map, two of the fort's gun emplacements do not have openings in the seawall for firing and, therefore, must have been elevated on the fighting deck shown on the map to fire over the wall. There were four cannon emplacements on the north and west walls, though none are depicted on the east wall. While Robertson did not depict a cross section of a stockade wall cannon emplacement, there are openings in the wall at each installation, indicating that the cannons fired through openings in the wall and were also on low ground platforms. Perhaps the cannon openings in the stockade wall were similar to those depicted in the Serres 1743 drawing of the fort at Presidio Santa Rosa (see figure 4.1). The 1763 Robertson map shows that the seawall had three sections of elevated fighting decks for firearms, measuring 65, 75, and 95 feet long, and the three curtain walls facing the interior also had long fighting decks. As shown in the cross section of the curtain walls, the fighting decks also served as covered ways along the walls.

In addition to fighting decks, cannons, and walls, bastions also protected Fort San Miguel. Documents state that engineer Feringan marked out triangular demibastions on each corner (Worth 2013: 11). While the 1761 Porlier map depicts four demibastions, the number varies on other historic maps. As indicated in the Ortíz-Feringan map, by 1763 there were only two bastions. The northeast bastion was symmetrical and diamond-shaped, but the southwest bastion was an irregular polygon. Both bastions had terrepleined walls 13 feet thick. The southwest bastion, named Baluarte del San Francisco, had six cannon emplacements with a thick wood plank floor for maneuvering its cannons. The northeast bastion, named Baluarte del Rosario, had 15 cannon emplacements mounted on low platforms on a low deck made of thick wood planks. The openings in the terrepleined bastion walls through which the cannons fired were lined and reinforced with posts similar to those on the seawall.

The west curtain wall and northeast bastion have been archaeologically documented. The west curtain wall was encountered first by Benchley (2007a: 44), shown in figure 5.6, and then by Benchley and April Holmes in 2018 (Benchley and Holmes, personal communication 2018). The construction trench is narrow, approximately 1 to 1.5 feet wide, with a flat base. The interior side of the

Figure 5.6. Presidio San Miguel archaeological remains of the west curtain wall of the 1757 Fort San Miguel from above showing post stains in wall trench. Scale is in feet. Courtesy of the Archaeology Institute, University of West Florida.

trench is vertical, and the upper half of the exterior side is angled outward about 45 degrees. There is clear evidence of the large posts (about one foot wide) that were once present (figure 5.6), though none of these post stains penetrate the base of the construction trench. The curtain wall post stains are likely from the subsurface portion of posts that remained in the ground after the above-ground portions were broken off at the surface during demolition by the British in 1767.

It is important to note that the dimensions of the wall trench for Fort San Miguel precisely match the dimensions of the wall trench documented for the stockade at Mission Escambe built in 1760. As discussed in chapter 4, Worth and colleagues (2015: 175–176) documented that the stockade at Mission Escambe was built from prefabricated wall sections made by laying posts out side by side and nailing long boards/planks to their bases. The sections of posts were then placed in the construction trench and raised. Two factors support the contention that the stockade walls of Fort San Miguel were constructed using the same pre-fab method documented at Mission Escambe. First, both wall trenches are the same narrow width (1 to 1.5 feet), have flat bases, and have posts that did not penetrate the base. Second, the same engineer, Feringan, designed and directed the construction of both stockades under pressure of imminent Indian attacks. This is a very different wall construction technique than that used at Fort San Carlos at Presidio Santa María, where posts were individually placed in wide and deep V-shaped construction trenches and posts often penetrated the base (figure 2.15).

Deborah Joy and I (Joy 1989a) discovered the remains of the northeast bastion, Baluarte del Rosario, in 1988. Although the British levelled the bastion in 1767 as part of a fort expansion, the lower portion remained intact. Excavated remains of the northeast bastion include six faggots or fascines (bundles of bound sticks or twigs) along with six posts and 15 timbers that were part of the framework of the low platform for the cannons inside this large bastion (Joy 1989a: 72). The cannon platform framework remains are illustrated in figure 5.7. Levelling of the upper portion of the terrepleined bastion walls filled in the bastion center, burying the entire cannon platform framework under two to three feet of sand. Only 10 pieces of ceramics were recovered in the bastion fill: six Coarse Earthenware, three Mexican Red Painted, and one Mexico City Green on Cream.

In sum, short-lived Fort San Miguel, was hurriedly built in 1757 to encompass an existing community of over 600 people and about 87 structures. Although unusual in its asymmetrical shape, the fort stood ready to defend against her enemies with a terrepleined seawall and bastions engineered to repel a naval attack. The remaining curtain walls were constructed as a single line of large posts with elevated fighting decks designed to ward off land attacks. Most of the fort cannons were mounted on low ground-level platforms and fired through openings in the wall. However, two cannon emplacements on the seawall appear to have been elevated to fire over the fort wall. Although Fort San Miguel was modest by period standards, it was the only safe haven for the entire community. The British demolished and cleared much of Fort San Miguel de Panzacola in 1767 during their two decades of occupation of Florida. However, many of the subsurface components of the fort lie intact beneath the deposition of over two and a half centuries of continual occupation of downtown Pensacola.

Inside Fort San Miguel

There were about 87 buildings inside Fort San Miguel. In addition to detailed maps of the location and size of the structures, map legends contain significant information about architectural details and building functions, and these legends often identify the residents. The function of some military buildings often changed through time, which is also reflected in map legends. For example, the

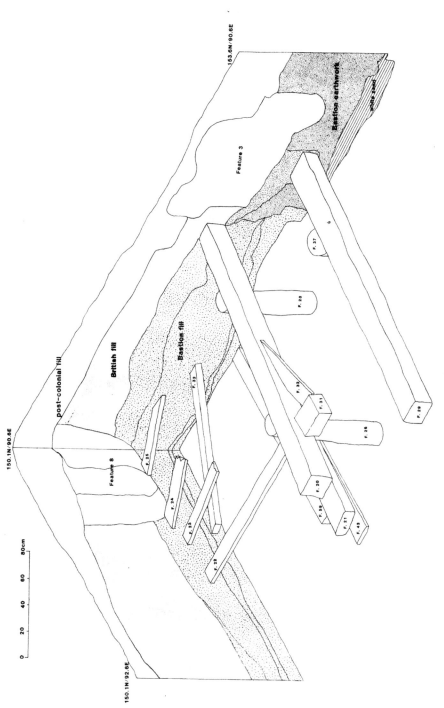

Figure 5.7. Presidio San Miguel, a 3-D drawing of wood support structure for cannon platform in Baluarte del Rosario, northeast bastion of Fort San Miguel. Courtesy of the Archaeology Institute, University of West Florida.

long structure on the north border of the plaza had three large internal sections used for five different purposes: barracks for forced laborers, officers' housing, resident housing, a hospital, and a galley or mess. Fortunately, a 1763 real estate document provides significant details about private property, including identification of the owner and descriptions of the use, construction, and value of all structures on the lot (see appendix VII, table VII.2).

The space enclosed within Fort San Miguel was divided into three general areas: a residential area of small cabins for married soldiers north of the central open plaza, large military buildings with differing purposes bordering the plaza, and a residential area ringing the central plaza and fort walls with large compounds for the highest-ranking residents along with the church and friary. As shown in figure 5.3, there are six residential compounds on the west and south sides of the central plaza. In addition, the large governor's compound is next to the east curtain wall, and in the southwest corner of the fort are compounds for the church, friary, and paymaster. Three of the occupants of the six residential compounds bordering the west and south sides of the plaza are known: the cavalry captain, commandant, and treasurer.

The detailed legend of the Ortíz-Feringan map reveals that the structures in the San Miguel presidio were constructed using timber framing with wood planks or cypress bark siding sometimes covered with a layer of clay, plaster, or lime. A few roofs were shingled, but most were covered with cypress bark. There were exceptions, however, such as the governor's residence, the powder magazine, the arsenal, and the long multipurpose structure on the north border of the plaza.

The largest residential compound inside the fort belonged to the governor and had seven buildings, including a residence, a kitchen with an attached bake oven, the original Punta Blanca warehouse with two internal offices, and a stable. The governor's household enjoyed the additional protection of two guardhouses, one just outside the compound's south entrance and the other next to the northeast corner of the compound. At the time of transfer to the British government, the governor's residence was described as a two-story, shingle-roofed house with a balcony, all in bad condition (Childers et al. 2007: 50). The Ortíz-Feringan map legend states that the house was 33 feet high with a stone foundation. Clinton Howard (1941: 371) describes the walls of the governor's house as filled with stone to about two feet above the surface, with clay and moss above that, covered with a coat of plaster on the exterior. The building also had a brick chimney. Howard (1941: 371) goes on to describe the floor of the second story as made of heavy timbers and wooden planks covered with two courses of bricks. He relates that the governor occupied one room on this floor and the adjutant major occupied the other. The first floor was used to store provisions and had two offices for the paymaster. Howard describes the attached kitchen as having a shingled roof and sides covered with cypress bark. Several workers lived and worked in the other structures within the governor's compound, including a master tailor, journeyman, silversmith, and shoemaker (Childers et al. 2007: 32).

Structures associated with gunpowder and weapons were made with very specific materials. According to the Ortíz-Feringan map legend (appendix VII, table VII.3), the powder magazine in the northwest corner of the fort was 22 by 20 feet and 13.8 feet high and made of stone. It had a brick roof with six tin drains and two wood doors covered with tin sheeting. The building also had a four-foot-high perimeter fence of mortared stone. The arsenal near the northwest corner of the plaza was also 13.8 feet high with a flat brick roof and walls of clay coated in lime.

In 1754–1755, Fort San Miguel's royal chapel and friary compound was one of the first structures engineer Feringan built in anticipation of the authorization that married soldiers would relocate their families from the island to the mainland (Worth 2013: 7). The church was 55 by 25 feet in size and facing east with a gallery over the doorway (Childers et al. 2007: 32). The 1763 Ortíz-Feringan map legend states that the church was made of cypress boards with a cypress bark roof. The friary building was just behind the west end of the church building. It was a rectangular structure about 19.5 by 46.8 feet in size and oriented north-south.

Three buildings on the plaza were designated as troop barracks. Two were parallel on the east end of the plaza, oriented north-south, and approximately 60 by 14 feet in size according to measurements from the map. The third was a longer structure (50 by 14 feet) with two internal rooms lining the southwest edge of the plaza. The 1763 Ortíz-Feringan map legend describes these buildings as made of cypress boards with cypress bark roofing. As noted above, the long, narrow structure bordering the north side of the plaza was 192 by 14 feet in size and divided into three large rooms. At the time the map was made, two rooms were used for laborers and officers, and the eastern room was used for the hospital. The map legend describes that the exterior of the two rooms housing the laborers and officers had walls of clay finished with lime and was roofed with cypress bark; it is likely that the entire structure had the same exterior treatment. There were four guardhouses inside the fort located in or near corners of the fort and close to the gates. The 1763 Ortíz-Feringan map legend describes the guardhouse as being near the northeast corner of the governor's compound and having walls of clay coated with lime, whereas the others were covered with only cypress bark. The legend also says that there was a room for the duty officer and prisoners in each guardhouse.

The area north of the central plaza was crowded with 40 small huts arranged in three rows and designated as housing for married soldiers and their families. The huts were built after the 1760 hurricane destroyed the two previously built quarters for the infantry and an open-sided shed used for San Miguel's convict laborers. The map legend also states that the small quarters were 8.2 feet high and had cypress bark for siding and roofing, but some are noted as having wood shingles (Childers et al. 2007: 34).

In sum, the interior of Fort San Miguel was organized into three areas: a central plaza/parade ground; long, narrow buildings bordering this plaza and serving a variety of military functions; and residential compounds surrounding the parade ground on the east, west, and south sides. North of the parade ground were rows of 40 small cabins for married soldiers. Other than the powder magazine and arsenal, structures were made of wood with timber framing and sided with cypress boards or sheets of cypress bark, and some were finished with plaster or clay. The roofs of almost all buildings were covered with sheets of cypress bark or, rarely, wooden shingles. The powder magazine and arsenal were fireproof and secure as they were built of stone and had flat brick roofs and heavy tin-lined doors. The interior of Fort San Miguel was a crowded place with hundreds of people living and working there.

Archaeological Investigations inside Fort San Miguel

As described earlier in this chapter, many archaeological projects have been conducted inside the walls of Fort San Miguel. This location lies in the heart of downtown Pensacola and has been continuously occupied since 1740. Luckily, paved streets and parking lots along with the construction of many low-impact buildings on piers or concrete slabs have preserved some of the remains of the San Miguel presidio. In the areas archaeologically investigated to date, the midden associated with the San Miguel community is largely compromised, but many features remain intact. While later materials are often intruded into the upper part of features, this part was excavated separately to preserve the integrity of the remainder.

All or part of 44 features inside Fort San Miguel are associated with the San Miguel occupation. The features were excavated as part of several UWF investigations since 1988 (Benchley 2007a, 2007b; Benchley et al. 2007; Bense 1995, 1999; Joy 1989a). Reanalysis of the early collections has resulted in some changes in component assignments of features, especially in the pre-2007 publications and reports by Benchley, Bense, and Joy. These changes must be taken into consideration if the reader chooses to use the original reports. Our understanding of early Spanish artifact assemblages and the historical record continues to expand and improve, and as is true in all scholarly fields, this understanding often produces new interpretations of previous information.

All of the archaeological projects inside the fort have been in the southwest area. Features inside the fort have been organized into three groups: the Ullate residential compound, pre–Fort San Miguel fence network, and general Fort San Miguel. All feature numbers, associations, functions, and total contents used in this analysis are presented in appendix VI, table VI.1. Using the latest projections of the buildings on historic maps, 22 features are within or tangent to the residential compound of cavalry Captain Don Luis Joseph de Ullate, who was the only resident for four years (1759–1763). Nine features are part of a network of fence lines that preceded the building of Fort San Miguel in 1757. The remaining 11 features are scattered in the southwest fort area and are associated with the presidio in general.

Captain Ullate's Residential Compound

Don Luis Joseph de Ullate was captain of a new cavalry unit established at Presidio San Miguel in 1759 to provide quick, mobile protection for the outlying settlements, including the Apalachee and Yamasee mission villages, cattle haciendas, brick kiln, and other Spanish interests. Ullate's residential lot was in the southwest corner of the fort and second in size only to the governor's compound on the opposite corner of the plaza. According to the 1763 inventory of unsold houses in Pensacola (appendix VII, table VII.2), the Ullate compound had a perimeter fence of pitch pine posts enclosing four wooden buildings: a residence, kitchen, storehouse, and second smaller house (figure 5.8). All of the structures had roofs of cypress bark sheets. The main residence was two stories and had plastered walls, a wood floor, a loft of boards, a second-story balcony, and two apartments on the upper floor. The small house had cypress bark siding.

UWF has conducted three archaeological investigations in the projected area of the Ullate residential compound (Bense 1995, 1999; Benchley 2007a). According to the latest projection of the 1763 Ortíz-Feringan map on the modern landscape (figure 5.8), all features were located behind the main residence in the center and along the east and west edges of the back yard. Archaeological features include three barrel wells, a cool storage facility, five wall trench segments, nine refuse pits, two postholes, and two posts.

Two of the barrel wells and the cool storage facility were clustered on the east edge of the compound (figures 5.8 and 5.9). Only the very base of the earliest well shaft was still intact; the rest was destroyed during the construction of an adjacent second well. As Benchley (2007b: 35) describes, the lower half of the second barrel shaft and most of the lowest barrel were still in situ. The

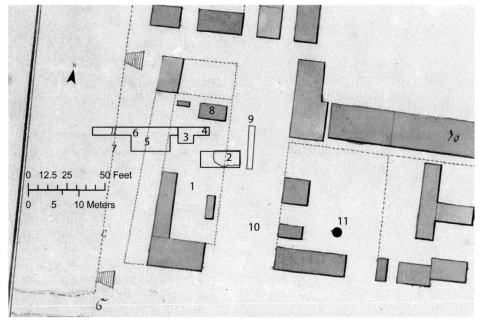

Figure 5.8. Location of Presidio San Miguel archaeological areas and some features in the southwest area of Fort San Miguel: *1,* Ullate residential compound; *2,* cluster of two barrel wells and cool storage facility; *3,* northern barrel well; *4,* outbuilding foundations; *5,* Ullate compound fence line; *6,* porcelain pit; *7,* west curtain wall of Fort San Miguel; *8,* probable Ullate kitchen; *9,* salvaged brick foundation; *10,* open walkway; *11,* Zaragoza Street refuse pit (Ortíz and Feringan 1763a, 1763b).

barrel base had holes drilled into it for water flow. As shown in appendix VI, table VI.1, the second well construction pit and well shaft (Feature 136) yielded a considerable amount of cultural material (1,618 counted items and 51.9 kg of weighed material). The second construction pit and barrel shaft fill both have TPQ dates of 1750 based on the presence of Aranama Polychrome Majolica and Brittany Blue and White Faience ceramics. A third barrel well was 18 feet northwest of the previous two wells in the center of the Ullate courtyard. It has a construction pit TPQ date of 1740, indicating it was probably earlier than the two wells to the south. Approximately a third of the construction pit of the northern well (Feature 164) was excavated, but it contained only 166 counted items and 6.4 kg of weighed material. This comparatively low amount of material supports the contention that this well was constructed during the earliest years of San Miguel's occupation before significant surface material had accumulated. It is unusual for three wells to be within just 20 feet of each other. At least part of the reason may be the presence of a thick muck/peat layer with cypress knees at the top of the permanent water table, which likely tainted the water soon after the installation of the wells. We encountered this muck/peat deposit with its brown, malodorous water during the placement of the well points in and around the wells.

A third large feature intersected the construction pit of the younger of the two southern barrel wells. At the base was a rectangular frame of timbers measuring four by six feet and extending about half a foot into the permanent water table (figure 5.9). Benchley (2007b: 35) describes that the lower portions of the corner posts, the side-by-side posts along the east wall, and the crossbeam of the floor support were all waterlogged and preserved in situ. From this evidence, Benchley concludes that it originally was a rectangular shaft lined with wood, extending into the permanent water table from the colonial ground surface. A large iron fastener and iron staining along the west edge of the shaft suggests that at least the sides of the wooden shaft were protected with metal sheeting. Benchley (2007b: 35) interprets this construction as a cool storage facility. This amenity was likely used to store perishable food, wine, and other provisions used in the nearby Ullate kitchen and household.

After the four large facilities described above were filled in, the area was used for refuse pits. Six pits, often intersecting, were dug into the top of the filled-in facilities and were relatively shallow (0.3–0.9 feet deep). Three were wide, ranging from 4.0 to 5.2 feet. Two of the refuse pits (Features 69 and 79) were stuffed with kitchen refuse (figure 5.10) and contained 2,218 counted

Figure 5.9. Presidio San Miguel, barrel wells and cool storage facility in Ullate back yard inside Fort San Miguel: *1,* base of earliest well shaft; *2,* second well construction pit and bottom barrel in situ; *3,* cool storage facility. Courtesy of the Archaeology Institute, University of West Florida.

Figure 5.10. Presidio San Miguel, in situ artifacts in two partially excavated intersecting refuse pits in Ullate back yard excavated into the top of previously filled-in wells and cool storage facility. Courtesy of the Archaeology Institute, University of West Florida.

items and 55.6 kg of weighed material (appendix VI, table VI.1). Another refuse pit was 20 feet north of this cluster, adjacent to the kitchen building, and contained several unusual items, including a complete alligator skull, a complete lower carapace of a sea turtle, and fitting pieces of a large porcelain bowl (figure 5.11).

After the early northern well was filled in, wall trenches from a rectangular or square structure were excavated into the well fill (Benchley 2007b: 41). Later, after this structure was demolished, a line of single posts set in a small trench was constructed there, probably serving as a fence line. Small posts measuring 0.4–0.6 feet in diameter were set side by side and had pointed ends that penetrated the base of the wall trench in which they were set. About 18 feet west of the northern well was a longer and larger north-south fence line wall trench in which all the posts also penetrated the base. This wall trench closely corresponds with the projection of the Ullate compound perimeter fence, shown in figure 5.8.

A large artifact assemblage was contained in the features associated with

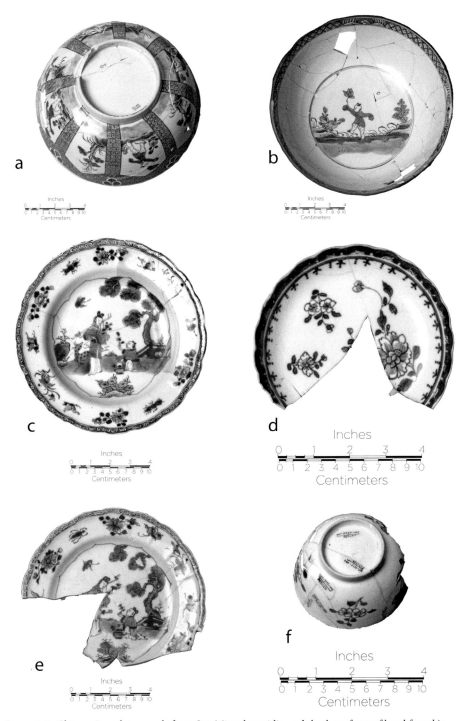

Figure 5.11. Chinese Porcelain vessels from San Miguel presidio: *a–b,* both surfaces of bowl found in Ullate refuse pit with alligator skull (93F-400–83); *c–f,* porcelain tableware in small pit near Ullate's fence line [*c,* complete plate (06F-5817–001); *d,* small bowl (06F-4634–001); *e,* partial porcelain plate (06F-5817–004); *f,* cup (06F-5550–005)]. Courtesy of the Archaeology Institute, University of West Florida.

the Ullate residential compound, totaling 6,090 counted items and 205.6 kg of weighed material. Almost all of the cultural material (94.5% of counted and 90.6% of weighed) was recovered from the concentration of six refuse pits and the four large, deep amenities. The wall trenches and posts contained very little cultural material.

Details of the artifact assemblage are provided in appendix VI, table VI.2. Architecture and Kitchen items make up 91.9 percent of counted artifacts, but the Activities and Architecture groups dominate by weight (91.4%). Metal is the largest artifact class by count (27.0%), and Modified Flora (wood posts and boards) and Building Material are the largest classes by weight. Almost all the metal consists of nails or fragments of large, deteriorated iron bands from around the second well barrel. Bricks, mortar, plaster, and tiles make up the building materials. The 1763 inventory of unsold houses states that the Ullate residence was made of wood, but the recovery of bricks, mortar, and tiles indicates that it had at least some masonry features, such as fireplaces, decorative tiles, or brick floors. Some of the recovered plaster has lathe marks and is painted and finished, corroborating the inventory description of plastered interior walls. Abundant nails and spikes support the use of wood for framing and boards.

Ceramics recovered from the Ullate compound features are 83.3 percent Euro-American and 16.7 percent Native American by count. Most of the Euro-American sherds by count are Other Coarse Earthenware (39.3%), Majolica (20.8%), Stoneware (16.2%), and Delft (12.5%). Faience, Porcelain, Redware, Creamware, and Earthenware are present in small amounts. Of the 726 typable ceramics, the most abundant Euro-American types are White Salt Glazed Stoneware (12.5%), El Morro (11.3%), Lead Glazed Coarse Earthenware (10.5%), and Plain Majolica (10.5%). There are 50 other ceramic types, each making up 7.0 percent or less of the assemblage. The classification of Euro-American ceramic types by wares and class is presented in appendix VI, table VI.2. Almost three quarters (72.5%) of the Other Coarse Earthenware by count are El Morro (37.6%) or Lead Glazed (34.9%). There are 14 additional types of Other Coarse Earthenware, but each is 7.8 percent or less of this ceramic class. Of the Majolicas, Plain (46.9%), Puebla Blue on White (31.5%), and Abo Polychrome (9.3%) are the most frequent. Most Stoneware are types of White Salt Glazed (90.1%). Almost all the Delft is either Plain (45.9%) or Blue on White (45.0%). Faience is primarily Plain (70.6%), but there are also single pieces of a drug jar, Moustiers Blue on White, and Polychrome. There are 29 pieces of typable Porcelain, primarily Chinese. Also present in small numbers are Glazed Redware, Clouded Creamware, and Mexican Indian Earthenware.

Over half of the Native American ceramic pieces in the Ullate lot features by weight are sand tempered (53.6%), followed by grog (17.6%), grit (16.1%), and shell tempering (9.9%), as listed in appendix VI, table VI.2. Of the 168 typable sherds, the most frequent ceramic types by weight are Sand Tempered Plain (21.6%), Marsh Island, *variety* Marsh Island (13.8%), Grog Tempered Plain (11.1%), and Grit Tempered Plain (11.0%). Plain surfaces are frequent (47.2%), and the surfaces of the remaining sherds are slipped red or brown, red painted or filmed, incised, or burnished. There is a variety of formal types with a few sherds each, including Chattahoochee Roughened, *variety* Chattahoochee; Marsh Island Incised, *variety* Marsh Island; Lamar Check Stamped, *variety* Leon; Mission Red, *variety* Kasita; Pensacola Red; and Pensacola Mission Red.

There is a large amount of faunal remains (40.4 kg) in the Ullate lot features, primarily in the cluster of six refuse pits on the east edge of the lot. Oyster shells and mammal bones are the dominant foods by weight in this collection. When shells are eliminated, mammals make up 29.6 percent of the meat sources, consisting mainly of cow, deer, and pig. There is a wide range of other animal food, including alligator, sea turtle, turkey, chicken, shark, gar, and mullet. This amount and variety of meat sources, paired with the high quantities of mammal remains, is probably a reflection of the privileged economic status and rank of Captain Ullate's household.

Aside from the relative high-quality food and the quality residence that afforded security and privacy within a crowded and bustling fort, other distinctive artifacts from the Ullate residential lot reflect Ullate's upper socioeconomic status. These items include jewelry, delicate stemmed glassware, buttons of bone, brass, and pewter, and a variety of metal buckles for clothes, belts, and shoes. Other interesting and indicative artifacts include a metal canteen, a nib for a writing pen, and a faience drug jar. In the Kitchen group, there are more benchmarks of Ullate's comfortable economic status, such as porcelain ceramics and glassware.

In sum, archaeological excavations at Captain Ullate's residential compound near the west gate of Fort San Miguel revealed four large amenities undocumented in the historical record: three barrel wells and a cool storage chamber. These amenities were concentrated in the back yard of the Ullate compound. After the wells and the cool storage chamber were filled, this area of the yard was used for refuse disposal and small structures. The archaeological assemblage from the Ullate lot features is large, with Building Material, Architecture, and Kitchen items making up most of the assemblage. The materials reveal that the residence had glass windows and brick elements that were likely fireplaces and hearths. The residence was also kept cleaner, cooler, and more comfortable than others because of its smooth, plastered, and painted walls. Materially, a wide range of artifacts reflected Ullate's high socioeconomic status in the community.

Captain Ullate certainly enjoyed some of the best food, housing, and other comforts that most residents of Presidio San Miguel de Panzacola did not.

Pre–Fort San Miguel Fences

Archaeological investigations revealed that Captain Ullate was not the first person to use what would become the southwest corner of Fort San Miguel. Both the west perimeter fence of Ullate's compound and the west wall trench of Fort San Miguel cut into an earlier network of small, perpendicular wall trenches, indicating that they existed before 1757 when the fort wall was constructed. The layout of the trenches consists of three long east-west sections and shorter north-south sections. The longest documented wall trench is an east-west section 35 feet long that continues to the west (Benchley 2007b: 45). The wall trenches are small, only about a foot wide, conical in profile, and have uneven bases. All contain mottled soil, apparently from pulling the posts. There were some impressions of small, pointed, side-by-side posts that were once in place, indicating the network was likely a line of small fence posts (Benchley 2007b: 45). Impressions of pulled fence posts were documented in all the fence wall trench segments in this network. The small size of the areas enclosed supports an interpretation that the fences probably enclosed vegetable gardens or animal pens.

Very little cultural material was contained in the fill of the fence line trenches (402 counted items and 3.1 kg of weighed material, as shown in appendix VI, table VI.1). While sparse cultural material supports an early date for the installation of the network of fence enclosures, the presence of four pieces of San Elizario Polychrome Majolica with a beginning date of 1750 indicates they likely were built in the post-1752 hurricane transition to San Miguel. Viewing the assemblage from all the fence trenches as a whole, Building Material makes up almost half (48.4%) the weight of the artifact classes, followed by Metal (17.1%) and Fauna (11.12%). Glass is the most abundant artifact class by count (26.7%), followed by Euro-American ceramics (21.8%). Most identifiable glass is from bottles, especially wine bottles (37.8%), but there are nine pieces of very thin glass. The most abundant artifact groups are Kitchen (61.0%) by count and Architecture (78.7%) by weight. The Euro-American ceramic sherds are primarily Other Coarse Earthenware (39.3%), Majolica (21.4%), and Stoneware (16.7%).

General Fort San Miguel Features

Thirteen additional features from the Fort San Miguel era occupation are scattered throughout the southwest area of the fort. Three notable features are a section of a large salvaged brick foundation with a tabby footer, a large refuse pit, and a small pit filled with porcelain. The seven other scattered features—a small refuse pit, five postholes, and the lower courses of a brick pier—contained very little cultural material. The three notable features are discussed below.

Salvaged Brick Foundation with Tabby Footer

According to the latest projections of the 1763 Ortíz-Feringan transfer map of Fort San Miguel, the architectural remains of part of an extremely large salvaged brick foundation with a tabby footer lie in a 40-foot-wide walkway about twelve feet east of the Ullate compound perimeter fence (see figure 5.8). The remains of the original construction trench of the brick foundation are six feet wide, half a foot deep, and rectangular in cross section with a flat base (figure 5.12). A layer

Figure 5.12. Presidio San Miguel, salvaged brick foundation with a tabby footer in six-foot-wide rectangular construction trench: *a,* construction trench; *b,* tabby footer; *c,* salvaged brick wall foundation. Courtesy of the Archaeology Institute, University of West Florida.

of oyster shell tabby 0.2–0.3 feet thick was poured on the base of the construction trench on which bricks were laid to stabilize the weight of the large wall. We do not know whether the wall had only a brick foundation or whether it was wholly or partially made of bricks. This is the only brick foundation and only tabby footer discovered at any of the West Florida presidio sites.

The construction trench fill contained a considerable amount of material (1,682 counted items and 33.1 kg of weighed material), indicating that an artifact-rich midden had accumulated in the immediate area when the wall was constructed. Unfortunately, no historic maps of Fort San Miguel, either Spanish or British, show a building at or near this wall trench location. The artifact assemblage in the five-foot section excavated of the salvaged wall clearly reflects the brick salvaging process, as Building Material makes up 93.4 percent of the assemblage. Brick fragments and mortar constitute 89.2 percent of the Architecture materials. The salvaged wall foundation contained eight datable Euro-American sherds, including one piece of Transfer Printed Creamware (1762) and one piece of Fruit and Vegetable (1755). The salvaged foundation contained a metal hinge, almost a hundred nail fragments, and a few other artifacts, including almost 50 pieces of broken wine bottles and part of the bone framework of a hand fan.

This building and its purpose remain something of a mystery. As of this writing, the best estimate is that the structure probably was built in 1754–1755 as part of the transition of the community from Santa Rosa Island to San Miguel. During these two transition years, many large public buildings were constructed in preparation for the community's move from the island, including barracks, a church, hospital, warehouse, commandant's residence, and new guardhouse. Maps of this phase of San Miguel have not yet been located. The salvaged brick foundation could have been one of these buildings or another structure not mentioned in the documents. Regardless of the initial construction date or its purpose for the San Miguel community, this substantial building was demolished prior to September 1763 as it is not on any of the maps made that year. Future research will, hopefully, shed more light on this unique, undocumented structure.

Zaragoza Street Refuse Pit

Another remarkable feature inside Fort San Miguel was discovered during this writing (2019) in an ongoing project in downtown Pensacola. Gulf Power, an electric utility company, is excavating trenches throughout historic downtown Pensacola for new underground electrical lines, and UWF archaeologists are performing cultural resource management compliance for this project. A portion of an unusually large refuse pit from the San Miguel occupation was discovered early in the project, and processing of the materials was expedited for inclusion in this publication.

On the latest projection of the 1763 map of the interior of Fort San Miguel, this refuse pit would have been in the center of an enclosed residential compound on the southwest corner of the plaza, across the walkway from Ullate's residential lot and across the street from the presidio church, shown in figure 5.8. The resident of this compound is not identified on any of the 1763–1764 map legends or in the historical records, but the householder must have been of very high rank or socioeconomic status to be given quarters in this privileged location.

Only part of the refuse pit was exposed in the utility trench, so the feature's true dimensions are unknown; the portion that was exposed measured six feet. The deepest excavated portion of the trash pit was just over four feet; however, the true base of the pit was not reached as it continued into the water table and project parameters did not allow further excavation. Even without being able to excavate the refuse pit in its entirety, we know that the Zaragoza Street refuse pit is the largest of those encountered thus far at San Miguel or at any of the other West Florida presidio sites.

The material recovered from the refuse pit included 1,520 counted items and 18.3 kg of weighed material (see appendix VI, table VI.3). There is an exceptional amount of faunal material (7.1 kg), making Fauna the largest artifact class by weight (39.6%); however, 61.1 percent is oyster shells. When oyster and other shells are removed, there is 2.8 kg of bone material, most of which is from mammals (68.2%), especially cow and deer. Pig and dog are also present. Fish make up 10.9 percent and include catfish, sheepshead/drum, mullet, and shark. There is also a small amount of chicken and turtle. As a whole, these are local sources of meat, and the food remains in this pit were probably raised, hunted, or caught in the immediate area.

Most of the materials are in the Kitchen and Architecture groups (table 5.1). Architecture-related items make up 53.3 percent and Kitchen-related materials are 42.5 percent of the weighed items. Kitchen group materials are primarily food bones (62.7%) and ceramics (27.2%) by weight. Architecture artifacts are primarily bricks and ladrillos along with small amounts of daub, mortar, and marked and finished plaster. There are also 148 nails and spikes.

The trash pit yielded 1,002 ceramic sherds, of which 80.8 percent are Euro-American and only 19.2 percent are Native American (table 5.1). Almost half of the Euro-American ceramics by count are Other Coarse Earthenware (46.5%), and 36.9 percent are Majolica. There are six other ceramic classes, but they each make up 6.5 percent or less. Of the 724 typable Euro-American sherds, the most abundant are El Morro (30.9%), Plain Majolica (15.3%), and Puebla Blue

Table 5.1. Artifact assemblage in Zaragoza Street refuse pit in Presidio San Miguel

Artifact Classes[a]	Count	%	Weight (g)	%
Fauna	-	-	7,074.0	39.6%
Building Material	186	12.3%	3,801.7	21.3%
Ceramics Euro-American	810	53.4%	3,104.1	17.4%
Metal	163	10.7%	2,349.6	13.1%
Ceramics Native American	192	12.7%	999.0	5.6%
Flora	-	-	283.4	1.6%
Glass	144	9.5%	142.3	0.8%
Lithics	3	0.2%	73.9	0.4%
Totals	1,498		17,828.0	
Artifact Groups[b]	**Count**	**%**	**Weight (g)**	**%**
Architecture	334	22.4%	5,263.4	53.3%
Kitchen	1,122	75.4%	4,200.0	42.5%
Activities	5	0.3%	360.9	3.7%
Personal	12	0.8%	29.1	0.3%
Tobacco	12	0.8%	16.3	0.2%
Arms	3	0.2%	4.5	[c]
Clothing	1	0.1%	3.2	[c]
Totals	1,489		9,877.4	
Euro-American Ceramic Wares and Classes	**Count**	**%**	**Weight (g)**	**%**
Other Coarse Earthenware	377	46.5%	2,302.7	74.1%
Majolica	299	36.9%	437.1	14.1%
Delft	53	6.5%	171.3	5.5%
Redware	31	3.8%	46.5	1.5%
Faience	17	2.1%	46.2	1.5%
Stoneware	11	1.4%	45.5	1.5%
Earthenware	7	0.9%	30.8	1.0%
Porcelain	3	0.4%	7.7	0.2%
Totals	798		3,087.8	
Native American Ceramic Tempers[b]				
Bone Charcoal Fiber Grog Shell	70	36.5%	582.8	58.3%
Sand	50	26.0%	181.1	18.1%
Grit	33	17.2%	83.9	8.4%
Shell	33	17.2%	60.9	6.1%
Grog	3	1.6%	4.3	0.4%
Mica	3	1.6%	86.0	8.6%
Totals	192		999.0	

[a] No Other
[b] No Unspecified
[c] Less than 0.1 percent.

on White Majolica (14.2%). There are 27 other ceramic types, but each is less than 7.0 percent of the total assemblage. Within the ceramic wares and classes, El Morro makes up 69.6 percent of the Other Coarse Earthenware, followed by Mexican Red Painted (15.2%) and Lead Glazed (10.9%). Most Majolicas are either Plain (41.1%) or Puebla Blue on White (38.1%). Almost all the Delft is Plain (54.7%) or Blue on White (39.6%). Stoneware is low in this feature, only 11 sherds. The complete quantified list of ceramic types is provided in appendix VI, table VI.3. An interesting aspect of the tableware in this refuse pit is the presence of many cross-mendable pieces from the same vessel, including several dainty majolica cups (*tazas*), small bowls (*escudillos*), and thin, white, glazed stoneware mugs. A fragment of a Delft pitcher and a large El Morro basin fragment with handles were also in this refuse pit.

Three Euro-American ceramic types in the Zaragoza refuse pit provide a TPQ date of post-1750 for this feature: 11 pieces of Aranama Polychrome Majolica (Deagan 1987: 87), one piece of Brittany Blue on White, and one piece of Provence Yellow on White Faience (Walthall 1991; Waselkov and Walthall 2002). The 1750 TPQ date reveals that this refuse pit was used by the population of Santa Rosa that moved to the mainland.

There are several unusual ceramic artifacts in the Zaragoza Street refuse pit artifact assemblage that warrant special attention. Two are fragments of small ceramic animal figurines made of coarse earthenware (figure 5.13). One fragment appears to be the head, neck, and shoulders of a horse, while the other is the lower back, rear, and stub of a tail of perhaps a dog or pig. Both are made of similar reddish buff clay paste. Both figurines are well made and hard fired, probably from the same batch of sand-tempered clay. No mold lines are present.

Other unusual ceramic pieces in this feature appear to be parts of two possible altarpieces used in home shrines. The altarpieces hold or surround special objects that held personal or religious significance to members of the household. One of the altarpiece fragments is about half of what appears to be a circular ring base and over half of a platform (4.5 inches in diameter) with a slightly depressed center (figure 5.13b). The outer edge of the platform has points, giving the impression of a celestial crown or the rays of the sun. Attached to the underside of the platform is a tall ring base 1.6 inches tall with a coarsely crenulated or pinched edge set 0.5–0.6 inches from the notched edge. The clay is micaceous, sand tempered, light gray in color, and quite hard. The second altarpiece is represented by less than half of its platform and has the same paste and notched edge suggestive of sunrays. The craftsmanship of these pieces is poor as they are asymmetrical and uneven, but the paste, firing, and shape are unique. A total of 14 more sherds of this grayish brown, hard fired

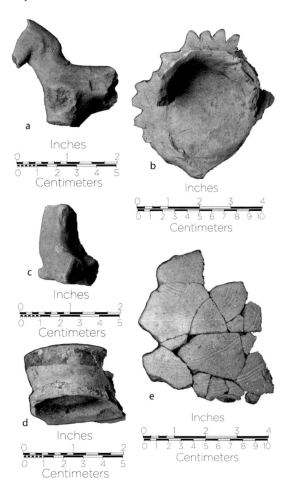

Figure 5.13. Presidio San Miguel artifacts in Zaragoza Street refuse pit: *a*, horse figurine (18N-0920–002); *b*, home altar display (18N-0918–001); *c*, animal rear (18N-0912–007); *d*, Guadalajara Polychrome pedestalled cup fragment (18N-0917–001); *e*, Kemper Combed, *variety* Pawticfaw mended sherds (18N-0912–002). Courtesy of the Archaeology Institute, University of West Florida.

clay were found in this trash pit, but they do not mend to either base or each other. The two potential altarpieces are unique to the West Florida presidios. A review of accessible literature yielded no similar items from other Spanish borderland sites, and home colonial altar-related artifacts remain understudied.

Small clay figurines have been recovered from only one other site in Spanish West Florida: Presidio Santa Rosa. As discussed in chapter 4, there are 27 figurines for which the represented figure could be determined: six are animals, 20 are humans, and one is a human and animal (Furlong 2008: 58). Almost all the figurines were made of coarse earthenware, but two were made of the distinctive Guadalajara paste and one was made of ivory. All but one figurine from Santa Rosa were hand molded, and one was hollow with mold lines. The two animal figurines from the San Miguel Zaragoza Street refuse pit fit well with the figurine assemblage from Santa Rosa. Similar small ceramic figurines of people and animals have been recovered from Presidio San Agustín in 1720–1740 contexts (Deagan 2002: 300). In addition, more small figurines similar to those recovered from the Santa Rosa and San Miguel presidio sites have recently been recovered in the early eighteenth-century San Agustín presidio context (Andrea White, personal communication 2019). Home shrines and altars for figurines of humans, animals, or saints have a long history in Mexico, and they continue to be popular today (Gutiérrez et al. 1997; Hammond 1989).

Also noteworthy in the refuse pit are the 11 pieces of Guadalajara Polychrome, including the lower portion and base of a small pedestalled cup, shown in figure 5.13. The small cup is 0.54 inches deep and has a flaring base with a red strip painted around its rim. Although the cup is broken, the pedestal is intact and is about one inch high. Guadalajara Polychrome is known to have been produced in Mexico in the eighteenth century and was used for bowls, lidded bowls, and novelty figurines. The vessels also were known to have special properties that were beneficial to the complexion (Deagan 1987: 46).

There are also 192 pieces of Native American vessels in this feature. As detailed in table 5.1, the most abundant temper (58.3% by weight) is present in 70 sherds tempered with a combination of bone, charcoal, fiber, grog, and shell, followed by sand temper (18.1%), and grit temper (8.4%). The distinctive multiple temper type is diagnostic of the Addis ceramic series. There are 63 pieces of the Addis series type Kemper Combed, *variety* Pawticfaw which has four parallel incisions applied simultaneously with a pronged implement (Little et al. 2016: 290). All 63 sherds of the variety Pawticfaw were from a single broken vessel, and many of the sherds mended together (figure 5.13). There are also seven pieces of Addis Plain, *variety* Addis. The presence of the multi-tempered Addis series at San Miguel is unique in the Spanish West Florida presidio communities. Kemper Comber, *variety* Pawticfaw, was originally defined by John Blitz (1985: 73, 1993: 5) and refined by Keith Little and colleagues (2016). This particular ceramic type is associated with the Choctaw in Mississippi thought to date to the late eighteenth- and nineteenth-centuries (Little et al. 2016; Voss and Blitz 1988: 137). A recent seriation of post-Choctaw ceramics by Little and colleagues (2020: 248) suggests that Kemper Combed pottery appeared sometime around 1760, but the authors lacked evidence to confirm this date from their research on Choctaw sites in Mississippi. The presence of Kemper Combed, *variety* Pawticfaw in the closed context refuse pit with a *terminus post quem* of 1750 and a *terminus ante quem* of 1763 inside Spanish Fort San Miguel in Pensacola confirms its appearance between 1750 and 1763. The vessel of Kemper Combed *variety* Pawticfaw in the Spanish refuse pit must have been imported through direct or indirect trade with the French via their Choctaw trade in Mississippi, especially at Fort Tombecbé. The remaining Native-made ceramics in this refuse pit have surfaces that are either plain, burnished, painted red, roughened, complicated stamped, or incised.

The Activity-related artifacts in this assemblage are almost all metal, and they include a barrel band, strap, container, handle, and lead weight. There are almost no Arms items (only three gunflint pieces) in the trash pit. One brass button is the only Clothing artifact. There are only twelve kaolin pipe fragments and one piece of personal jewelry.

In sum, the available portion of the Zaragoza Street refuse pit assemblage was only a small part of the very large pit with a TPQ date of 1750. It was full of material from Kitchen activities, especially ceramics and food bones. The assemblage contains several noteworthy items, particularly two small ceramic figurines and two possible altarpiece fragments that were likely part of a household shrine. The dainty pedestalled cup of Guadalajara Polychrome is also remarkable. The Indian-made pottery assemblage also had surprises, specifically the presence of the late Choctaw pottery type Kemper Comber, *variety* Pawticfaw. Its presence in a feature that dates from 1750 to 1763 provides the earliest date for this type.

Porcelain Pit

Another notable feature inside the fort was located between Ullate's residential compound fence and the west wall of Fort San Miguel. It was a small refuse pit but contained 46 pieces of Chinese porcelain and very little else. The pieces mended into four vessels: a large plate, shallow bowl, teacup, and saucer (figure 5.11c–f). The concentration of 46 fragments of porcelain in this small pit is unique at the West Florida presidio sites. Both the quantity and pristine condition of the porcelain fragments suggests that the four vessels were broken at the same time and disposed of soon afterward. Datable items in this pit include one sherd each of Jackfield and White Salt Glazed stoneware, which set 1740 as the TPQ date of this pit. The few other artifacts excavated from the pit include three pieces of a barrel band, five nails, a part of an iron knife, and small fragments of bricks and mortar that likely were accidentally included from the surrounding midden in the pit backfill. Although there is no direct connection with Captain Ullate, the location of a pit full of expensive and unused but broken porcelain vessels just outside his residential compound suggests that they could have originated from his residence.

Summary of the Archaeological Assemblage from inside Fort San Miguel

All or part of 44 closed features are associated with the San Miguel occupation. Groups of features are associated with a pre-1757 fence network and the 1759–1763 residential lot of Captain Ullate. Other features are comfortably associated with the general San Miguel occupation. The total artifact assemblage from all the San Miguel features inside the fort is quite large: 10,927 counted items and 317.1 kg of weighed material. As shown in table 5.2, most of the assemblage by weight was recovered from the Ullate lot features (64.8%) and the general Fort San Miguel features in the southwest area of the fort (34.2%).

An analysis of the artifact classes reveals an unusually high amount of Modified Flora (62.2 kg) from the large waterlogged timbers and posts of the cool storage facility's framework and the waterlogged wooden barrel, which together make up 96.1 percent of that artifact class. When the posts and timbers are removed from the assemblage calculations, Modified Flora is the *smallest* class in the assemblage, making up only 0.7 percent, which is typical of the assemblages from the other two presidio locations on Pensacola Bay. With the waterlogged timbers and barrel staves removed from the analysis, Building Material makes up just over half the material classes by weight (51.7%), followed by Fauna (21.7%) and Metal (13.5%). The significant weight of the metal artifacts in this assemblage is primarily due to the iron barrel bands in the second barrel well.

Of the artifact groups, Architecture (72.5%) and Activities (19.3%) are greatest by weight. The weight of architectural materials is usually high as a result of the heaviness of building materials such as bricks and iron fasteners. However, the Activities artifact group is substantial (47.3 kg) because of the many wooden barrel pieces. There are very few Arms artifacts (N=63), and of these, 50 are pieces of shot and the remainder are gunflint fragments.

Ceramics make up 22.1 percent of the counted materials from inside the fort. Of the 2,357 sherds, 82.4 percent are Euro-American and 17.6 percent are Native American. As shown in table 5.2, Other Coarse Earthenware is the most frequent Euro-American ceramic class by count (41.7%), followed by Majolica (26.8%), Stoneware (9.7%), and Delft (9.4%). Porcelain (5.0%), Faience (3.1%), and Redware (3.0%) are present in low quantities. The appearance of nine Creamware sherds is a sign of the lateness of the San Miguel occupation as well as the presence of resident British traders, which is discussed in detail in the following section. The proportion of Porcelain by weight (14.5%) is high for the West Florida Spanish presidio sites and is explained by the recovery of five almost-complete, large porcelain vessels that were broken into almost 100

Table 5.2. Artifact assemblage inside Fort San Miguel

Inside the Fort Totals	Count	%	Weight (g)	%
Pre-Fort Fence Line Network	402	3.7%	3,146.9	1.0%
Ullate Residential Compound	6,090	55.7%	205,614.8	64.8%
General Southwest Fort San Miguel	4,435	40.6%	108,307.9	34.2%
Totals	10,927		317,069.6	
Artifact Classes[a]	**Count**	**%**	**Weight (g)**	**%**
Building Material	3,800	35.6%	126,636.7	51.7%
Fauna	311	2.9%	53,055.5	21.7%
Metal	2,072	19.4%	33,127.9	13.5%
Ceramics Euro-American	1,943	18.2%	10,569.5	4.3%
Glass	1,754	16.4%	7,534.8	3.1%
Flora	67	0.6%	7,246.3	3.0%
Lithics	310	2.9%	5,080.6	2.1%
Ceramics Native American	414	3.9%	1,623.3	0.7%
Fauna Modified	8	0.1%	56.4	c
Totals	10,679		244,931.0	
Artifact Groups[b]	**Count**	**%**	**Weight (g)**	**%**
Architecture	5,416	54.6%	178,017.6	72.5%
Activities	297	3.0%	47,282.5	19.3%
Kitchen	3,969	40.0%	19,768.7	8.0%
Personal	31	0.3%	239.2	0.1%
Tobacco	91	0.9%	105.5	c
Clothing	46	0.5%	98.5	c
Arms	63	0.6%	58.7	c
Furniture	5	0.1%	11.7	c
Totals	9,918		245,582.4	
Euro-American Ceramic Wares and Classes	**Count**	**%**	**Weight (g)**	**%**
Other Coarse Earthenware	810	41.7%	4,876.2	46.1%
Majolica	521	26.8%	839.4	7.9%
Stoneware	189	9.7%	2,358.8	22.3%
Delft	183	9.4%	520.7	4.9%
Porcelain	98	5.0%	1,531.1	14.5%
Faience	60	3.1%	102.8	1.0%
Redware	59	3.0%	256.9	2.4%
Earthenware	13	0.7%	51.7	0.5%
Creamware	9	0.5%	31.2	0.3%
Refined Earthenware	1	0.1%	0.8	c
Totals	1,943		10,569.5	

Native American Ceramic Tempers	Count	%	Weight (g)	%
Sand	179	43.2%	607.2	37.4%
Grog Shell	68	16.4%	546.4	33.7%
Grit	64	15.5%	174.2	10.7%
Shell	67	16.2%	132.3	8.2%
Grog	29	7.0%	109.9	6.8%
Bone Charcoal Fiber Grog	7	1.7%	53.3	3.3%
Totals	414		1,623.3	

[a] No Other or Flora Modified
[b] No Unspecified
[c] Less than 0.1 percent.

pieces. The ceramic assemblage is very diverse, as only El Morro (19.6%) and Plain Majolica (11.9%) have double digit percentages out of 65 ceramic types in the 1,675 typable sherds. The predominance of just two or three ceramic types and a long list of types with very low proportions continues in all the wares and classes. For example, as shown in appendix VI, table VI.4, of the 19 types of Other Coarse Earthenware, three-quarters are either El Morro (54.6%) or Lead Glazed (20.7%). Of the 11 types of Majolica, 78.4 percent are either Plain (43.4%) or Puebla Blue on White (34.9%).

As shown in table 5.2, most Native American ceramics are tempered with sand (37.4%) or grog shell (33.7). However, the high percentage of grog-shell-tempered ceramics is directly related to one large, shattered Kemper Combed, *variety* Pawticfaw vessel. The full list of ceramic types by temper is listed in appendix VI, table VI.4. In addition, the presence of seven sherds of the multi-tempered Addis Plain, *variety* Addis also stands out. Both Kemper Combed and Addis Plain vessels were made by the Choctaw in north Mississippi and undoubtedly arrived in San Miguel through trade. They are unique in the assemblages from the four presidio sites. Local Native-made ceramics were usually tempered with sand, grog, or shell and have plain or burnished surfaces. When the heavy Kemper and Addis sherds are taken out of the analysis, Sand Tempered Plain, Fine Burnished, and Grit Tempered Plain are the most frequent by both count and weight, making up 43.2 percent of the assemblage. When surfaces are treated, they are usually painted red, incised, or roughened. Of the 375 typable ceramics, Kemper Combed is still the most abundant by weight of the Indian-made ceramics found inside the fort.

In the total assemblage from inside Fort San Miguel, there are 232 artifacts generally considered as high-status indicators, and the vast majority were in features from Captain Ullate's residential lot. Some examples of the finer items are a hand fan, cuff links, Guadalajara Polychrome, porcelain tableware, stemmed glasses, and window glass. The Zaragoza Street refuse pit appears to have been from a large kitchen and contained very few expensive or harder-to-obtain artifacts and none of the quality cuts or desired exotic foods such as the alligator or sea turtle remains recovered from Ullate's compound. Collectively, these data support the contention that the refuse was likely generated from a soldier's kitchen or mess (such as the one destroyed in the August 1760 hurricane) rather than from meals prepared for San Miguel's officers.

The population living in the southwest area inside Fort San Miguel produced a rich archaeological assemblage. Judging from the historical maps, the residents of this area were high status individuals, primarily officers, senior administrators, and friars, along with their household attendants (clerks, stable hands, cooks, and servants). However, the materials in the huge Zaragoza Street refuse pit seem to be from people who were not part of the well-provisioned minority. These folks were likely the regular soldiers or civilian servants of higher status individuals and took their meals communally. The architectural remains in this area reveal that structures were built on post-on-sill foundations, with the exception of the brick foundation laid on a tabby footer in the six-foot-wide construction trench. This was an active area of the community both before and after the walls of Fort San Miguel were raised.

Outside Fort San Miguel

Similar to that of other Spanish colonial settlements, the population of Presidio San Miguel outside the fort was segregated by ethnicity and socioeconomic rank. Generally, Spanish civilians and military members clustered their residences north and west of Fort San Miguel whereas refugee Yamasees and Apalachees lived east of the fort along the shoreline. As shown in figure 5.5, there were about nine residential compounds outside the fort, the largest of which was that of Feringan, the military engineer who designed and supervised the construction of Fort San Miguel and the smaller garrison fort at Mission Escambe. The 1763 inventory of unsold houses describes several residences outside the fort, though most are not located on any known map. Residences outside the fort were generally more modest than those inside Fort San Miguel. An example of a more typical residential compound is that of Mather Padrón, described in the 1763 Ortíz inventory as having three houses made of wood and finished with plastered walls and cypress bark roofs (appendix VII, table VII.2). Another example is the home of Don Francisco de Abreu, which was 27 by 16 feet and had wood floors and walls and a cypress bark roof.

Archaeological investigations have been conducted at four San Miguel–era residential compounds outside the fort. Shown in figure 5.5, these investigations include two side-by-side residential compounds just northwest of the fort (8ES981) in modern-day Plaza Ferdinand, an unmapped residential area just east of the fort (8ES49), and a residential lot in the area known as Punta Rasa II near the east wall of the fort on the bay shore (8ES115).

Plaza Ferdinand Residential Compounds

Fortunately, we have historical and archaeological information for one of the large private residences built and occupied during the Presidio San Miguel years. The residential compound is one of two adjacent household lots in a downtown Pensacola park (Plaza Ferdinand). The house lots are depicted on a 1765 color-coded map by Elias Durnford as built by the Spanish (figure 5.5). The largest substantial house lot was second in size only to engineer Feringan's estate, noted above. Measuring on the Durnford map, the large lot had a perimeter fence 150 by 200 feet, an internal fence enclosing a large residence, two outbuildings, and what appears to be a well. The primary residence was on the south edge of the lot, facing two main paths leading to the west and north gates of Fort San Miguel. The residence was comparatively large, 63 by 40 feet, with an indented porch or second-story loggia in the center of the long north and south walls.

While documents do not identify the Spaniard who constructed and lived in this large residential compound, there is strong circumstantial evidence that it belonged to Carlos Antonio Ricardos, a wealthy Spanish trader and dealer in British contraband (Benchley and Whitaker 2007: 80). The largest outbuilding in this enclosed compound could have been his warehouse. Documents describing the Spanish evacuation of Pensacola state that merchant Ricardos had so many possessions he needed the cargo space of three ships to transport all of his goods. After the Spanish left Pensacola, the residential compound appears to have been purchased by British merchant Alexander Moore, who came to Pensacola via Havana with considerable property (Benchley and Whitaker 2007: 70, 80). Support that Moore utilized the Spanish-era compound is found in the documents related to the first expansion of fort, which the British military renamed Fort of Pensacola (Benchley and Whitaker 2007: 70). Buildings lying too close to the expanded fort walls were demolished in the summer of 1767, and as the large house was within 50 feet of the new fort wall, Moore's structures were ordered to be torn down (Benchley and Whitaker 2007: 70, figure 18). From this information, Benchley and April Whitaker are confident that Spanish trader Ricardos built and occupied the structures and British merchant Moore purchased and occupied them from 1765 to mid-1767.

Archaeological excavations at the Ricardos lot targeted the primary dwelling, the northwest outbuilding, and part of the back yard. Benchley and Whitaker (2007: 71) exposed the 2.5-foot-wide construction trench of the north wall of the residence, shown in figure 5.14, and determined that this wall of the large house was supported by a series of upright, squared posts set in large, earth-filled foundation trenches. Judging from the debris left behind after the building was dismantled, the aboveground space between the wall timbers had been chinked with Spanish brick fragments and mortar, and the exterior wall surface was finished with plaster. In the area of the north wall's porch or loggia, excavations revealed the wall chinking was with pieces of limestone rather than bricks. Limestone does not occur naturally in Pensacola and probably was recycled ship ballast gathered in the St. Marks area, where it is easily collected. A rectangular concentration of shells similar to tabby was just outside the back porch or loggia close to the centerline of the structure, and it may have served

Figure 5.14. Presidio San Miguel, an image of northwest corner of Ricardos residence showing construction trench (21) and back yard features. Courtesy of the Archaeology Institute, University of West Florida.

either as a footer for a large support post for a second-story porch or as the landing for a set of stairs (Benchley and Whitaker 2007: 71).

The south wall or front of the residence in the area of the porch or loggia was less substantially built than the north wall, as there were only two widely spaced posts without any chinking. Based on this method of construction, Benchley and Whitaker (2007: 78) interpret that the south loggia may have been an open gallery or porch. The southwest corner of the residence was located, and it had a 2.5-foot-wide construction trench, though there was no evidence of chinking.

Archaeological investigations also revealed foundations of two structures not on the Durnford 1765 or 1767 town plan maps. Both structures were within a few feet of the Ricardos residence and likely were additions to it. The first was an addition seven feet north of the residence and identified by a 2.5-foot-wide construction trench that paralleled the north wall of the residence and contained a series of posts set three feet apart. There was little cultural material or features between this wall and the residence, which led Benchley and Whitaker (2007: 78) to suggest that this structure was attached to the main Ricardos house and had a covered floor.

The second addition was just west of the residence and was in alignment with its southern wall. The width of this east-west wall trench was narrow, only 1.5–2.0 feet, containing five large, irregularly placed posts. Demolition debris included limestone and ironstone rocks, British-made bricks, tiles, wrought nails, and mortar (Benchley and Whitaker 2007: 78). There were two smaller wall trenches perpendicular to the east-west wall trench and extending to the north, probably representing the base of interior walls. Cultural material in the demolition debris suggests that the addition probably stood into the British period.

The adjacent lot was much smaller than the Ricardos household compound. As recorded on the Durnford town plan map, it measured only 90 by 120 feet. The map shows a perimeter fence and an internal fence enclosing four small structures. Measuring 18 by 36 feet in size, the main residence was on the southern border of the lot, outside of the internal fence, and facing the trails into the fort. Two small outbuildings were located along the internal fence line, and a third was in the back yard near the house. The fifth structure was a small outbuilding just east of the primary residence.

Archaeological investigations in the smaller residential lot targeted the yard midden and refuse pits along the western perimeter of the enclosure away from the house (Benchley and Whitaker 2007: 86–91). Features associated with the presidio occupation included a narrow, 0.7-foot-wide, flat-based east-west wall trench that Benchley and Whitaker (2007: 89) suggest was part of the southern lot fence line. There was also a north-south row of five large posts in the ground about 1.5 feet in diameter and regularly set on 4.5-foot centers, located along the west lot line. This too may have been part of the lot line fence. One small refuse pit was excavated within this line of posts and contained household refuse.

The vast differences in size between the house lots is a contextually reliable indicator of the difference in property value and monetary worth of the occupants. The Ricardos residence is four times the size of the neighboring house, with excavations documenting substantial foundations, large support posts, and the additional architectural strengthening and weatherproofing provided by stone and brick chinking in some walls. Additionally, the Ricardos household enjoyed two loggias for comfortable and shaded space outdoors, finished plastered walls indoors, and probably a second story. Although the structures on the adjacent lot were not targeted for investigation, the Durnford map reveals that the size, quality, and comfort of the Ricardos residence far surpassed that of the more modest neighbors.

The size of the artifact assemblages from closed features on the two lots is just as telling as the residences themselves (see appendix VI, table VI.5). The Ricardos assemblage has 2,137 counted artifacts and 61.1 kg of weighed material, while the small lot yielded only 681 counted items and 10.8 kg of weighed material. However, it should be noted that much more area was excavated in the Ricardos house lot. The proportions of artifact classes and groups in the assemblages from the two house lots are quite similar. For example, Building Material and Architecture-related items dominate both assemblages. The Kitchen group is either the first or second largest by count in each house lot, and Activities artifacts are fourth in proportion by count. The assemblages are also similar in the low proportions of items in the Furniture and Tobacco artifact groups as well as in the Flora and Native American Ceramics artifact classes.

Within the Building Material artifact class in the Ricardos assemblage, 2.2 kg of daub was recovered from a posthole of the northwest outbuilding. Made from a mixture of clay and moss, daub is rarely preserved when exposed to harsh weather, as it gradually dissolves with rain and ground water. Only a small amount of daub (17 g) was recovered from Santa Rosa, and none was recovered from Santa María. The use of limestone as a building material in the Ricardos house is unique; it was not found in the other locations of the West Florida presidio. Tiles, some painted plaster finishes, and glass windowpanes were also used as architectural elements in this large house.

Ceramics from the two house lots held the most surprises in the residential lot artifact assemblages. Of the 619 sherds recovered from both lots, 95.4 percent are Euro-American and only 4.6 percent are Native American. This percentage of Euro-American sherds is by far the highest in any context across the four sites of the presidio. Also surprising is the composition of the ceramic classes recovered from the Ricardos house lot. Creamware is the most abundant ceramic ware (35.7%) followed by Delft (29.9%). This is the only site area in the entire San Miguel community with such high counts of these ceramic classes. Diving deeper into the provenience of the Creamware, almost all (96.0%) were in the back yard and recovered from two refuse pits and five nearby postholes. There were also a few pieces in the wall trench of the southern addition to the residence. Only three Creamware sherds were recovered from the adjacent house lot.

There are 31 ceramic types in the combined Euro-American assemblage of the house lots. Almost three-quarters (73.1%) of the 513 typable sherds are either Clouded Creamware (30.6%), Delft Blue on White (17.9%), Plain Delft (12.7%), or White Salt Glazed Stoneware (11.9%). Within the ceramic wares and classes, almost all (92.9%) of the Creamware sherds are Clouded, and a few are Fruit and Vegetable (6.5%). Delft types are either Blue on White (57.5%) or Plain (40.6%). The presence of British Creamware and Delft ceramics in such high proportions from the same features is likely connected to the occupation of the primary householder, Carlos Antonio Ricardos, who was a wealthy Spanish trader known for dealing in British contraband (Benchley and Whitaker 2007: 80).

Despite the significant differences in lot and house sizes, both assemblages have only a small number of high-status items such as window glass, porcelain, beads, and stemmed glass. For these adjacent households both built and occupied during the waning years of San Miguel and the earliest years of the British occupation of Pensacola, the foremost differences lie in the size and architectural details of the main residences and lots.

Old Christ Church Residential Area

The second residential area archaeologically investigated outside Fort San Miguel was just 90 feet from the east wall (figure 5.5) preserved beneath the floor of Old Christ Church, one of the oldest surviving church buildings in Florida, constructed in 1832. None of the Spanish or early British maps made between 1763 and 1765 show any structures in or near this location, yet the archaeological record revealed that it was once a substantial residential area. There are two reasons for its absence on the available maps: first, there are no pre-1763 detailed maps of the San Miguel community, and second, all structures within a musket shot (about 300 yards) of the walls of Fort San Miguel were burned and cleared in June of 1761 to create a defensive open space around the fort in the face of a perceived imminent attack by the Creek Indians on the Spanish community (Childers et al. 2007: 30; Worth 2013: 11–12).

There have been three archaeological investigations at the Old Christ Church site, both under the church and in the surrounding yard. The first two studies focused on post–San Miguel components (Joy 1989b; Shaeffer 1971). In 1997–1998, UWF archaeologists mitigated the impact of installing new ductwork beneath the church floor, and the remains of the San Miguel–era occupation were discovered (Stringfield and Benchley 1997). Later, two UWF master's theses analyzed the results of the project (McMahon 2017; C. Williams 2004).

The San Miguel component consists of 25 wall trench segments and three refuse pits. The wall trench segments were substantial, 1.2–1.5 feet wide and 1.2–1.6 feet deep, with flat or slightly concave bases. An example of one of the large wall segments is shown in figure 5.15. In addition, one wall trench was followed outside the building (Johnson 1992). As only the side areas of the church interior were investigated, the wall trench segments could not be connected. However, two very similar wall trench segments were in alignment and appeared to be part of the same wall. As both wall trench segments extended outside the church, they were either part of a very large building or a perimeter wall enclosing a residential compound (McMahon 2017: 121). Attached to the southern wall segment were two short wall trenches with small posts in the ground, similar to the documented small enclosures at Presidio Santa María attached to the exterior wall of a structure and the fort wall. Another wall trench segment under the church floor was similarly large, deep, and had a flat base, and it is thought to have been part of a separate structure (McMahon 2017: 122). An additional wall trench segment much larger than the others (figure 5.15) suggests the presence of yet another substantial structure within the boundaries of this unmapped and unrecorded San Miguel–era household complex. All of the wall foundation trenches under the church floor were larger and deeper than those documented at the other two Pensacola presidios, which is likely due to the exceptional preservation environment under the raised floor built in 1832.

There is convincing archaeological evidence supporting the contention that all the structures were burned. Almost every wall trench and post was rich in charcoal, as was the surrounding midden. There was also a charred post or timber lying next to the small enclosure wall trench. Patricia McMahon (2017: table 6, 141) performed a charcoal density analysis of the features that supports the deduction of a fiery demise of the residential compound. There were also three pits under the church, one of which had the shape and size of a cask. Although no traces of the cask were preserved, there was a layer of charcoal near the bottom covered by layers of laminated soil, and it contained a variety of kitchen and personal artifacts and architectural materials.

Despite the relatively high number of features in the small area investigated

Figure 5.15. Presidio San Miguel, typical large wall trench with posthole below Old Christ Church floor sills. Courtesy of the Archaeology Institute, University of West Florida.

under and adjacent to Old Christ Church, the amount of cultural material recovered from the features is low, only 408 counted artifacts and 4.4 kg of weighed material. Wall trench segments and refuse pits contained the most material, and the majority of posts produced very little. Expectedly, as shown in appendix VI, table VI.6, the Architecture group makes up just over half (56.5%) of the recovered materials by weight and consists primarily of bricks and mortar, most of which (81.0%) were contained in two refuse pits. The remainder of the brick and mortar fragments were scattered in small amounts in 12 other features. Material markers that are indicative of high status include eight pieces of window glass (one quite large), fragments of a drinking glass and porcelain vessel, a metal button, and a silver half-real cob minted under Philip III between 1609 and 1620. The half-real cob is described in detail in appendix VIII.

The ceramic assemblage of 207 sherds is 76.8 percent Euro-American and 23.2 percent Native American. The Euro-American ceramics are primarily Other Coarse Earthenware (61.0%) and Majolica (28.3%). There are only a few pieces of Faience, Delft, Porcelain, and Stoneware. In the small assemblage of 101 typable ceramics, El Morro (46.7%) and Puebla Blue on White Majolica (19.8%) are the most frequent. Within the ceramic wares and classes, almost all Other Coarse Earthenware are El Morro (82.5%), with only a few sherds of Mexican Red Painted, Reyware, Guadalajara Polychrome, and one sherd of Olive Jar. The Majolicas are primarily Puebla Blue on White (50.0%) and San Luis Polychrome (35.0%). The ceramic TPQ date of the assemblage is 1740 based on the beginning date of one piece of Rouen Faience.

Most of the Native American sherds are tempered with grit (50.9%) or shell (29.0%), but some are tempered with grog shell (13.7%) and sand (6.3%). Of the 46 typable sherds, Grit Tempered Plain (51.5%), Mississippi Plain, *variety unspecified* (12.8%), and Grog Shell Tempered Plain (10.2%) are the most frequent. Most surfaces of Native American pottery are plain (82.0% by weight), and the remainder are decorated with red paint or incising. McMahon (2017: 86) also notes that some of the Euro-American and Native American ceramics were burned.

Based on a ceramic TPQ date of 1740 recovered archaeologically, the earliest possible date of the residences is 1740–1741 when the outpost of San Miguel was built. The terminal date of the residences is 1761 when the structures, if still standing, were burned and cleared from the area. Clearly, the danger of structural fires was ever present at San Miguel, and these buildings could have burned at any time within this 21-year span.

Mission San Antonio de Punta Rasa II

The third residential area investigated outside the walls of Fort San Miguel was about 625 feet from the former east wall of the fort (8ES115; figure 5.5). A noteworthy aspect of this portion of the Presidio San Miguel de Panzacola community is that it was not occupied until 1761 when it became the residential area for refugee Yamasee and Apalachee Indians. As Worth and colleagues (2011: 3) and Jennifer Melcher (2015: 21) relate, both the Yamasee and Apalachee mission villages were destroyed in 1761 by British-allied Creeks as part of the English's attempt to take Spanish Florida during the Seven Years War. Survivors fled to Fort San Miguel where they sought and were granted refuge and protection from the Spanish Crown (Worth 2018b: 327; Worth et al. 2011: 3).

Initially, the Native American refugees lived inside the fortified walls of Fort San Miguel. In May 1761, a muster roll for San Miguel listed 184 Christian Indians from the two destroyed mission villages. These survivors were given daily rations of corn, beans, and chiles, and care was given to 10 individuals confined to the hospital with unspecified illnesses and injuries (Worth 2018b: 328). That same month, Yamasee Chief Andrés Escudero presented himself to the leadership at Fort San Miguel as a representative of both Apalachees and Yamasees and requested permission to establish a new town adjacent to the presidio. By October 1761, an agreement was reached as Governor Miguel Román reported that an adjoining settlement for the Indian refugees contained 26 new houses (Worth 2018b: 329).

No known Spanish-era maps of Presidio San Miguel and its surrounds include the location of this refugee community; however, it is included on two early British maps. It first appears on a 1764 British map of Pensacola Bay by George Gauld, which depicts the newly renamed Fort of Pensacola and a long row of residences just east of the fort labeled "Indian Town" (figure 5.16). The 1765 Durnford town plan map (figure 5.5) depicts a row of Spanish-built houses just east of the fort. From the 1764 Gauld map and the bureaucratic records the Spanish produced, we know that the refugees from the mission villages of

Figure 5.16. Presidio San Miguel, part of 1764 Gauld map of Pensacola Bay showing location of "Indian Town" also known as Punta Rasa II as well as a brick kiln (Gauld and Lindsay 1764).

Punta Rasa I and Escambe settled in the area the Spanish called Punta Blanca near the east wall of Fort San Miguel (Worth 2018b: 329). This Indian barrio of the San Miguel community was referred to as Mission San Antonio de Punta Rasa despite the fact that the original Punta Rasa mission village across the bay was for Yamasees and was destroyed. Both the Apalachees and Yamasees lived in the new community near Fort San Miguel, and for clarity, archaeologists refer to it as Mission Punta Rasa II (Melcher 2015: 22).

In about 1765, Gauld made a detailed sketch of the shoreline of the Pensacola settlement that included part of "Indian Town" (figure 5.17). This rendering shows several buildings arranged end to end with gabled roofs, rounded doorways, no windows, roofs of cypress bark fastened with strips of wood, and exteriors finished with smoothed clay (Benchley 2004: 10). The buildings appear to

Figure 5.17. Presidio San Miguel, close-up of ca. 1765 Gauld painting of Pensacola waterfront showing the structures in the area called "Indian Town" (Gauld ca. 1765).

have been single-family homes as well as larger structures divided into several sections for multiple households. The west ends of at least two of the shoreline houses are depicted with exposed framing, and there are at least four houses with exposed rafters. Interestingly, Benchley interprets the exposed framing as an indicator of the demolition required to clear the area around the fort for defensive purposes (Elizabeth Benchley, personal communication 2019). In Durnford's 1765 town plan map (figure 5.5), at least 10 Spanish-built and five newly built British homes east of the fort were in the area to be cleared. In 1765, the 26 Punta Rasa II homes were only four years old, and the buildings were most likely sold, dismantled, and the components salvaged for reuse.

The Apalachee and Yamasee vacated the reformulated Mission Punta Rasa II in 1763 as a result of the forced evacuation of the Spanish and their Indian allies. In a 1763 letter to the new governor, Principal Chief Escudero listed 111 residents who wanted to immigrate to Mexico along with the evacuating Spanish; once in Veracruz, 103 Apalachees and Yamasees were identified as new immigrants as of September 1763 (Worth 2018b: 329).

Today, the Lee House site is located in the heart of Pensacola's historic district, but in 1761–1763 it was the approximate center of the shoreline homes of Mission Punta Rasa II. As no other buildings are known to have been constructed in this area during the San Miguel period, the Spanish-built structures on the Durnford map are thought to have been residences in Mission Punta Rasa II and lived in by Yamasee or Apalachee families. These structures are within the confines of the modern Lee House site area.

UWF archaeologists Benchley and Norma Harris directed archaeological salvage investigations at the Lee House site in 2007 just ahead of construction of the Lee House. UWF archaeologist Melcher's (2015) draft report of the investigations at Lee House serves as the primary source of archaeological data in the discussion below. The property has been continuously occupied since the Presidio San Miguel period, resulting in a plethora of features and midden deposits from all historic periods. Three wall trench segments are linked to two Spanish-built structures enclosed by a fence on the east side of the lot. One wall trench foundation segment 9.5 feet long is thought to be part of the west wall of the northern Spanish building (Melcher 2015: 41). Two wall trench segments are separated by a four-foot gap that Melcher suggests may be part of the same building, and the gap could be a doorway connecting all the wall trenches. If so, the discontinuous wall trench measures at least 18.5 feet long, which is close to the length of the structures on Durnford's map. The northern wall trench segment contained the most cultural material, and the other two had very little. There were several small posts or pit features between the two buildings enclosed by a fence on the eastern side of the lot, and these features also contained very little cultural material. On the western edge of the lot, several pits or posts ran in a linear pattern and are associated with the nearby fence line.

The Punta Rasa II artifact assemblage in the Lee House lot features has 896 counted items and 10.6 kg of weighed material. When the assemblage is broken down by material class, Building Material (58.6%), Fauna (17.8%), and Glass (9.6%) represent most of the materials by weight (appendix VI, table VI.7). Artifacts of glass, metal, and ceramics predominate the counted materials (84.6%). Interestingly, glass artifacts are 42.3 percent of the total counted assemblage. Almost all the glass by weight is from bottles: 80.2 percent wine and 9.4 percent case bottles. By count, wine bottle fragments are 46.5 percent and case bottle are 13.6 percent. There are only six bottle bases and they comprise 46.0 percent of the glass weight. Included is a small fragment from a large unique carboy bottle that held at least five gallons of liquid and one heavy, rough pontil base weighing 243 g. The other identifiable glass artifacts include a single piece of window glass, four fragments of drinking glasses, nine very thin glass fragments, and a single seed bead. The distribution of the bottle fragments across the house lot was uneven; three quarters were recovered from four features, three of which are associated with the northern structure inside the fenced yard. The fourth feature with a notable glass count is in the center of the household compound yard. An abundance of faunal remains was also recovered from the lot. Although oyster shells make up most of the faunal material weight, there are also remains of turtles and a variety of fish.

Surprisingly, 80.7 percent of the 187 ceramic sherds recovered from this Native American household compound are Euro-American, and only 19.3 percent are Indian made. Euro-American ceramics by count are primarily utilitarian Other Coarse Earthenware (33.3%), Stoneware (22.0%), Redware (11.3%), and Delft (10.0%). Majolica makes up only 8.7 percent of the Euro-American ceramics. Other ceramic classes are 6.0 percent or less each. Of the 124 typable Euro-American ceramics, the most abundant ceramic types are Glazed Redware (12.9%), White Salt Glazed Stoneware (12.1%), and Mexican Indian Earthenware (7.3%). Within the ceramic wares and classes, almost two-thirds of the Stoneware are White Salt Glazed (45.5%) or Scratch Blue (18.2%). The few Majolicas include pieces of Aranama and San Elizario Polychrome. One of the three pieces of Faience recovered was a large piece of a Moustiers Blue and White small bowl (appendix VI, table VI.7).

Just over half of the 36 Native American sherds by weight are sand tempered (58.9%), followed by shell (15.3%), grit (13.3%), and grog (12.1%). Of the typable sherds, 36.4 percent are Sand Tempered Plain and 15.5 percent are Sand Tempered Brown Slipped. Plain surface treatment is present on 43.3 percent of Native American ceramics though some are slipped (brown and red) and burnished (painted and incised). There is one piece of Mission Red, *variety* Kasita; one of Lamar Incised, *variety* Ocmulgee Fields; and two of Jefferson Check Stamped, *variety* Leon. Though small, this assemblage contains ceramic types associated with both the Apalachee and Yamasee and signals continuing material traditions of the two ethnic groups in the Punta Rasa II community.

When the assemblage is analyzed from the functional perspective, almost all the artifacts by weight are in either the Architecture group (79.4%) or the Kitchen group (19.8%). By count, the proportion of these two groups is reversed. All other artifact groups make up 2.1 percent or less by both weight and count. Building materials recovered are primarily bricks, tiles, and mortar, with some pieces of pink-colored mortar, plaster, and fasteners. There is one piece of window glass. The abundance of building materials is appropriate as 18 of the 25 features on this residential lot were architectural.

The recovered architectural materials associated with the northern structure reveal that it had some lathe walls covered with daub or finished with plaster, at least one window with glass panes, and at least one structural element containing tile work. The artifact assemblage contains very few artifacts associated with high status or privileged households: two pieces of porcelain, very thin glass, and one large piece of Moustiers Blue and White Faience.

In sum, the 1765 Durnford town plan map indicates that the Lee House site was once part of the Punta Rasa II residential compound with three structures: two on the east side were enclosed with an internal fence and the third was on the west side of the lot. From Durnford's 1765 town plan, we know that this was the only multi-structure residential compound in the Punta Rasa II community and it had the largest lot. The remains of one and possibly two structures were archaeologically documented along with several associated refuse pits and postholes. From the large size of the house lot, number of structures, and abundance of recovered bottle glass, it is possible that this lot was the residential compound of the highest-ranking member of the refugee community: Andrés Escudero, chief of the Yamasees and governor general of the Tallapoosas and Apiscas. In 1757, Escudero had been granted a license by Presidio Governor Román to establish a store in his house from which he could distribute brandy and other consumables to the Yamasee when they were living at the mission village of San Antonio de Punta Rasa I (Worth 2018b: 325). The quantity and type of bottle fragments recovered at this site suggest that Escudero may have continued selling liquor from his new home in Pensacola.

The Lee House lot provides the first archaeological window into the Mission Punta Rasa II Yamasee-Apalachee community at Presidio San Miguel. It is notable in the circa 1765 Gauld engraving of Pensacola's shoreline that all the structures there are architecturally Spanish. The Lee House confirms this architectural style with its method of wall foundations, finishing techniques, and tile elements, all of which are consistent with architectural findings across the community of Spanish-built San Miguel, both inside and outside the fort. The architecture and artifact assemblage at Punta Rasa II is different than that found at either of the previous mission villages (as described in chapter 4). At this residence in Punta Rasa II, the assemblage is reminiscent of Spanish households at San Miguel. Ever the survivors, the Apalachee and Yamasee were used to dealing with the Spanish, and the assemblage hints at how they were willing to adapt available materials in their homes and on their tables.

Summary of Information outside Fort San Miguel

Investigations at three residential areas outside Fort San Miguel provided the first view of civilian life in the presidio community. Two of the residential areas are on the 1765 Durnford town plan map: two side-by-side household compounds about 250 feet northwest of the fort and a residential compound in the Apalachee and Yamasee barrio of Mission Punta Rasa II just east of Fort San Miguel on the bay shore. Each area contained multiple structures that the 1765 Durnford map identified as Spanish built. The third residential area is not on any historic map, yet it was located about 90 feet from Fort San Miguel's eastern wall. Across the three residential areas identified thus far outside the fort walls, a portion of at least four (and possibly up to seven) residences, one outbuilding, and one attached enclosure were archaeologically identified.

Architecturally, the large house northwest of the fort located in today's Plaza Ferdinand is unique in terms of construction technique, and it is the third largest residence on the maps of the community. The foundations consisted of upright squared posts set at three- to six-foot intervals in a substantial 2.5-foot-wide construction trench. The home also had two indented porches on the long walls and may have had two stories. Above the earth-filled foundation in the north wall, the spaces between the support posts had chinking primarily of Spanish bricks and mortar, but limestone was used in the center of the structure. The other residences were all built on post-on-sill foundations set in construction trenches. The largest of these were the structures beneath today's Old Christ Church. The substantial size of these foundation features is undoubtedly due in part to the unique and exceptional preservation environment under the raised floor of a church constructed in 1832.

Of the four to seven primary residences documented archaeologically outside of Fort San Miguel, the largest belonged to a Spanish trader known to deal in illegal British goods, Carlos Antonio Ricardos from Havana. The homes in the Old Christ Church area belonged to residents who must have been of solid economic means. The structure in the Mission Punta Rasa II community likely belonged to Andrés Escudero, chief of the Yamasees. House lots inside and outside Fort San Miguel included a primary residence as well as freestanding outbuildings for cooking and storage and often pens for gardens and animals. Archaeological excavations outside the walls of Fort San Miguel have thus far documented one outbuilding belonging to the Ricardos household and a small enclosure attached to a large structure at the Old Christ Church residential site. The Ricardos outbuilding was constructed with widely set posts while the Old Christ Church enclosure was constructed with three walls of closely set posts in a construction trench and attached to the wall of a large residence.

The artifact assemblage recovered from the residential compounds in the community outside the fort walls consists of 4,190 counted items and 97.0 kg of weighed material. Well over half (67.3%) of the counted and three quarters of the weighed materials were recovered from the two house lots northwest of the fort. This proportion was expected, as much more area was excavated at this site than at the others. As detailed in table 5.3 and appendix VI, table VI.8, almost half of the total residential assemblage by weight is Building Material (48.3%), primarily mortar, stone, tiles, ladrillos, and bricks, in that order. Almost all of the stone is the limestone used to chink part of the walls of the Ricardos residence.

A total of 1,019 fragments of ceramic vessels were recovered outside the fort. Most (89.0% by count) are Euro-American and only 11.0 percent are Native American. Euro-American ceramics are diverse and do not have a dominant ware or class. The most abundant are Other Coarse Earthenware (25.9%), Delft (20.1%), Creamware (19.5%), Stoneware (15.5%), and Majolica (11.4%). Other wares present in small amounts (2.4% or less) include Faience, Redware, Porcelain, and Earthenware. Unrepresentative of the wider community are the high proportions of Creamware and Delft recovered from the Ricardos house lot (96.6% of Creamware and 87.9% of Delft), resulting from the Ricardos householder's occupation as a trader in British contraband.

A full presentation of the ceramic assemblage by class and ceramic type is given in appendix VI, table VI.8, with only highlights presented here. Of the 741 typable sherds classified into 49 ceramic types, Clouded Creamware (21.6%), Delft Blue on White (13.6%), White Salt Glazed Stoneware (10.5%), and Plain Delft (9.7%) make up 55.5 percent. Of the 119 typable sherds within the Other Coarse Earthenware, El Morro makes up just over half (56.3%), and Lead Glazed and Olive Jar are 6.7 percent each. The remainder is distributed between 10 different ceramic types with 5.0 percent or less each, including North Devon Gravel Tempered and Guadalajara Polychrome. Almost all the Delft (97.8%) is either Blue on White (57.1%) or Plain (40.7%). Almost all the

Table 5.3. Artifact assemblage outside Fort San Miguel

Outside the Fort Totals	Count	%	Weight (g)	%
Plaza Ferdinand	2,818	67.3%	71,880.3	74.1%
Lee House	891	21.3%	10,637.6	11.0%
Old Christ Church	407	9.7%	4,383.5	4.5%
Old City Hall	74	1.8%	10,065.2	10.4%
Totals	4,190		96,966.6	
Artifact Classes[a]	**Count**	**%**	**Weight (g)**	**%**
Building Material	635	16.5%	42,521.6	48.3%
Lithics	27	0.7%	18,842.9	21.4%
Fauna	336	8.8%	8,956.8	10.2%
Metal	768	20.0%	7,608.6	8.6%
Glass	884	23.0%	3,183.2	3.6%
Ceramics Euro-American	907	23.6%	3,111.7	3.5%
Flora	160	4.2%	2,111.0	2.4%
Flora Modified	7	0.2%	1,471.0	1.7%
Ceramics Native American	112	2.9%	226.4	0.3%
Fauna Modified	1	c	0.4	c
Totals	3,837		88,033.6	
Artifact Groups[b]	**Count**	**%**	**Weight (g)**	**%**
Architecture	1,188	37.5%	62,753.2	83.2%
Kitchen	1,820	57.4%	6,498.8	8.6%
Activities	31	1.0%	5,942.1	7.9%
Arms	52	1.6%	159.3	0.2%
Tobacco	57	1.8%	50.5	0.1%
Clothing	12	0.4%	15.1	c
Furniture	3	0.1%	4.7	c
Personal	7	0.2%	2.9	c
Totals	3,170		75,426.5	
Euro-American Ceramic Wares and Classes	**Count**	**%**	**Weight (g)**	**%**
Other Coarse Earthenware	235	25.9%	893.5	28.7%
Delft	182	20.1%	634.3	20.4%
Creamware	177	19.5%	514.1	16.5%
Stoneware	140	15.5%	580.3	18.6%
Majolica	103	11.4%	218.1	7.0%
Faience	22	2.4%	111.1	3.6%
Redware	21	2.3%	48.3	1.6%
Porcelain	14	1.5%	35.8	1.2%
Earthenware	11	1.2%	75.4	2.4%
Refined Earthenware	1	0.1%	0.7	c
Totals	906		3,111.6	

[a.] No Other
[b] No Unspecified
[c] Less than 0.1 percent.

Creamware sherds are Clouded (91.4%), and 73.3 percent of the Stoneware are types of White Salt Glazed. Majolicas are Plain (29.5%), Puebla Blue on White (29.5%), and San Luis Polychrome (11.5%). The remaining pieces of Majolica represent six types including Aranama and San Elizario Polychrome from the Punta Rasa II Indian household, which fall nicely into the 1761–1763 construction and occupation dates. There are very few pieces of Porcelain, Faience, and Mexican Indian Earthenware. Overall, the Euro-American ceramic assemblage is diverse. Also noticeable is the abundance of Creamware and Delft as well as the decline in the proportion of Majolica compared to the three earlier sites of the West Florida presidio.

Of the 112 Native American sherds, the tempering agents are also diverse with no dominant ingredient. The tempers are divided relatively evenly by weight between shell (31.9%), grit (29.2%), and sand (27.0%). Of the 104 typable sherds, the more abundant are Grit Tempered Plain (29.7%), Sand Tempered Plain (17.4%), Pensacola Red (9.6%), and Mississippi Plain, *variety* unspecified (7.2). The trend of undecorated plain surfaces is seen on over half the sherds (58.8%), and the remainder are slipped or painted red, brown slipped, stamped, incised, or burnished. Pensacola Red is the most abundant formal type by weight, followed by Mission Red, *variety* Pensacola; Mission Red, *variety* Kasita; Mission Red Filmed 1; and Jefferson Check Stamped, *variety* Leon.

In the other artifact classes, glass was recovered from all residential areas outside the fort, and the Ricardos household had twice as much as the Lee House lot, but there was very little from the Old Christ Church residential area. Almost all of the classifiable glass pieces are from bottles, especially wine. To date, only 15 pieces of window glass have been recovered from households outside the fort, and most are from the Old Christ Church residences and the Ricardos house lot. The finer and more costly glassware fragments were recovered from the Ricardos compound, including clear and stemmed flint glasses, flint and clear drinking glasses, and an engraved, fire-polished drinking glass. The Mission Punta Rasa II household also yielded a stemmed, fire-polished flint drinking glass, a large (at least five gallon) glass carboy container, and an engraved wine bottle.

Most metal artifacts (86.2%) were recovered from the residences northwest of the fort, and the Punta Rasa II house lot and the residences at Old Christ Church had the second and third most metal artifacts, respectively. The most abundant metal artifacts by weight are pieces of barrel bands and fasteners (nails and spikes). The remainder of the metal artifacts include a few pieces of shot and sprue, buttons, pins, a coin, some wire, and jewelry.

Almost three quarters (72.0%) of the faunal remains were recovered from the two residential compounds west of the fort. The domestic faunal assemblage includes oyster, fish, turtle, deer, cow, and chicken eggs. Floral material is almost all carbonized wood (99.9%), but there are a few seeds and nuts. A large, heavy, weight-bearing post cut to a point at its base was recovered from the south wall of the Ricardos residence. Only one worked bone artifact (a button) was found from the remains of Punta Rasa II at today's Lee House lot.

When artifact groups are considered, Architecture and Kitchen materials predominate and are in reverse order when counted or weighed. The Ricardos residence has the highest proportion of Architecture materials by weight (86.7%), but the proportion is also high at the Punta Rasa II residential lot (79.4%). The proportion of Kitchen materials by count is highest at the residential area near the east fort wall (75.6%), followed by the Punta Rasa II residence (62.0%) and the house lots northwest of the fort (52.8%). Arms artifacts were scarce and consist of only 50 pieces of shot and two gunflint fragments; most were recovered from the Old Christ Church residential area. The Punta Rasa II Yamasee or Apalachee residence produced the only fishing weight and piece of ochre. Overall, there was not a strong pattern in distribution of the other artifact groups between the sites.

The house lot adjacent to the Ricardos compound was modest in size by comparison. While much less area was excavated and a smaller artifact assemblage was recovered from the site, there are some significant differences in the ceramic assemblages from the Ricardos lot and the adjacent small house lot. An example is the proportion of Creamware: 2.5 percent at the small lot and 36.0 percent at the Ricardos lot. While the numbers are small, the typable Native American ceramics are very similar from both lots, with Pensacola Red and Sand Tempered Plain most abundant by weight.

High status makers were relatively low in number outside the fort, only 71 artifacts out of 4,190 despite the facts that all the structures were average- to high-quality constructions and located close to the fort that served as the heart of the entire community in Pensacola. Over half of the high-status markers are from the two domestic compounds west of the fort, a third are from the Punta Rasa II residence, and the remainder are from the Old Christ Church residential area.

Despite the low number of expensive or coveted imported tableware and personal possessions, the combined historical and archaeological information from the three residential areas considered here supports the contention that the principal individuals or families of each of these households enjoyed the available material comforts of the middle- and high-status residents in Pensacola. The Ricardos house lot was constructed near the west wall of the fort, directly on the main paths to the west gate of Fort San Miguel. This compound was the largest and most substantially built across the entire community of homes outside the fort walls. The use of brick and stone chinking in the north wall, the size of the primary dwelling, and even the well-built outbuildings place the occupants in the company of only one other household in Pensacola during the late first Spanish San Miguel era: the governor's residence inside the fort. Notably, however, the artifact assemblage recovered from the Ricardos lot features suggests a conservative lifestyle with few outward signs of wealth or status other than their large and spacious home.

Excavations at the Punta Rasa II (Lee House site) residential compound revealed that one and possibly two structures were there between 1761 and 1763. According to the 1765 town plan map from British engineer Durnford, this house lot was the largest in the Punta Rasa II community. The compound contained three structures enclosed by a perimeter fence and an additional internal fence similar to that seen at the Plaza Ferdinand household compounds. The one or two structures archaeologically investigated were post-on-sill and fastened with nails and spikes. At least some of the structural walls were finished with plaster. A single glass window pane fragment was also recovered from the site. The Punta Rasa II assemblage had a high proportion of faunal remains, indicating an ample diet for at least some members of the household. The archaeological assemblage also includes an unusually high proportion of glass bottles. Overall, the architectural details and artifact assemblage suggest a principal resident who enjoyed a materially secure economic position in the community. Paired with several lines of historical data, the archaeological remains at this lot can be tentatively associated with Yamasee chief and governor general of the Tallapoosas and Apiscas, Andrés Escudero. Escudero was the highest status Native American in the community and had been granted license to run a store from his residential property at Mission Punta Rasa I. Though unconfirmed in the historical records, perhaps Escudero was able to transfer that private business to his household compound at Punta Rasa II just outside the east wall of Fort San Miguel.

One of the best surprises of our research outside but near Fort San Carlos was the discovery of part of a residential area hidden and well preserved under Old Christ Church. This small area contained the remains of at least two, and perhaps four, structures that had been burned and demolished. The date of occupation of the residences is bracketed by ceramic TPQ dates of 1740 to 1761 when the structures, if still standing, were burned and cleared from the area. There is a possibility that these structures were part of the original Punta Blanca outpost settlement, but the current interpretation is that these substantial residences were probably built in 1754–1755 as the general population of the presidio was transitioning from Santa Rosa Island to the mainland. In 1761, with the threat of an imminent Indian attack, all structures near the fort walls were ordered burned and cleared for defensive purposes.

What we have learned from our study of the residences outside the confines of Fort San Carlos is that while some homes and compounds were substantial, the residents lived quite modestly with little outward symbols of their status and wealth. This lifestyle was very different from that of Captain Ullate, whose rank resulted in many expenses and responsibilities. He and other captains provided aid to soldiers and their family members between situados (John Worth, personal communication 2020). There were many military social requirements of senior officers, such as elegant entertaining of his and other officers and the requirement to display one's rank on clothing, uniform, and accessories.

Presidio San Miguel de Panzacola: The Fort and Community

The first occupation of the area that became Presidio San Miguel began in 1740 immediately after a hurricane almost destroyed the presidio on Santa Rosa Island. To prevent another loss of critical supplies in a storm on the vulnerable barrier island at Santa Rosa, a new warehouse and guardhouse were built on the mainland and guarded by a small squadron of soldiers. The location was named San Miguel de Punta Blanca, and it remained in use as a small outpost for the next 12 years. In 1752, another direct hit from a hurricane destroyed the presidio on Santa Rosa Island. This time the Spanish had had enough of the island's vulnerability to storms and began what became a five-year-long transfer of the community to the mainland. The original fortified warehouse eventually became part of the governor's domestic compound within the walls of Fort San Miguel, and it was still standing 23 years later when Florida was ceded to the British.

Unfortunately, there are no detailed maps of San Miguel until 1763. However, historical documents from the 1752–1756 transfer period provide information about San Miguel's transition from an outpost to a presidio and its development until secession to the British in 1763. The combined analysis of historical documents and the continuous refinement of projections of the 1763 Ortíz-Feringan transfer map of Fort San Miguel and internal buildings on the modern city grid has been very useful in associating many of the archaeological deposits with the specific buildings and residential compounds of San Miguel.

Important to remember is that during the two decades between 1740 and 1761, Apalachee and Yamasee Indians lived in their mission villages of Escambe and Punta Rasa I, not at the Pensacola presidio. From these distinctive village communities, the Yamasee and Apalachee maintained autonomy while continuing trade relationships that provided significant amounts of food, supplies, and information for the Spanish residents of San Miguel. When English-led Creek attacks destroyed the mission villages of Escambe and Punta Rasa I in 1761, the residents of both communities fled to the safety of Presidio San Miguel. Housing for the Native American refugees was soon constructed outside the fort close to the east wall and was designated Mission Punta Rasa II. Additional soldiers also arrived in 1761 anticipating an Indian attack and swelling the population to over 1,100 counted residents.

When looking at the San Miguel's population as a whole, the relatively distinct social groups are identifiable within the community: officers and civilian administrators of Spanish descent born in New Spain, soldiers and forced laborers/convicts of mixed ethnicities from New Spain, and Native Americans. Although San Miguel was structured as a military community first, it is important not to forget the other people within this demographic who were underreported, if reported at all. These "others" include wives, children, kinfolk, household servants, and often, the families of these individuals. There were also many support staff and craftsmen such as stewards, stable masters and groomsmen, cooks and kitchen staff, skilled carpenters and laborers, masons, and clerks.

An obvious difference between those living inside or outside the walls of Fort San Miguel is population density. In 1763, hundreds of people lived in over 80 structures within the confines of Fort San Miguel, which enclosed only about 4.8 acres of land. Conversely, the population living outside the fort was dispersed in residential compounds scattered around the fort, as well as in the Indian housing at Punta Rasa II (figure 5.5). The archaeological remains directly reflect the density differential, as more than 2.5 times the number of counted artifacts and 3.3 times the amount of weighed materials were recovered from only 44 features inside the fort as opposed to the 92 features outside the fort.

The archaeological and historical records for San Miguel are rich in architectural information. The historical record—especially the 1763 Ortíz-Feringan map and inventory of unsold Spanish houses of the same year—contains detailed descriptions of 28 structures. From these official documents, we know that almost all the structures at San Miguel were made of wood. They had wood framing with board siding, interior walls of boards or lathe often finished with plaster, and roofs covered with sheets of cypress bark. However, a few special-use buildings had specific construction features, such as the powder magazine, arsenal, and governor's residence.

Archaeological remains of portions of at least eight and possibly eleven different structures have been documented at San Miguel. As listed in table 5.4, the documented structures include four to seven houses, one unknown building, and three outbuildings. The post-on-sill construction method was the most frequent type of foundation and wall framing. However, the Ricardos house was post-in-ground with large foundation trenches and walls reinforced with chinking of brick and limestone in the ground floor walls. The structure also had indented porches or loggias on both of its long sides. Another architectural exception to the post-on-sill wall trench construction was the brick foundation of a building inside the fort. It was a full six feet wide (the largest encountered at any of the presidio sites) with a tabby footer to support a heavy wall. Three outbuildings were documented and each was constructed differently. The Ricardos outbuilding had a frame of wide-spaced single posts. The enclosure in the Old Christ Church residential area was attached to a compound wall or house with walls of posts set close together in a small trench. The outbuilding in the backyard of the Ullate compound had a post-on-sill wall trench foundation.

At San Miguel, with the exception of the brick foundation trench, there was very little cultural material in wall trenches or postholes. This low amount of material is likely due to the structures being erected within a very short period of time (two to four years) as the Spanish population transitioned from Santa Rosa Island and an artifact-rich midden had not yet accrued on the surface. In addition, the structures of San Miguel were occupied for nine years at most. Conversely, the non-architectural features such as refuse pits and wells had a plethora of architectural materials. As shown in table 5.5, Architecture-related

Table 5.4. Houses and outbuildings archaeologically documented in Presidio San Miguel

Structures	Construction Method
Houses outside Fort San Miguel (4 to 7)	
Old Christ Church 2–4	Post-on-sill
Punta Rasa II 1–2	Post-on-sill
Ricardos House Lot 1	Single posts in large trench
Unknown Building inside Fort San Miguel (1)	
Building with salvaged brick foundation	Bricks on tabby footer in large trench
Outbuildings (3)	
Ullate possible kitchen	Post-on-sill
Enclosure-Old Christ Church	Posts-in-trench
Ricardos House Lot outbuilding	Single set spaced posts

items make up almost two-thirds (63.0%) of the weighed total artifact assemblage, and Building Material makes up half (51.0%) of the classes of materials recovered. Significant architectural details can be deduced within the Building Material class. A good example is plaster. While fragments of plaster make up only 8.0 percent of the weight of the building materials, they reveal details about the wall treatments on many of the buildings with which they can be associated, such as the presence of lathe and plaster walls and whether they were whitewashed or painted. Bricks and ladrillos make up 73.4 percent of the building materials and were consistently present in many types of features, signifying the consistent use of these materials for specific architectural features such as fireplaces, floors, walls, and baking ovens. Another example of architectural details gathered from non-architectural features is window glass. Glass window panes were expensive and difficult to produce and transport. Consequently, fragments of glass window panes are indicators of either the high status of the residents or the importance of the structure. Only 27 pieces of window glass have been recovered from all San Miguel contexts, and they were found in the three residential areas outside the fort and Captain Ullate's compound inside the fort. The presence of only 27 pieces of window glass out of the 15,117 total artifacts underscores the rarity of glass windows at San Miguel and stands in stark contrast to over 2,000 nails and spikes excavated across the site. The great quantity of nails stands as yet another enduring testament to the almost unvarying use of wood as the primary construction material in all structures across the community.

Fort San Miguel itself was the central feature dominating the physical and social spaces across the community. The long fort walls, cannons, jutting bastions, and guarded entryways controlled and directed the flow of people, vehicles, animals, information, and all manner of everyday things for the entire community. Historic maps of the fort in 1763 provide a great deal of information about its design and defensive elements. This asymmetrical, irregular-shaped fort was hurriedly built in 1757–1758 *after* a large community of evacuees had already settled at San Miguel because of the devastating effects of a hurricane on the island presidio at Santa Rosa.

Fort San Miguel was constructed with two different types of wall designs: a sand-filled double wall and a stockade line of single posts. The terrepleined walls included the seawall and at least two of the fort's bastions. The east, west, and north walls were all single-post stockade lines. The double wall of the northeast bastion and part of the west stockade wall have been documented archaeologically. Remarkably, at least the west wall of the fort appears to have been constructed in pre-fabricated sections with the sill fastened to the base of several large posts while aboveground. The sections of the stockade were then

Table 5.5. Total Presidio San Miguel artifact assemblage

Artifact Classes[a]	Count	%	Weight (g)	%
Building Material	4,441	30.6%	167,411.2	51.0%
Fauna	649	4.5%	62,265.9	19.0%
Metal	2,860	19.7%	41,066.6	12.5%
Lithics	83	0.6%	23,114.4	7.0%
Ceramics Euro-American	2,849	19.6%	13,675.1	4.2%
Glass	2,646	18.2%	10,729.4	3.3%
Flora	471	3.2%	7,204.5	2.2%
Ceramics Native American	528	3.6%	1,854.8	0.6%
Fauna Modified	9	0.1%	56.8	[c]
Totals	14,536		327,378.7	
Artifact Groups[b]	**Count**	**%**	**Weight (g)**	**%**
Architecture	6,620	48.3%	238,259.3	63.0%
Kitchen	6,408	46.7%	88,043.4	23.3%
Activities	321	2.3%	51,319.5	13.6%
Personal	38	0.3%	242.1	0.1%
Arms	118	0.9%	218.6	0.1%
Tobacco	147	1.1%	154.2	[c]
Clothing	59	0.4%	113.7	[c]
Furniture	8	0.1%	16.4	[c]
Totals	13,719		378,367.1	
Euro-American Ceramic Wares and Classes	**Count**	**%**	**Weight (g)**	**%**
Other Coarse Earthenware	1,045	36.7%	5,768.0	42.2%
Majolica	624	21.9%	1,057.5	7.7%
Delft	367	12.9%	1,156.1	8.5%
Stoneware	327	11.5%	2,938.3	21.5%
Creamware	186	6.5%	545.3	4.0%
Porcelain	113	4.0%	1,568.0	11.5%
Faience	82	2.9%	213.9	1.6%
Redware	80	2.8%	305.2	2.2%
Earthenware	22	0.8%	121.3	0.9%
Refined Earthenware	2	0.1%	1.5	[c]
Totals	2,848		13,675.0	

Native American Ceramic Tempers	Count	%	Weight (g)	%
Sand	219	41.6%	656.6	35.4%
Grog Shell	73	13.9%	562.7	30.4%
Grit	92	17.5%	251.5	13.6%
Shell	97	18.4%	208.8	11.3%
Grog	39	7.4%	120.9	6.5%
Bone Charcoal Fiber Grog	7	1.3%	53.3	2.9%
Totals	527		1,853.8	

[a] No Other or Flora Modified
[b] No Unspecified
[c] Less than 0.1 percent.

raised and dropped into a narrow trench. This rapid technique of stockade wall construction was also documented at Mission Escambe (Worth et al. 2012: 9), an Apalachee satellite village whose fortifications were overseen by the same engineer, Feringan, who designed and supervised the construction of Fort San Miguel.

The total assemblage of cultural material from 136 closed context features of the Presidio San Miguel community is robust: 15,117 counted items and 414 kg of weighed material (table 5.6). The material classes are skewed by the cool storage facility as well as the heavy waterlogged barrel, timbers, and posts from the Ullate compound wells. They have been removed from this analysis in order to more accurately highlight class proportions across the artifact assemblage. Almost three-quarters (72.3%) of the artifacts were recovered from inside the fort, reflecting both the high population density and increased archaeological investigations there. Most cultural material inside the fort was recovered from the Ullate compound (64.8%), and most outside the fort was recovered from the Ricardos compound (52.2%).

By both count and weight, the Kitchen group is second in abundance, just surpassed by the Architecture group by count (table 5.5). Only 38 personal items were recovered from San Miguel, which is a surprisingly low number considering the large population that lived there and the very large artifact assemblage they left behind. Most of the personal items are either glass beads (14) or pieces of Guadalajara Polychrome (15) in the form of small jars and pots for makeup or medicinal unguents. There is also part of an iron canteen, a hand fan, a pen nib, and four jewelry parts. Clothing items are primarily straight pins (20) and seed beads (19), but there are also fasteners, including four buckles, eight buttons of metal and three of bone, and two cuff links.

Table 5.6. Site area artifact totals of Presidio San Miguel

Site Area	Count	%	Weight (g)	%
Outside Fort				
Plaza Ferdinand	2,818	67.3%	71,880.3	74.1%
Lee House	891	21.3%	10,637.6	11.0%
Old Christ Church	407	9.7%	4,383.5	4.5%
Old City Hall	74	1.8%	10,065.2	10.4%
Subtotals	4,190		96,966.6	
Inside Fort				
Pre-Fort Fence Line Network	402	3.7%	3,146.9	1.0%
Ullate Compound	6,090	55.7%	205,614.8	64.8%
Unassociated features	4,435	40.6%	108,307.9	34.2%
Subtotals	10,927		317,069.6	
Grand Totals	15,117		414,036.2	

A total of 3,377 ceramic sherds were recovered from San Miguel features, 84.4 percent Euro-American and 15.6 percent Native American. Other Coarse Earthenware is the most abundant ceramic class by both count (36.7%) and weight (42.2%), followed by Majolica (21.9%), Delft (12.9%), and Stoneware (11.5%) by count. Creamware, Porcelain, and Faience together total less than 14.0 percent of the Euro-American sherds. A complete list of all ceramic types and quantities is provided in appendix VI, table VI.9. Of the 2,414 typable sherds, no one type is dominant. Only one type, El Morro, is in the double digits (16.4%), followed by Plain Majolica (9.2%) and White Salt Glazed Stoneware (8.3%). The remaining 76 types comprise 7.6 percent or less. Within the Other Coarse Earthenware, just over half are El Morro (54.8%), followed by Lead Glazed (18.4%) and Mexican Red Painted (9.3%). The remaining 126 pieces of Other Coarse Earthenware are distributed between 18 different ceramic types. Most Majolicas are either Plain (41.4%) or Puebla Blue on White (34.1%). However, 19.1 percent of the Majolica types are polychromes: San Luis, Playa, Abo, Aranama, and San Elizario. Almost all the Delft sherds are either Blue on White (49.7%) or Plain (45.3%). There are 13 types of Stoneware and most are types of Salt Glazed (82.8%), especially White (61.3%), Dot Diaper and Basket (11.0%), and Bead and Reel (4.9%). Most Porcelain is Chinese (87.8%) with only a few pieces of Hand Painted, Hand Painted over Glaze, and Brown-Backed. Redware are primarily glazed (81.3%). There is a variety of Faience with Faience Plain (54.7%), Rouen Style (13.3%), and Blue on White (12.0%) as the most frequent types. Most Creamware is Clouded (89.1%), with only a few pieces of Fruit and Vegetable, Plain, and Transfer Printed.

As table 5.5 shows, the most abundant Native American ceramic temper types by weight are sand (35.4%), grog shell (30.4%), grit (13.6%), and shell (11.3%). Of the 481 typable sherds, the most abundant by weight are Kemper Combed (30.1%), Sand Tempered Plain (11.1%), and Grit Tempered Plain (9.8%). The ceramic types are quantified in appendix VI, table VI.9. Of the Native American ceramic sherds, 30.2 percent have plain surfaces and 17.6 percent are burnished. The most abundant named types are Kemper Combed, *variety* Pawticfaw (30.1%); Mission Red varieties (3.4%); Marsh Island Incised, *variety* Addis (4.3%); and Chattahoochee Roughened, *variety* Chattahoochee (2.4%). The most unusual type in this assemblage is Kemper Combed, *variety* Pawticfaw. All 63 sherds of this type are from the same large vessel recovered from the Zaragoza Street refuse pit. The Choctaw in northern Mississippi, strong allies of the British, made this ceramic type. Its presence in Spanish Presidio San Miguel reflects either direct or indirect trade with the Choctaw, likely through the refugee mission village of Escambe.

In sum, a combined archaeological and historical analysis of Presidio San Miguel reveals a community on the rise until the Indian wars of 1761. Borderland town though it remained, San Miguel at the end of the Presidio Period in Spanish West Florida was a military settlement with a growing civilian community. The community at San Miguel differed from Pensacola's prior presidio communities in significant ways, especially with the successes of official governmental solicitation for entrepreneurs and other skilled immigrants with families. The presence of a new cavalry unit strengthened the military presence at Pensacola and not only served its broader *raison d'être* but also protected the Native American villages, surrounding farms, haciendas, and nascent industries spread out across the countryside. The Indian attacks in 1761 once again destroyed the mission villages and outlying cattle ranches and farms, and the community retreated inside the walls of the presidio fort. Florida's becoming a British territory in 1763 was undoubtedly met with disappointment as the Spanish had endured the violent aggressiveness of the British and their Creek allies since 1698.

6

West Florida Presidio Integration

After the peak expansion of Spanish Florida in the mid-seventeenth century, all that was left by the turn of the eighteenth century was the peninsula with one settlement on the Atlantic, the San Agustín presidio, and a mission system extending 200 miles west to the Apalachicola that was under attack. The West Florida presidio extended Spanish control 200 more miles west to Pensacola Bay on the Gulf coast, anchoring the western border of Spanish Florida. The West Florida presidio survived despite the unremitting problems of almost continuous violence, many destructive hurricanes, and three relocations. Four hundred miles west of San Agustín, the western presidio was a strategic safeguard protecting the Gulf coast and western border against invasion by French and British competitors. Located on the edge of the Spanish colonial empire, the West Florida presidio was a frontier military community far from the nearest permanent Spanish settlements of Presidio San Agustín and Veracruz. Though there were four locations of the West Florida presidio between 1698 and 1763, the community was surprisingly cohesive as many presidio residents moved from one location to the next, staying together in Spanish West Florida.

Fortuitously for archaeologists and historians, the relocation of the Pensacola presidio over a 65-year period created four distinct archaeological sites and associated historical records. Collectively, these sites offer the rare opportunity to identify both small- and large-scale cultural consistencies and changes for a Spanish borderland community within the tumultuous early eighteenth-century Southeast. With details available from archaeological and historical analyses of the four presidio locations, two missions, and a shipwreck presented in previous chapters, this chapter now addresses the West Florida military frontier community as a whole. The topics include demographics, settlement pattern, fortifications, architecture, and material culture. By integrating, comparing, and contrasting the four geographically separate and chronologically sequential data sets, it is possible to unpack much of how this Hispanic frontier military community was governed, populated, supplied, adapted, and grew within the political and environmental conditions of the Spanish West Florida borderlands between 1698 and 1763.

Demographics

That there were four separate Spanish presidio communities planned, funded, and built in Spanish West Florida during the first seven decades of the eighteenth century seemingly contradicts the fact that the cultural and ethnic composition of the presidio populations remained relatively stable over time. However, the majority of people sent to the Spanish West Florida presidio were consistently from central New Spain, specifically Mexico City and Veracruz. What also remained stable were the areas of those cities targeted for fresh recruits: the poorest neighborhoods, slums, and prisons. What did shift significantly over the course of 65 years was an increase in women sent to the presidio (wives and fiancées) and the recruitment of soldiers with families.

Pensacola's presidio population was culturally Hispanic, composed primarily of people of mixed Spanish, African, and Indian descent who were part of the regulated casta system in New Spain that structured Spanish colonial social organization. Spanish West Florida presidio communities reflected the colonial era ethnic diversity of New Spain, where ethnic mixing had been occurring since the spring of 1519 when Hernán Cortéz began his conquest of the Aztec Empire.

By 1698, Iberian nobility were solidifying earlier attempts to classify the minor nobility, ruling elite, and common citizenry of New Spain into *castas* or *castes* (Carrera 2012). As a legal and social construct, the castas were specifically aimed at delimiting Creole power and influence by defining hierarchal racial categories based on observed physical characteristics and reported or assumed familial genealogy. The top of the hierarchy was always Iberian-born nobility. The castas conflated race with assumed personality traits, prospective socioeconomic rank, and even suitable occupations (Carrera 2012; Katzew 1996). However, in real life and real time, the casta system was a fluid social construct, contextually dependent and malleable. A person's casta designation was indeed a legal status, but that status was flexible and could change during one's lifetime for a variety of reasons, such as the accumulation or loss of wealth, marriage, immigration, or misfortunes. As discussed below, in the military and borderlands context of the eighteenth-century Spanish West Florida presidio communities, the importance of one's official casta was diminished and sometimes ignored.

Across all Spanish West Florida presidio locations, the size of the Hispanic population was not regularly recorded, and when it was, only certain people were counted. Through decades of occupation there were about 300 to 500 people living in the West Florida presidio communities. Military families were always present as part of this community, as were several old Spanish Florida families originally from East Florida via the mission system. The number of military families increased through time, and their presence was sought and valued as a stabilizing factor for the long-term success of the community. The last two decades of West Florida's presidio included native Spanish Floridian families such as the Florencias and active military families living alongside civilian and ex-military families who had immigrated from New Spain and decided to make Spanish West Florida their permanent home.

Despite having to relocate the presidio three times after its initial founding, as a community, Spanish West Florida residents displayed surprising cohesion over the seven decades of the presidio's existence. That cohesion came from the continuity of the people themselves as they settled the region and became the first generations of colonial-era West Floridians. Alongside the Spanish subjects, communities of Apalachee and Yamasee people moved into the western Florida Panhandle after 1718, living in quasi-independent mission villages after negotiating with the Spanish for economic and structural support and military protection in return for their allegiance and trade.

Social Organization

Available historical documentation for the first and third presidio communities, Santa María and Santa Rosa, has thus far yielded the most detailed demographic information. Three incomplete lists of the casta designations of residents have been located thus far: a 1708 census at Santa María, a 1733 list of 20 convict laborers arriving at Santa Rosa, and a partial list of civilians arriving at Santa Rosa in 1741. As shown in table 6.1, most people on these lists were classified as español, mestizo, and mulatto. The lists contain interesting details about Pensacola's newest immigrants. For example, two of the convicts arriving in 1733 were classified as *peninsulares*, but apparently, they had committed crimes egregious enough to be sentenced to hard labor at a borderland presidio. While such details are fascinating, ongoing archival research makes clear that while the people who came to West Florida were part of the regulated casta system in New Spain, the military assigned them a position within the presidio military and social ranks. Krista Eschbach's (2019) recent, in-depth study of the social makeup of the Spanish West Florida presidio population makes clear the decreased importance of casta categories in West Florida. Even in official bureaucratic correspondence concerning individuals within the community, casta designation was rarely noted. With the exception of persons falling into the "Indio" category in reference to Spanish West Florida's Native Americans, a person's official casta label in New Spain actually had little relevance for those living at the frontier presidio (Eschbach 2019: 237).

The West Florida presidio was first and foremost a military installation where official military rank conferred economic and social standing. Across the community were five hierarchical social categories that by and large cross-cut casta categories and the perception of an individual's race and ethnicity (table 6.2). As Eschbach's (2007, 2019) research has revealed, there was a basic top-down hierarchy in Pensacola consisting of officers/senior administrators, craftsmen/artisans, regular soldiers, convicts/slaves, and Native Americans. Officers and senior administrators were of Spanish descent usually born in New Spain. Craftsmen were generally from the craft guilds in New Spain or individuals locally trained through apprenticeships. Soldiers were from many castas (usually lower), and presidio documents indicate that they were treated as social peers. At the bottom were convicts and slaves, also from many castas, as well as Africans and some Native Americans. Local Native Americans were

Table 6.1. West Florida presidio casta lists

Casta	Santa María 1708[a]	Santa Rosa 1733[b]	Santa Rosa 1741[c]
Mestizo	41.0%	70.0%	7.5%
Spanish (Español)	34.0%	-	50.0%
Mulatto	21.0%	10.0%	15.0%
Parda	-	-	15.0%
Castizo	-	10.0%	7.5%
Morisca	-	-	5.0%
Zambo	4.0%	-	-
Peninsulares	-	10.0%	-
Total counted	unknown	20 convicts	40 settlers

[a] Data from Clune et al. (2003: 25).
[b] Data from Childers (2003a: 21).
[c] Data from Eschbach (2019: 231).

Table 6.2. Social ranks in West Florida presidio communities

Social Categories	Casta or Ethnicity
Officers and administrators	Españoles
Craftsmen/artisans	Craft guilds in New Spain; locally trained individuals; Indios
Soldiers	Many castas between Españoles and Indios
Convicts/slaves	Usually lower castas, but occasionally Españoles and Indios
Native Americans	Indios

always treated as outsiders and usually hired as laborers, hunters, or skilled laborers, and military men sometimes took Indian women as wives. The top ranked officers, appointed administrators, soldiers, and convicts resided in strictly separate spaces, while craftsmen, servants, laborers, and slaves were usually scattered in the community, living either in their place of work or in the compounds of the person they served. Segregation of physical space notwithstanding, the reality of such a small community most assuredly saw people of every social, economic, and military rank interacting with a greater degree of familiarity and frequency than may have been possible in the larger towns and cities of Spain's colonies. For persons wishing to establish (or mitigate) a reputation, the porousness of society in a borderland community such as the West Florida presidio made it a better place to live than the more socially rigid society of New Spain.

Population Size

Uneven archival resources have made the task of determining the exact number of people living in the West Florida presidio community at any one time difficult. A second problem with population counts is that their recorded numbers could vary greatly over the course of a single season or year due to a high attrition rate among the enlisted soldiers and convict laborers from desertion, mutiny, disease, and death. In addition, diseases such as scurvy and beriberi ravaged the early communities, especially Santa María, and there were many medical evacuations to Veracruz. Starting in 1702, waves of Yellow Fever swept through Santa María, killing scores of people (Clune et al. 2003: 31). These deaths, along with the frequent practice of freeing convicts only to enlist them as regular soldiers, further compound the difficulty of determining the number of soldiers and convicts at any one point in time. Native American refugees, shipwreck survivors, and the arrival of large military units also temporarily swelled the population. The most consistent record of the population is the number of official positions or *plazas*. Officials in New Spain calculated the situado for Pensacola on the basis of both reported and authorized *plaza* numbers. However, as John Clune and colleagues (2003: 32) point out, the *plaza* numbers were not actual counts of people but only estimates that aided in the calculation of salaries and rations.

One of the most accurate counts of the entire population at a presidio comes from the evacuation of 1763 when Florida was transferred from Spanish to British hands. As R. Wayne Childers and colleagues (2007: 22) describe, in September of 1763, approximately 773 people were evacuated from San Miguel to Veracruz or Havana. The specific social categories of 724 people were identified: 252 soldiers, 68 wives of soldiers, 72 children, 106 convict laborers, 118 civilians (17 male, 41 female, and 60 children), and 108 Christian Indians (38 males, 30 females, and 40 children). Seven high-status administrators were also among the evacuees identified: the governor, two Franciscan priests, the adjutant major, a surgeon, the senior official of the paymaster's office, and the military engineer. Childers and colleagues (2007: 22) note that 42 people of various families had departed earlier for Veracruz along with an unknown number of servants and enslaved persons serving them. Based on this information, there were at least 815 people living in San Miguel in 1763.

Despite the problems inherent in quantifying the population, there is some information available for each of the locations of the presidio, shown in figure 6.1, and the source for each entry is presented in appendix VII, table VII.1. Overall, population fluctuated between two lows of 80 at Santa María in 1700 and Santa Rosa in 1737 and a high of about 1,200 at San José in 1719. There were three spikes in population related to extraordinary but temporary situations. In 1704, at least 800 refugee Native Americans arrived at Santa María after fleeing the destruction of the missions. Though most left within a few months of their arrival, they added to the existing population for a total of about 1,100. In 1719, 800 troops arrived at Santa María and recaptured it from the French; later that year, two large military units numbering 1,200 men were

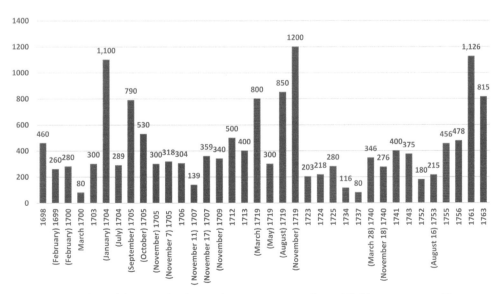

Figure 6.1. Bar chart of the West Florida presidio community population (Childers 2001, 2003a; Clune et al. 2003; Coker and Childers 1998; Eschbach 2019; Harris and Eschbach 2006).

on St. Joseph Bay constructing and occupying West Florida's second presidio. For a few months in 1761, Pensacola hosted an influx of troops from Havana and Veracruz sent as additional protection during the Indian War, and the population spiked to 1,126. Including highs and lows, the average population at the West Florida presidio was about 450, and excluding the spikes, the average was about 332 people. From the available information, it appears that there was an average resident population at the presidio communities of between about 300 and 500 people.

Families

Although the origin of the presidio population was consistent over time, what *did* change was the gender ratio of the population and the number of families and civilian settlers. The number or estimate of military men was usually recorded in all population counts, but prior to 1741, women were counted only under special circumstances such as receiving a salary or rations for working as a laundress or being a military widow (Childers 2003a: 23–25). For example, in 1706 at Santa María, the widow Ynes de Bracamonte and her sons were recorded as receiving rations and salaries, along with four other single women earning salaries as laundresses employed to wash linens and clothes for the hospital and friars (Clune et al. 2003: 28). Other families at Santa María were Spanish refugees from Apalachee. Eight families arrived from Mission San Luis in 1704 along with 31 other Spanish women, three of whom were married to presidio soldiers (Coker and Childers 1998: 36). Three years later, only 14 of the Spanish and Indian women from Apalachee remained at Santa María (Holmes 2012: 62). Families continued to be an increasing part of the population in the West Florida presidio. For example, three members of the Spanish Florencia family born at Mission San Luis were officers assigned to San José and were living there with their families. In 1722, a French priest visiting San José stated that most of the officers had their families there (Charlevoix 1923 [1761]: 323).

Many of the families living at San José moved to Santa Rosa on Pensacola Bay in early 1723, and by then, both husbands and wives were receiving rations. There were also 19 women connected to the two military companies at Santa Rosa in 1724 and 1725 who received a salary (Childers 2003a: 23). In 1734, there were also 19 women attached to the two companies (Clune et al. 2006: 42–43). The first time children were counted was in 1741 with the arrival at Santa Rosa of six families of civilian settlers who had 65 children in total. Their arrival was part of the push to increase and diversify the population. By 1753, the number of families had grown to 32 (Clune et al. 2006: 41). In 1754, 35 young women volunteers arrived at the presidio who either were wives of enlisted men or had plans of marrying upon arrival. In 1756, 95 more women, one of whom had a 10-year-old son, disembarked at San Miguel, and each received clothing and a food ration (Childers et al. 2007: 24). In that same year, women born in Pensacola continued to receive rations and salaries as an incentive to stay in the settlement. By 1760, there were 40 small cabins for married soldiers inside Fort San Miguel. Finally, in 1763 when Spanish Florida was handed over to the British, there were 68 military families totaling 172 family members living in Pensacola (Childers et al. 2007: 22; Clune et al. 2006: 41).

Community Cohesion

Despite moving the entire community three times, turnover of military assignments, and a high sickness and death rate, there was considerable continuity in the population. The most disruptive of the moves was in 1719 when the French captured Santa María and sent the Spanish officers, sailors, and marines to France and 600 soldiers to Havana. While many of the 1,200 troops assembled a few months later at the second presidio location on St. Joseph Bay were new to West Florida, a sizeable number of the soldiers and artillerymen were previously stationed at Santa María. They were captured by the French, taken to Havana, and sent to Veracruz, where they were assigned to the squadron sent to San José in West Florida (Coker and Childers 1998: 74).

The soldiers and officers from Santa María and San José, along with their families, formed a culturally continuous community through the locational changes of the West Florida presidio. When the presidio community returned to Pensacola Bay, first to Santa Rosa Island in 1723 and then to San Miguel in 1754–1755, most of the same people transferred from one location to the next. By the time of Santa Rosa, some of the Spanish families had lived in West Florida for several generations. An example is the powerful Florencia clan who started at San Luis, where Juan Fernández de Florencia became the deputy governor of Florida and turned his ranching business into a "fiefdom" in the last quarter of the seventeenth century (Hann and McEwan 1998: 54–61). His extended family filled most of the administrative posts in the Apalachee province. Magdalena de Florencia, wife of Diego Ximénez de Alfonso, and her five children arrived at Santa María in 1704 as refugees following the collapse of the Spanish mission system. After assignments in Cuba and San Agustín, the military family returned to Santa María in 1713, and Diego Ximénez de Alfonso served as an adjutant there (Coker and Childers 1998: 31). Diego was captured by French forces in 1719; after being released, he was assigned to San José where his family joined him. Diego and his family were then transferred to the Santa Rosa presidio where Diego served as the first captain of an infantry unit. In 1733, Diego's sons Nicholás and Pedro Ximénez de Florencia, both born at San Luis, were captains of the two infantry companies at Santa

Rosa (Childers 2003a: 23). Nicholás Ximénez de Florencia also served as acting governor at the West Florida presidio three different times. In 1752, their sister Petrona Ximénez was one of 10 women attached to the second infantry unit and receiving rations, which any woman born at the presidio had a legal right to receive. Petrona was living at San Miguel in 1756 and is thought to have been evacuated in 1763 (Childers 2003a: 25). This branch of the Florencia family can truly be called the first family of Spanish West Florida.

Another Spanish family with multigenerational roots in the West Florida presidio community was that of Ygnacio de Soliz y Carcamo. He and his wife Doña Magdalena Garcia served at San José and had two sons there. In 1741, Ygnacio and Magdalena were documented at Santa Rosa, living with their now-adult children and the rest of their family (Eschbach 2019: 225). In addition to these two families, other multigenerational families settled at Santa Rosa, later moving to the mainland at San Miguel. Community investment and cohesion only increased after 1741 with the recruitment of new civilian families and the retention of military families with incentives of free land grants and promises of military-backed security and property protections if they stayed after completing their service.

Native Americans

After the collapse of the Apalachee mission system in 1704, Apalachees and Chacatos were often hired as laborers and hunters, living at Santa María with their families during periods of employment. After the Yamasee War in 1718, a group of Apalachee returned to live with the Spanish in West Florida. Negotiating support and protection from the presidio, they started a new mission village at the mouth of the Escambia River, Nuestra Señora de Soledad y San Luis, living separate and quasi-independently from the Spanish presidio community from that point onward. Yamasees fleeing Spanish San Agustín arrived in Pensacola in 1741 after a devastating British attack on that settlement. Like the Apalachee, the Yamasee negotiated support and protection from the presidio and established a separate mission village on Escambia Bay. Both Yamasee and Apalachee mission villages had repositioned to the two major trading paths to the interior. The two groups provided essential avenues of trade to the Spanish while also serving as outguards for the presidio communities. In return, presidio leaders pledged military support, religious leadership, food rations, and supplies to the village residents. Spanish soldiers were stationed at the villages to monitor illicit trade with English-allied Indians, and as hostilities increased, a small fort was constructed at the Apalachee village of Escambe.

From the earliest years of the Spanish occupation of Pensacola, various Southeastern Indians regularly resided at the presidios as wage laborers, allied fighters, and refugees. Native American men, women, and children were a part of the community, including some Native women who were the wives of Spanish soldiers and officers. Rations were requested for scores of Native Americans at every location of the Spanish West Florida presidio, a pattern evidencing the Spanish colony's continuous need for Indian presence and support (Eschbach 2007; Harris 1999; Holmes 2012).

Settlement Pattern

Spanish West Florida extended for about 150 miles between the Apalachicola and Perdido Rivers, encompassing most of the north coast of the Gulf of Mexico. This region was designated as a maritime province administered under the viceroy and the Windward Fleet that patrolled the Gulf and Caribbean (Childers 2004: 27). In eighteenth-century Spanish Florida, there was a consistent constellation of three types of settlements: presidios, military outposts, and mission villages. In Spanish West Florida, there was a total of four presidio locations, six different military outposts, and six allied mission villages. In reality, at any one time, there were only one or two mission villages and outposts because several locations were used for outposts at different times and the Native American groups moved their settlements at least once (table 6.3). However, when the location of the presidio changed, the locations of the outposts also changed. The presidio was a coastal one located on the shore of two deep-water harbors along this stretch of coastline: Pensacola and St. Joseph Bays. The coastal positions of the presidio were strategic and defensive to deter rival European naval attacks and to allow easy access for ships, which were the lifeline for the frontier military installation.

Outposts were also strategically placed to protect entrances to bays and rivers, shipping lanes, supply warehouses, and allied Native American villages. The interior was occupied by Native American groups who lived in the larger river valleys, often along the trading paths from the interior to the coast. The majority of the resident Native Americans in West Florida were refugee Christians allied with the Spanish, but hostile bands from the interior who roamed the region and had short-term settlements in the northern portion of the region were allied with the British, and they were a constant menace to the Spanish and their allied Natives. Except for brief periods of peace, the enemy bands, usually Creeks, moved around West Florida harassing and attacking the presidio, work groups from the presidio, and Spanish-allied Native American villages. Together, the outposts and Indian villages formed a protective and supportive buffer for the coastal presidio.

The presidio itself was the largest of the three types of settlements in the

Table 6.3. Spanish settlement pattern in West Florida during the Presidio Period (1698–1763)

Presidio	Outpost(s)	Native American Mission Villages
Santa María de Galve: 1698–1719	Pensacola Bay mainland	Chacato: San Jose de Valladares 1700–1703/4
	St. Joseph Bay 1700–1703/4; 1718–1719	Apalachee: Perdido River, name unknown 1705–1710(?)
	Punta de Sigüenza 1703–1704; 1718–1719	Nuestra Señora de Soledad y San Luis 1718–1741
San Joseph de Panzacola: 1719–1722	Peninsula, St. Joseph Bay	San Andres 1720–1722?
	–	Nuestra Señora de Soledad y San Luis 1718–1741
		Apalachee: Nuestra Señora de Soledad y San Luis 1718–1741
		San Joseph de Escambe 1741–1761
Santa Rosa Punta de Sigüenza: 1723–1756	Santa Rosa Island, Pensacola Bay	
	San Miguel de Punta Blanca 1741–1756	Yamasee: Yamasee Town 1740–1749
		San Antonio de Punta Rasa I 1749–1761

San Miguel de Panzacola: 1756–1763		
Pensacola Bay mainland	Santa Rosa 1757–1763	Apalachee: San Joseph de Escambe 1741–1761
		Yamasee: Punta Rasa I 1749–1761
		Yamasee and Apalachee: Punta Rasa II 1761–1763
		Lower Creek: Los Tobases[a] 1759–1761
		Talacayche[a] 1759–1761

[a] Non-mission Native American villages.

region. Housing hundreds of people from New Spain, the presidio was the administrative and military headquarters for the region. Outposts were much smaller military installations with a specific defensive purpose and usually were fortified. There was typically only one outpost for a presidio at any one time, supported by a small military unit with 10–25 soldiers who rotated from the regular garrison at the presidio. San José may have had an outpost at East-point, but it is unsubstantiated. Mission villages were composed of Christian refugee families with a leader or governor. Each mission village had a Catholic church and a resident missionary/friar supported by the presidio. The Indian villagers worked, traded, and received rations from the Spanish presidio, but the village was their home. The mission villages were between 10 and 30 miles from the presidio, an agreeable buffer between the two populations. When the Spanish moved the presidio to within a few miles of the mission villages, Native American leadership responded by moving their own communities farther away. Using table 6.3 as a guide, the four patterns of Spanish settlements are described below.

Santa María de Galve, 1698–1719

After considerable debate, the location of the first presidio on Pensacola Bay was on the bluffs overlooking the entrance to the bay. There were four short-lived outposts for Santa María, two allied Apalachee mission villages on Pensacola Bay, and a supporting Chacato village on St. Joseph Bay (figure 6.2). The first two outposts were established in 1700 on Pensacola and St. Joseph Bays. The installation on St. Joseph Bay was to protect the shipping lane between San Marcos and Santa María, and 200 allied Chacato Indians were relocated from Apalachee nearby to hunt game for the population at Santa María (Coker and Childers 1998: 25). The outpost on Pensacola Bay was on Sigüenza Point at the entrance to Pensacola Bay on the western tip of Santa Rosa Island. The British destruction of the Apalachee mission system spelled the end for both outposts and the Chacato village.

It was not until 1718 that the two outposts were re-established at their former locations, this time to thwart French aggression in the area. The French had secretly constructed a fortified outpost on St. Joseph Bay in 1718, but the Spanish had forced its abandonment a few months later. As a precaution, the Spanish established their own outpost there and began construction of a new fort across the bay. In the same year, 90 miles east of St. Joseph Bay, the outpost of Fort San Marcos was rebuilt under the auspices of Presidio San Agustín in East Florida, further fortifying the northern Gulf coast against more French intrusions. The fourth and final outpost for Santa María was rebuilt on Sigüenza Point in 1718 at the entrance to Pensacola Bay.

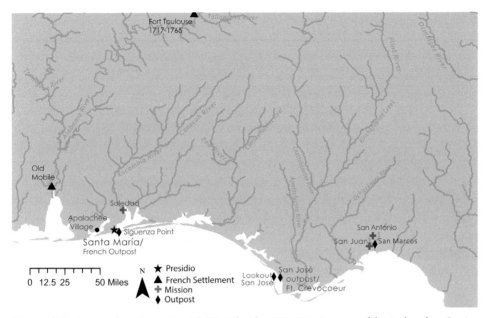

Figure 6.2. Settlements in and near Spanish West Florida, 1698–1719. Courtesy of the Archaeology Institute, University of West Florida.

The first Native American village in Spanish West Florida was established in 1705 when a group of 200 refugee mission Apalachees received some support from the Spanish and established a short-lived village on Perdido Bay about eight miles from Santa María (figure 6.2; Childers and Cotter 1998: 89; Coker and Childers 1998: 34; Worth 2008: 5). In 1718, Apalachee Governor Juan Marcos Fant led another group of refugee Apalachees and successfully negotiated with the Spanish for support to establish a new village at the mouth of the Escambia River about 15 miles from Santa María: Nuestra Señora de la Soledad y San Luis (Harris 2003a: 276–277; Worth et al. 2011: 3). Two additional new refugee mission Indian villages were also established at this time around Fort San Marcos, one by the Apalachee (San Juan) and one by the Yamasee (San Antonio) (Worth 2018b).

Presidio San José de Panzacola, 1719–1722

Threatened by the French need for a new port on the Gulf and immediately after taking the French outpost on St. Joseph Bay in 1718, the Spanish started construction of a second large fort near the tip of a long, thin barrier peninsula that forms the western side of the bay (figures 3.1 and 6.3). With the fall of Santa

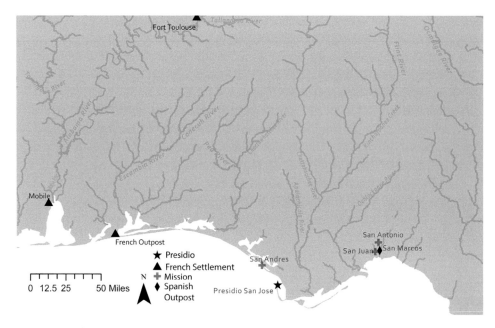

Figure 6.3. Settlements in and near Spanish West Florida, 1719–1722. Courtesy of the Archaeology Institute, University of West Florida.

María to the French in late 1719, the Spanish retreated to their outpost on St. Joseph Bay and quickly completed the new fort out on the peninsula, and it became the second site of the West Florida presidio. In addition, at least one new allied Apalachee mission village was established on St. Andrew Bay. After just three years, in 1722, the treaty ending the War of the Quadruple Alliance returned Pensacola Bay to Spain. Because Pensacola Bay was still viewed as the best harbor in West Florida, King Philip V ordered San José abandoned and the presidio returned to Pensacola Bay.

Isla de Santa Rosa, Punta de Sigüenza, 1723–1752

The few years spent away from Pensacola on the long, narrow barrier peninsula on St. Joseph Bay was free of land raids, and for this reason the Spanish placed the new Pensacola presidio in a similar position on the tip of Santa Rosa Island, naming it Isla de Santa Rosa, Punta de Sigüenza. The Santa Rosa presidio had one outpost and two allied mission villages (figure 6.4). Despite choosing the island for safety-through-isolation over the conveniences of the mainland, the British-allied Creek raids and attacks resumed. Documents describe hostile non-Christian Indians regularly crossing the narrow bay

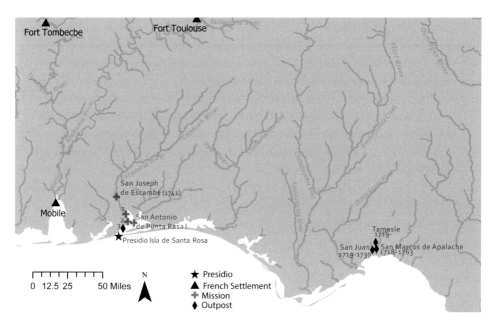

Figure 6.4. Settlements in and near Spanish West Florida, 1723–1756: *1,* Apalachee mission village of Nuestra Señora de Soledad y San Luis 1718–1741; *2,* Yamasee Town 1740–1949; *3,* San Miguel de Punta Blanca outpost 1741–1756, Presidio San Miguel, and Punta Rasa II; *4,* Apalachee mission village of Escambe; *5,* Punta Rasa I; *6,* Apalachee mission village of San Juan, 1718–1763; *7,* Spanish outpost of San Marcos de Apalachee; *8,* Yamasee mission village San Antonio (New Tamasle), 1723–1763. Courtesy of the Archaeology Institute, University of West Florida.

entrance in canoes and attacking and raiding the community (Rivera and Almonacid 1727).

The only outpost for Santa Rosa was across the bay on the mainland, San Miguel de Punta Blanca. This outpost was established in 1740 immediately after the severe hurricane damage to the island presidio. It consisted of a fortified warehouse to protect the island community's supplies in case of another storm (and there were several). There was also a guardhouse inside the stockade, small cabins on the bayshore, and a kiln built nearby the next year.

After their return to Pensacola, officials at Santa Rosa renewed relations with the Apalachee mission village of Soledad at the mouth of the Escambia River. In 1741, Soledad was moved about 12 miles upstream and changed its name to San Joseph de Escambe (figure 6.4). The reasons behind this move were twofold: first, the new outpost of San Miguel apparently was too close for comfort for the Apalachees, and second, in 1741, a group of refugee Yamasee Indians from San Agustín had moved into the area and established a village, probably named Yamasee Town, near the San Miguel outpost on Escambia

Bay (Pigott 2015: 30; Worth 2018b: 322). In 1749, the Yamasee moved across Escambia Bay to Garcon Point, where their new mission village was renamed San Antonio de Punta Rasa I. The new locations of both mission villages were strategically placed on well-travelled trading paths into Alabama and Georgia, and the two groups were heavily engaged in trade with interior Native American communities and gathered intelligence for the Spanish on their activities. As English-led Creek hostilities intensified in West Florida in the early 1750s, a small garrison of Spanish soldiers was stationed permanently at each mission village.

San Miguel de Panzacola, 1753–1763

The fourth and last location of the West Florida presidio was an outpost-turned-presidio. After a hurricane destroyed the Santa Rosa presidio community in 1752, the presidio was officially moved to the mainland in 1756 and named San Miguel de Panzacola. The former location of the Santa Rosa presidio on the island became the sole outpost for the San Miguel presidio, as its location near the entrance to the bay was still strategic (figure 6.5). This outpost was active until the evacuation in 1763.

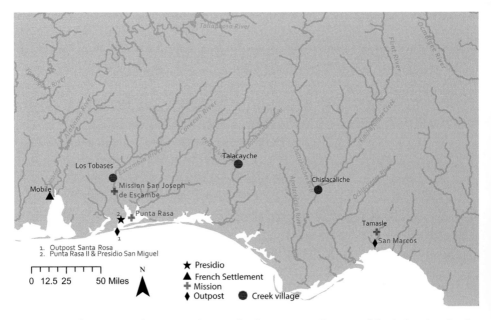

Figure 6.5. Settlements in and near Spanish West Florida, 1757–1763. Courtesy of the Archaeology Institute, University of West Florida.

The two mission villages of Escambe and Punta Rasa I remained in alliance with the Spanish during their short duration, but they came to a violent end in 1761. Two other short-lived Creek towns were also formed in the interior and pledged alliance to the Spanish, Los Tobases and Talacayche. After the destruction of the two mission villages, the Apalachee and Yamasee fled to the San Miguel presidio for safety. It is important to note that the settlement pattern during the San Miguel Period also included four cattle ranches in the countryside as well as lime production areas and two brick kilns, but these were all were destroyed by the Creeks in the 1761 Indian War.

Forts

The Spanish occupation of West Florida for most of the Presidio Period was marked by hostilities caused by their English and French rivals. As a result of the hostile environment, fortifications were essential. A total of 11 forts were constructed in West Florida during the 65 years of Spanish occupation. Six forts were constructed in the presidio locations and five smaller fortifications were constructed, four at outposts and one at the Apalachee mission village of Escambe. The three largest forts were at Santa María, San José, and San Miguel, and the fort on Santa Rosa Island was diminutive by comparison. Available information about the presidio forts is mixed. To date, there is rich historical documentation related to the first and last presidio forts of San Carlos and San Miguel, and there is very little information about the forts at San José and Santa Rosa.

Presidio Forts

Described in detail in previous chapters, the forts at the four presidio locations are compared here. Points of comparison in construction, layout, and armament are identified in table 6.4. The forts were in service for between 3 and 21 years (San José and Santa María, respectively). The first two forts at Santa Rosa were destroyed by hurricanes and rebuilt each time.

Military engineers usually designed and supervised at least the start of construction of three presidio forts. Engineer Jaime Franck designed Fort San Carlos at Santa María; José de Berbegal designed the fort at Santa Rosa; and Phelipe Feringan Cortés designed Fort San Miguel. Unfortunately, we do not know who designed the fort for San José. Fort San Carlos was a classic Vauban design consisting of a square with large, diamond-shaped bastions on each corner. From the brief observations of it, Fort San José could also have been a Vauban design with bastions on the corners, but this is not confirmed. The three small forts at Santa Rosa appear to have been square

Table 6.4. Specifications of Spanish West Florida presidio forts

Specifications	San Carlos	San José	Santa Rosa	San Miguel
			Presidio Forts	
Dates	1698–1719	1720–1723	1723–1740 1741–1752 1753–1763	1757–1763
Shape	square; corner diamond bastions	4 sides; 2 bastions	rectangular; bastions	irregular quadrilateral; corner demi-bastions
Size (ft)	square: 275 bastions: 112x43	unknown	1741–1752: 158x48(est.)	630x375x660x440
Acres enclosed	2.5	unknown	1.2	6.7
Wall construction	terreplein and stockade	earth walls with top palisades	all stockades	terreplein and stockade
Cannons: number and position	14–30, top of terrepleined walls	unknown	8–12, on ground	36 on ground of terrepleined walls; 2 probably on platforms of stockade walls
Internal structures	up to 20	unknown, but many	14	87
Demise	burned to ground	abandoned	first 2 destroyed by storms; 3rd abandoned	abandoned

Sources: Buscarons (1731–1733); Childers (2001); Franck (1699); Roberts and Jefferys (1763); Robertson (1763).

stockades, and there are mentions of at least one bastion on each fort. Fort San Miguel was an irregular polygon and initially is described as having a demi-bastion on each corner, but by 1763, there was one full bastion and one demi-bastion.

The size of the three forts for which we have information varied widely. San Miguel was by far the largest, enclosing about 6.7 acres, which is 2.7 times the 2.5 acres Fort San Carlos enclosed. The smallest presidio fort was at Santa Rosa, and the second fort there is estimated to have enclosed only about 1.2 acres.

Forts San Carlos and San Miguel had two types of walls: sand-filled terrepleins and stockades. Terrepleined walls were limited to seawalls and bastions and designed to withstand cannon fire, but they were constructed differently at each fort. At San Carlos, there was a framework of large posts set in two parallel rows every three or four feet and connected with lintels. The interior wall was vertical and the outside wall was angled inward. The outer wall framing was covered with horizontally laid logs fastened together, and the inside wall was covered with vertical posts, logs, and planks that acted as a retaining wall (Renacker 2001: 36). The space between the outer and inner walls was filled with sand excavated from the moat surrounding the exterior of the fort. The height of the terrepleined walls at Fort San Carlos is not clear in the documents. As Judith Bense and Harry Wilson (2003: 99–105) and Bense (2004) describe, the curtain walls were made of posts set side by side in long U- or V-shaped trenches (see figure 2.15).

The terrepleined seawall and bastions of Fort San Miguel consisted of two parallel vertical stockade walls about 10 feet apart and filled with sand (see figure 5.4). The curtain walls were set in a narrow trench just wide enough for the foot-wide posts (Benchley 2007a: 44). It is thought that the stockade wall of San Miguel was constructed with a series of prefabricated sections of side-by-side posts fastened at the base to a horizontal timber and placed into the construction trenches. This method of construction was much faster than the method used at Fort San Carlos, though both forts were built under threat of an imminent attack.

Both historical and archaeological records reveal that the stockade walls of San Carlos were frequently repaired during the fort's 21 years of existence, as decay, fire, and eight years of violent attacks took their toll on the wooden fortification. This was not the case at Fort San Miguel, which was in use for only six years by the Spanish. No evidence of repair or replacement of the fort walls at San Miguel has been documented, but only small areas of the west wall have been observed archaeologically.

An interesting difference between Fort San Carlos and San Miguel is the placement of cannons. At San Carlos, cannons were mounted on parapets or fighting decks and fired *over* the fort walls. At San Miguel, cannons were placed on low platforms on the ground and fired *through* reinforced openings in the walls (see figure 5.4). It is not completely clear from the historic maps whether the cannons on the curtain walls of San Miguel were on the ground or on the raised fighting decks, although the former seems more likely.

Only scanty archival records and no drawings have been located of the fort at Santa Rosa. There is a brief description of the first fort, built in 1723, in the 1731–1733 account book of the paymaster and quartermaster Don Benito Buscarons. Buscarons (1731–1733) describes the fort at that time as a stockade with half of its support posts held together with ribbands (strips of metal or wood), one bastion facing the water, two outside traverses fastened to the stakes, and two sentry boxes. The second fort at Santa Rosa is depicted in the 1743 Dominic Serres etching (see figure 4.1). This image shows a stockade wall with eight cannons on the ground that fired *through* small openings in at least one wall. While the 1743 Serres sketch of the fort at Santa Rosa shows no bastions, the post-1752 hurricane damage descriptions mention a bastion for the second fort that had been destroyed (Clune et al. 2006: 37). The third fort at Santa Rosa was built quickly after the 1752 hurricane, reportedly about a half-mile east of its previous location(s). The fort is shown on the 1756 López de la Camara Alta map as a small square fort with four corner bastions (see figure 5.2).

There is even less archival information about the short-lived fort at San José. In 1722, a visiting French priest described this briefly occupied fort as having earth walls topped with palisades and defended with numerous artillery (Charlevoix 1923 [1761]). This description suggests that the fort was probably large, with four walls and at least two bastions. Natural parallel east-west dune ridges 8–12 feet high characterize the sandy peninsula where Fort San José was constructed (see figure 3.1). These dune ridges could have been used for earthen fort walls topped with palisades, as described in 1722; however, this is only speculation.

The number of structures inside the three presidio forts for which we have information ranges from 4 at Santa Rosa to 87 inside Fort San Miguel. At all the fort locations, large or small, there were a few essential structures secured inside the fort walls: supply warehouse(s), the powder magazine, and guardhouses. At Santa María, the number of structures initially inside the fort consisted only of the governor's residence, a warehouse, a powder magazine, and a guardhouse (see figure 2.6). By 1702, documents state that the church and barracks were inside the fort, and eventually there were at least 20 buildings surrounding an open central plaza or parade ground (see figure 2.5).

The structures inside Fort San Carlos lining the plaza were large community buildings and facilities such as the church, hospital, warehouses, and governor's residence. Barracks and administrative offices lined the fort walls. Officers' barracks and administrative offices were along the southern walls nearest the bluff and farthest from the dangerous powder magazine and ovens in the north bastions. The barracks for soldiers and convicts were along the north and west walls closest to volatile facilities.

Fort San Miguel enclosed the highest number of buildings (87). Much like those at Fort San Carlos, the buildings inside Fort San Miguel were organized around a large central plaza or parade ground (see figure 5.3), but the parade ground was lined with military barracks and high-status residential compounds. San Miguel had large, multi-structure residential compounds, but in the smaller, cramped Fort San Carlos, officers and administrators lived in barracks or sections of multi-room buildings lining the fort walls. Both forts had the powder magazine in the northwest bastion with housing for lower ranking soldiers and convicts nearby. The church inside Fort San Carlos was on the central plaza, but it was in the southwest corner of Fort San Miguel. The governor lived in the eastern area of both forts. The differences in the spatial organization and building layout of the two forts are likely related to two factors. First, at Fort San Carlos, the governor's residence and two community buildings—a church and a warehouse—were already on the central plaza/parade ground when the community moved inside for protection. Second, at Fort San Miguel, the structures and residential compounds were built without the restriction of fort walls, leaving the upper echelon of officers and administrators free to mark out spacious areas for themselves.

Little is known about the structure of Fort San José, but existing documents indicate that everyone lived inside. The visiting French priest in 1722 did observe that the officers and their families lived in private houses lining sandy streets (Charlevoix 1923 [1761]: 323–324).

The fort at Santa Rosa was the smallest by far and acted more as secure storage than a protective fortification for the population. The fort was located on the perimeter of the presidio settlement, not at its center, and supported the fewest number of cannons (eight). The two rebuilds of the fort appear to have reproduced the same small structure with up to four corner bastions. The fort housed only four buildings: two warehouses, a silo-shaped structure that was likely a powder magazine, and a dilapidated house the artillerymen used. It is curious that the two presidio locations positioned on similar landforms (barrier island and barrier peninsula) apparently had very different-sized forts.

Forts at Outposts and a Mission Village

Outposts and mission villages were an important part of the constellation of settlements associated with each location of the West Florida presidio (figures 6.2–6.5; table 6.5). Of the five outposts, four are known to have been fortified, as was the Apalachee mission village of Escambe. All the forts were wood stockades, two had bastions, and one had a moat. Two outpost stockades enclosed warehouses and one enclosed a guardhouse. There were two outposts for Santa María on St. Joseph Bay. The first (1700–1703/4) was not fortified, but the second (1718–1719) was on the site of an intrusive French outpost (Fort Crèvocoeur). Fort Crèvocoeur is described as a square stockade with corner bastions and five cannons enclosing a warehouse (Coker and Childers 1998: 69). The two outposts for Santa María were both at the entrance of Pensacola Bay on Punta de Sigüenza. The second outpost is known to have had a fort and is described as a redoubt of stakes with sand parapets and a moat. A chapel and huts for the soldiers were also erected there (Coker and Childers 1998: 72–73).

In 1741, the only outpost for Santa Rosa was built on the mainland to protect a new supply warehouse on the shore of Pensacola Bay. Named San Miguel de Punta Blanca, the outpost consisted of a warehouse and guardhouse surrounded by a stockade for a small military detachment. When the presidio moved to San Miguel, the former site of the Santa Rosa presidio was used as an outpost because of its proximity to the entrance to Pensacola Bay. The Santa Rosa outpost consisted of a small fort with four bastions and four other undefined buildings, shown on the 1756 Camara Alta map of the Pensacola Bay area (see figure 5.2).

The fortification of mission Escambe in 1760 was intended to include a small, square stockade fort along with a warehouse, barracks, and stables. However, a strong hurricane struck during construction, badly damaging the newly built fort and stables along with a warehouse (Worth et al. 2015: 50–51). The fort has been documented archaeologically, and it was constructed using prefabricated sections of posts nailed to a sill and set in a narrow trench (Worth et al. 2015: 102).

Throughout the Presidio Period, outposts and mission villages were crucial elements in the constellation of settlements supporting and protecting the presidio. Five of the six outposts had a fort and all had a military contingent. All the fortifications at the outposts and mission village were made of stockade post walls. Some of the forts had bastions and enclosed a few buildings, including warehouses and guardhouses. Outposts buffered the presidio communities from attacks, monitored illegal trade, guarded critical entrances of bays and rivers, and provided protection for crucial supplies.

Table 6.5. Fortification specifications at outposts and mission village

Outposts	Dates	Presidio	Fort Shape and Construction	Cannons	Other Buildings
San José	1700–1703/4	Santa María	unknown	unknown	lookout station
Punta de Sigüenza	1718–1719	Santa María	wood stockade with moat	3	chapel and huts
San José	1718–1719/20	Santa María	wood stockade with corner bastions	5	warehouse
San Miguel	1740–1757	Santa Rosa	wood stockade	none	warehouse and guardhouse
Santa Rosa	1757–1763	San Miguel	wood stockade square fort with corner bastions	unknown	four buildings
Missions					
Escambe	1760–1761	San Miguel	square stockade	none	barracks and stable

Architecture

There is a wealth of architectural information from historical documents, historic maps and their legends, and archaeology for all or part of about 205–209 structures at the West Florida presidio locations. The information about the structures is uneven in detail, but together it provides a relatively good understanding of the variety and style of buildings constructed at the four communities. As expected for such complex archaeological sites, the number of structures represented by overlapping and parallel wall trench segments is usually an estimate at best. The foundation of only one complete structure has been uncovered, and the myriad of other wall segments extended beyond the boundaries of excavation units. Occasionally, an estimate was not possible and only a range of the number of structures encountered was possible. The historical record, however, has provided considerable details about a wide range of structures.

As shown in table 6.6, 123 (60%) of the buildings for which we have information were for housing, and there is information for 30 public/community buildings: 11 warehouses, nine churches, seven hospitals, and three administrative buildings. Information is also available for 11 guardhouses, two arsenals, six powder magazines, three administrative buildings, and 33 outbuildings. While there were hundreds of other structures built at the presidio locations,

Table 6.6. Documented structures at West Florida presidio locations

Type of structure	Santa María	San José	Santa Rosa	San Miguel	Total
Individual residences	3	-	9	33–37	45–49
Outbuildings	2	-	-	31	33
Barracks	9	-	2	3	14
Soldiers' housing	0	-	24	40	64
Warehouses	4	-	5[a]	2[a]	11
Churches	4	1	3	1	9
Administrative buildings	1	-	1	1	3
Hospitals	3	-	3[a]	1	7
Arsenals	-	-	1	1	2
Powder magazines	2	-	2	2	6
Guardhouses	3	-	4	4	11
Totals	31	1	54	119–123	205–209

[a] One warehouse and one hospital used by both Santa Rosa and San Miguel.

outposts, and mission villages, the information available for the 205–209 buildings provides a strong base for analysis and understanding the built environment in Spanish West Florida during the Presidio Period.

Building Materials and Architectural Style

Materials used in building construction combined local and imported resources throughout the Spanish West Florida Presidio Period, and they changed
through the years as builders became more knowledgeable about the harvest
and use of local resources. By 1741, there was a kiln for local production of
ceramics such as bricks and tiles, and lime was produced from oyster shells for
mortar, plaster, and whitewash. This developed knowledge reduced the need to
supply the presidio with building materials from New Spain. Wood remained
the dominant building material for all structures, and the four presidios were
wooden communities. Other than temporary huts, all the structures the Spanish built in West Florida were constructed in the Spanish style: square or rectangular in shape with windows and gabled or shed roofs. Most structures had
a single story, but some special buildings and residences had two stories. Individual homes often had perimeter and internal fences and outbuildings. The
1743 Serres drawing of Santa Rosa (see figure 4.1) is useful for visualizing what
the built environment in the West Florida presidio communities looked like.

The most basic structures the Spanish built for short-term residence were
huts made of a bent sapling frame covered with thatch. Huts were used initially
at Santa María while the fort was under construction and later for soldiers after
the first barracks burned. Huts were also used at the Sigüenza Point outpost in
1718–1719 and as temporary housing at the San Miguel outpost after the 1740
hurricane destroyed most of the structures at Santa Rosa.

Thatch was made of palmetto fronds and was often used as a temporary siding and roofing material to cover timber frames of many types of structures, as
this method allowed a building to be occupied or used immediately after framing. Thatch was usually replaced with more durable materials. The use of thatch
for siding and roofing is illustrated on the 1699 Franck map of Santa María (see
figure 2.8). Thatch was the primary roofing material used at Mission San Luis
and San Agustín. In West Florida, fronds of the dwarf palmetto (*Sabal minor*)
were used for thatch. While this small palm is abundant, it produces small
fronds that require frequent replacement and repair when used for thatching.

Wood was the primary construction material at the West Florida presidio
communities, and the types of wood used changed through time. At Santa
María, pine was used exclusively for entire structures: framing, siding, roofing,
flooring, and wall covering. Pine logs were cut in the local forests and floated
to the presidio for cutting into lumber. Cypress is also an abundant local tree

and makes excellent lumber, but the trunks of old, large virgin trees do not float well and can sink because of a bacteria they acquire with age (Hurst 2005). When cypress trees were first cut down for use at Santa María, the very largest trees were selected, but as the logs sunk, they could not be transported and used at the presidio. As a result of this problem, only pine was used in construction there. While pine is ubiquitous in the region and has tall and straight trunks, it has the serious drawbacks of quick decay and insect damage. At Santa María, the exclusive use of pine for construction necessitated constant repair and replacement of all structures and fortifications.

When the presidio moved to St. Joseph Bay, the Spanish avoided the use of pine as a building material by importing cedar timbers and boards from Veracruz. Cedar is a more durable wood as it is resistant to decay and insects. While at San José, the Spanish learned to harvest cypress bark and use it as a roofing, and it is documented in the inventory of building materials brought to Santa Rosa (table 4.1; Griffen 1959: 258). In the spring, cypress bark can be easily peeled from the trunk (Demrow 2009), and extremely large sheets up to 40 by 25 feet in size could be peeled from the abundant local stands of huge virgin cypress trees. Because the bark is resistant to decay and insects, sheets of cypress bark quickly became the almost-exclusive material used for roofing during the three-year occupation of Presidio San José. While the presidio was on Santa Rosa Island, the Spanish made a breakthrough in the use of cypress as a building material; while the older, larger virgin cypress tree trunks sink due to a bacterial infection acquired with age, the trunks of smaller, younger cypress trees are not infected and will float (Hurst 2005). As a result of this new knowledge, cypress trees felled in the swamps could be floated to the presidio settlement to be processed into lumber. Like cedar, cypress is an excellent building material for structures in Florida's humid environment because like its bark, the wood also resists decay and insects. In 1723, all the initial buildings at Santa Rosa were made of cedar timbers and lumber imported from Veracruz (see table 4.1), but in the 1763 inventory of unsold buildings at San Miguel, almost all the structures were built of local cypress lumber (see appendix VII, table VII.2). Despite its vulnerabilities, pine was consistently used for poles, especially for stockades, throughout the Presidio Period. The abundant local pines have long, straight trunks without branches for 20–40 feet and make excellent poles for fort walls as well as for ship masts and spars.

In 1741, a kiln was constructed near San Miguel to take advantage of local clay deposits, thereby reducing the need to import bricks and other ceramic products from New Spain (Worth 2013: 2). A second kiln is thought to have been added later. It is probable that in addition to bricks, ladrillos and ceramic containers were also produced in the kiln for local use. In her recent study of utilitarian wares from the three Pensacola presidio sites, Eschbach (2019: 494) concludes that more than 10 percent of lead glazed sherds from ceramic containers were locally made by people of mixed European, African, and Native descent. There are abundant high-quality clay sources exposed in many places on the Escambia Bay bluffs and gullies near San Miguel. Additionally, lime was produced in several areas during the San Miguel presidio occupation by burning shells from the abundant local oyster beds. The locations of several oyster beds and areas of clay are shown on the 1756 Camara Alta map of the Pensacola Bay system (see figure 5.2). Lime was used primarily for mortar and plaster, but the use of whitewash is also documented. While local production of bricks, ladrillos, and lime was much cheaper and easier than importing from Veracruz, these materials were still more expensive than the local lumber always available in the surrounding forests and swamps. The abundance of cheap local wood sources, paired with a growing knowledge of where and how to use specific species, resulted in the continued domination of wood as a building material throughout the Presidio Period. Bricks and ladrillos were used for special features in the wooden buildings, such as hearths, chimneys, and floors. Only three structures out of the hundreds constructed are known to be made of brick and stone: the second hospital, second powder magazine, and the King's House at Santa Rosa. Several ovens made of ladrillos are mentioned in the house lots noted in the inventory of the unsold houses at San Miguel (appendix VII, table VII.2). Other important building materials, especially iron fasteners, stone, glass, and other iron hardware, were always imported.

Regardless of where, when, or what materials were used, the architectural style of buildings in Spanish West Florida was Spanish. Adjustments in building materials used to construct Spanish-style buildings had begun with the earliest settlements in the Caribbean and continued in New Spain, San Agustín, and the missions, especially San Luis. For example, prior to the burning of San Agustín in 1702, the buildings were much like those at the West Florida presidio communities. They were built in the Spanish style with post-in-ground frames, board siding, and thatch or shingle roofs. After the fire, the Spanish architectural style continued, but most new building foundations and walls were made with blocks of local coquina stone or tabby made from lime mortar and oyster shells and finished with plaster (Manucy 1992: 64–65). Within the new coquina or tabby buildings, flooring materials changed to a well-packed base of oyster shells or coquina chips covered with about two inches of a poured tabby flooring of lime, sand, and crushed coquina or oyster shells (Manucy 1992: 118–119). Another example of changes in building materials is at Mission San Luis, where there was a shift in wall construction of Spanish-style residences from lumber to wattle covered with daub, a technique the local Apalachee had previously developed. The wattle and daub walls were finished with traditional whitewash (Scarry and McEwan 1995: 490).

From the above discussion, it is clear that having to build four new communities in short succession in West Florida provided community builders with opportunities to experiment with different and potentially better materials without having to demolish and rebuild or remodel existing structures. All four West Florida presidio communities started from scratch, and they were either burned to the ground (Santa María), dismantled (San José), destroyed by hurricanes (Santa Rosa), or abandoned (San Miguel). These calamities offered a clean slate at each new location. The quick succession of four new locations in 65 years has also enabled historians and historical archaeologists to detect changes in requested and harvested building materials for each presidio and archaeologically document changes that are often difficult to expose as a result of continuous repair and rebuilding in one place through time. Once a settlement is built, the main construction activity is maintenance and repair. Had the community remained in one place for those six and a half decades, there would have been much less reason to experiment and a much lower demand for local production of building materials.

Residences

There is architectural information for 45–49 individual residences at all locations of the West Florida presidio. Most homes archaeologically documented are at San Miguel (33–37); nine are documented at Santa Rosa and three at Santa María. At San José, there are only general descriptions of officers' homes. From the beginning, documents, maps, and archaeology reveal that at least some senior officers lived in private residences both outside and inside the forts. At Santa María, Captain Juan Jordán de Reina had a home just outside the fort with a portico partially enclosed with a perimeter fence, shown on the 1699 Franck map (see figure 2.8). Part of the foundation of another private residence was encountered archaeologically outside the fort in the central village area of Santa María (see figure 2.11). The foundations of this structure were post-on-sill with a large corner post, and the building measured eight feet wide. The third residence was identified on a 1719 map as a private house for an unidentified captain located in the southwest bastion of Fort San Carlos (see figure 2.5).

At San José, the visiting French priest Father Charlevoix noted in his letter that the officers had neat and spacious houses (Charlevoix 1923 [1761]: 323–324). From the descriptions of the initial buildings at Santa Rosa constructed from materials from dismantled structures at San José (table 4.1), the buildings at San José were made with cedar boards and cypress bark roofing (Griffen 1959: 258).

At the Santa Rosa presidio, Captain Primo de Rivera occupied the same house he had lived in at San José, which had been disassembled, transported, and reconstructed; it was 20 feet long, 10 feet wide, and 10 feet high (see table 4.1; Griffen 1959: 258). The other officers at Santa Rosa initially occupied eight larger dwellings constructed of cedar boards with cypress bark roofs brought from San José. The paymaster's house at Santa Rosa is described in Buscarons' (1731–1733) account book as long and narrow, 54.8 by 16.2 feet in size, and made of wood and boards with a roof of cypress boards. The roof boards of the home were described at the time as rotten and in need of replacement, as were several supports. Sergeant Major Don Juan Joseph de Torres at Santa Rosa donated his house to the king, and Buscarons (1731–1733) described it as 32.9 by 16.4 feet in size with a living room, bedroom, kitchen, and outbuildings. In addition, of the 40 houses depicted in the 1743 Serres drawing of Santa Rosa (figure 4.1), 14 appear to have second stories.

At San Miguel, the 1763 inventory and appraisal of 28 unsold houses reveals that four belonged to military officers, one to a sergeant, and 23 to private citizens (see appendix VII, table VII.2). The residential compounds of three officers—Captains Santiago Benito Eraso and Don Luis Joseph de Ullate and Lieutenant Don Pedro Amoscotigui y Bermudo—were inside the fort, west and south of the parade ground (see figure 5.3). The location of the remaining private residence of an unidentified officer and sergeant is not known. Eraso's compound directly bordered the southeast edge of the parade ground (see figure 5.3) and contained two houses and a detached kitchen. Captain Ullate's lot was the largest of the officers' residential compounds, containing a large two-story house with a balcony, plastered walls, two loft apartments, and three outbuildings, one of which was a kitchen. Lieutenant Bermudo had a smaller lot with a house and detached kitchen. Ensign Don Bernardo Gallega is recorded as having a two-story house but no adjacent outbuildings. Sergeant Cardenas' residence had two loft apartments with new plaster; one apartment was used as a kitchen. At San Miguel, all residences were rectangular with at least three structures sporting a second story: the civilian Ricardos residence was outside the fort near the west gate and the Ullate and Turbal homes were inside the fort.

Residence foundations encountered archaeologically were either post-on-sill or post-in-trench. Separate corner posts were recorded at only one residence in the Santa María village and possibly at one house on the east edge of Santa Rosa (Smith 1965). Post-in-trench constructions had both regularly and irregularly set posts, often with many replacement posts. The foundations at the large Ricardos residence outside Fort San Miguel had the widest wall trenches encountered for a private home (2.5 feet) with large, squared posts set every three to six feet. Of the two additions to this residence, one had wall

trenches as wide as those of the main residence with posts set at three-foot intervals, and the second addition had more narrow construction trenches with
posts set at irregular intervals. From archival sources, we know that there was
at least one exception at Santa Rosa to the two foundation methods documented archaeologically. After the devastating hurricane of 1740 left almost all
of Santa Rosa in ruins, some of the new houses are documented to have been
raised on stakes to prevent flooding during storms (Clune et al. 2006: 35).

As with foundations, exterior siding materials were usually vertical boards
and/or cypress bark. In the circa 1765 Gauld view of Pensacola (figure 5.17),
Spanish-built buildings have vertical board siding with occasional horizontal
boards on the ends of structures. However, the structures in the Apalachee and
Yamasee barrio or sector known as Punta Rasa II, also built by the Spanish,
have several unique elements (see figure 5.17). The buildings have rounded
doorways, no windows, and a smooth exterior resembling surfaces finished
with clay, daub, or plaster. Of the 22 residences in San Miguel that have their
exteriors described in the 1763 inventory of unsold houses, ten were covered
with boards, two were covered only with cypress bark, and ten were covered
with both boards and cypress bark. Many Spanish-built residences in the
Gauld rendering have windows on both sides of the doorway and often several
more at the same height along the wall, usually in a symmetrical arrangement.
Additionally, most of the residences in the 1743 Serres drawing of the Santa
Rosa presidio community have windows, and often on what appears to be the
second story.

Interior wall coverings are described for 21 of the 28 unsold houses in San
Miguel. Eleven had walls finished with plaster over boards, eight were bare
boards, and two were covered with cypress bark. Plaster was recovered archaeologically at all the presidio locations, but the amount is very small from
Santa María. A little more was recovered at Santa Rosa (52 g), and by far the
most was found at San Miguel (1.3 kg). It is also noteworthy that the only lathe
impressions on plaster archaeologically recovered are from San Miguel residences, both inside and outside the fort.

Eleven residences in the 1763 inventory had lofts, ten full lofts and one half
loft. All lofts are described as made of cypress boards, and all full lofts had
apartments. Four lofts had two apartments and one had three. Homeowners likely rented the loft apartments to soldiers for an additional source of
income. One of the 28 houses had a balcony and another had a new porch.
In sum, there were many styles and qualities of living arrangements available
across San Miguel, and the same was likely true for Santa Rosa and perhaps
for San José.

Roofing material of houses across Presidio San Miguel is also described in the 1763 inventory of unsold houses made at the time of Florida's transfer to British authority. Four residences had roofs covered with cypress boards that were in turn covered with cypress bark; two homes had cypress boards covered with shingles, another had only shingles, and 17 were covered only in strips of unfurled cypress bark. The preference for cypress bark roofing at San Miguel is also documented in the reports of the damage of the 1760 hurricane, where the cypress bark roofs of *all* the buildings blew off and could not be replaced all winter since cypress could not be harvested until spring (Coker 1999: 20). In the Gauld view of Pensacola (figure 5.17), it appears that the roofs of most structures were covered with unrolled cypress bark sheets fastened to rafters with long, narrow strips of wood.

Size is recorded for 23 of the residences in the 1763 inventory of unsold houses at San Miguel, and it ranged between 166 and 901 square feet with an average of 317 square feet. Some of the residential compounds were enclosed at all the presidio communities. At Santa María, the large house of Captain Juan Jordán de Reina was enclosed with a horseshoe-shaped fence that seems to have been made of regularly set posts connected at the top with a railing of sorts. Of the 40 buildings depicted in the Serres drawing of Santa Rosa, 38 appear to be residences and six had yards enclosed with vertical board fences (like today's privacy fences). At San Miguel, 12 residences listed in the inventory have fenced yards, and five were located inside Fort San Miguel according to the 1763 Ortíz-Feringan map; the fences are described as composed of juniper or pitch pine posts set side by side. The recorded size of fenced yards at San Miguel ranged from 840 to 6,609 square feet, averaging about 2,741 square feet.

In sum, most private residences in the West Florida presidio communities were one story, but some at Santa Rosa and San Miguel had two stories. Foundations were either post-in-trench or post-on-sill, and a few were said to be raised on stakes. Interior walls were usually covered with boards. Some homeowners at San Miguel enjoyed the comfort and cleanliness of plastered and smooth interior walls. The use of cypress bark for roofing started at San José and continued at Santa Rosa and San Miguel. Boards were also used for roofing at all locations, though at San Miguel most houses were recorded as having cypress bark roofs and a few had roofs of both materials. Shingles were also used on a few structures at San Miguel and Santa María. Board planks covered the exterior of most residences at all locations of the presidio community. Some were covered with sheets of cypress bark, and a handful were finished with plaster or clay on the exterior. Homes appear to have been small at San Miguel, averaging 317 square feet. Many residential yards were enclosed and secured with board or post fences.

Outbuildings

There were at least 33 outbuildings associated with residences at Santa María and San Miguel. The 1699 Franck map of Santa María shows two small outbuildings just outside the front of Captain Reina's compound that were likely used as servants' quarters or storage (see figure 2.8). At San Miguel, there were 31 outbuildings: 11 documented in the unsold inventory, 14 shown inside Fort San Miguel on the 1763 Ortíz-Feringan transfer map (figure 5.3), and 6 shown outside the fort in two residential compounds (figure 5.5). The number of outbuildings in any one household compound ranged from one to four.

Nine of the eleven outbuildings in the San Miguel inventory were listed as detached kitchens, and two residential compounds had ovens made of ladrillos. All the detached kitchen buildings were wood construction with seven roofed with bark. The kitchens belonging to the governor and commander had shingled roofs. The 1763 inventory of unsold houses also identifies two outbuildings used for storage. All the outbuildings at San Miguel were rectangular, but there are few details in the inventory about their construction. Three outbuildings are noted as having had plastered walls, and siding materials were either boards or cypress bark. Two outbuildings had both board and cypress bark siding. All but one outbuilding had a cypress bark roof. The exception was Eraso's kitchen, which was sided with boards and cypress bark and roofed with shingles.

Foundations of two outbuildings have been encountered archaeologically, one in the Ullate compound and one in the Ricardos residential compound. The outbuilding in the Ricardos lot had regularly set single posts without a construction trench. Fragments of plaster were found in posthole fill, suggesting some walls were finished with it (Benchley et al. 2007: 78). The outbuilding encountered in the Ullate rear yard had a post-on-sill foundation and could have been the kitchen. The dimensions of these two outbuildings were not recorded in the 1763 inventory, and our knowledge of these structures is from archaeological excavation and analysis.

Overall, San Miguel had all but two of the 33 known outbuildings at the presidio communities. At San Miguel there was more space, the residential compounds were far larger, and the residents constructed more buildings in residential compounds than they did at the earlier locations. The community's relative airiness is due to the fact that it was built without the restrictions of fort walls. There was room to subdivide domestic spaces in a fashion more familiar to the Hispanic residents who were, for the most part, immigrants from New Spain. Outbuildings were rectangular, probably had gabled roofs, and were usually placed behind the main residence in the rear and side yards.

Most were kitchens, but a handful were designated for storage. One example of a post-on-sill and one example of a post-in-ground outbuilding foundation were documented. San Miguel was battered by one strong hurricane in 1760, but it did not suffer the level of destruction of home and property that Santa Rosa Island regularly experienced. Relatively free from the major storms and direct attacks that plagued the communities at Santa María and Santa Rosa, San Miguel achieved a relatively higher level of development than the previous three iterations of the West Florida presidio were able to achieve.

Barracks and Other Military Housing

Barracks were present at all presidio locations, though the total number of these structures built is unknown. Like most structures throughout the Spanish presidio communities, barracks were accidentally and purposefully burned, demolished, destroyed by storms, or deteriorated in the harsh panhandle climate, usually with little or no recorded details. There is some historic documentation for 14 barracks buildings (table 6.6): nine at Fort San Carlos, two at Santa Rosa, and three inside Fort San Miguel. There is archaeological information for three of the nine barracks inside Fort San Carlos.

The first barracks at Santa María were built inside Fort San Carlos in 1702, but no descriptions are available and they were destroyed in the fire of 1704 (Clune et al. 2003: 49–50). In 1708, soon after the Creek raids had driven the community inside the fort, five new wooden barracks were constructed with thatch roofs. As Clune and colleagues (2003: 50) describe, these barracks were nearly square in shape (13.8 by 13 feet in size and 13.8 feet high) and each housed eight soldiers. The next year, two long structures described as sheds, 151 by 19.3 feet in size, were constructed for the troops. Three years later, in 1712, two more troop sheds were added, each 110 feet long (Clune et al. 2003: 50). Barracks appear on three maps of Fort San Carlos (figures 2.4 and 2.5), and while they vary in size and number, they all are located along the curtain walls of the fort.

Two barrack buildings were among the first structures raised at Santa Rosa, both 40 by 18 feet in size and 8 feet high (see table 4.1). They were constructed from cedar boards and cypress bark brought from San José. Both barracks had a solid floor made of cedar boards imported from Veracruz.

There were at least three troop barracks inside Fort San Miguel, shown on the 1763 Ortíz-Feringan transfer map (figure 5.3). As the scale of this map is not calibrated, the exact dimensions of the buildings are not known. The map legend describes the barracks as made of wood and roofed with cypress bark sheets. A long, narrow building lining the north edge of the plaza/parade ground had three partitioned sections, two of which were used for housing.

One is labelled as a gallery for forced laborers and the other was designated as housing for officers and residents. This building is described in the legend as having clay walls coated with lime and a bark roof. All the barracks inside Fort San Miguel were long and narrow and bordered the central plaza/parade ground near the fort's center.

Comparing the variation in the location and shape of the barracks buildings inside Fort San Carlos and Fort San Miguel, it is clear that there was not a standard size or placement of military barracks inside Spanish forts. In Fort San Carlos, barracks lined three curtain walls opposite the main gate, but in Fort San Miguel, the barracks lined the plaza/parade ground in the fort's center. The differences in location of the barracks in the two forts are probably related to fort size and circumstances. Fort San Miguel was 2.7 times larger than Fort San Carlos, and its central plaza/parade ground and barracks were constructed prior to enclosure by the fort walls. At Fort San Carlos, the barracks were built after the fort walls were completed, and several large buildings (church, guardhouse, and hospital) already lined the central plaza/parade ground. Therefore, the only available space for the San Carlos barracks was along the curtain walls.

Part of three barracks inside Fort San Carlos were documented archaeologically: barracks for officers, regular soldiers, and convict/laborers. There are significant differences in the construction standards of the barracks directly related to the rank and status of the occupants. The officers' barracks had substantial post-on-sill foundations with large corner posts, a covered floor, and glass windows. The back wall of the soldiers' barracks had a substantial post-in-trench foundation, but the side and front wall were post-in-ground with a dirt floor and a large pit in the center. The rear wall of the convicts' barracks was a less substantial post-in-trench foundation with irregularly placed small posts, and the other walls only had small posts-in-ground, similar to the soldiers' barracks. There was much more evidence of repair and replacement in the convicts' barracks, and it had the lowest quality construction materials.

Only at Fort San Miguel are individual houses for married soldiers documented. After the 1760 hurricane destroyed the quarters the infantry used, 40 small buildings were built inside the fort for married soldiers and their families. The Ortíz-Feringan map legend (appendix VII, table VII.3) describes the small buildings as 8.2 feet high with cypress siding and roofing, though some are noted as having wood shingles (Childers et al. 2007: 34).

In sum, military housing consisted of both barracks and private residences. Barracks were long, narrow structures lining either curtain walls (San Carlos) or the central plaza/parade ground (San Miguel). All barracks were built of wood, and roofs were covered with thatch, boards, cypress bark, or shingles.

Officers and administrators either lived in separate barracks, segregated portions of barracks, or private houses.

Governor's Residences

There was an official governor's residence at each presidio location with at least some historical but no archaeological documentation. The 1699 Franck map of Santa María shows that a large governor's residence was constructed inside the fort near the main gate only a few months after arrival. Figure 2.8 shows a sketch of the structure that reveals it was about 52 feet long and tall enough to have two stories (27.4 feet). The siding appears to be boards with the lower half oriented horizontal and the upper half vertical. Window openings were symmetrically placed in the upper half of the structure. The roof appears to have been thatch at the time. Fourteen years later, however, the 1713 Spanish map of Fort San Carlos shows that the original governor's residence was gone, and at that time, the new residence was along the south fort wall near the southeast bastion (see figure 2.4). This residence was much smaller in size than the governor's first residence, and by 1719, no governor's residence is identified, only a director's area that was part of the barracks lining the curtain wall.

At San José, descriptions of the governor's house indicate it was small, measuring just 20 by 10 feet in size and 10 feet tall (Griffen 1959: 258). At Santa Rosa, the only information about the governor's house is the depiction on the 1743 Serres shoreline-perspective drawing of the community (see figure 4.1). In this rendering, the building labeled the governor's house is a huge two- or three-story building with three domed towers. There is skepticism among researchers about the reality of this structure, which is by far the largest and most exotic of any structures depicted in the West Florida presidio communities.

At San Miguel, the governor lived in a large compound stretching along the entire east curtain wall inside Fort San Miguel encompassing approximately 20 percent of the fort interior (see figure 5.3). There were seven buildings in the governor's compound, four of which are identified: a new warehouse, the old warehouse built in 1740, stables, and a kitchen with an attached bake oven. The governor lived in a large apartment above the new warehouse that had a stone foundation, was two stories tall (32.9 feet), and had a brick chimney (Childers et al. 2007: 50; Howard 1941: 371). The ground floor was the provisions warehouse and also had two dedicated rooms for the paymaster's offices. The second story was divided into two large living areas with the governor on one side and the adjutant major housed on the other. Childers and colleagues (2007: 32, 50) and the Ortíz-Feringan map legend (see appendix VII, table VII.3) describe the building's supporting framework as post-in-ground with wall interstices chinked with stone for about two feet above the ground with clay and moss above the stone. The exterior was covered with plaster. The second-story floor was made of large timbers and planks overlaid with two courses of brick. Many people worked and resided in this large compound, including a master tailor, journeyman, silversmith, shoemaker, and convict and free laborers.

In sum, at Santa María, San José, and San Miguel, the governor lived inside the fort. However, at Santa Rosa, the governor lived in the community alongside everyone else. At San Miguel, the governor lived in a large apartment on the second story of a warehouse in a large compound protected by two guardhouses. At San José and Santa Rosa, the governor's residence was quite small. At Santa María, the first residence was large, but in 1713, it was small and along a curtain wall; by 1719, there was no dedicated governor's residence.

Administrative Buildings/Offices

In addition to the governor, other senior administrators were present at the presidio. Some had offices or residences in or near warehouses and officers' barracks, and others were in separate structures. The only administrative office/residence known at Santa María is identified on the 1719 Devin map that shows an enlarged room for the director at the east end of the soldiers' barracks lining the south curtain wall (see figure 2.5). This same building was identified as the governor's house on the 1713 map (see figure 2.4). At Santa Rosa, one of the initial buildings was a paymaster's office that was 20 by 9 feet in size and 9 feet high (see table 4.1). At San Miguel, the "King's House" or treasury was in a large corner compound across the street from the governor's compound on the southeast corner of the central plaza/parade ground (see figure 5.3). Also in Fort San Miguel, the paymaster had a residential compound of three small structures in the fort's southwest corner, just west of the church/friary complex. Located within larger buildings were other administrators such as the adjutant major at San Miguel who was located in the provisions warehouse.

Warehouses

Secure warehouses are always an essential facility at any military installation as they hold materials necessary for survival and defense. Warehouses were especially significant at the isolated Spanish colonial presidio in West Florida, where there was little chance of receiving replacement or supplemental supplies for months on end. There is information available for 11 warehouses constructed at the four locations of the West Florida presidio. Clune and colleagues (2003: 42–49) detail a series of four sequential warehouses at Santa María, three inside and one outside the fort. The first warehouse was described as a temporary supply shed outside the fort, and it burned in the January 1699 fire. The second warehouse was inside the fort and was 19.3 feet on a side, 6.9

feet high, made of boards, and roofed with shingles. It was also burned in either the 1701 or the 1704 fire. The third warehouse, built in 1705, was a larger structure. It was a two-story building that was 55 by 25 feet in size and had a roof of caulked boards with ends sealed with lead sheets. This warehouse is depicted on the 1713 Spanish map as situated in front of the officers' barracks (see figure 2.4). In 1712, the third warehouse was so deteriorated that it was recommended to be demolished. This warehouse was archaeologically documented, and it was discovered that the structure had a cellar pit over eight feet deep and was supported by six large perimeter posts (Bense 2004; Bense and Wilson 2003: 134–142). Excavation revealed no evidence of burning, and the cellar pit had been filled in, supporting the 1712 recommendation that the structure be torn down. On the 1719 Devin map of San Carlos, the third warehouse is gone, and a former hospital in front of the soldiers' barracks is identified as the fourth warehouse. The building is first identified as a hospital on the 1713 Spanish map, but later it was apparently converted to a warehouse (figures 2.4 and 2.5). The hospital/warehouse structure was documented archaeologically as 40 feet wide (Bense and Wilson 2003: 144–148), and historic maps show it to be rectangular and about 60 feet long. The building was supported by a series of large perimeter posts with small post-in-trench construction for the interior walls (see figure 2.22). It also had a covered entryway and solid floor. Driplines along the east and south walls were also documented during excavations.

Unfortunately, there is no information available for warehouses at Presidio San José. At Santa Rosa, there were at least five warehouses. The first was inside the small fort as part of the initial settlement on the island. It is described as 40 by 20 feet, 20 feet tall, and constructed of cedar boards and nails brought from Veracruz (see table 4.1; Clune et al. 2006: 35). Given the height of this warehouse, it could have had two floors for storage. It appears that by 1725, there were at least two more warehouses at Santa Rosa located just outside the fort, one for food and one for military materials. Buscarons (1731–1733) described the food warehouse as 32.9 by 22 feet in size and tall enough to include an attic of cedar boards. The building was covered with board planks and cypress bark and was secured with locks on the exterior and interior doors. The 1740 hurricane destroyed these three warehouses and two new warehouses were quickly built, one on the mainland and one at the battered presidio site.

Some supplies in the badly damaged, large, two-story warehouse inside the first fort at Santa Rosa survived the hurricane and were transferred to the new warehouse at San Miguel on the mainland (Faye 1941: 162; Worth 2013: 2). The warehouse built in 1740 when San Miguel was an outpost was still standing in 1763, and the Ortíz-Feringan map legend notes that it still had clay walls with a roof of cypress bark at that time (see figure 5.3). Across from the original 1740 warehouse, the new warehouse at San Miguel was a two-story building that served two purposes. The first floor stored provisions and the second floor had two apartments for the governor and adjutant major.

In total, we know of at least 11 warehouses at the four locations of the West Florida presidio. They all were constructed of heavy timbers, and roofing was either bark, shingles, or sealed boards. With the exception of the earliest shed-like, temporary, square warehouses at Santa María, all the other warehouses for which we have dimensions were large, rectangular structures. Two warehouses at Santa María had a solid floor and one had a deep cellar. Five of the warehouses are known to have been two-story structures. The upper story of one warehouse inside Fort San Miguel had apartments for the governor and adjutant major.

Churches

The Catholic Church was the most distinguishing characteristic of a Spanish colonial settlement, and it was usually the most prominent structure. We know of nine churches at the four locations of the West Florida presidio. Four were raised at Santa María, one at San José, three at Santa Rosa, and one at San Miguel. Information about the churches is far from complete, but some information has been gleaned from documents, map legends, and archaeology. Cemeteries associated with the churches were either nearby or beneath the church floor. Aside from the church structures, there was usually a friary or convent building associated with the churches at Santa María and San Miguel.

The first church at Santa María was built immediately upon arrival, and engineer Franck described it as a crude palmetto thatched hut (Clune et al. 2003: 46). It burned two months later in the January 1699 fire, and its replacement, along with a nearby friary, is illustrated on the May 1699 Franck map (see figure 2.8). Both buildings appear to have had board siding and thatch roofs at that time. Both had double front doors, and the friary had a portico over the front doorway. Before 1702, a third church was erected inside the fort and is described as having board walls with an initial palmetto thatch roof that was eventually replaced with shingles (Clune et al. 2003: 47). This third church burned in 1704, and the fourth and last church was built in 1706 inside the fort. This last house of worship boasted an interior vault, board walls, and glass windows purchased from the French at Mobile (Clune et al. 2003: 47). The fourth church has been documented archaeologically, where a unique construction method was recorded. The framework consisted of large interior posts set on 12-foot centers supporting the rafters and roof. The southern edge of the church building was quite clear with a line of wall posts and a sharp boundary of subfloor burials (see figure 2.23). The subfloor cemetery was crowded with the remains of at least 24 people in the 600 square feet exposed during the field investigation. There were disarticulated human remains throughout the cemetery as the remains of previous burials were disturbed by later interments.

The church at San José carried that name, but very little else is known about it. There were three churches at the presidio location on Santa Rosa Island. Surprisingly, the church is not specifically mentioned among the first structures constructed, but Wauchope's 1723 inventory references furnishings for the church, and a year later church supplies were received; therefore, it must have been one of the initial buildings constructed (Eschbach 2007: 97). The first specific mention of the presence of a church is in 1731–1733 when Buscarons (1731–1733) described it as being 41.1 by 22 feet in size, 8.2 feet high, built of wood, and roofed with cypress bark. It had a choir loft and three wooden doors lined and covered with cypress bark. Buscarons (1731–1733) said the church was useless at the time because of wood rot. In 1735, Friar Salazar complained that the church had no sacristy (Salazar 1735). Destroyed in the 1740 hurricane, the church was rebuilt in 1742 and had a post-on-sill framework with supporting pillars mounted on timbers, a roof of cypress bark, and a subfloor cemetery (Childers 2003b: 4). This church was destroyed in the monstrous 1752 hurricane when water swept through the church with such force that it washed away the coffins and all human remains except for one skull found outside the remains of the church (Quixano et al. 1752).

The remains of two churches were encountered archaeologically at Santa Rosa. The foundations consisted of wall trenches oriented to the cardinal directions, a signature distinction of many colonial Catholic churches and unique among the plethora of other wall trenches excavated across the Santa Rosa site, all of which were oriented roughly 15 degrees east of north. As described in chapter 4, the foundations of the church walls were parallel and within a few feet of each other. The latest wall foundation was documented for 37 feet, and it continued outside the excavation units. There were only four posts in the long wall trench, which correlates well with the historical description of post-on-sill framing for the second church. The second wall trench preceded and paralleled the last church wall. This earlier structure could have been the remains of the first church at Santa Rosa.

The third church at Santa Rosa was a repurposed hospital built of stone and brick and was one of only three buildings that survived the 1752 hurricane (Andreu 1753). The other buildings to survive were the King's House and powder magazine, both made of stone and brick. The repurposed hospital appears to have served as a church for the military outpost stationed there until 1763.

There was only one church at San Miguel. It was built in 1754–1755, measuring 44 by 22 feet and oriented east-west, and it had a timber frame, board walls, and a cypress bark or shingled roof. The interior of the church included a sacristy and two rooms used for living quarters for two priests (Eraso 1752; Ortíz-Feringan 1763a). On the 1763 Ortíz-Feringan transfer map, there is a rectangular friary building behind the church building (see figure 5.3). The church and friary were enclosed with a fence, and the map legend identifies the church as the "Royal Chapel."

Hospitals

Hospitals were a necessity at all locations of the presidio, as sickness, accidental injury, and violence were chronic issues throughout the settlement's existence. There is information for seven hospitals at three presidio locations: three at Santa María, three at Santa Rosa, and one at San Miguel. The first two hospitals at Santa María were outside the fort in the village that sat along the bay bluff edge. The first hospital was recorded as about 35 by 23.5 feet in size (Clune et al. 2003: 48), and it was fortuitously spared in the fires of 1699 and 1704. A second and larger hospital with board walls and a thatch roof was built outside the fort at Santa María in 1707, though it was partially dismantled under pressure of Creek and English raids (Clune et al. 2003: 48). The third hospital was inside Fort San Carlos and is described as poorly constructed with a perpetually leaking roof and separating board walls. By 1713, the third hospital was deemed unserviceable (Clune et al. 2003: 48–49). On the 1713 Spanish map of Fort San Carlos (figure 2.4), this hospital is shown and labeled on the west side of the central plaza/parade ground in front of the soldiers' barracks. By 1719, it had been converted to a warehouse as indicated on the French Devin map made that year (figure 2.5a). This structure was documented archaeologically as 40 feet wide and 60 feet long, with a covered floor, gabled roof, and covered entryway (see chapter 2 for additional details).

Unfortunately, there is no mention of a hospital at San José, though there surely was one. At Santa Rosa, the first mention of a hospital is in 1727 when it was located outside the fort. This structure was destroyed in the 1740 hurricane, and it was suggested that a private house on the mainland should be purchased for use as a hospital in the rebuilt community until a new one could be constructed. It was one of three buildings to survive the devastation and was used as a church after the storm as the new hospital was built on the mainland at San Miguel where the population was relocating (Andreu 1753).

A hospital was built at San Miguel that was 44 by 22 feet in size and had walls of clay and timber filled in with lime. It was first roofed with palm fronds, but these were soon replaced with cypress bark (Eraso 1752). On the 1763 Ortíz-Feringan transfer map of Fort San Miguel, a hospital is located in the eastern portion of the long, three-room multipurpose building lining the north side of the plaza/parade ground. The map legend describes the building as having walls of clay and a cypress bark roof. Inside the hospital were two rooms for the sick, a medium-sized room used as a pharmacy and lodging for the doctor, a short room for the storage of bedclothes, and another that served as a kitchen.

Of the seven hospitals for which we have information, all were stand-alone buildings except the one in Fort San Miguel, which occupied one of three partitions in a long building on the northern edge of the plaza/parade ground. There is significant structural information from archaeology about the third hospital at Santa María and detailed historical information about the one at San Miguel. It should be noted, however, that makeshift or temporary structures and private homes served as hospitals when needed, such as during epidemics, destruction of hospitals by storms or fires, and episodic violence.

Powder Magazines and Arsenals

Six powder magazines were constructed at the West Florida presidio locations, two each at Santa María, Santa Rosa, and San Miguel (see table 6.6). All the maps of Forts San Carlos and San Miguel show the powder magazine in the northwest bastion of the forts. Only at Fort San Carlos were the magazines buried. The first powder house was constructed by May 1699 and is portrayed on the 1699 Franck map (see figure 2.6). Clune and colleagues (2003: 50) found documents that reveal it was constructed of boards planed on site and was about 9.3 by 13.8 feet in size and 11 feet high; the depth to which the magazine was buried is unknown. It survived the 1704 fire, but by 1706 it was described as collapsing. While fireproof materials for a new magazine were being requested, the powder was piled in the middle of the fort and covered with cattle hides (Clune et al. 2003: 51). However, as the requested ladrillos and lime to construct a masonry magazine were not delivered, the second magazine was built much like the first, in a cellar lined with boards (Clune et al. 2003: 51).

The first powder house at Santa Rosa was made of cedar boards; the building was 15 by 10 feet in size, five feet tall, and covered with cured cowhides (Childers 2003b: 8). It was destroyed in the 1740 hurricane and a second magazine was built out of stone and brick (Clune et al. 2006: 34). The tall domed structure inside the fort in the 1743 Serres drawing may be the second powder magazine (see figure 4.1). In a report of Santa Rosa after the 1752 hurricane, the stone and brick powder house appears to have survived, but the fort bastion next to it was torn off and the sea was within nine feet (Andreu 1753).

The first powder magazine at San Miguel was in engineer Feringan Cortés's fortified estate on the west edge of the settlement (see figure 5.5). In his report following the 1752 hurricane, Captain Eraso describes an ill-shaped turret made of timbers under construction at the Feringan estate for a powder house that was 13.7 by 11 feet in size with clay walls filled with lime and a shingled roof (Eraso 1752). The second powder magazine at San Miguel was inside the northwest bastion of the fort (see figure 5.3). The legend of the Ortíz-Feringan map describes the second magazine as made of stone with walls 13.8 feet high, a flat brick roof, tin gutters, and two cedar board doors covered in tin with an iron lock and key. The magazine was surrounded by a wall of stone coated in lime about 4.1 feet high.

Documents describe two arsenals or armories, one at Santa Rosa and one at San Miguel. At Santa Rosa, the armory was large, 82.2 by 11 feet in size and 8.2 feet high, and it had three interior rooms, each 27.4 feet wide. The building was made of wood and boards covered with cypress bark, but Buscarons (1731–1733) states that it was in such a state of disrepair that it was useless. The arsenal at San Miguel was much more substantial but smaller. The legend of the Ortíz-Feringan map states it was 13.7 feet high and had walls of clay coated in lime, a flat roof of brick, and a wood door with a lock and key of iron. The arsenal was positioned on the northwest corner of the San Miguel plaza/parade ground (see figure 5.3).

Guardhouses

There are 11 documented guardhouses associated with the West Florida presidio locations. As shown in table 6.6, there were three at Santa María, four at Santa Rosa, and four at San Miguel. At Fort San Carlos, a guardhouse was one of the first two buildings inside the fort, and it is shown on the May 1699 map (see figure 2.8). It housed soldiers who guarded the three gates of the fort and was placed close to the covered gate in the terrepleined south wall. The guardhouse was rectangular shaped with a gabled roof and appears to have been open on at least one end. This guardhouse burned in the 1701 fire, and its replacement burned in the 1704 fire that swept through the community. Both buildings had roofs of palmetto fronds (Clune 2003: 50). A third guardhouse was built in 1705 or early 1706, but by 1712 it was reported to be in poor condition. This guardhouse apparently was repaired or reconstructed and served an additional function as soldiers' quarters until 1719 (Clune et al. 2003: 50). This guardhouse was located next to the east gate of the fort on the plaza/parade ground. It is depicted on both the 1713 Spanish map and 1719 French map of Fort San Carlos (figures 2.4 and 2.5).

Of the four guardhouses at Santa Rosa mentioned in the documents, the first was the smallest. It was one of the initial buildings at the settlement, only eight by ten feet in size, eight feet high, and made of cedar boards brought from San José (Childers 2003b: 7). Buscarons' (1731–1733) account book describes another larger guardhouse that could have been a replacement for the small initial building. It was 32.8 by 16.4 feet in size, 8.2 feet high, made of boards covered with cypress bark, had a covered floor, and was in poor repair (see table 4.1). This second guardhouse was replaced in December 1731 with a "Principal Guardhouse" inside the fort. It was larger still, 43.8 by 22 feet, 8.2 feet high, made of wood, lined and roofed with cypress bark, and had a covered floor (Buscarons 1731–1733). At the same time, there was a fourth and smaller guardhouse outside the fort that was 32.9 by 16.4 feet in size, 6.9 feet high, and made of the same materials as the third guardhouse. All the guardhouses were destroyed in the 1740 hurricane, and an undescribed replacement was built and later destroyed by the 1752 hurricane.

At San Miguel, the 1763 Ortíz-Feringan map shows four guardhouses inside the fort (see figure 5.3). All were rectangular in shape and different in size. The largest was near the governor's residential compound near the south gate of the fort. The map legend describes the guardhouse near the governor's compound as having clay walls coated with lime. The other three guardhouses were covered with cypress bark. Each guardhouse had a room for the officer on guard and any prisoners.

The 11 guardhouses built at the four West Florida presidio locations did not follow a standard building plan. They were usually located at or near the fort gates. The guardhouses were not standardized and all were different, even within a single fort. One guardhouse was expanded into a general soldiers' quarters inside Fort San Carlos, and it had clay walls. We know nothing about the guardhouses at San José, and only a few details are known for those at Santa Rosa. However, guardhouses were important, built early, and rebuilt as necessary in order to aid in the protection and security of the presidio community.

Architecture Summary

It is clear that the West Florida presidio settlements were wooden communities. Wood was plentiful in the surrounding forests and swamps, and there is a clear evolution in the types and parts of trees used in construction as adaptions were made to local resources. Pine was exclusively used at Santa María. At San José, techniques were developed to harvest cypress bark for its use as roofing and siding, but cedar boards and timbers were imported from Veracruz. In the first years at Santa Rosa, cedar lumber continued to be imported, but by 1731, the Spanish had determined methods of harvesting local cypress trees. At San Miguel, cypress was almost the exclusive source of lumber, but the use of local red cedar in a few structures was documented for the first time. Cypress bark continued to be the dominant roofing material. Iron hardware, especially fasteners, always had to be imported. Pine logs were used for fort walls at all locations. A kiln was built on the mainland in 1741 and a second was in operation by 1754–1755. The bricks and ladrillos produced locally were used for floors, hearths, and ovens inside the wooden structures. Lime was produced after 1741, enabling local production of plaster, mortar, and whitewash.

Housing was the most frequent type of structure documented at the presidio locations. We have documentation for 64 small houses for soldiers, 45–49 individual residences with 33 associated outbuildings, and 14 barracks. There is additional information for 11 warehouses, 9 churches, and 7 hospitals. Three administrative structures, 11 guardhouses, 2 arsenals/armories, and 6 powder magazines are also documented.

Construction of all structures across the presidio community was in the Spanish style, with rectangular-shaped structures and timber framing set either on post-on-sill or in post-in-ground foundation trenches. Some houses at Santa Rosa were elevated to avoid flooding. Roofs were either gabled or single sloped (shed) and covered with thatch, bark, boards, or shingles. Walls were primarily covered with boards inside and out. At San Miguel, however, interior walls were usually covered with plaster, and there are also examples of plaster applied to lathe-covered walls. Moreover, some exterior walls at San Miguel were covered with clay and finished with a coat of lime or plaster. What is referred to as "clay" was probably local clay mixed with crushed oyster shells.

Material Culture

The total artifact assemblage recovered from the four locations of the Spanish West Florida presidio is remarkable in size and diversity. A combined assemblage of 94,501 counted items and 1,285.4 kg of weighed material has been recovered from 545 closed features and sealed midden contexts. As table 6.7 reveals, the assemblage from the Santa Rosa site makes up almost half the counted items (46.5%), owing to two extensive excavations and storm-battering of the sandy island site. The assemblage from Santa María makes up 33.9 percent of the counted assemblage and slightly less of the weighed (31.0%). San Miguel contributes only 16.0 percent of the counted but 31.5 percent of the weighed assemblage because of the smaller area excavated and the high number of large, waterlogged wooden parts of three wells and a cool storage facility, as well as the massive amount of brick rubble in the salvaged brick foundation. The assemblage from San José is considered only as a general collection, as the documentation has been lost from the only excavation Florida State University (FSU) conducted in 1965 and the site is now completely disturbed by water and bulldozing. The assemblage from San José was included in large-scale analyses, but it is excluded from finer-grained analyses where appropriate.

Table 6.7. Total presidio artifact assemblage: Artifact classes and groups

Presidio Location	Count	%	Weight (kg)	%
San Miguel	15,156	16.0%	405.3	31.5%
Santa María	32,018	33.9%	398.4	31.0%
Santa Rosa	43,899	46.5%	369.6	28.8%
San José	3,428	3.6%	112.2	8.7%
Totals	94,501		1,285.4	
Artifact Classes[a]	Count	%	Weight (g)	%
Building Material	6,335	6.7%	447,200.0	36.3%
Ceramics Euro-American	37,642	40.1%	227,975.8	18.5%
Metal	13,595	14.5%	157,425.9	12.8%
Fauna	717	0.8%	122,801.6	10.0%
Ceramics Native American	20,127	21.4%	98,712.7	8.0%
Flora Modified	118	0.1%	64,935.5	5.3%
Lithics	1,842	2.0%	53,219.7	4.3%
Glass	13,013	13.9%	31,522.6	2.6%
Flora	486	0.5%	27,392.9	2.2%
Fauna Modified	30	c	127.9	c
Totals	93,905		1,231,314.5	
Artifact Groups[b]	Count	%	Weight (g)	%
Architecture	14,794	16.0%	596,111.3	51.3%
Kitchen	67,147	72.4%	464,344.2	40.0%
Activities	1,629	1.8%	79,572.3	6.8%
Arms	4,574	4.9%	16,839.5	1.4%
Tobacco	1,455	1.6%	1,903.9	0.2%
Personal	894	1.0%	1,639.0	0.1%
Clothing	2,063	2.2%	920.1	0.1%
Furniture	157	0.2%	330.7	c
Totals	92,713		1,161,661.0	

[a] No Other
[b] No Unspecified
[c] Less than 0.1 percent.

Artifact Classes and Groups

The proportions of artifact classes and groups for the total assemblage from the four presidio sites are shown in table 6.7 and figure 6.6. In the combined assemblage, 61.5 percent of the artifact classes by count are ceramics, of which 65.2 percent are Euro-American and 34.8 percent are Native American. Metal items make up 14.5 percent of the assemblage by count and 12.8 percent by weight. Artifacts made of glass are 13.9 percent of the assemblage by count but only 2.6 percent by weight. Ceramics and glass are hardy materials but tend to meet a quick end via accident and breakage. On the other hand, metal items, especially iron, break up slowly through time, which increases their count in an archaeological context. As expected, heavy Building Materials make up the largest artifact class by weight (36.3%), followed by Euro-American Ceramics (18.5%), Metal (12.8%), and Fauna (10.0%). Almost all the assemblage is associated with the Architecture or Kitchen artifact groups (88.4% by count, 91.3% by weight). Each other group makes up 4.9 percent or less by count and 6.8 percent or less by weight.

Comparing the assemblages from the three Pensacola presidio sites by function, the Kitchen and Architecture artifact groups by weight at Santa María and Santa Rosa are very similar (figure 6.6; appendix VII, table VII.4). However, San Miguel has proportionately more Architecture material and less Kitchen material by weight. The high proportion of the Architecture group at San Miguel reflects the rapid construction of scores of buildings during its short 10-year occupation and the high number of architectural features excavated archaeologically. The high proportion by weight of the Activities group at San Miguel is skewed from the inclusion of heavy, wet barrel well staves and cool storage timbers. However, the count of Activities items at San Miguel is comparable to that of the other Pensacola locations, and it has the lowest number of Activities items of the three collections.

Arms artifacts by count and weight make up a low proportion of each assemblage recovered from the Pensacola presidio locations (0.1%–3.2% by weight). By count, the proportions of the Arms group range from 0.7 percent to 7.4 percent, reflecting the large number of shot (3,169) and gunflint fragments (1,276). When shot and gunflint fragments are removed, there are only 42 arms artifacts in the total assemblage: 32 from Santa Rosa, 10 from Santa María, and none from San Miguel. The only location of the presidio to have significant and prolonged warfare was Santa María, where the population suffered eight years of raids and guerrilla warfare by British-led Indian armies and two major naval attacks by the French in 1719. Arms from Santa María include three cannons and cannon balls, a cannon screw, a musket butt plate, and two sword/rapier

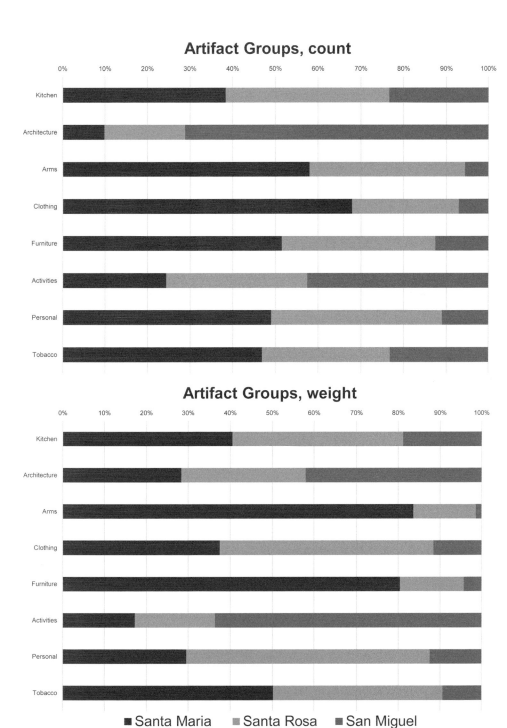

Figure 6.6. Proportions of artifact groups at the three Pensacola Bay presidio locations.

hilts. Many of the arms artifacts from Santa Rosa are quite small, such as a ramrod thimble, gun ferrules, gun cocks, trigger guards, and scabbard tips. As noted, the scattering of residents' belonging during many storm events and the site's soft, sandy matrix are the likely causes of the high numbers of small arms artifacts there.

Personal artifacts make up only a small amount (1.2% or less) of the artifact assemblage at the presidio sites by count and weight (figure 6.6). The low numbers of these deeply personal artifacts seemingly belies their significance in the lives of Pensacola's *presidiales*, yet we understand that the opposite is true. The number and proportion of personal items from Santa María and Santa Rosa are similar, but very few personal possessions were recovered from San Miguel. Almost half of the 872 total items of personal possession are fragments of Guadalajara Polychrome jars (47.4%), and 33.4 percent are rosary spacers or decorative beads. Other personal items such as keys, coins, dice, and pen nibs were recovered as well. Medicinal and cosmetic materials were primarily pieces of Guadalajara Polychrome, and as previously described, this particular ceramic type was believed to have both cosmetic and medicinal value for women and was also commonly used in Spanish colonial church contexts (Deagan 1987: 45).

The assemblage includes 287 beads from jewelry, especially necklaces, but some of these beads are undoubtedly from rosaries and five are metal rosary bead spacers. Most of the beads are made of glass (86.1%), but 26 are jet and amber, materials commonly used for rosary beads in this period. A handful of beads (21) are made of ceramic, gold, brass, and copper. There are also 55 pieces of jewelry and jewelry fragments, including five metal finger rings of brass, copper, and lead. Of the five finger rings, two are Jesuit rings from a burial at Santa María and were reinterred after examination. Other jewelry includes pendants of gold, brass, silver, and glass. Also of note are a higa of jet from Santa María and metal necklace parts such as hooks and chain. Unusual personal items include a brass music box key and three iron keys from Santa Rosa, writing nibs from San Miguel and Santa Rosa, a brass crucifix and part of a bone fan from San Miguel, and a mirror fragment from Santa Rosa. The low number of personal items in the San Miguel assemblage is curious, but this artifact assemblage is also the smallest of the three Pensacola presidio sites (15,156 counted items).

In the Personal artifact group, twenty coins were recovered from the three presidio locations on Pensacola Bay, but only 17 were available for this analysis. Of these 17, 15 are Spanish/Mexican cobs and two are French deniers. Table 6.8 offers a summary of the more detailed analysis in appendix VIII. Of the 15 silver cobs available for study, 13 are valued at a half-real, and two are valued at a full real. Thirteen of the Spanish coins were minted in Mexico City and two in the Potosí mint in Bolivia. The two French coins were struck at La Rochelle, France. Five of the cobs and the two French coins have readable dates, and the remaining Spanish cobs were dated by the known reigns of Spanish kings stamped on the coins. All the minting dates are in alignment with the occupation dates of the West Florida presidio. The oldest half-real cob was found at San Miguel, issued between 1609 and 1620 by Philip III of Spain. The two French coins, both recovered from Presidio Santa Rosa, were issued in 1721 and 1722 under the reign of Louis XV. An incredible 104 Spanish cobs have been recovered from two French colonial sites on Mobile Bay (Old Mobile and Port Dauphin) occupied during the Spanish West Florida Presidio Period. As detailed in appendix VIII, the values, mint sources, and manufacturing dates of the coins from French Mobile are the same as those of the coins recovered in Spanish Pensacola. In truth, the Spanish cobs came from Pensacola to Mobile and reflect the active trade between the colonial settlements that is well documented historically and discussed previously in this work. The French coveted Spanish coins and needed them to purchase supplies since they were poorly supported by France.

In the Kitchen group, ceramics are the most abundant items in the combined assemblage (82.7%). However, at San Miguel ceramics make up only half (50.1%) of the Kitchen group by count. Glass makes up 16.1 percent of the Kitchen group by count, and most artifacts are bottle fragments by both count (86.9%) and weight (95.6%). In the combined assemblage from the Pensacola presidio sites, fragments of wine bottles were the most abundant (41.6% by weight) followed by case bottles (33.1%). Other bottle types are condiment, pharmaceutical, and carboy. Fragments of tumblers, drinking glasses, and stemmed glasses were recovered from each presidio site. As shown in appendix VII, table VII.5, San Miguel had by far the highest percentage of glass fragments (18.1%). The assemblage from the three Pensacola presidio sites includes some unusual glass items, such as glass bottle stoppers, a large carboy at San Miguel, two jars and a pitcher at Santa Rosa, and a decanter, bowl, and three flasks at Santa María.

Food remains consistently reflect a preference for large animals, especially cow and deer, along with medium-sized mammals such as sheep, goat, and pig and small animals, especially chicken. The bay provided a wide variety of fish, oysters, and clams. Wild game meat was limited to deer and turkey, but alligator and sea turtle were consumed at San Miguel. Almost 16.0 percent of the San Miguel assemblage was faunal remains by weight, the highest proportion of the three Pensacola presidio sites (see appendix VII, table VII.5).

Metal kitchen tools provide an interesting array of 590 items, including fragments of 27 knives, five spoons, three forks, a cleaver, and three other utensils.

Table 6.8. Coins recovered from the Pensacola presidio locations

Presidio Location	Value	Metal	Nationality	Date or Date Range	Ruler	Mint
San Miguel	½ real	silver	Spanish/Mexican	1609–1620	Philip III	Mexico City
Santa Rosa	½ real	silver	Spanish/Mexican	1668–1699	Charles II	Mexico City
Santa Rosa	½ real	silver	Spanish/Bolivian	1718	Philip V	Potosí
Santa Rosa	1 real	silver	Spanish/Mexican	1731	Philip V	Mexico City
Santa Rosa	½ real	silver	Spanish/Mexican	1715–1727	Philip V	Mexico City
Santa Rosa	1 real	silver	Spanish/Mexican	1731	Philip V	Mexico City
Santa Rosa	1 real	silver	Spanish/Mexican	1732	Philip V	Mexico City
Santa Rosa	9 deniers	copper	French	1721	Louis XV	La Rochelle
Santa Rosa	9 deniers	copper	French	1722	Louis XV	La Rochelle
Santa María	½ real	silver	Spanish/Mexican	1715–1727	Philip V	Mexico City
Santa Maria	½ real	silver	Spanish/Mexican	1701–1728	Philip V	Mexico City
Santa María	½ real	silver	Spanish/Mexican	unknown	Philip ?	Mexico City
Santa María	½ real	silver	Spanish/Mexican	1678–1697	Charles II	Mexico City
Santa Maria	½ real	silver	Spanish/Mexican	1668–1697	Charles II	Mexico City
Santa María	1 real	silver	Spanish/Bolivian	1669	Charles II	Potosí
Santa María	½ real	silver	Spanish/Mexican	1706–1728	Philip V	Mexico City
Santa Maria	½ real	silver	Spanish/Mexican	1677–1697	Charles II	Mexico City

There are also pieces of eight pots, five lids, a pan, two caps, and four cups. Iron is the dominant metal in the combined assemblage (90.0% by weight, 68.3% by count), but there are many items made of other metals: lead (bale seals, fishing weights, and shot), steel (scabbard tip), brass (candlesticks, jewelry, buckles, and compasses), silver (aglet, brocade, and pendants), pewter (buckles, spoon, cuff links, and buttons), and copper (pan, utensils, and furniture escutcheon plate).

Clothing artifacts make up between 0.4 percent and 4.1 percent of the presidio site assemblages. Though few in number (2,042), these artifacts are revealing of status, as clothing and related accoutrements were important symbols of rank and status to Spain's colonial subjects. Just over two-thirds of the clothing-related artifacts were recovered from Santa María (64.5%), primarily owing to the 1,064 clothing seed beads from the clothes of the deceased laid to rest in the cemetery beneath the church floor. In line with the smaller proportion of personal items from San Miguel discussed above, this assemblage yielded very few clothing artifacts (only 59), while the Santa Rosa assemblage produced 32.6 percent of the clothing items. Clothing fasteners in the combined assemblage include 139 buckles for belts, shoes, and general clothing; almost 300 straight pins; 108 buttons, most of them metal; and 15 hooks and eyes. There also are three metal aglets as well as needles, thimbles, and a tang.

Ceramics

Ceramics make up 61.5 percent of the counted artifacts and 26.5 percent of the weighed material recovered from the four presidio sites (see table 6.7). The assemblage includes 57,769 sherds, 65.2 percent Euro-American and 34.8 percent Native American. Table 6.9 presents the three Pensacola presidio sites' Euro-American ceramic assemblage of 37,641 sherds by wares and classes along with the distribution of the ceramic classes at each presidio location on Pensacola Bay. In the combined Pensacola presidio assemblage, there are 29,706 typable Euro-American ceramics, the counts and weights of which are presented in appendix VII, table VII.6. There are 97 individual ceramic types but only ten make up 83.3 percent of the counted sherds (table 6.10). Not surprisingly, they are all Coarse Earthenware, including five Majolica types, four Other Coarse Earthenware types, and one Delft type. The remaining 88 ceramic types each make up only 1.4 percent or less of the Euro-American assemblage.

Euro-American Ceramics

The ceramic data for the Native American mission villages of San Joseph de Escambe and San Antonio de Punta Rasa I are presented in full in appendix IV. At Escambe, the Euro-American ceramic assemblage makes up only 3.3 percent of the ceramics. In both missions, Coarse Earthenware predominate

Table 6.9. Euro-American ceramic wares and classes from Pensacola presidio locations

Ceramic Ware	Ceramic Class	Count	%
Coarse earthenware	Other Coarse Earthenware	19,231	51.1%
Coarse earthenware	Majolica	15,280	40.6%
Coarse earthenware	Delft	994	2.6%
Coarse earthenware	Faience	636	1.7%
Coarse earthenware	Redware	375	1.0%
Coarse earthenware	Earthenware	53	0.1%
Coarse earthenware	Greyware	2	0.0%
Porcelain	Porcelain	483	1.3%
Refined earthenware	Creamware	186	0.5%
Refined earthenware	Refined Earthenware	2	0.0%
Stoneware	Stoneware	399	1.1%
Total		37,641	

	Santa María		Santa Rosa		San Miguel		Total	
Ceramic Wares and Classes	Count	%	Count	%	Count	%	Count	%
Other Coarse Earthenware	7,719	57.1%	9,570	48.4%	1,045	36.7%	18,334	50.7%
Majolica	5,466	40.5%	8,580	43.4%	624	21.9%	14,670	40.6%
Delft	15	0.1%	612	3.1%	367	12.9%	994	2.8%
Faience	87	0.6%	467	2.4%	82	2.9%	636	1.8%
Porcelain	165	1.2%	205	1.0%	113	4.0%	483	1.3%
Stoneware	28	0.2%	45	0.2%	327	11.5%	400	1.1%
Redware	30	0.2%	265	1.3%	80	2.8%	375	1.0%
Creamware	-	-	-	-	186	6.5%	186	0.5%
Earthenware	-	-	31	0.2%	22	0.8%	53	0.1%
Greyware	-	-	2	0.0%	-	-	2	0.0%
Refined Earthenware	-	-	-	-	2	0.1%	2	0.0%
Totals	13,510		19,777		2,848		36,135	

Table 6.10. Total Pensacola presidio ceramic assemblage: Top ten Euro-American and Native American ceramic types

Top 10 Euro-American Ceramic Types	Count	%	Weight (g)	%
El Morro	8,911	30.0%	30,474.6	18.0%
Majolica Puebla Blue on White	3,805	12.8%	4,018.3	2.4%
Lead Glazed Coarse Earthenware	2,709	9.1%	16,607.1	9.8%
Olive Jar	2,364	8.0%	64,689.5	38.2%
Majolica Puebla Polychrome	1,912	6.4%	8,007.2	4.7%
Majolica San Luis Polychrome	1,318	4.4%	1,615.2	1.0%
Coarse Earthenware Unglazed	1,205	4.1%	6,333.0	3.7%
Majolica Abo Polychrome	1,040	3.5%	4,461.9	2.6%
Majolica Blue on White	961	3.2%	994.3	0.6%
Delft Blue on White	533	1.8%	1,895.6	1.1%
Totals	24,758	83.3%	139,096.5	82.2%
Top 10 Native American Ceramic Types	**Count**	**%**	**Weight (g)**	**%**
Grog Tempered Plain	4,172	29.9%	20,199.5	28.3%
Sand Tempered Plain	2,426	17.4%	9,160.7	12.8%
Grog Tempered Burnished	1,068	7.7%	6,363.5	8.9%
Grog Shell Tempered Plain	427	3.1%	2,530.0	3.5%
Sand Tempered Burnished	492	3.5%	2,319.6	3.2%
Mississippi Plain, *variety* unspecified	282	2.0%	1,897.9	2.7%
Grit Tempered Plain	442	3.2%	1,680.5	2.4%
Jefferson Plain	138	1.0%	1,633.8	2.3%
Pensacola Plain	373	2.7%	1,503.2	2.1%
Chattahoochee Roughened, *variety* Chattahoochee	327	2.3%	1,489.7	2.1%
Totals	10,147	72.7%	48,778.2	68.3%

(97.2%), and almost all (91.3%) are Majolica and Other Coarse Earthenware. The additional Coarse Earthenware classes such as Delft (2.6%) and Cream-ware (0.5%) are very small.

The three large Euro-American ceramic assemblages from the sites of three spatially separate and chronologically sequential presidios on Pensacola Bay provide a rare opportunity to determine if there are temporal trends in the Euro-American ceramics. Seriation of ceramic wares, classes, and types has identified temporal trends at each of these levels of classification. Looking at the proportions of ceramic wares in the assemblages from the three Pensacola sites (table 6.9; figure 6.7), the similarity between Santa María and Santa Rosa (1698–1752) is striking. Both large ceramic assemblages (13,510 from Santa María; 19,777 from Santa Rosa) are almost completely composed of Coarse Earthenware (98.6% and 98.7%, respectively), and there are only tiny amounts of Porcelain and Stoneware. The proportion of Coarse Earthenware in the San Miguel Period drops significantly to 77.9 percent with a corresponding increase in other wares (11.5% Stoneware, 6.6% Refined Earthenware, and 4.4%

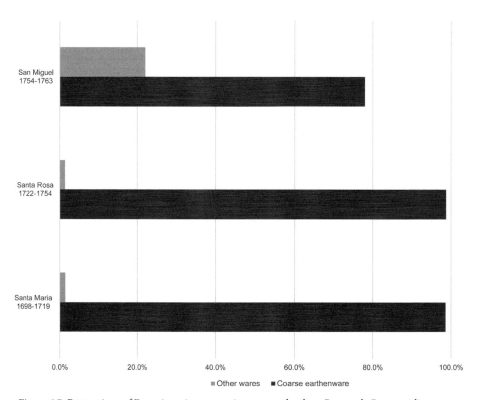

Figure 6.7. Proportions of Euro-American ceramic wares at the three Pensacola Bay presidio locations.

Porcelain). Interestingly, the Euro-American ceramic assemblage collected from San José (N=1,510) is 100 percent Coarse Earthenware.

When seriating ceramic classes, once again Santa María and Santa Rosa are nearly identical, and the San Miguel assemblage is significantly different (figure 6.8). At San Miguel, the proportion of Other Coarse Earthenware and Majolica is significantly lower with a coinciding sharp increase in other ceramic classes, which are all non-Spanish made (French Faience, Dutch Delft, English Creamware and Stoneware, and Chinese Porcelain), illustrated in figure 6.9. The proportions of non-Spanish-made ceramics are very small at Santa Rosa (6.8%) and Santa María (2.2%). The dramatic increase in the proportion of non-Spanish-made ceramics at San Miguel (37.8%) is a strong indicator of the San Miguel Period (1756–1765). The influx of non-Spanish ceramics is attributed to the change in Spanish trade policy of allowing merchants in their colonies to conduct trade directly with other countries. Several merchants in the San Miguel presidio were engaging in brisk, multi-national trade during the presidio's decade of existence.

Seriation of the 99 Euro-American ceramic types in the combined assemblage of 29,706 typable sherds identified four ceramic types that are abundant, have a peak in proportion at different presidio locations through time, and are present in all three Pensacola presidio assemblages. Figure 6.10 reveals that three abundant ceramic types peak at Santa María (1698–1719): Puebla Polychrome, San Luis Polychrome, and Olive Jar. The most abundant of these ceramic types is Puebla Polychrome, which makes up over half (52.2%) of the Majolicas at Santa María but is very low at the other locations. San Luis Polychrome makes up 25.2 percent of the Majolicas at Santa María but drops to 7.2 percent and 5.5 percent at the later Pensacola presidio sites. Olive Jar sherds make up 27.7 percent of the Other Coarse Earthenware in the Santa María period but only 5.5 percent or less at the other locations. At Santa Rosa, Puebla Blue on White jumps to 54.5 percent of the Majolicas from only 4.5 percent at Santa María, and it drops to 29.8 percent at San Miguel. While there is no single, distinctive, high-percentage ceramic type marker for San Miguel, the significant ceramic indicator is the distinctive sudden swell of non-Spanish-made ceramics (37.8%). As discussed above, non-Spanish-made ceramics make up only 6.7 percent or less in both previous periods (figure 6.8).

In sum, seriation of the three large Euro-American ceramic assemblages from three spatially and chronologically separate locations of the West Florida presidio on Pensacola Bay has revealed temporally sensitive indicators in ceramic wares, classes, and types. Ceramic wares and classes in the assemblages of Santa María and Santa Rosa are strikingly similar, but there are differences in the proportions of two abundant types of Majolica and Olive Jar. The San

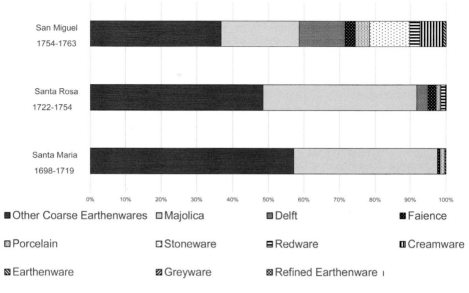

Figure 6.8. Ceramic trends of Euro-American ceramic classes at the three Pensacola Bay presidio locations.

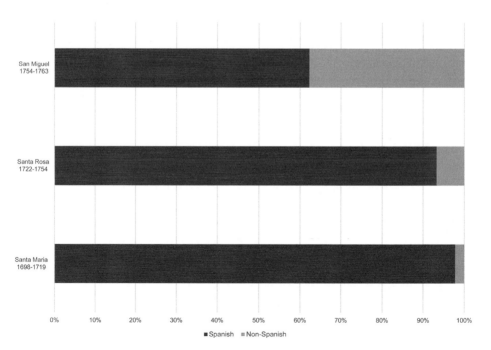

Figure 6.9. Ceramic trends of Spanish/non-Spanish ceramics at the three Pensacola Bay presidio locations.

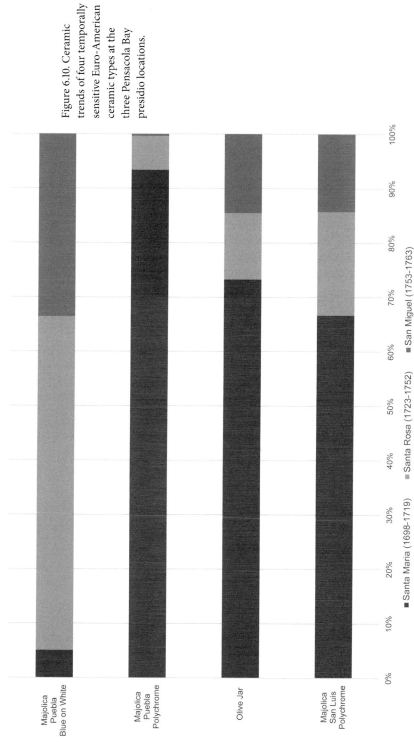

Figure 6.10. Ceramic trends of four temporally sensitive Euro-American ceramic types at the three Pensacola Bay presidio locations.

Miguel assemblage stands out as a result of the reduction in Spanish-made ceramics and the significant increase in non-Spanish-made ceramics. Given the size of the Euro-American ceramic assemblage (37,641 sherds, 29,706 of which are typable), the identified temporal assemblage indicators should be credible.

Native American Ceramics

Native American ceramics comprise 34.8 percent of the total ceramic assemblage collected from the West Florida presidio sites on Pensacola Bay. As shown in figure 6.11, the proportion of Native American ceramics at Santa María and Santa Rosa varies by only a few percentage points (38.5% and 33.8%, respectively). However, at San Miguel, the proportion of Native American ceramics drops significantly to 14.7 percent. The high proportion of Native American ceramics at the early presidios likely reflects an inadequate supply of and access to Euro-American ceramic containers. As a result of this undersupply, for over half a century, the Spanish supplemented their need for ceramic containers by obtaining them from local Native Americans, and after 1740, "casta manufacturing" by

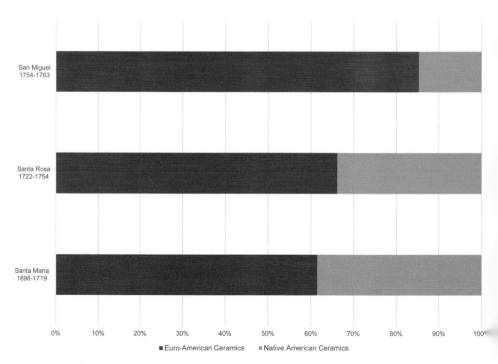

Figure 6.11. Proportions of Euro-American and Native American ceramics at the three Pensacola Bay presidio locations.

Hispanic presidio community members contributed to locally made utilitarian containers (Eschbach 2019: 496). San Miguel experienced an increase in the supply of and access to Euro-American ceramics, and the percentage of Native American-made containers drops significantly to 14.7 percent with a coinciding increase in the proportion of non-Spanish-made Euro-American ceramics. Both ceramic assemblage changes at San Miguel are a direct reflection of the relaxing of the Spanish monopoly on trade, which greatly increased the community's access to non-Spanish Euro-American ceramics.

As explained in chapter 4, Worth (2012) points out that Native American groups continued using traditional ethnic tempering agents during the Presidio Period, but surface treatments were much more flexible. The Native American ceramic assemblage from the Pensacola presidio sites consists of 18,992 sherds weighing 87.4 kg (table 6.11). Of the 16 tempers identified in the assemblage, 98.8 percent are tempered with the following ingredients: grog, sand, shell, grog shell, and grit. The remaining 11 tempers are combinations of these five materials plus a few new ingredients. In order to see tempering patterns more clearly, I have excluded the 1.2 percent with a wide variety of mixed tempers from the following analysis.

The proportions of the five dominant temper types by weight at each of the presidio locations on Pensacola Bay are shown in figure 6.12, and several patterns are evident. Sand tempering was consistently used throughout the Presidio Period, ranging from 26.7 to 36.5 percent. The use of grog temper seriates well as it has a classic battleship frequency pattern, peaking at Santa María (55.8%), markedly declining at Santa Rosa (33.6%), and falling very low at San Miguel (6.7%). This trend in grog tempering indicates that a high percentage (50.0% or more) of grog tempering by weight is a good marker for the Santa María Period, and when it is about 30.0 percent, it is an indicator of the Santa Rosa period.

Shell tempering also seriates well and is present in significant amounts in the Pensacola presidio assemblages. Shell tempering reaches its peak at Santa Rosa (29.2% by weight) and is significantly less at the previous and following presidio sites. Shell tempering is associated with several Native American groups west of Pensacola Bay in both the Mobile Bay area and the interior river valleys that have their confluence there. The high proportion of shell tempering at Santa Rosa is thought to reflect both direct and indirect down-the-line trade with members of the many ethnic groups who visited Santa Rosa (Harris and Eschbach 2006). This proportion also reflects the return of refugee Apalachees from the interior, who probably adapted shell tempering from the Lower Creeks living there. There was also heavy trade between Santa Rosa and Mobile, where French traders from the interior sold

Table 6.11. Native American ceramic tempers from Pensacola presidio locations

Pensacola Presidio Locations	Count	Weight (g)		
San Miguel	528	1,854.8		
Santa Rosa	10,120	46,008.7		
Santa María	8,461	40,892.6		
Totals	19,109	88,756.1		

Native American Ceramic Tempers	Count	%	Weight (g)	%
Majority Tempers				
Grog	6,695	35.3%	36,650.2	41.9%
Sand	7,653	40.3%	24,974.3	28.6%
Shell	2,942	15.5%	16,515.1	18.9%
Grog Shell	629	3.3%	4,126.0	4.7%
Grit	847	4.5%	3,403.8	3.9%
Subtotals	18,766	98.8%	85,669.3	98.0%
Minority Tempers				
Grit Grog	123	0.6%	1,017.7	1.2%
Sponge spicules	9	a	115.0	0.1%
Mica	8	a	114.1	0.1%
Mica Shell	20	0.1%	99.2	0.1%
Grog Mica	17	0.1%	97.8	0.1%
Grit Shell	22	0.1%	85.8	0.1%
Limestone	7	a	61.4	0.1%
Grit Mica	9	a	59.2	0.1%
Bone Charcoal Fiber Grog	7	a	53.3	0.1%
Grit Grog Shell	2	a	23.0	a
Charcoal Grog	2	a	12.0	a
Subtotals	226		1,738.5	
Grand Totals	18,992		87,407.8	

a Less than 0.1 percent.

their goods, which could have included Native American ceramic containers (Worth 2015). Regardless of the reason, when about one-third of a Native American ceramic assemblages is shell tempered, it is a good indicator of the Santa Rosa years (1723–1752) in West Florida. Grit tempering, though low in proportion, also has a distinct temporal pattern. It is 14.0 percent of the Native American assemblage at San Miguel and significantly lower at the

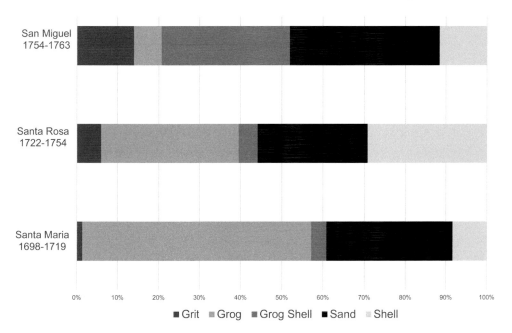

Figure 6.12. Ceramic trends of Native American temper types at the three Pensacola Bay presidio locations.

earlier locations. A maximum proportion of 14.0 percent is too low to be a determining temporal indicator, but it is a supporting one.

There are 143 Native American ceramic types in the total West Florida assemblage, but only 10 make up 68.3 percent of the assemblage by weight (appendix VII, table VII.7). The most abundant types are Grog Tempered Plain (28.3%), Sand Tempered Plain (12.8%), and Grog Tempered Burnished (8.9%). The remaining top 10 ceramic types each make up 3.5 percent or less of the assemblage. A distinguishing characteristic of Native American pottery throughout the West Florida Presidio Period is that regardless of temper, over two-thirds (68.8%) have either plain (57.5%) or burnished (11.3%) surfaces. Other surface treatments occur in low amounts, such as roughened (6.8%), stamped (4.3%), and slipped and painted (1.9%). The wide variety of Native American ceramic types is a reflection of the many ethnic groups that passed through West Florida during this time, traded ceramics to the presidio communities, and moved on. Mixing and merging of Native American groups was occurring throughout West Florida and the greater Southeast during this time, disrupting traditional ceramic surface decorating and, consequently, the application of archaeologists' traditional ceramic classification system. Typology of Native American ceramics during the late seventeenth and early eighteenth centuries in the Southeast needs revising to better understand the connection to people.

Colono Ware

Native American ceramics with European features have been noted in Spanish colonial assemblages from the very beginning of research into this period in the Southeast (Smith 1948a, 1948b). Deagan's (1987: 103–104) description of these ceramics as "locally produced, handbuilt ceramics of non-European origin that were used by Europeans in the New World colonies" has been the benchmark definition for over three decades. Jennifer Melcher (2008, 2011) and Worth and Melcher (2015) have conducted new research on this generally neglected Colono Ware ceramic type from Mission Escambe and the three Pensacola presidio locations. The discussion below uses the database Melcher and Worth developed for their research. Their reanalysis of these ceramics used the type-variety system with temper as the primary typing feature, surface decorations as varieties, and vessel form as subtypes. Five varieties of Mission Red Filmed were defined based on temper, and two new types, Mission Slipped and Colonial Red Painted, were defined. See Melcher (2011: appendix C) and Worth and Melcher (2015) for the definitions of the new types and varieties.

There is little Colono Ware (N=583, 3.0 kg) in the large Native American ceramic assemblage of 20,127 sherds weighing 98.7 kg from the Pensacola presidio sites. Melcher (2008) suggests that the low amount may be due to the difficulty in identifying undecorated body sherds as Colono Ware. The complete list of types in the Colono Ware assemblage is shown in appendix VII, table VII.8. The most abundant types by weight are Grog Tempered Plain (26.7%); Mission Red, *variety* San Luis (20.0%); and Mission Red, *variety* Pensacola (11.8%). Almost all (93.6%) of the Colono Ware was recovered from Santa María and Santa Rosa in almost equal amounts. Three-quarters of the Colono Ware at Santa María is grog tempered, but there is only 39.3 percent from Santa Rosa, which corresponds with the temporal distribution of the tempering agents of grog and shell discussed above. Eighty percent of the red filmed ceramics at Santa María are grog tempered, but only 15.0 percent are grog tempered at Santa Rosa. Melcher (2011: 100–104) correlates the shifts in Colono Ware and red filming at the two presidio locations with changes in the Native American populations at both sites. The Native American population at Santa María was predominately Apalachee, who used grog to temper their clay. At Santa Rosa, there was a change in the Native American population on Pensacola Bay with the immigration of Apalachees from the interior who probably adapted red filming and shell tempering from the Lower Creeks. There is very little Colono

Ware in the San Miguel assemblage (N=96, 194.1 g); grog tempering continues to decline, and sand is the preferred tempering agent. Melcher (2008) suggests that the preference for sand temper could have been due to the immigration of Yamasees into the Pensacola Bay area.

Colono Wares were made into tableware, primarily platos and brimmed plato forms. There is an increase in lebrillos (straight sided shallow bowls) at Santa Rosa (Bense and Wilson 2003: 178; Melcher 2011: 104). Another interesting feature of Colono Ware is a preciseness in manufacturing at Santa María and its decline at Santa Rosa. Melcher (2011: 106–107) suggests that the precise replicas of Spanish tableware at Santa María are related to direct contact with the Spanish as many Indians lived at the presidio. However, at the Santa Rosa location of the presidio, Apalachees lived in a separate village in the Escambia River valley some 35 miles away and had much less direct contact with the Spanish. This reduction in direct contact, Melcher (2011) suggests, resulted in manufacturing and decorating tableware forms from memory rather than direct observation, producing pottery that was less precise and had a wider range of variation than the pottery at Santa María.

Overall, Colono Ware is present in all three locations of the Pensacola presidio, but in small amounts. Just over half (54.7%) the pieces are tempered with grog, followed by shell (21.1%) and sand (14.7%). There are differences in temper and vessel forms between Santa María and Santa Rosa, which are attributed to a shift in the Native American settlement pattern away from the presidio community. Worth and Melcher's (2015) recent study of this Colono Ware assemblage provides useful new types that integrate well into the type-variety system of Native American ceramic typology in the Southeast.

Ceramic Assemblage Summary

Overall, a large ceramic assemblage of 57,769 sherds weighing 326.7 kg was recovered from the four locations of the West Florida presidio. Almost two-thirds are Euro-American (65.1% by count, 69.7% by weight) and one-third is Native American. The ratio of Euro-American and Native American ceramics is about 2:1 at Santa María and Santa Rosa but significantly drops at San Miguel to almost 7:1. The Euro-American ceramic assemblages at Santa María and Santa Rosa are quite similar and both had a low diversity. However, the San Miguel assemblage is much more diverse and includes some refined earthenware. One of the distinctions of the San Miguel assemblage is that almost 40.0 percent of the Euro-American ceramics are not Spanish made.

The most abundant ceramic types in the combined assemblage are El Morro, Puebla Blue on White Majolica, and Lead Glazed Coarse Earthenware. Four ceramic types are temporally sensitive, three of which have proportions specific to Santa María: San Luis and Puebla Polychrome majolicas and Olive Jar. Puebla Blue on White majolica is most abundant in the Santa Rosa assemblage.

Temper is the most informative feature of Native American ceramics as it appears to be associated with ethnic groups rather than surface decoration during this tumultuous period in lower southeastern North America. Overall, grog and sand are the most abundant tempers. However, grog and shell tempering agents are temporally sensitive and indicative of the Santa María and Santa Rosa assemblages, respectively. There is a wide variety of types of Native American ceramics and over two-thirds of surfaces are plain or burnished.

Material Culture Summary

The artifact assemblage recovered from the four presidio locations on Pensacola Bay is very large: 94,501 counted items and 1,285.4 kg of weighed material (see table 6.7). The largest individual assemblage by count is Santa Rosa (46.5%), and the largest by weight is San Miguel (31.5%) followed by Santa María (31.0%). The combined assemblage's large size provides an excellent view of the material culture that has survived the elements and lends credibility to the temporally sensitive indicators and distinctive patterns identified in its analysis. The most abundant artifact classes across this large assemblage are Building Material by weight and Ceramics by count, followed by Metal and Fauna. Almost all the materials are associated with the Architecture and Kitchen artifact groups, but the remaining groups offer a wealth of information about the people and their communities who lived in the four locations of the West Florida presidio.

The analysis of the material culture has focused on the large assemblages recovered from the three presidio locations on Pensacola Bay. The collection from San José is more limited in its analytical usefulness, though it does have some utility. In general, the assemblages from Santa María and Santa Rosa are quite similar by many measures, and the San Miguel assemblage is quite different. The patterns and trends in the assemblages across space and time reflect changes in the demographic composition of the communities, shifting Spanish policies on outside trade and private enterprise, and chronic problems of dependability of the situado. Seriation of the ceramic assemblages has identified temporal indicators at the levels of ware, class, and type. The fortunate (for archaeologists) geographic and temporal segregation of the three presidio locations on Pensacola Bay has provided unusually strong temporal bracketing of the archaeological record that has enabled tracking of many aspects of the material culture used by the Hispanic military community in West Florida.

Integration Summary

With the exception of a few foreigners and Native Americans, residents of the West Florida presidio were subjects of New Spain. These men and women were sent willingly and unwillingly from Veracruz and Mexico City to the isolated garrison on the western frontier of Spanish Florida. The community at Pensacola was established during a time when the Spanish Crown was grappling with the seemingly infinite variety of peoples, cultures, languages, and diversity of experiences among her New World colonial subjects. In this environment, the *sistema de castas* took root among the elite in an effort to control, understand, and ultimately, contain the growing economic and social power among wealthy Spanish and criollo colonial families. However, despite the expansion and refinement of casta categories and their related social and legal regulations for the populace of New Spain, the West Florida presidio was first and foremost a military community with the mission of protecting Spanish West Florida from intrusion by European rivals. In the presidio community, military rank came first and crosscut the more rigid racial or social hierarchy in New Spain. Within this framework of military order, the presidio population had five basic hierarchical categories of occupation and social standing: officers/ senior administrators, craftsmen, soldiers, convicts/slaves, and Native Americans. At the top, officers and senior administrators were criollos, people of Spanish descent born and raised in New Spain. Craftsmen either were from the established guilds in New Spain or were locally trained apprentices. Soldiers and convicts were from many lower castas, as were the servants of officers and administrators, but they had the same social rank at the presidio. Native Americans, in general, were considered outsiders and were often hired as temporary laborers, skilled craftsmen, and builders throughout the Presidio Period. In addition, some soldiers married or lived with Native American women.

Aside from servants and enslaved persons who lived within the households of their masters, these five social groups generally lived in physically separate spaces across the presidio community but interacted regularly and with a level of familiarity particular to very small and geographically isolated settlements. Despite the disruptions of moving the entire presidio community three times, the regular turnover in military assignments, and a high sickness and death rate, there was cultural continuity within the immigrant population for the 65 years of its existence. This continuity grew out of a shared cultural background among the majority of Pensacola's *presidiales*, both officers and enlisted soldiers as well as their dependents. Starting in 1741, there was an increased emphasis on recruiting military men with families to serve at the West Florida presidio, with offered incentives of free workable land and military-backed property protection after their enlisted service ended. New military families met resident-established Spanish families who had been thriving in Florida for decades since the preceding mission period of Spanish East Florida. Civilian families and single adults also began to arrive in Pensacola at this time and were offered the same incentives to put down roots. When Spain turned over Florida to Britain in 1763, a burgeoning multi-generational community of Spanish West Floridians was displaced.

As noted, historians and archaeologists have had a difficult time determining the exact number of people living at the Pensacola presidio community. Obstacles to an accurate count include sporadic records, high turnover of military positions, uncounted population loss from desertion, mutiny, and disease, and the common practice of not always counting servants, women, children, and the small but present group of enslaved people. The shifting Native American refugee populations associated with the Pensacola community also generally went uncounted and underreported, as did the occasional group of shipwreck survivors, temporarily stationed military units, Native American refugees fleeing the destruction of the mission system, and shipwreck survivors. All these groups of people briefly swelled the population several times throughout the Presidio Period. The most consistent part of the counted population was the group of people occupying official positions or *plazas* and receiving rations. Despite these problems, available records indicate that the population fluctuated from a low of 80 to a high of 1,200. Overall, however, the average population at the West Florida presidio appears to have been between 300 and 500 people.

Regardless of where the presidio was located, there was a consistent constellation of three settlement types in Spanish West Florida: the presidio itself, military outposts, and Native American mission villages. Presidios were always situated on the bay shores with direct access to the Gulf. Military outposts were strategically located to protect supply warehouses, shipping lanes, and the entrances to bays and rivers. Refugee Native mission villages were located between about 14 and 34 miles from the presidios. While the Native Americans lived in separate mission villages, many worked for wages, traded, and lived for periods of time at the presidio, and many others received regular rations.

Eleven forts were constructed in West Florida during the 65 years of Spanish occupation. There was a single fort at three of the presidio locations, three forts at Santa Rosa, four at outposts, and one in a mission village. Three of the presidio forts were sizable and equipped with many cannons: San Carlos, San José, and San Miguel. The fort at Santa Rosa was diminutive in comparison and was twice destroyed by storms and rebuilt. The basic Vauban fort design of a square stockade with corner bastions has been documented at Fort San Carlos. Fort San Miguel was built urgently after the community was already built and occupied, and as a result, it had an irregular polygon shape with two to four bastions. Seawalls and bastion walls were terrepleined at San Carlos and San Miguel, and their design evolved from a sand-filled stanchion frame with a low, angled exterior wall of horizontal logs at San Carlos to two parallel, vertical, sand-filled stockade walls at San Miguel. Curtain walls were single post stockades, but the construction method changed from individual log placement in a long, wide, and deep trench at San Carlos to pre-fabricated post sections in a narrow trench at San Miguel. Placement of cannons also changed from mounting on the top of walls at San Carlos to placement on low ground platforms to allow firing through openings in the walls at Santa Rosa and San Miguel. The number of structures inside presidio forts varied from 4 to 87. Regardless of their size, inside all of the forts were a few structures essential to the survival of the presidio: supply warehouse(s), powder magazine, and guardhouses.

The fort structure was the initial construction project at the first three presidio locations, and it was the last construction at San Miguel. Structures inside Forts San Carlos and San Miguel were organized around a central plaza/parade ground with two surrounding rings of buildings. At San Carlos, the plaza was lined with large community buildings and barracks lining the curtain walls, but at San Miguel, the plaza was lined with military barracks and large, multi-structure, high-status residential compounds.

Some architectural information is available for a total of 205–209 buildings. Most (60.0%) of the buildings were for housing, but there is some information for 30 public/community buildings: 11 warehouses, 9 churches, 7 hospitals, and 3 administrative buildings. Preferred building materials changed over time as builders became more knowledgeable about local resources and began local production of bricks, tiles, and lime, thereby reducing their dependency on imports from New Spain. Wood was the dominant building material for all structures, and all four presidio communities were wooden. The types of wood used in construction changed from pine, to imported cedar from Veracruz, to sheets of local cypress bark, and finally to cypress lumber. Bricks and tiles were used for specific features of structures. Long, straight pine poles were used for all fort walls.

The most numerous structures at the presidio locations were military housing and residences, followed by warehouses, guardhouses, churches, administrative buildings, hospitals, and powder magazines. With the exception of temporary thatch huts, the architectural style was Hispanic, originally derived from Spain and modified in the Caribbean, San Agustín, and Mission San Luis. Buildings were rectangular in shape with gabled roofs.

The structure framing method was consistent at all locations of the West Florida presidio. Foundations were either post-on-sill or post-in-trench, and walls were framed with vertical posts. Almost all buildings had gabled roofs covered with thatch, boards, cypress bark, or shingles. Exterior walls were covered with palmetto fronds, boards, and clay and sometimes finished with plaster or lime. Almost all homes were one-story structures. Some large buildings such as warehouses, churches, and high-status residences had two floors with large and substantial foundations, balconies, and rental apartments upstairs. The function of some structures changed over time, with a hospital becoming a warehouse, private homes being used as hospitals, and a hospital becoming a church.

Powder magazines were special structures and their construction varied. They were in cellars, out in the open covered with hides, and made of stone and brick. All powder magazines were inside the fort, usually in a bastion. Arsenals were also specially constructed and secured.

The artifact assemblage recovered from the four presidio locations is large, totaling 94,501 counted items and 1,285.5 kg of weighed material. The largest assemblages of counted items are from Santa Rosa (46.5%) and Santa María (31.9%). San Miguel (31.5%) and Santa María (31.0%) are the heaviest assemblages. The large size of the assemblage as a whole provides confidence that the patterns and proportions in the assemblage and through time are credible reflections of the material culture. In general, the assemblages recovered from Santa María, San José, and Santa Rosa are very similar, and the San Miguel assemblage is different.

The composition of the artifact assemblages also reflects the shift in Spanish policies toward outside trade and private enterprise, as well as the chronic problems of poor supply and corruption of local officials. The fortunate geographic and temporal segregation of the four presidio locations has provided unusually short and wide windows into the evolution and adaptations of the Hispanic and Native American populations as reflected in their material culture. Building Material and Ceramics are the most abundant artifact classes in this large assemblage, followed by Metal and Fauna. Almost all the materials are associated with either the Architecture and Kitchen artifact groups, but items in the remaining artifact groups provide considerable information related to status, activities, and gender. With this large of a sample of the material culture in use at the presidio locations, several small but telling items have been recovered. For example, though scarce, porcelain has identified new and corroborated other high-status persons and households while inexpensive majolica tableware has not. The presence of rare fragments of writing implements (nibs, slates, and ink bottles) has revealed where literate persons lived and shown that they were not always of high status, as indicated by those recovered from the convicts' barracks at Fort San Carlos. Scores of fragments of unusual, small ceramic figurines corroborated the site of two churches at

Santa Rosa. Unique French religious items such as Jesuit rings and Man-in-the-Moon glass beads found in the remains of the church and subfloor cemetery at Santa María reflected the presence of the French priest La Maire who served there for a short while. Then there are the three cannon tubes quickly buried inside Fort San Carlos, one of which contained part of a linen gunpowder bag. There are many more special artifacts in this large assemblage from closed contexts carefully excavated over the course of almost four decades.

The huge ceramic assemblage of over 57,000 sherds shows the full range of both the Euro-American and Native American containers used at these settlements. Internally and in the assemblage as a whole, almost all the 37,642 Euro-American ceramics are Coarse Earthenware, with Majolica and Other Coarse Earthenware predominating. The most abundant types are El Morro, Puebla Blue on White, Lead Glazed Coarse Earthenware, and Olive Jar. The primary tempers of Native American ceramics are grog, sand, and shell. Sand Tempered Plain, Grog Tempered Plain, and Grog Tempered Burnished are the most frequent ceramic types. Colono Wares, though few, are also present in the large ceramic assemblage.

Being able to separate the 65-year presidio into four internal chronological intervals has enabled the identification of several ceramic temporal trends and markers. Examples of documented temporal ceramic trends include changes in proportions of Euro-American and Native American ceramics, identification of four abundant Euro-American ceramic types that are distinctive of specific time periods, and the sudden rise in non-Spanish ceramics in the San Miguel Period. The proportions of temper types also have distinct differences through time.

Overall, the information gathered about the people of the presidios, their settlement patterns, their fortifications, and their adaptations to the building materials available in West Florida has provided valuable insight into life in Spanish West Florida between 1698 and 1763. Far from home, undersupplied, and besieged by French and English enemies and their allied Native American fighters, a small, motely military and civilian community of Spanish subjects found themselves transplanted from New Spain. Once settled, these early West Floridians held the western border of what was left of Spanish Florida for the Crown for nearly seven decades. The residents of the Spanish West Florida presidio communities learned from and adapted to their environment while also holding fast to their Hispanic culture that had characterized Spain's colonies since the sixteenth century.

7

Conclusions

This book is the culmination of over three decades of research (1995–2018) on the Spanish occupation of West Florida. This endeavor began as the second step in historical archaeology research in West Florida following a decade of archaeological experience in historic downtown Pensacola, occupied since 1754. The presidios project was begun relatively early in my career, and the perspectives and methodologies brought to it were a result of my academic training in anthropology, the development of a community-level interest in Pensacola's archaeology and historic preservation, and my involvement in the growing interdisciplinary field of historical archaeology. The development of these issues and their influence on the long-term research synthesized in this book are summarized below.

Throughout my academic education, a "four-field" approach to anthropology, which included courses and training in archaeology, linguistics, biological anthropology, and archaeology, predominated. The object of anthropology is to gain an understanding of human culture, and the goal of anthropological archaeologists is to develop research projects capable of shedding light on this uniquely human phenomenon among people in the past. Within the archaeological subdiscipline of anthropology, I was initially trained at Florida State University (FSU) in the methodologies and interpretative models developed at the University of North Carolina (UNC) by Joffre L. Coe, which stressed the application of the scientific method and meticulous field methods over long-term, large-scale excavations of strategically selected sites (Ferguson 2002). Coe included the historic period in his research, as evidenced in his students' work, especially the work and writings of Stanley A. South (1977). Coe's sway in American archaeology remains strong; his particular emphasis on the application of scientific methods in archaeology was foundational in the development of "processual" models of archaeology by another of his students, Lewis R. Binford (1972).

Yet another of Coe's students, David S. Phelps, taught at FSU in the 1960s, and it was through Phelps that I was trained in the "Coe School" of archaeology as I earned my bachelor's and master's degrees there between 1963 and 1969.

One of the most important principles of this training was thoroughness and meticulousness in the field, with all subsequent analyses and conclusions only as good as the fieldwork. No shortcuts, rushing or sloppiness in excavation, photography, notes, or scale drawings were tolerated. Essential to the process of archaeology was determining an accurate chronology and using seriation based on stratigraphy and various radiometric dating methods. Phelps followed Coe in his quickness to include new developments from other disciplines into archaeology, especially zooarchaeological analysis and ecological studies.

In the doctoral program at Washington State University (WSU), I continued the four-field anthropology education in a Quaternary Studies interdisciplinary program that combined fieldwork and coursework in botany, ecology, geomorphology, and archaeology. A recent archaeological find of human remains dating to 10,000–11,000 B.P. at the Marmes rock shelter in the Snake River Valley (Fryxell et al. 1968) had led to significant funding for the Quaternary Studies program, and I was fortunate enough to be selected to join it (1969–1972). This program opened my eyes to the value of truly interdisciplinary research and the information it could provide to archaeologists in terms of the wider environmental context in which humans are adapting and making strategic decisions.

This academic education was quickly applied when I led a large scale testing and excavation of 11 Archaic sites that were in the path of the construction of the Tennessee-Tombigbee Waterway in Alabama and Mississippi. By including soil scientists, a new developing dating method (archaeomagnetism), geomorphologists, and advisors such as Bennie C. Keel and James B. Griffin, we were able to extract a wealth of information from the deeply stratified midden mounds in the floodplain of the swampy headwaters of the Tombigbee River, which revealed much about the Early and Middle Archaic bands of people and the environmental conditions in which they lived (Bense 1987a; Bense and Pettry 1989).

It was with the mindset of four-field anthropology, the processual theoretical approach, interdisciplinary research, the scientific method, and the Coe mandate of meticulous fieldwork that I found myself in 1983 as the only archaeologist in a new anthropology program at the University of West Florida (UWF), watching the looting of historic period features at the construction site of a new city hall in downtown Pensacola, Florida. As I have described elsewhere, I simply could not turn a blind eye any longer to this destruction of the plethora of in situ historical archaeological deposits being destroyed in my community (Bense 1985b, 1987b, 1987c, 1991a, 1991b). This realization of my responsibility was a significant turning point in my career.

While the public was well aware of its rare colonial history, no one but me and a handful of others, plus the looters, knew there were intact archaeological remains of that past still preserved under the city. Despite knowing literally nothing about post-Columbian history or the artifact assemblages, I and four other local people who were aware of the historic period deposits under downtown Pensacola decided to find a way to educate city leadership and the public about the buried historic period deposits and to actively insert archaeology into the development construction process. This proactive stance resulted in my approaching Gulf Power Company to support an archaeological survey at the site of their new headquarters downtown on the bay shore. The company agreed, and the project known as Hawkshaw identified and mitigated a single component Early Woodland site and most of a post–Civil War historic Black neighborhood scheduled for destruction. As there was no compliance required, my approach to Gulf Power was based on developing a way to mollify the bad publicity the project was drawing over the destruction of an African American neighborhood to build a luxurious new waterfront headquarters. I proposed that through archaeology and history the company could provide many public products about the Native and African Americans who once lived there that would have otherwise been lost forever if not for their efforts. This first attempt at the proactivist approach at the local level was a huge success, and public archaeology in West Florida was begun. Gulf Power Company and I were awarded the first Department of the Interior National Public Service Award for archaeology, and the project stands as a testament to how to make significant but silent buried archaeological remains valuable to a large private corporation (Bense 1985b, 1985c).

The next steps in the process of local archaeology proactivism were to form a local activist group and to begin to educate the general public about the archaeological remains in our area through public media and public participation. We also continued our activism to alert the designers of all pending construction projects about the negative impacts on potentially significant archaeological deposits in the city. I have described these next steps in the development of public archaeology in Pensacola in detail elsewhere (Bense 1987b, 1991a, 1991b, 1992).

I immediately urged the city council to conduct a survey of city-owned property and to pass an archaeological policy that is a local version of Section 106 of the National Historic Preservation Act. The council agreed, but funding for the survey and compliance projects was inadequate. As our fledgling anthropology program had neither resources nor a large cadre of students, I sought help from the general public. I advertised in the jobs section of the local newspaper classified ads for out-of-work people to volunteer on the survey.

This strategy worked, and volunteers began to be part of all our archaeological projects. These volunteers led directly to the formation of the local interest and activist group the Pensacola Archaeological Society (PAS).

It was our proactivism that led directly to the first encounter with the remains of Presidio San Miguel (1757–1763) that lie under downtown Pensacola. In 1985, construction associated with the federal urban renewal program had begun in downtown Pensacola and focused on upgrading utilities under the streets in the historic areas. As the street pavements were removed, hundreds of features, primarily colonial, were exposed. PAS members and I approached the City about the necessary compliance required with federal funds and their responsibility to conserve our heritage, and thus began a decade of historical archaeology in downtown Pensacola. The compliance projects led to follow-up research projects of colonial Pensacola funded primarily by state historic preservation grants to UWF. The projects were the training ground of many archaeological field schools with growing numbers of students and volunteers working side by side in downtown Pensacola.

As the urban renewal program ended and construction projects in downtown Pensacola slowed in the mid-1990s, I synthesized the archaeological and historical information generated from 17 projects into a book, *Archaeology of Colonial Pensacola* (Bense 1999). As I was writing this synthesis, I reflected on the value that historical documents brought to understanding and interpreting the archaeological remains of a community. While both historical and archaeological records are biased and incomplete, together they provide a richer and more accurate picture of the past reality than either can produce alone. Once again, the interdisciplinary approach proved to be the best path. Interpreting the pre-Columbian archaeological record of Native American cultures is complicated and fraught with cultural misunderstandings. Historical archaeology offers two primary advantages to understanding and more accurately interpreting the archaeological record. First, the discipline makes use of information from historical documents written by and about the actual members of the communities, and second, we as members of a western European colonial-based culture have an insider's perspective of the culture under study. As an archaeological researcher of Culture with a "Capital C," these two advantages were an irresistible draw to historical archaeology. This subdiscipline of archaeology can sharpen the archaeologist's ability to understand the associations between behaviors and artifacts.

In my reflection on the decade of historical archaeology experience in downtown Pensacola, I also realized the high value of public participation and interest in archaeology. It was clear that without the public's participation and support, we would have accomplished and learned much, much less. Therefore,

I knew that public interest should play an important role in determining the next phase of my research.

It just so happened that as I was synthesizing the decade of downtown archaeology, the Cold War had ended and one of the outcomes was for military installations to become better contributing members of their host communities. In 1986, I was involved in the recording of the suspected site of the "first" permanent Pensacola community, Presidio Santa María de Galve (1698–1719) on Naval Air Station Pensacola (NASP), and in 1991, the site was impacted, revealing preserved midden and features associated with Santa María (Neilsen et al. 1992). In 1994, a representative of the naval command at NASP asked if I would be interested in determining if the site actually was that of the "first" Pensacola and said, if so, the Navy would like to have it documented and studied as their contribution to the 300th anniversary celebration of its founding in 1998. They also offered initial funding with a Legacy grant.

All the pieces for determining the next historical archaeology research effort then fell together. Public interest was high in the Early Spanish Period (1698–1763), as very little was known about it and there was public curiosity about this early colonial occupation of Pensacola. I was also curious and knew that the site was in an excellent location for a large scale investigation that could be the beginning of a long-term study of all four presidio communities and that would be a quality contribution to understanding the early Spanish colonial culture in West Florida. Previous long-term seminal work on the colonial missions in North Florida by John Hann and Bonnie McEwan (Hann 1988; Hann and McEwan 1998; McEwan 1993; Worth 1998) and Presidio San Agustín by Kathleen Deagan (1976, 1983) had provided information and explanations about the rest of seventeenth- and eighteenth-century East Spanish Florida, leaving Spanish West Florida as the only missing piece of Spain's domain in the Southeast. Thus, the study of the people and their way of life in Early Spanish West Florida began in 1995 at Presidio Santa María de Galve.

This research has applied the field methods and documentation that is the legacy of Coe and Phelps along with the if-then scientific method and mid-range theory of Coe and Binford throughout the research to test a myriad of mid-level hypotheses that were the topics of theses, reports, and articles. It is time now for the upper level explanations of the overt and covert cultural processes that were in operation during those 65 years in the presidio and Native American communities holding the West Florida portion of the perimeter of the Spanish Empire in the Americas.

European Colonialism and Ethnogenesis

To understand and explain the cultural processes occurring in the early eighteenth-century in Spanish West Florida, it is necessary to place them in the context of European colonization of the Americas, especially by Spain. Historical archaeology from its beginnings has contributed to the understanding of the complex processes and repercussions of colonization in the Americas. As McEwan and Gregory Waselkov (2003: 1) relate, the legacies of European colonialism pervade our societies today and have helped shape the consciousness of Americans in all the nations in the Western Hemisphere. Various forms of colonization and migration have been documented by many societies for many reasons over the millennia to the present day. The sudden and unexpected discovery of the Western Hemisphere by a Spanish-sponsored trading venture involved two parts of the world that had no prior knowledge of the other's existence. As Deagan (2003: 3) describes, the discovery of the New World led to a Spanish colonial empire that was the largest ever known in the Americas, and it endured for three centuries.

The general overarching approach of European colonialism was characterized by "finders-keepers" and "steal it, keep it." Since the Middle Ages, European states were extremely competitive rivals with shifting alliances and many wars between them. The different histories and enmities of the European countries greatly affected the development of different versions of European colonization. But the Spanish had found and claimed the Americas first, and their empire became an extraordinarily diverse array of societies, ethnic groups, geography, and polities. They imposed a relatively consistent yet somewhat flexible set of political, religious, and social patterns in their colonies. Despite the diversity of cultures colonized by the Spanish, there were four pervasive elements throughout the Spanish Empire: a central government, monolithic Catholicism, an emphasis on life in towns, and formalized notions of class and race (Deagan 2003: 3). Spain's most outstanding discovery was the gold and silver deposits in New Spain and Peru, and the priority of exploitation and transportation of these most valuable minerals on earth rivaled their papal justification for colonization, which was the conversion of all people to Catholicism in their colonial Empire.

In southeastern North America, the primary European colonizers were French, British, and Spanish, and the colonizers of each nation immediately and consistently mixed both biologically and culturally with the indigenous people they encountered and Africans brought there. Each colonizing European state had varying restrictions on marriages and consensual relations between European men and Native women, but they were often relaxed or ignored. The

Spanish were most accepting of mixed marriages as long as both partners were Catholic, and the English were least accepting of mixed unions. The European-Indian-African mixed marriages and their offspring began the genesis of new ethnic groups characterized by a mix of biological and cultural traits. Deagan (1973) has used the term *mestizaje* to refer to people of mixed racial and cultural ethnicities, and this ethnogenesis occurred in all areas colonized by Europeans. The resulting new hybrid ethnic groups differed because of the cultural mixes and the attitudes of the colonizing European cultures toward them.

Despite two unsuccessful French attempts to invade Spanish Florida and New Spain in the sixteenth and seventeenth centuries, the French approach to colonization was a form of mercantile capitalism that developed the lucrative fur trade in Canada in the mid-seventeenth century (Moussette 2003: 30). It required a network of only a few French traders who purchased furs procured by Native Americans with inexpensive European manufactured goods, and it generated a huge profit for the large private fur trading companies such as the Compagnie de la Nouvelle France. The male French traders usually took Native American women as wives, who facilitated trade and mutual aid relationships between her ethnic group and the trader. The daughters of these mixed marriages often became other fur traders' wives. The offspring of French traders and Indian women began the ethnogenesis process of a new ethnic group called *métis* (St-Onge et al. 2012).

British colonialism in southern North America from its beginnings at Jamestown in 1607 and Charleston in 1670 was also a capitalist form of colonialism. Investors formed companies and recruited colonists from the home country with various incentives to provide profitable products for the company such as tobacco, sugar, indigo, and cotton (Sirmans 2013; Weir 1983). In general, British colonialization was focused on producing wealth for companies and individuals. Cotton and rice plantations and the Native American trade, especially in Native war captives and deerskins, were very successful business enterprises in the British colonies of the Southeast (Gallay 2002). British traders often took Indian wives who facilitated trading partnerships with Native American groups. Their mixed ethnicity offspring often became successful traders and leaders of Native groups, serving as important negotiators between the British and Indian groups.

Spanish colonialism was very different from the capitalistic goals of the British and French. For the Spanish Crown, religious conversion of indigenous people to Catholic Christianity was the sole authority for colonization, and it was as important as economic exploitation. However, to the Spanish colonists on the ground, Indians were seen as a subhuman source of labor. In the Spanish colonies, the intermarriage of Spanish (mostly men) with Indians and Africans (mostly women) was frequent and a crucial element of ethnogenesis in creating, transforming, and stabilizing the social milieus in the Spanish-American colonies. Deagan thinks the high frequency of Spanish/Indian relationships was not necessarily due to the shortage of Spanish women but to the influence of the Catholic church following the centuries-long duration in Spain of living and mixing with multiple ethnicities (Deagan 2003: 8). The offspring of unions between Spanish, Indian, and African people began the ethnogenesis of the *mestizaje,* especially mestizos and mulattos (African and Spanish) throughout the Spanish Empire. These new groups grew rapidly, and by 1646, they made up 12.8 percent of the population in New Spain; by 1742, they made up over a quarter (27.2%) of the population (20.1% mestizos and 7.1% mulattos) (Chance 1979: 155). In New Spain, the large mixed race *mestizaje* was formally institutionalized into more than 25 formal categories or castas. While hierarchical and racially based, the castas formally integrated the *mestizaje* into Spanish society and legitimized virtually any combination of racial attributes. However, the castas were flexible and could be manipulated as individuals might have self-identified differently in different situations to gain an advantage.

Ethnogenesis of the Hispanic ethnicity occurred in San Agustín in East Florida in the late seventeenth and eighteenth centuries (Deagan 1973, 1983); however, it did *not* occur in Spanish West Florida. There were some marriages recorded between soldiers and Indian women in West Florida, but in general, *mestizaje* women were sent from New Spain, especially wives and groups of single women intending to marry soldiers. Except for a very few *peninsulares* and *españoles,* all the people sent to West Florida were members of the lower castas of the mixed race *mestizaje,* also known as Hispanic, from central New Spain. For most of the 65 years of occupation of Spanish West Florida, this Hispanic population of military men, convicts, and a few civilian *españoles* along with some of their families were isolated in a defensive military colony surrounded by hostile French and British forces who held them captive in their fortified presidio. While there were some periods of peace, they were short lived. The refugee Native American population in the few mission villages was low, and they lived apart from the Spanish. Spanish West Florida was a violent place for the newcomers to West Florida who were caught in the cross fire of the violent rivalry of France, Britain, and Spain in southeastern North America. It was a dangerous frontier.

The Spanish West Florida Frontier

While ethnogenesis *per se* did not occur in Spanish West Florida, some cultural changes did take place in this frontier society. As in all culture areas, the expressions of a culture differ in its core and periphery. In the large picture, the core of Spanish colonial culture in North America was central New Spain, especially between Mexico City, Zacatecas, and Veracruz, and the peripheral areas were northern New Spain, Spanish Florida, and Alta California. Maintaining a presence in the peripheral areas was very important politically as these areas and settlements were the outguards for the core area that included most of the population and resources. In the core area, there was a strong military presence, relative safety, towns and cities, markets, and a structured society. The peripheral borderlands had few Spanish or Hispanic people, and because of their few numbers, hostile European rivals and their allied Native Americans posed a dangerous threat. The frontier in the borderlands was a place of isolation, sickness, and poor support from the core. There were two primary reasons people left the core area of New Spain for the dangerous and unpredictable frontier; they were forced through military assignment, conscription, or prison sentence, or they volunteered to take advantage of opportunities and incentives.

Regardless of the reasons that brought people to the frontier of Spanish West Florida, there were economic, social, and political opportunities that were absent in New Spain. As Laurie Wilkie (2019: 127) puts it, there was more social freedom in the frontier military society, and for many men and some women, the opportunity for advancement offset the risks of hardships and potential physical violence that were common across contested frontier communities. While the West Florida presidio community was first and foremost a military one, the limitations or advancement of a person's standing based on perceptions of blood purity that predominated in New Spain were quieted in presidio communities such as those in West Florida. Rank, not race, was most important in the military society of West Florida. This disregard of one's racial casta is evidenced by its pervasive absence in the many historical documents that identify the people who were going to and from the West Florida military community. The casta of soldiers or convicts was only rarely recorded, and when it was, it was self-identified, which encouraged inflating one's casta. The frontier military society in West Florida had only a few ranks or statuses: laborer (free or prisoner), soldiers, craftsmen, officers, and administrators. When a person's casta happened to be recorded, each tier of the population consistently included people of many different castas, from high born to low. As a result of the diminishment of a person's casta, the West Florida frontier military society offered economic, social, and professional opportunities for people, especially in the lower castas, that were closed to them in the core area of New Spain. In addition, a person's rank or status could change frequently. For example, documents from the West Florida Presidio Period state that convicts were regularly offered and accepted their freedom as well as the rank of enlisted soldier in return for risky assignments and as a reward for defense of the presidio during an enemy attack. Soldiers were often authorized to apprentice as carpenters, blacksmiths, and other tradesmen because of the lack of members of the established guilds on the frontier. These advancements meant an increase in salary and social standing. These types of promotions and social maneuvers were difficult to achieve in the core area of New Spain but were born from necessity across the Spanish borderlands.

The result of the relaxation of casta regulations on the frontier of Spanish West Florida was that the Hispanic population underwent another change characterized by opportunities for advancement on the frontier through individual accomplishments. In essence, the military's disregard for the casta system was transferred to the Hispanic community outside the presidio, and the process of ethnogenesis began to develop in the last decades of the Spanish occupation of West Florida. One's social position was not defined by racial category but by one's accomplishments and economic success. *Españoles* were still at the top and laborers/convicts were still at the bottom, but a broad social middle ground was developing where one's formal casta was simply irrelevant.

The Cultural Effect of Subsidization

Another important result of our research was the discovery that the frontier military communities in Spanish West Florida generally did not adapt to the region and its resources. There was no significant development of new subsistence, social, or ideological systems by the population over the course of 65 years because the settlement was subsidized and not expected to adapt. The military-based population was expected to continue their Hispanic way of life, and they did. Our research has demonstrated that the imprint of a culturally Hispanic West Florida presidio community was manifest throughout the historical and archaeological records they left behind. The architectural traditions and structures, expressions of rank and status, food traditions, religion, burial practices, and material culture of this community were markedly Hispanic. Some adaptations were made in local building materials, local food sources, and Hispanic traditions such as the use of basalt manos and metates and Guadalajara Polychrome pottery adopted from the indigenous population of New Spain. People at every level in Spanish West Florida sought to maintain and improve their way of life within a racial, cultural, and socioeconomic structure that had been maturing for centuries. After all, the purpose of the presidio was to demonstrate the Spanish Crown's power and control over West Florida. This outward show of permanence was reinforced with a professional military presence, armed fortifications, and the acculturating presence of Catholic missions, churches, and Christian Indian mission village communities.

As detailed in the previous chapter, both the material and documentary records reveal that there were few meaningful cultural changes through time during the 65 years of occupation in Spanish West Florida. The communities were so similar that I suspect that if we did not know which presidio an assemblage or documents was from, we would not be able to identify it. Only the four ceramic temporal markers noted in the previous chapter and the dates and place names on the documents of the first three communities identify them. San Miguel is the exception, as the influx of non-Spanish ceramics is very noticeable. Cultural change was purposefully stymied as a result of continual subsidization and the dominance of the conservative Catholic and military ways of life. The population started out with and retained their Hispanic/Latin *mestizaje* way of life in West Florida for over six decades.

Kathleen Deagan's (1983) seminal study of the early eighteenth-century San Agustín presidio community found this same situation there. She notes that, in fact, the Spanish Crown took great efforts to preserve and develop Iberian cultural norms across the expanding New World colonies. The San Agustín presidio was a very necessary military installation along the Atlantic-facing border of La Florida because it assisted in the protection of shipping flotas carrying the bullion gathered in Havana to the Iberian Peninsula. Deagan (1983: 267) reasons that because San Agustín was always a subsidized garrison, it was unnecessary for residents to develop a new, self-sufficient way of life. Deagan's work revealed that in St. Augustine, as in West Florida, colonists did include local food sources and adapted local building materials in their architecture. The ethnogenesis process in San Agustín included the frequent practice of Spanish men marrying Indian and mestizo women with the resulting addition of Native American materials in households in the female-related areas, especially the kitchen. However, in public areas, architectural style, construction methods, and military-political materials were Spanish. In both San Agustín and the West Florida presidio communities, material culture and documentary evidence combine to support a direct connection between the firm retention of a colonial Hispanic culture and the subsidization of the two presidios.

The two presidios that bookended La Florida at the beginning of the eighteenth century were intimately tied to a larger system of Hispanic colonial life that had been developing since 1492. On the Atlantic and Gulf coasts, residents of both communities were the king's subjects and generally looked like it, even when circumstances were dire. The plethora of information about the population of the West Florida and San Agustín presidios leads to the conclusion that Spanish-subsidized frontier military communities were resistant but not immune to the processes of culture change. The key factors in understanding the culture of Spanish Florida and the continued conformity to Spanish ideals are the presidio's dependency for survival on the situado, the logistical success of the colonial system, and the isolation from the Hispanic world at the periphery of New Spain. Fortified frontier military installations served crucial strategic and symbolic purposes for colonial agents in their quest to maintain control over local lands, resources, and people (Lightfoot 2019: 171). The Spanish Florida presidio communities were classic examples of site unit intrusions by professional military units placed in strategic defensive and fortified locations without the expectation of self-support.

Next

A wealth of information has been gathered in the four decades of historical archaeological investigations of Spanish West Florida. This synthesis has brought together frontline information produced by scores of theses, papers, reports, articles, chapters, and books into a database of 94,501 artifacts from the four presidio and two mission village sites that were used in the analyses of the individual and combined assemblages. This synthesis has addressed only a few of the possible topics that can be explored using the available historical and archaeological information. Three areas of future research using this information will be rewarding: borderland area ethnogenesis comparisons, Native American-Spanish relations, and the process of ethnogenesis.

One particularly fruitful area of research that is possible now that the "missing piece" of Spanish West Florida is in place is the comparison of ethnogenesis in the three Spanish borderland areas of Florida, northern New Spain, and Alta California. Especially interesting avenues of interest are demographic composition and its evolution and the various forms of ethnogenesis that took place. Another productive topic is the evolution of the relationships of the Native American and Spanish colonists in the Spanish borderlands in the eighteenth century. The area of ethnogenesis has greatly expanded in the last few decades, especially in the Spanish, French, and British colonial cultures. The different twist on ethnogenesis in Spanish West Florida is that the colonial population was started with a group of mixed race Hispanic people and classified into hierarchical racial castas. The quick diminishment of the importance of one's casta in the military and the eventual transfer of it to the new civilian community with a large middle social ground warrants further study. There are similar examples of a founding Hispanic population in the presidios in northern New Spain and Alta California. Did the same cultural processes take place? How did the community of San Agustín with its ethnogenesis-in-place differ from that in contemporary New Spain and the post-ethnogenesis populations in the rest of the borderlands?

There are also many other productive research topics such as the shifting value of material culture on the frontier, the roles the new mixed race hybrid groups played in the different colonial societies, and legal and illegal trade on the colonial frontier. The frontier was and is very different than the home culture area. Some social rules were waived, new ones developed, and new opportunities arose that draw people on the low rungs of the social and economic ladders to the opportunities in a dangerous and unpredictable frontier.

Our own American culture was derived by the process of ethnogenesis driven by Christian and primarily British legal and capitalist values. This blending has resulted in a culture that is similar to but quite different from our European cultural roots. The modern conflicts in the United States of inequality of race and gender are directly related to our colonial roots, and capitalism with its goal of wealth generation is at the core of many socioeconomic conflicts in our society. The violent taking of North America from the indigenous Native Americans marked our imperial beginnings, and our struggles with the ramifications of our capitalist heritage are difficult. But the first step in finding solutions is to understand the problem, and it is my hope that this research can somehow help in that understanding.

References Cited

Primary Sources

Andreu

1753   Report of Dr. Andreu, August 16, 1753 in Autos of the Hurricane of the 2nd, 3rd and 4th of November of 1752. Mexico 2448, Archivo General de Indias, Seville, Spain.

Anonymous

1713   Carta de la costa de Pansacola desde Santa Rosa hasta Massacra, MDCCXIII. Map 34, Mapas y Planos—Florida y Luisiana, Archivo General de Indias, Seville, Spain. http://pares.mcu.es/ParesBusquedas20/catalogo/show/19169, accessed May 7, 2020.

1752a   Petition of the Infantry, November 8, 1752. Mexico 2448, Archivo General de Indias, Seville, Spain.

1752b   Second Examination (of storm damage), November 8,1752, in Autos of the 2nd, 3rd, and 4th of November of 1752. Mexico 2448, Archivo General de Indias, Seville, Spain.

1752c   First Examination (of storm damage), November 8,1752, in Autos of the 2nd, 3rd, and 4th of November of 1752. Mexico 2448, Archivo General de Indias, Seville, Spain.

Arriola, Andrés de

1698   Mapa de la bahía de Santa María de Galve, o de Pensacola, delineada por Andrés de Arriola y mandada fortificar por orden del virrey conde de Moctezuma. Map 91, Mapas y Planos—Mexico, Archivo General de Indias, Seville, Spain. http://pares.mcu.es/ParesBusquedas20/catalogo/show/20916, accessed May 7, 2020.

Buscarons, Benito

1731–1733   Libro Manual de Cargo y Data de todos los generos de bastimentos, pertrechos, armas, y muniziones que son al cargo de mi, D.n Benito Buscarons, Pagador, y Thendor actual del Presidio de la Ysla de Santa Rosa, Punta de Sigüenz, alias Santa María de Galbe. Expediente 4, Caja 6568, Cárceles y Presidios, Archivo General de la Nación, Mexico City, Mexico. Translated by John E. Worth. Manuscript on file, Archaeology Institute, University of West Florida, Pensacola, 2018.

Devin, Valentin

1719   Carte de l'Entrée du Port et Rade de Pensacole. Map bound with Jean de Beaurain's manuscript copy of *Journal historique concernant l'etablissement des Français a la Louisiane,* by Bénard de La Harpe, 1724, following p. 52. MMC 2653, Louisiana Miscellany, Manuscript Division, Library of Congress, Washington, DC.

c1720   Carte de l'entré du port, et rade de Pensacola. In *Cartes marines: a la svbstitvtion dv Valdec proche Solevre en Svisse, MDCCXXVII.* Ayer MS, map 30, sheet 85, Newberry Library, Chicago.

Durnford, Elias

1765   Plan of the New Town in Pensacola and county adjacent, shewing the gardens and situation of the Blockhouses. CO 700, Florida 20/1, The National Archives, Kew, England. https://discovery.nationalarchives.gov.uk/details/r/C6744131, accessed May 7, 2020.

Eraso, Santiago Benito

1752   Report of Santiago Benito Eraso, no date, in Autos of the Hurricane of the 2nd, 3rd and 4th of November of 1752. Mexico 2448, Archivo General de Indias, Seville, Spain.

Franck, Jaime

1699   Real Fuerza de San Carlos de Austria, en la nueva población de Santa Maria de Galve, o Pensacola [May 16, 1699]. Map 93, Mapas y Planos—Mexico, Archivo General de Indias, Seville, Spain. http://pares.mcu.es/ParesBusquedas20/catalogo/show/20919, accessed May 7, 2020.

1700   Letter to the King, June 3, 1700. Mexico 618, Archivo General de Indias, Seville, Spain.

Gauld, George

c1765   A view of Pensacola, in West Florida. Prints and Photographs Division, Library of Congress, Washington DC. https://www.loc.gov/item/2004672419/, accessed May 7, 2020.

Gauld, George, and Sir John Lindsay

1764   A plan of the harbour of Pensacola in West-Florida. Geography and Map Division, Library of Congress, Washington DC. http://hdl.loc.gov/loc.gmd/g3932p.ar165600, accessed May 7, 2020.

López de la Camara Alta, Agustín

1756   Plano de la Baia y Puerto de Santa Maria de Galbe, y del Presidio llamado Pansacola cituado en la Ysla de Santa Rosa. Biblioteca Virtual del Ministerio de Defensa. http://bibliotecavirtualdefensa.es/BVMDefensa/i18n/consulta/registro.cmd?id=83804, accessed May 7, 2020.

Matamoros de Ysla, Juan Pedro

1718   Letter to the King, July 9, 1718. Santo Domingo 2533, Archivo General de Indias, Seville, Spain.

Ortíz Parrilla, Diego, and Phelipe Feringan Cortés

1763a   Plano del Presidio de San Miguel de Panzacola. MR/42/426, Biblioteca Nacional de España, Madrid, Spain. http://bdh-rd.bne.es/viewer.vm?id=0000033172, accessed May 7, 2020.

1763b   Plano de Panzacola. Map 64, Mapas y Planos—Florida y Luisiana, Archivo General de Indias, Seville, Spain. http://pares.mcu.es/ParesBusquedas20/catalogo/show/19202?nm, accessed May 7, 2020.

Porlier, Joseph

1761   Plano del Puerto de Panzacola cituado Enla Latitud de 30 Grados y 14 minutos, y enla Longitud, de 284 Grados y 27 minutos Segun el meridiano de Thenerif [July 1761]. Biblioteca Digital Hispánica, Biblioteca Nacional de España. http://bdh-rd.bne.es/viewer.vm?id=0000033175, accessed May 6, 2020.

Quixano, Fray Luis, Fray Joseph Nodal, Fray Gabriel de Llerena, Joseph de Yberri, Pedro Ximénez de Florencia, Joseph de Escobar, Joseph de Navarro, Medina [sic], Pedro Amoscotegui y Bermudo, Francisco Canelas, Carlos Cuellar, Luis Garcia Narro, Augustin de Serna, and Joseph Augustin Hidalgo

1752   2nd Examination (of storm damage), November 8, 1752 in Autos of the Hurricane of the 2nd, 3rd, and 4th of November of 1752. Mexico 2448, Archivo General de Indias, Seville, Spain.

Rivera, Joseph Primo de

1723   Letter to the King, May 24, 1723. Santa Domingo 849, Archivo General de Indias, Seville, Spain.

Rivera, Pedro Primo de, and Bernardino de Almonacid

1727   To the King, October 22, 1727. Coleccion de Documentos para la Historía de Florida, Dos Tomos (Tomo I), Biblioteca Nacional de España, Madrid, Spain.

Roberts, William, and Thomas Jefferys

1763   A North View of Pensacola, on the Island of Santa Rosa. Plate 3 in *An Account of the First Discovery and Natural History of Florida*, p. 9. T. Jefferys, London. Internet Archive. https://archive.org/details/accountoffirstdi00robe/page/n37/mode/2up, accessed May 7, 2020.

Robertson, Archibald

1763   Plan of the Fort at Pensacola, 1763 [Copy from the original in the War Office records, Caxton House, London, number Z/30/1]. Spencer Collection, New York Public Library Digital Collections. http://digitalcollections.nypl.org/items/be0f6d75-d1ee-1529-e040-e00a18065909, accessed May 7, 2020.

Salazar, Fray Marcos de Hita

1735   To the Holy Office, March 15, 1735. Inquisicion 835, Expediente 6, Archivo General de la Nación, Mexico City, Mexico.

Urueña, Juan de

1741   Report of the Previous Accountant, don Juan de Urueña, August 12, 1741 in Autos of the Hurricane of the 2nd, 3rd, and 4th of November of 1752. Mexico 2448, Archivo General de Indias, Seville, Spain.

Yberri, Joseph de

1753   Report of don Joseph de Yberri, August 29, 1753 in Autos of the Hurricane of the 2nd, 3rd, and 4th of November 1752. Mexico 2448, Archivo General de Indias, Seville, Spain.

Secondary Sources

Arnade, Charles W.

1959   *Florida on Trial, 1593–1602.* University of Miami Hispanic-American Studies No. 16. University of Miami Press, Coral Gables, Florida.

1996   Raids, Sieges, and International Wars. In *The New History of Florida*, edited by Michael Gannon, pp. 100–116. University Press of Florida, Gainesville.

Azzarello, Jennifer

1997   Archaeological Investigations on the St. Joseph Peninsula, Florida. Paper presented at the Gulf Coast History and Humanities Conference, Pensacola, Florida.

Azzarello, Jennifer, and Christine Hamlin

1997   *Results of Trip to 8Gu8, March 21 and 27, 1997.* Bureau of Archaeological Research, Division of Historical Resources, Florida Department of State, Tallahassee.

Baker, Henry A.

1975   *Archaeological Investigations at Fort George, Pensacola, Florida.* Miscellaneous

Project Report Series No. 34. Division of Archives, History and Records Management, Bureau of Historic Sites and Properties, Florida Department of State, Tallahassee.

Beck, Robin A., Jr., David G. Moore, and Christopher B. Rodning
2006   Identifying Fort San Juan: A Sixteenth-Century Spanish Occupation at the Berry Site, North Carolina. *Southeastern Archaeology* 25(1):65–77.

Beck, Robin A., Jr., David G. Moore, and Christopher B. Rodning (editors)
2016   *Fort San Juan and the Limits of Empire: Colonialism and Household Practice at the Berry Site.* University Press of Florida, Gainesville.

Benchley, Elizabeth D.
2004   Domestic Architecture at Presidio San Miguel de Panzacola (1754–1763) Florida. Manuscript on file, Archaeology Institute, University of West Florida, Pensacola.
2007a   *2006 Investigations at the Commanding Officer's Compound (8ES1150).* Report of Investigations No. 156. Archaeology Institute, University of West Florida, Pensacola.
2007b   *Archaeology of Old Pensacola: 2005 Investigations at the Commanding Officer's Compound (8ES1150).* Report of Investigations No. 152. Archaeology Institute, University of West Florida, Pensacola.

Benchley, Elizabeth D., and Judith A. Bense
2001   *Archaeology and History of St. Joseph Peninsula State Park: Phase I Investigations.* Report of Investigations No. 89. Archaeology Institute, University of West Florida, Pensacola.

Benchley, Elizabeth D., R. Wayne Childers, John J. Clune, Jr., Cindy L. Bercot, David B. Dodson, April L. Whitaker, and E. Ashley Flynt
2007   *The Colonial People of Pensacola: History and Archaeology of the Community Associated with Spanish San Miguel de Panzacola (1754–1763) and British Pensacola (1763–1781).* 2 vols. Report of Investigations No. 107. Archaeology Institute, University of West Florida, Pensacola.

Benchley, Elizabeth D., and April L. Whitaker
2007   Archaeological Results. In *The Colonial People of Pensacola: History and Archaeology of the Community Associated with Spanish San Miguel de Panzacola (1754–1763) and British Pensacola (1763–1781)*, pp. 66–93. Report of Investigations No. 107. Archaeology Institute, University of West Florida, Pensacola.

Bense, Judith A.
1985a   *Reconnaissance Survey of Prehistoric Archaeological Sites on Santa Rosa Island, Northwest Florida: Ft. Pickens and Santa Rosa Areas of the Gulf Islands National Seashore.* Report of Investigations No. 8. Office of Cultural and Archaeological Research, University of West Florida, Pensacola.
1985b   Archaeological Resource Management Plan in Pensacola, Florida and the Hawkshaw Project. *Florida Anthropologist* 38(1–2):120–123.
1985c   *Hawkshaw: Prehistory and History in an Urban Neighborhood in Pensacola, Florida.* Report of Investigations No. 7. Office of Cultural and Archaeological Research, University of West Florida, Pensacola.
1987a   *The Midden Mound Project, Final Report.* Report of Investigations Number 6. Office of Cultural and Archaeological Research, University of West Florida, Pensacola.
1987b   Development of a Management System for Archaeological Resources in Pensacola, Florida. In *Living in Cities: Current Research in Urban Archaeology*, Edited by Ed-

ward Staski, pp. 82–89. Special Publication Series No. 5. Society for Historical Archaeology, Pleasant Hill, California.

1987c   *Report of the Pensacola Archaeological Survey 1986 Season.* Report of Investigations No. 10. Office of Cultural and Archaeological Research, University of West Florida, Pensacola.

1991a   Archaeology at Home: A Partnership in Pensacola. In *Protecting the Past*, edited by George S. Smith and John E. Erenhard, pp. 117–122. CRC Press, Boca Raton, Florida.

1991b   The Pensacola Model of Public Archaeology. In *Archaeology and Education: The Classroom and Beyond*, edited by K. C. Smith and Francis P. McManaman. Archaeological Assistance Study No 2. U.S. Department of the Interior, National Park Service, Cultural Resources, Washington, DC.

1992   Public-Private Partnerships in Archaeology. In *The Public Trust and the First Americans*, edited by Ruthann Knudson and Bennie C. Keel, pp. 145–155. Oregon State University Press for the Center for the Study of the First Americas, Corvallis, Oregon.

1995   *The Colonial Archaeological Record in Pensacola, Florida.* Report of Investigations No. 74. Archaeology Institute, University of West Florida, Pensacola.

1998   Archaeology at the Presidio Santa María de Galve. In *Santa María de Galve: A Story of Survival*, edited by Virginia Parks, pp 99–134. Pensacola Historical Society, Pensacola, Florida.

2002   *Field Report 2002, Archaeological Evaluation Presidio Isla de Santa Rosa (8ES22).* Report of Investigations No. 105. Archaeology Institute, University of West Florida, Pensacola.

2004   Presidio Santa María de Galve (1698–1719): A Frontier Garrison in Spanish West Florida. *Historical Archaeology* 38(3):47–64.

Bense, Judith A. (editor)

1999   *Archaeology of Colonial Pensacola.* University Press of Florida, Gainesville.

2003   *Presidio Santa María de Galve: A Struggle for Survival in Colonial Spanish Pensacola.* University Press of Florida, Gainesville.

Bense, Judith A., and David E. Pettry

1989   Anthropic Epipedons in the Tombigbee Valley of Mississippi. *Soil Science Society of America Journal* 52(2): 505–511.

Bense, Judith A., and Harry J. Wilson

1999   *Archaeology and History of the First Spanish Presidio: Santa María de Galve in Pensacola, Florida (1698–1719): Interim Report of the First Three Years of Research, 1995–1997.* Report of Investigations No. 67. Archaeology Institute, University of West Florida, Pensacola.

2003   Archaeological Remains. In *Presidio Santa María de Galve: A Struggle for Survival in Colonial Spanish Pensacola*, edited by Judith A. Bense, pp. 83–209. University Press of Florida, Gainesville.

Binford, Lewis R.

1972   *An Archaeological Perspective.* Seminar Press, New York.

Blitz, John H.

1985   *An Archaeological Study of the Mississippi Choctaw Indians.* Archaeological Report No. 16. Mississippi Department of Archives and History, Jackson.

1993   Ceramics from Historic Choctaw Sites, East-Central Mississippi: Eastern and Southern Divisions. Unpublished manuscript.

Boyd, Mark F., Hale G. Smith, and John W. Griffin

1951   *Here They Once Stood: The Tragic End of the Apalachee Missions*. University of Florida Press, Gainesville.

Brading, D. A.

2008   *Miners and Merchants in Bourbon Mexico, 1763–1810*. Cambridge University Press, Cambridge, England.

Braley, Chad O.

1979   *Archaeological Investigations at Fort Barrancas, Bateria San Carlos, and Advanced Redoubt in the Fort's Section, Gulf Islands National Seashore*. Southeast Conservation Archaeology Center, Florida State University, Tallahassee.

Bratten, John R.

2003   *The Santa Rosa Island Shipwreck Project: 1998–2003*. Report of Investigations No. 109. Archaeology Institute, University of West Florida, Pensacola.

Bruseth, James E. (editor)

2014   *La Belle: The Ship That Changed History*. Texas A&M University Press, College Station.

Bruseth, James E., Jeffrey J. Durst, Tiffany Osburn, Kathleen Gilmore, Kay Hindes, Nancy Reese, Barbara Meissner, and Mike Davis

2004   A Clash of Two Cultures: Presidio La Bahía on the Texas Coast as a Deterrent to French Incursion. *Historical Archaeology* 38(3):78–93.

Bruseth, James E., Bradford M. Jones, Amy A. Borgens, and Eric D. Ray

2017   The Archaeology of a Seventeenth-Century Ship of New World Colonization. In *La Belle: The Archaeology of a Seventeenth-Century Vessel of New World Colonization*, pp. 805–829. Texas A&M University Press, College Station.

Bushnell, Amy Turner

1994   *Situado and Sabana: Spain's Support System for the Presidio and Mission Provinces of Florida*. Anthropological Papers of the American Museum of Natural History No. 74. University of Georgia Press, Athens.

1996   Republic of Spaniards, Republic of Indians. In *The New History of Florida*, edited by Michael Gannon, pp. 62–77. University Press of Florida, Gainesville.

Carrera, Magali M.

2012   *Imagining Identity in New Spain: Race, Lineage, and the Colonial Body in Portraiture and Casta Paintings*. University of Texas Press, Austin.

Chance, John K.

1979   On the Mexican Mestizo. *Latin American Research Review* 14(3):153–168.

Chapman, Ashley A., II

1998   Predictive Model of the Archaeological Remains of the Presidio Santa María de Galve (1698–1722): Results of the First Year of Field Research (1995). Master's thesis, Department of History, University of West Florida, Pensacola.

Charlevoix, Pierre-Francois-Xavier de

1923   [1761] *Journal of a Voyage to North America*, Vol. II. Translated and edited by Louise Phelps Kellogg. The Caxton Club, Chicago. https://www.google.com/books/edition/Journal_of_a_Voyage_to_North_America/79A0AQAAMAAJ?hl=en&gbpv=1&dq=

Pierre+Charlevoix+Voyages+Volume+II&printsec=frontcover, accessed August 19, 2020.

Childers, R. Wayne

2001   Appendix 1: History of T.H. Stone Park, St. Joseph's Peninsula, Florida. In *Archaeology and History of St. Joseph Peninsula State Park: Phase I Investigations*. Report of Investigations No. 89. Archaeology Institute, University of West Florida, Pensacola.

2003a   Supplies for the Presidio of Santa Rosa Punta de Sigüenza 1722–1755. Technical report on file, Archaeology Institute, University of West Florida, Pensacola.

2003b   Construction and Planning, Santa Rosa Punta de Sigüenza 1723–1755. Technical report on file, Archaeology Institute, University of West Florida, Pensacola.

2003c   Personnel at Santa Rosa Punta de Sigüenza: 1723–1755. Technical report on file, Archaeology Institute, University of West Florida, Pensacola.

2004   The Presidio System in Spanish Florida 1565–1763. *Historical Archaeology* 38(3):24–32.

Childers, R. Wayne, John J. Clune, Jr., and Cindy L. Bercot

2007   Settlers, Settlement, and Survival: A Comparative Study of Spanish San Miguel de Panzacola (1754–1763) and British Pensacola (1763–1781). In *The Colonial People of Pensacola: History and Archaeology of the Community Associated with Spanish San Miguel de Panzacola (1754–1763) and British Pensacola (1763–1781)*, pp. 14–65. Report of Investigations No. 107. Archaeology Institute, University of West Florida, Pensacola.

Childers, R. Wayne, and Joseph Cotter

1998   Arrested Development: The Economy at the Royal Presidio of Santa María de Galve, 1698–1719. *Gulf South Historical Review* 14(1):76–103.

Cleland, Charles E.

1972   From Sacred to Profane: Style Drift in the Decoration of Jesuit Finger Rings. *American Antiquity* 37(2):202–210. DOI:10.2307/278206, accessed July 9, 2019.

Cleland, Charles E. (editor)

1971   *The Lasanen Site: An Historic Burial Locality in Mackinac County, Michigan*. Publications of the Museum of Michigan State University, Anthropological Series Vol. 1(1). Michigan State University, East Lansing.

Clune, John J., Jr.

2003   Historical Context and Overview. In *Presidio Santa María de Galve: A Struggle for Survival in Colonial Spanish Pensacola*, edited by Judith A. Bense, pp. 12–24. University Press of Florida, Gainesville.

Clune, John J., Jr., R. Wayne Childers, William S. Coker, and Brenda N. Swann

2003   Settlements, Settlers, and Survival: Documentary Evidence. In *Presidio Santa María de Galve: A Struggle for Survival in Colonial Spanish Pensacola*, edited by Judith A. Bense, pp. 25–82. University Press of Florida, Gainesville.

Clune, John J., Jr., R. Wayne Childers, and April L. Whitaker

2006   Documentary History of Santa Rosa Pensacola (1722–1752): Settlement, Settlers and Survival. In *Presidio Isla de Santa Rosa Archaeological Investigations 2002–2004*, pp. 19–48. Report of Investigations No. 133. Archaeology Institute, University of West Florida, Pensacola.

Coker, William S.

1975   Pedro de Rivera's Report on the Presidio of Punta de Sigüenza, alias Panzacola, 1744. *Pensacola Historical Society Quarterly* 8(2):1–22.

1978   The Rise and Fall of San Carlos. *Scenic Hills Singing Kettle* 18:14–15.

1979   The Financial History of Pensacola's Spanish Presidios, 1698–1763. *Pensacola Historical Society Quarterly* 9(4):1–20.

1984   The Village on the Red Cliffs. *Pensacola History Illustrated* 1(2):22–26.

1996   Pensacola, 1686–1763. In *The New History of Florida*, edited by Michael Gannon, pp. 117–133. University Press of Florida, Gainesville.

1997   The Name Panzacola (Pensacola) Keeps Getting Newer and Newer. *Pensacola History Illustrated* 5(2):29.

1998a   Pensacola's Medical History: The Colonial Era, 1559–1821. *Florida Historical Quarterly* 77(2):181–192.

1998b   Admiral Andrés de Paz, "Pensacola's Hero." In *Santa María de Galve: A Story of Survival*, edited by Virginia Parks, pp. 1–9. Pensacola Historical Society, Pensacola, Florida.

1999   Pensacola, 1686–1821. In *Archaeology of Colonial Pensacola*, edited by Judith A. Bense, pp. 5–60. University Press of Florida, Gainesville.

Coker, William S., and R. Wayne Childers

1998   The Presidio Santa María de Galve: The First Permanent European Settlement on the Northern Gulf Coast, 1698–1722. In *Santa María de Galve: A Story of Survival*, edited by Virginia Parks, pp. 11–98. Pensacola Historical Society, Pensacola, Florida.

Coker, William S., and G. Douglas Inglis

1980   *The Spanish Censuses of Pensacola, 1784–1820: A Genealogical Guide to Spanish Pensacola*. Perdido Bay Press, Pensacola, Florida.

Coker, William S., and Thomas D. Watson

1986   *Indian Traders of the Southeastern Spanish Borderlands: Panton, Leslie, & Company and John Forbes & Company, 1783–1847*. University of West Florida Press, Pensacola.

Connelly, N.D., and David M. White

1968a   Stabilization and Public Presentation of the 1968 British Guardhouse Excavations: An Advisory Report. Report to the Pensacola Historical Restoration and Preservation Commission. Manuscript on file, Archaeology Institute, University of West Florida, Pensacola.

1968b   Archaeological Report of the Tivoli House of Pensacola. Report to the Pensacola Historical Restoration and Preservation Commission. Manuscript on file, Archaeology Institute, University of West Florida, Pensacola.

Cook, Gregory D., John R. Bratten, and John E. Worth

2016   *Exploring Luna's 1559 Fleet: Final Report for Florida Division of Historic Resources Special Category Grant SC 503*. Report of Investigations No. 202. Archaeology Institute, University of West Florida, Pensacola.

Darby, Mike

1965   Spaniards 1st Settlers in Area: Evidence Found on Citizens 250 Years Ago. *Panama City News Herald* 22 July. Panama City, Florida.

Darley, Mike

1965   Excavations Yield 18th Century Artifacts: Archaeologist Faces Facts. *Panama City News Herald* 25 July. Panama City, Florida.

Deagan, Kathleen

1973   Mestizaje in Colonial St. Augustine. *Ethnohistory* 20(1):55–65.

1976   *Archaeology at the National Greek Orthodox Shrine, St. Augustine, Florida: Micro-*

change in Eighteenth-Century Spanish Colonial Material Culture. Florida State University Notes in Anthropology No. 15. University Presses of Florida, Gainesville.

1983   *Spanish St. Augustine: The Archaeology of a Colonial Creole Community.* Academic Press, New York.

1987   *Artifacts of the Spanish Colonies of Florida and the Caribbean, 1500–1800, Vol. 1: Ceramics, Glassware, and Beads.* Smithsonian Institution Press, Washington, DC.

1993   St. Augustine and the Mission Frontier. In *The Spanish Missions of La Florida,* edited by Bonnie G. McEwan, pp. 87–110. University Press of Florida, Gainesville.

2002   *Artifacts of the Spanish Colonies of Florida and the Caribbean, 1500–1800, Vol. 2: Portable Personal Possessions.* Smithsonian Institution Press, Washington, DC.

2003   Colonial Origins and Colonial Transformations in Spanish Americas. *Historical Archaeology* 37(4):3–13.

2007   Eliciting Contraband through Archaeology: Illicit Trade in Eighteenth-Century St. Augustine. *Historical Archaeology* 41(4):98–116.

2009   *Historical Archaeology at the Fountain of Youth Park Site (8SJ31) St. Augustine, Florida 1934–2007.* Final Report on Florida Bureau of Historical Resources Special Category Grant No. SC 616. Florida Museum of Natural History, University of Florida, Gainesville.

2016   *Investigating the 1565 Menéndez Defenses: Field Report on the 2011–2015 Excavations at the Fountain of Youth Park Site, St. Augustine.* Miscellaneous Papers in Archaeology No. 62. Florida Museum of Natural History, University of Florida, Gainesville.

Demrow, Carl
2009   Peeling Logs. *Northern Woodlands Magazine* 60. 7 May:73.

DePratter, Chester B., and Stanley South
1990   *Charlesfort: The 1989 Search Project.* Research Manuscript Series 221. South Carolina Institute of Archaeology and Anthropology, University of South Carolina, Columbia. https://scholarcommons.sc.edu/archanth_books/221/, accessed July 9, 2019.

DePratter, Chester B., Stanley South, and James B. Legg
1996   Charlesfort Discovered! *Legacy* 1(1):1, 5, 8–9.

Duffy, Christopher
1985   *The Fortress in the Age of Vauban and Frederick the Great, 1660–1789.* Siege Warfare Vol. 2. Routledge & Kegan Paul, London.

Eschbach, Krista L.
2007   An Examination of Eighteenth-Century Spanish Colonial Socio-Economics as Seen at Presidio Isla de Santa Rosa. Master's thesis, Division of Anthropology and Archaeology, University of West Florida, Pensacola.

2019   Mechanisms of Colonial Transformation at the Port of Veracruz and the Northwest Florida Presidios. PhD dissertation, Department of Anthropology, Arizona State University, Tempe.

Esri
2019   Aerial image of modern-day downtown Pensacola. Esri, DigitalGlobe, GeoEye, i-cubed, USDA FSA, USGS, AEX, Getmapping, Aerogrid, IGN, IGP, swisstopo, and GIS User Community, accessed August 27, 2019.

Falkner, James
2015   *The War of the Spanish Succession, 1701–1714.* Pen & Sword Military, Barnsley, South Yorkshire, England.

Faye, Stanley

1941   Spanish Fortifications of Pensacola, 1698–1763. *The Florida Historical Quarterly* 20(2):151–168.

1946a   The Contest for Pensacola Bay and Other Gulf Ports, 1698–1722: Part I. *The Florida Historical Quarterly* 24(3):167–195.

1946b   The Contest for Pensacola Bay and Other Gulf Ports, 1698–1722: Part II. *The Florida Historical Quarterly* 24(4):302–328.

Ferguson, Leland

2002   Joffre Lanning Coe (1916–2000). *American Anthropology* 104(1):294–297.

Ford, Lawrence Carroll

1939   *The Triangular Struggle for Spanish Pensacola, 1689–1739.* Catholic University of America Press, Washington, DC.

Fryxell, Roald, Tadeusz Bielicki, Richard D. Daugherty, Carl E. Gustafson, Henry T. Irwin, and Bennie C. Keel

1968   A Human Skeleton from Sediments of Mid-Pinedale Age in Southeastern Washington. *American Antiquity* 33(4): 511–515.

Furlong, Mary M.

2008   Expressions of Religion and Ideology in the Material Culture of Pensacola's Presidios Santa María de Galve and Isla de Santa Rosa. Master's thesis, Department of Anthropology, University of West Florida, Pensacola.

Gallay, Alan

2002   *The Indian Slave Trade: The Rise of the English Empire in the American South, 1670–1717.* Yale University Press, New Haven, Connecticut.

Greene, James N.

2009   Architectural Variations in Pensacola's Three Presidios. Master's thesis, Department of Anthropology, University of West Florida, Pensacola.

Gremillion, Kristen J.

2002   Archaeobotany at Old Mobile. *Historical Archaeology* 36(1):117–128.

Griffen, William B.

1959   Spanish Pensacola, 1700–1763. *The Florida Historical Quarterly* 37(3/4):242–262.

Grinnan, Joseph J.

2013   Molino Mills: The Maritime Cultural Landscape of a Reconstruction Era Sawmill in Molino, Florida. Master's thesis, Department of Anthropology, University of West Florida, Pensacola.

Gutiérrez, Ramón A., Sal Scalora, William H. Beezley, and Dana Salvo

1997   *Mexican Home Altars.* University of New Mexico Press, Albuquerque.

Hammond, Norman

1989   The Function of Maya Middle Preclassic Pottery Figurines. *Mexicon* 11(6):111–114.

Hann, John H.

1988   *Apalachee: The Land between the Rivers.* University Presses of Florida, Gainesville.

Hann, John H., and Bonnie G. McEwan

1998   *The Apalachee Indians and Mission San Luis.* University Press of Florida, Gainesville.

Harris, Norma J.

1999   Native Americans of Santa María de Galve 1698–1722. Master's thesis, Department of History, University of West Florida, Pensacola.

2003a   Native Americans. In *Presidio Santa María de Galve: A Struggle for Survival in Co-*

lonial Spanish Pensacola, edited by Judith A. Bense, pp. 257–314. University Press of Florida, Gainesville.

2003b   *Field Report 2003, Archaeological Evaluation Presidio Isla de Santa Rosa (8ES22)*. Report of Investigations No. 114. Archaeology Institute, University of West Florida, Pensacola.

2004a   *Annual Report 2003, Archaeological Evaluation Presidio Isla de Santa Rosa (8ES22)*. Report of Investigations No. 119. Archaeology Institute, University of West Florida, Pensacola.

2004b   *Field Report 2004, Archaeological Evaluation Presidio Isla de Santa Rosa (8ES22)*. Report of Investigations No. 128. Archaeology Institute, University of West Florida, Pensacola.

2007   Eighteenth Century Native American Migration and Interaction on the Spanish Frontier: Yamassee/Apalachee and Chisca Missions of Pensacola, Florida. Paper presented at the 40th Annual Conference of the Society for Historical Archaeology, Williamsburg, Virginia.

Harris, Norma J., and Krista L. Eschbach

2006   *Presidio Isla de Santa Rosa Archaeological Investigations 2002–2004*. Report of Investigations No. 133. Archaeology Institute, University of West Florida, Pensacola.

Heintzelman, Nicole

2003   Appendix 2.17: Report of Human Remains Investigated at 8Es1354, Presidio Santa María de Galve, 1698–1719, Naval Air Station Pensacola, Florida. In *Presidio Santa María de Galve: A Struggle for Survival in Colonial Spanish Pensacola*, edited by Judith A. Bense, pp. 393–402. University Press of Florida, Gainesville.

Henderson, Kad Michael

2020   Mahogany and Iron: The Construction of the *Nuestra Señora del Rosario y Santiago Apostòl*. Master's thesis, Department of Anthropology, University of West Florida, Pensacola.

Higginbotham, Jay

1977   *Old Mobile: Fort Louis de la Louisiane, 1702–1711*. University of Alabama Press, Tuscaloosa.

Holmes, April A.

2012   Demographic Patterns at Presidios Santa María de Galve and Isla de Santa Rosa (1698–1752): An Analysis of Historical Documents and Personal Adornment Artifacts. Master's thesis, Department of Anthropology, University of West Florida, Pensacola.

Holmes, Jack D. L.

1967   Dauphin Island's Critical Years: 1701–1722. *Alabama Historical Quarterly* 29(182): 39–63.

Holmes, Jack D. L. (editor)

1968   *José de Evia y sus reconocimientos del Golfo de México, 1783–1796*. Colección Chimalistac No. 26. José Porrua Turanzas, Madrid, Spain.

Howard, Clinton L.

1941   Colonial Pensacola: The British Period Part III: The Administration of Governor Chester, 1770–1781. *The Florida Historical Quarterly* 19(4):368–401.

Hunter, James W., III

2001   A Broken Lifeline of Commerce, Trade and Defense on the Colonial Frontier: Historical Archaeology of the Santa Rosa Island Wreck, an Early Eighteenth-Century Spanish Shipwreck in Pensacola Bay, Florida. Master's thesis, Department of History, University of West Florida, Pensacola.

Hunter, James W., III, John R. Bratten, and J. Cozzi

2000   *Underwater Field Investigations 1999: The Santa Rosa Island and Hamilton Ship-wrecks.* Report of Investigations No. 81. Archaeology Institute, University of West Florida, Pensacola.

Hurst, Christopher A.

2005   Sinker Cypress: Treasures of a Lost Landscape. Master's thesis, Department of Geography and Anthropology, Louisiana State University and Agricultural and Mechanical College, Baton Rouge.

Johnson, Patrick Lee

2012   Apalachee Agency on the Gulf Coast Frontier. Master's thesis, Department of Anthropology, University of West Florida, Pensacola.

2013   Apalachee Identity on the Gulf Coast Frontier. *Native South* 6:110–141.

2018   Vengeance with Mercy: Changing Traditions and Traditional Practices of Colonial Yamasees. PhD dissertation, Department of Anthropology, The College of William & Mary, Williamsburg, Virginia.

Johnson, Sandra L.

1992   Archaeological Field Notes, University of West Florida Archaeological Excavations, September 1992. Manuscript on file, Archaeology Institute, University of West Florida, Pensacola.

1999   Pensacola and Franco-Spanish Trade and Interaction on the Northern Gulf. Master's thesis, Department of History, University of West Florida, Pensacola.

2003   External Connections. In *Presidio Santa María de Galve: A Struggle for Survival in Colonial Spanish Pensacola*, edited by Judith A. Bense, pp. 315–340. University Press of Florida, Gainesville.

Joy, Deborah

1988   *Archaeological Investigations behind Old City Hall, Pensacola, FL.* Report of Investigations No. 14. Office of Cultural and Archaeological Research, University of West Florida, Pensacola.

1989a   *The Colonial Archaeological Trail in Pensacola, Florida: Phase I.* Report of Investigations No. 27. Institute of West Florida Archaeology, University of West Florida, Pensacola.

1989b   *Excavations under Old Christ Church in Pensacola, Florida.* Report of Investigations No. 25. Institute of Archaeology, University of West Florida, Pensacola.

Katzew, Ilona

1996   *New World Orders: Casta Painting and Colonial Latin America.* Americas Society Art Gallery, New York.

Kuethe, Allan J., and Kenneth J. Andrien

2014   *The Spanish Atlantic World in the Eighteenth Century: War and the Bourbon Reforms, 1713–1796.* Cambridge University Press, New York.

Leonard, Irving A.

1936   The Spanish Re-Exploration of the Gulf Coast in 1686. *The Mississippi Valley Historical Review* 22(4):547–557.

1939   *Spanish Approach to Pensacola, 1689–1693.* Quivira Society, Albuquerque, New Mexico.

Lightfoot, Kent G.

2019   Commentary: Frontier Forts—Colonialism and the Construction of Dynamic Identities in North America. *Historical Archaeology* 53(1):170–180. DOI:10.1007/s41636-019-00165-z, accessed October 18, 2019.

Little, Keith J., Ashley A. Dumas, Hunter B. Johnson, and Travis Rael

2020   A Refinement of Post-Contact Choctaw Ceramic Chronology. *Southeastern Archaeology* 39(4):235–258.

Little, Keith J., Hunter B. Johnson, Travis Rael, Katherine Wright, and J. Rocco de Gregory

2016   *Archaeological Excavations along Chickasawhay Creek, Kemper County, Mississippi,* Vol. I. Special Investigation 6. Tennessee Valley Archaeological Research, Huntsville, Alabama.

Long, George A.

1976   *Archaeological Study for the Pensacola Shoreline Drive.* Miscellaneous Project Report Series No. 36. Division of Archives, History, and Records Management, Bureau of Historic Sites and Properties, Florida Department of State, Tallahassee.

Lorenzini, Michele, and Karlis Karklins

2000–2001 Man-in-the-Moon Beads. *Beads* 12/13:39–47.

Lyon, Eugene

1976   *The Enterprise of Florida: Pedro Menéndez de Avilés and the Spanish Conquest of 1565–1568.* University Presses of Florida, Gainesville.

1996   Settlement and Survival. In *The New History of Florida*, edited by Michael Gannon, pp. 40–61. University Press of Florida, Gainesville.

Manucy, Albert

1959   The Founding of Pensacola: Reasons and Reality. *The Florida Historical Quarterly* 37(3/4):223–241.

1992   *The Houses of St. Augustine, 1565–1821.* University Press of Florida, Gainesville.

Mays, Dorothy A.

2008   Pensacola during the War of the Quadruple Alliance. In *The Encyclopedia of North American Colonial Conflicts to 1775: A Political, Social, and Military History*, Vol. II, edited by Spencer C. Tucker, James R. Arnold, and Roberta Wiener, pp. 602–603. ABC-CLIO, Santa Barbara, California.

McEwan, Bonnie G. (editor)

1993   *The Spanish Missions of La Florida.* University Press of Florida, Gainesville.

McEwan, Bonnie G, and Gregory A. Waselkov

2003   Colonial Origins: The Archaeology of Colonialism in the Americas. *Historical Archaeology* 37(4):1–2.

McGrath, John T.

2000   *The French in Early Florida: In the Eye of the Hurricane.* University Press of Florida, Gainesville.

McKay, Derek, and Hamish M. Scott

1983   *The Rise of the Great Powers, 1648–1815.* Longman, London.

McMahon, Patricia L.

2017   A Study of the First Spanish Occupation of the Old Christ Church Site (8ES49B) in

Downtown Pensacola, Florida. Master's thesis, Department of Anthropology, University of West Florida, Pensacola.

Melcher, Jennifer A.

2008   Colon Ware, Colono-ware, Colonoware, Colono Where. Paper presented at the 66th Annual Meeting of the Southeastern Archaeological Conference, Mobile, Alabama.

2011   More Than Just Copies: Colono Ware as a Reflection of Multi-Ethnic Interaction on the 18th-Century Spanish Frontier of West Florida. Master's thesis, Department of Anthropology, University of West Florida, Pensacola.

2015   2007 Investigations at the Lee House Lot (8ES115). Manuscript on file, Archaeology Institute, University of West Florida, Pensacola.

Milanich, Jerald T.

1999   *Laboring in the Fields of the Lord: Spanish Missions and the Southeastern Indians.* Smithsonian Institution Press, Washington, DC.

Moussette, Marcel

2003   An Encounter in the Baroque Age: French and Amerindians in North America. *Historical Archaeology* 37(4):29–39.

Neilsen, Jerry, Neil Robinson, and Ernie Seckinger

1992   *Archaeological Investigations of Underground Electrical Utilities and Fort San Carlos de Austria, Site 8ES1354 Naval Air Station, Pensacola, Florida.* Report prepared by the U.S. Army Corps of Engineers, Mobile District, Mobile, Alabama.

Panama City News Herald (PCNH)

1965   Artifacts Tell of 1st Colonies. 20 July. Panama City, Florida.

Parker, Catherine B.

2003   Zooarchaeological Remains. In *Presidio Santa María de Galve: A Struggle for Survival in Colonial Spanish Pensacola,* edited by Judith A. Bense, pp. 210–228. University Press of Florida, Gainesville.

2006   Faunal Analysis. In *Presidio Isla de Santa Rosa Archaeological Investigations 2002–2004,* pp. 198–212. Report of Investigations No. 133. Archaeology Institute, University of West Florida, Pensacola.

Pigott, Michelle M.

2015   The Apalachee after San Luis: Exploring Cultural Hybridization through Ceramic Practice. Master's thesis, Department of Anthropology, University of West Florida, Pensacola.

Pokrant, Marie E.

2001   The Santa María Village: Archaeology and History at First Pensacola, 1698–1719. Master's thesis, Department of History, University of West Florida, Pensacola.

Priestley, Herbert Ingram (editor and translator)

1928   *The Luna Papers: Documents Relating to the Expedition of Don Tristán de Luna y Arellano for the Conquest of La Florida in 1559–1561.* 2 vols. Florida State Historical Society, Deland.

Quinn, David Beers (editor)

1979   *New American World: A Documentary History of North America to 1612,* Vol. II. Arno Press, New York.

Renacker, George M.

2001   A Study of Military Architecture at Fort San Carlos de Austria at Santa María de Galve. Master's thesis, Department of History, University of West Florida, Pensacola.

Roberts, Amanda D.

2009   Secret Exchange: Alternative Economies of Presidios Santa María de Galve and Isla de Santa Rosa. Master's thesis, Department of Anthropology, University of West Florida, Pensacola.

Ruhl, Donna L.

2003   Archaeobotanical Remains. In *Presidio Santa María de Galve: A Struggle for Survival in Colonial Spanish Pensacola*, edited by Judith A. Bense, pp. 229–256. University Press of Florida, Gainesville.

Saccente, Julie H. Rogers

2013   Archaeology of the Early Eighteenth-Century Spanish Fort San José, Northwest Florida. Master's thesis, Department of Anthropology, University of South Florida, Tampa.

Saccente, Julie Rogers, and Nancy Marie White

2015   Fort San José, a Remote Spanish Outpost in Northwest Florida, 1700–1721. In *Archaeology of Culture Contact and Colonialism in Spanish and Portuguese America*, edited by Pedro Paulo A. Funari and Maria Ximena Senatore, pp. 297–311. Springer International Publishing, Cham, Switzerland.

Sappington, Ericha E.

2018   Facilitating Trade on the Florida Frontier: An Historical and Archaeological Analysis of Fort San Marcos de Apalachee, 1639–1821. Master's thesis, Department of Anthropology, University of West Florida, Pensacola.

Saunders, Rebecca

1996   Mission-Period Settlement Structure: A Test of the Model at San Martín de Timucua. *Historical Archaeology* 30(4):22–36.

Scarry, John F., and Bonnie G. McEwan

1995   Domestic Architecture in Apalachee Province: Apalachee and Spanish Residential Styles in the Late Prehistoric and Early Historic Period Southeast. *American Antiquity* 60(3):482–495.

Shaeffer, James B.

1971   *Historic District Archaeological Survey*. Historic Pensacola Preservation Board, Pensacola, Florida.

Shapiro, Gary, and Richard Vernon

1992   Archaeology at San Luis Part Two: The Church Complex. *Florida Archaeology* 6:177–277.

Shorter, George W., Jr.

2002   Status and Trade at Port Dauphin. *Historical Archaeology* 36(1):135–142.

Sims, Cynthia L. Smith

2001   Searching for Women at the Presidio Santa María de Galve: A New Approach to Examining Women through Material Culture and History. Master's thesis, Department of History, University of West Florida, Pensacola.

Sirmans, M. Eugene

2013   *Colonial South Carolina: A Political History, 1663–1763*. University of North Carolina Press, Chapel Hill.

Skowronek, Russell K.

2002   Global Economics in the Creation and Maintenance of the Spanish Colonial Empire. In *Social Dimensions in the Economic Process*, edited by Norbert Dannhaeuser and Cynthia Werner, pp. 295–310. JAI, Boston.

Smith, Hale G.

1948a   Two Historical Archaeological Periods in Florida. *American Antiquity* 13(4):313–319.

1948b   Results of an Archaeological Investigation of a Spanish Mission Site in Jefferson County, Florida. *Florida Anthropologist* 1:1–10.

1949   *Two Archaeological Sites in Brevard County, Florida.* Florida Anthropological Society Publications No. 1. University of Florida, Gainesville.

1965   *Archaeological Excavations at Santa Rosa, Pensacola.* Notes in Anthropology Vol. 10. Florida State University, Tallahassee.

1972   Historic Figurines from Florida and Mexico. *Historical Archaeology* 6(1):47–56.

1994   Ventures into the Unknown. In *Pioneers in Historical Archaeology: Breaking New Ground*, edited by Stanley South, pp. 79–84. Springer, Boston.

Smith, Marvin T.

2002   Eighteenth-Century Glass Beads in the French Colonial Trade. *Historical Archaeology* 36(1):55–61.

Smith, Roger C. (editor)

2018   *Florida's Lost Galleon: The Emanuel Point Shipwreck.* University Press of Florida, Gainesville.

South, Stanley A.

1977   *Method and Theory in Historical Archaeology.* Academic Press, New York.

Spirek, James D., Della A. Scott, Michael Williamson, Charles Hughson, and Roger C. Smith

1993   *Submerged Cultural Resources of Pensacola Bay.* Florida Bureau of Archaeological Research, Division of Historical Resources, Florida Department of State, Tallahassee.

St-Onge, Nicole, Carolyn Podruchny, and Brenda Macdougall

2012   *Contours of a People: Metis Family, Mobility, and History.* University of Oklahoma Press, Norman.

Stojanowski, Christopher Michael

2005   Biological Structure of the San Pedro y San Pablo de Patale Mission Cemetery. *Southeastern Archaeology* 24(2):165–179.

Stone, Lyle M.

1974   *Fort Michilimackinac, 1715–1781: An Archaeological Perspective on the Revolutionary Frontier.* Anthropological Series Vol. 2. Michigan State University, East Lansing.

Stringfield, Margo S., and Elizabeth D. Benchley

1997   *Archaeological Testing of the Old Christ Church Restoration Project.* Report of Investigations No. 61. Archaeology Institute, University of West Florida, Pensacola.

Sutton, Leora M.

1964   *Amateur Archaeologist Exploratory Probe of the Panton Leslie Trading Post Site.* Report to Board of County Commissioners, Escambia County, Pensacola Historical Society, Pensacola, Florida.

1976   *Archaeological Investigations, Block Three and Eleven, Old City Plat of Pensacola.* Report to Board of County Commissioners, Escambia County, Pensacola Historical Society, Pensacola, Florida.

Swann, Brenda N.

2000   Supplies at Presidio Santa María de Galve (1698–1712): A Study of the Historical and Archaeological Records. Master's thesis, Department of History, University of West Florida, Pensacola.

Tesar, Louis D.

1973   *Archaeological Survey and Testing of Gulf Islands National Seashore, Part I: Florida.* Edited by Hale G. Smith. Department of Anthropology, Florida State University, Tallahassee.

Thompson, Amanda D. Roberts

2012   Evaluating Spanish Colonial Alternative Economies in the Archaeological Record. *Historical Archaeology* 46(4):48–69.

US Department of Agriculture (USDA)

2018   NAIP digital ortho photo image of Santa Rosa Island. USDA-FSA-APFO Aerial Photography Field Office, Salt Lake City, Utah.

US Geological Survey (USGS)

2016   2004 aerial photo of a new breach across Santa Rosa Island formed by Hurricane Ivan. Electronic document, https://archive.usgs.gov/archive/sites/coastal.er.usgs.gov/hurricanes/ivan/photos/florida.html, accessed May 6, 2020.

Voss, Jerome A., and John H. Blitz

1988   Archaeological Investigations in the Choctaw Homeland. *American Antiquity* 53(1):125–145.

Walthall, John A.

1991   Faience in French Colonial Illinois. *Historical Archaeology* 25(1):80–105.

Wampler, Morgan H.

2012   The Social Identity of the Crew Aboard the *Nuestra Señora Rosario del Santiago y Apóstol.* Master's thesis, Department of Anthropology, University of West Florida, Pensacola.

Ware, John D.

1982   *George Gauld, Surveyor and Cartographer of the Gulf Coast.* Revised and completed by Robert R. Rea. University Presses of Florida, Gainesville.

Waselkov, Gregory A.

1991   *Archaeology at the French Colonial Site of Old Mobile (Phase 1: 1989–1991).* Anthropological Monograph 1. University of South Alabama, Mobile.

1994   Apalachee Indians and the French at Old Mobile. *Old Mobile Project Newsletter* 11:2.

1999   *Old Mobile Archaeology.* Center for Archaeology Studies, University of South Alabama, Mobile.

2002   French Colonial Archaeology at Old Mobile: An Introduction. *Historical Archaeology* 36(1):3–12.

Waselkov, Gregory A., and Bonnie L. Gums

2000   *Plantation Archaeology at Rivière aux Chiens, ca. 1725–1848.* Archaeological Monograph 7. Center for Archaeological Studies, University of South Alabama, Mobile.

Waselkov, Gregory A., and John A. Walthall

2002   Faience Styles in French Colonial North America: A Revised Classification. *Historical Archaeology* 36(1):62–78.

Weber, David J.

1992   *The Spanish Frontier in North America.* Yale University Press, New Haven, Connecticut.

Weddle, Robert S.

1968   *San Juan Bautista: Gateway to Spanish Texas.* University of Texas Press, Austin.

1985   *Spanish Sea: The Gulf of Mexico in North American Discovery, 1500–1685.* Texas A&M University Press, College Station.

1991   *The French Thorn: Rival Explorers in the Spanish Sea, 1682–1792.* Texas A&M University Press, College Station.

2002   Kingdoms Face to Face: French Mobile and Spanish Pensacola, 1699–1719. *Alabama Review* 55(2):84–95.

Weir, Robert M.

1983   *South Carolina: A History.* KTO Press, Millwood, New York.

Wilkie, Laurie A.

2019   At Freedom's Borderland: The Black Regulars and Masculinity at Fort Davis, Texas. *Historical Archaeology* 53(1):126–137. DOI:10.1007/s41636-019-00161-3, accessed October 18, 2019.

Williams, Carrie A.

2004   Land Use at the Site of Old Christ Church Pensacola, Florida. Master's thesis, Department of History, University of West Florida, Pensacola.

Williams, Jack S.

2004   The Evolution of the Presidio in Northern New Spain. *Historical Archaeology* 38(3):6–23.

Wilson, Harry J.

2000   Archaeological Site Transformation Processes and the Spanish Presidio Santa María de Galve (1698–1998). Master's thesis, Department of History, University of West Florida, Pensacola.

Worth, John E.

1998   *The Timucuan Chiefdoms of Spanish Florida, Vol. I: Assimilation.* University Press of Florida, Gainesville.

2008   Rediscovering Pensacola's Lost Spanish Missions. Paper presented at the 65th Annual Meeting of the Southeastern Archaeological Conference, Charlotte, North Carolina.

2012   Bridging History and Prehistory: General Reflections and Particular Quandaries. Paper presented at the 69th Annual Meeting of the Southeastern Archaeological Conference, Baton Rouge, Louisiana.

2013   From Island to Mainland: The Spanish Transfer from Presidio Santa Rosa to San Miguel de Panzacola. Paper presented at the 65th Annual Meeting of the Florida Anthropological Society, St. Augustine, Florida.

2015   Shifting Landscapes of Practice in the Eastern Gulf Coastal Plain during the Colonial Era. Paper presented at the 72nd Annual Meeting of the Southeastern Archaeological Conference, Nashville, Tennessee.

2017   What's in a Phase?: Disentangling Communities of Practice from Communities of Identity in Southeastern North America. In *Forging Southeastern Identities: Social Archaeology, Ethnohistory, and Folklore of the Mississippian to Early Historic South*, edited by Gregory A. Waselkov and Marvin T. Smith, pp. 117–156. University of Alabama Press, Tuscaloosa.

2018a   Archaeological and Documentary Insights into the Native World of the Luna Expedition. Paper presented at the 75th Annual Meeting of the Southeastern Archaeological Conference, Augusta, Georgia.

2018b   The Yamasee in West Florida. In *The Yamasee Indians: From Florida to South Carolina*, edited by Denise I. Bossy, pp. 309–338. University of Nebraska Press, Lincoln.

2018c   Linking Archaeological and Documentary Evidence for Material Culture in Mid-

Sixteenth-Century Spanish Florida: The View from the Luna Settlement and Fleet. Paper presented at the 51st Annual Conference of the Society for Historical Archaeology, New Orleans, Louisiana.

Worth, John E., Elizabeth D. Benchley, Janet R. Lloyd, and Jennifer A. Melcher

2019   The Discovery and Exploration of Tristán de Luna y Arellano's 1559–1561 Settlement on Pensacola Bay. *Historical Archaeology* 54(2):453–471.

Worth, John E., Norma J. Harris, and Jennifer Melcher

2011   San Joseph de Escambe: An 18th-Century Apalachee Mission in the West Florida Borderlands. Paper presented at the 44th Annual Conference of the Society for Historical Archaeology, Austin, Texas.

Worth, John E., Norma J. Harris, Jennifer Melcher, and Danielle Dadiego

2012   Exploring Mission Life in 18th-Century West Florida: 2011 Excavations at San Joseph de Escambe. Paper presented at the 45th Annual Conference of the Society for Historical Archaeology, Baltimore, Maryland.

Worth, John E., and Jennifer Melcher

2015   Revised Typology for Historic Period Native American Ceramics in Northwest Florida. Manuscript on file, Archaeology Institute, University of West Florida, Pensacola.

Worth, John E., Jennifer Melcher, Danielle Dadiego, and Michelle Pigott

2015   Archaeological Investigations at Mission San Joseph de Escambe 2009–2012. Manuscript on file, Archaeology Institute, University of West Florida, Pensacola.

Index

Page numbers in italics refer to illustrations.

Presidio Isla de Santa Rosa, 134, 136, 137, 143, 167, 171, 178, 179, 182, 188, 242, 265, 275, 280, 287, 289, 290, 291, 293; in 1741, at Presidio Isla de Santa Rosa, 137; in 1742, at Presidio Isla de Santa Rosa, 190; in 1751, at Presidio Isla de Santa Rosa, 135, 137; in 1752, at Presidio Isla de Santa Rosa, 15, 134, 135, 137, 169, 182, 190, 210, 242, 270, 278, 289, 291, 293; in 1754, at Presidio Isla de Santa Rosa, 191; in 1760, at Fort San Miguel/Presidio San Miguel de Panzacola, 202, 222, 281, 283, 284; in 2004, at Presidio Isla de Santa Rosa, 138; definitions of, 136; unspecified date, at Mission San Joseph de Escambe, 272; unspecified date, at Presidio Isla de Santa Rosa, 180, 181, 182; unspecified date, on Santa Rosa Island, 283

Indian Town. *See* Mission San Antonio de Punta Rasa II
Indian War, 149, 249, 267
Industry: and 1761 Indian War, 267; brick and tile production, 161, 182, 188, 190, 192, 267, 275, 277, 293–94, 317; ceramics manufacture, 276–77; fishing, 139, 192; lime production, 192, 267, 275, 277, 294, 317; logging, 22, 49, 52, 53, 57, 96, 97, 275, 276, 293. *See also* Ranching

Jacksonville, FL, 6
Jamestown, VA, 6, 326
Jesuits. *See under* Catholics
Johnson, Patrick Lee, 145, 146–47, 148–49
Johnson, Sandra, 25, 116
Joseph de la Cruiz Cui Native American refugee settlement, 142
Joy, Deborah, 198, 202

Keel, Bennie C., 321

La Belle (ship), 90
La Florida, 21, 330
La Maire, Father, 90, 92, 105, 319
Landeche, Andrés de, 49, 50, 52
La Rochelle, France, 299
La Salle, Réné-Robert Cavelier (Sieur de La Salle), 9, 18, 90, 116
Laws of the Indies, 8
Lazarus, William, 150
Le Moyne, Antoine (Sieur de Châteaugué), 105
Le Moyne, Jean-Baptist (Sieur de Bienville): and

1719 attack on Presidio Santa María de Galve, 107, 109; and British blockade of Port Dauphin, 55; family of, 22, 105, 107, 108; and Fort Crèvocoeur, 105, 106; and Louisiana colony, 22; on Native refugees in Mobile Bay, 35
Le Moyne, Pierre (Sieur d'Iberville), 22
Little, Keith, 217
Lloyd, Jan, 150
Los Tobases village, 12, *13,* 144, 261, *266,* 267
Louisiana, 8, 9, 18, 22, 105, 107, 142
Louis XIV, king of France, 24, 27
Louis XV, king of France, 299, 300
Low Countries/Holland, 24, 106–7
Lower Creek Indians: as British allies, 10, 54; and British provinces, 144; and ceramics, 158, 309, 312; and Creek Indians, 23; locations of, 10, 23, 143, 144, 261; and Panzacola Indians, 23; and repopulation of Apalachee Province, 54; as Spanish allies, 10; and trade, 100, 144. *See also* Creek Indians; Native peoples
Lowery, Woodbury, xviii
Luna y Arellano, Tristán de, 3, 20

Maldonado, Francisco, xvii
Manucy, Albert, 27
Marmes rock shelter, 321
Matamoros de Ysla, Juan Pedro, 62, 99, 100, 106, 107, 108, 109
McEwan, Bonnie, 324, 325
McMahon, Patricia, 228, 230
Melcher, Jennifer, 147, 233, 312, 313
Menendez, Pedro de Avilés, 7
Mestizaje: categories of, 327; and culture, 330; definition of, 9, 10, 326, 327; and mestizos, 327; and mulattos, 327; from New Spain, 327; population of, 253; protection of, 10; and socioeconomic status, 10, 117, 327, 331; supplies for, 10; women as, 327
Métis, 326
Mexico: Apalachee and Yamasee refugees in, 233; British and, 22; ceramics production in, 80, 217; colonial administration in, 190–91; historical documentation in, xviii; home shrines and altars in, 217; and shipping routes, 8; viceroys of, 106
Mexico City, Mexico: Apalachee leaders in, 99; conscripts and convicts from, 38, 117, 140; and culture, 328; map of, *6;* minting in, 48, 70, 104, 115, 162, 299; settlers from, 10, 251, 315; soldiers from, 33, 38, 140

372 · Index

Presidio San Miguel de Panzacola, population at: administrators, 243; children, 184, 243, 254, 255, 257; civilians, 184, 185, 236, 243, 249, 254–55, 279; convicts and forced laborers, 185, 191, 192, 243, 254; craftsmen, 243; density of, 243; families, 135, 185, 191, 192, 249, 257, 258; figures for, 254–55, 257; merchants, 305; Native persons, 184, 230, 243, 255, 267; officers, 192, 243, 279; origins of, 135, 184, 185, 243, 282; servants, 243; soldiers, 135, 185, 191, 243, 249, 254, 279; Spanish, 243; support staff, 243; women, 184, 191, 243, 254, 255, 256–57. *See also* Fort San Miguel: population at

Presidio San Miguel de Panzacola, structures at: 1761 clearing of, 227, 228, 230, 233, 241; 1767 demolition of, 197, 198, 223; construction of, 237, 240–41, 244, 245–47, 282, 283, 296; dating of, 230, 241; fences, 281; historical documentation on, 222, 223, 243, 276, 277, 278, 279, 280, 282; layout of, 282–83; maps of, 223, 225, 226, 227, 231, 233, 236; materials for, 222, 243, 244, 245, 276, 277, 280–81, 282, 287, 291–92, 293, 294; military housing, 222; number of, 198, 282; occupation of, 244; outbuildings, 206, 237, 244, 282–83; ovens, 277, 282; pier, *194*; residences, *195*, 222, 227, 243–44, 278, 279, 280–81; Ricardos compound, 223–25; and socioeconomic status, 222, 226, 236–37, 245; stockade, 198; storehouses, *206*, 283; unidentified/unspecified, 227–30; warehouses, 287–88. *See also* Fort San Miguel, structures at

Presidio Santa María de Galve: 1707–1715 sieges/attacks on, 39, 53, 54–56, 57, 80, 84, 92, 96–97, 118, 283, 290, 296; 1719 attacks on/destruction of, 10, 15, 64, 87, 98, 107, 108–10, 120, 128, 257, 263–64, 278, 296; 1719 recapture of, 255; 1722 destruction of remains of, 131; agriculture and husbandry at, 23, 27; attacks of unspecified dates on, 23; bureaucratic oversight of, 8; as capital of Louisiana, 107; dates of, 11, 39, 260; diagrams and illustrations of, *28, 46;* diet at, 48, 80, 102, 120; diseases and epidemics at, 33, 254; establishment of, 4, 8, 22, 29, 33, 117; evacuations from, 10, 33, 98, 254, 257; fires at, 38, 49, 53, 54, 87, 118, 275, 286, 287, 288, 290; as French outpost, 12, *14,* 15, 98, 109, *263;* historical documentation on, 29, 37, 48–49, 100, 141, 252, 278; hurricanes at, 38, 49, 54; leaders of, 25, 40, 56, 106; location of, 8, 10, 15, 22, 27–28, 54, 128, 187, 260, 262, 324; logging

at, 97; maps of, *13, 14, 19,* 27, 29, *30, 32,* 39–43, 45, 87, 101, *263,* 275, 278, 282, 288; as maritime province, 80; and mission villages, 260, 262, 263; operating rules for, 8; as protected government property, 188; purposes of, 8; scholarship on, 25, 27, 48–49, 185; shipping lane near, 120; and socioeconomic status, 101; and Spanish outposts, 260, 262, 272, 273; Spanish prisoners of war from, 121; and trade, 23, 24–25, 56–57, 80, 96, 109, 116, 118; village area of, 39–41, 53, 54, 100–105, 110, 117, 118; and Yamasee War, 97–98. *See also* Fort San Carlos de Austria

Presidio Santa María de Galve, archaeology at: of cemetery, *28,* 29, 43, *46,* 101, 118, 298; funding of, 29; historical documentation informing, 40–41; identifying location for, 27–28, 29; maps and diagrams of, *46, 47;* of village area, 29, 43–49, 54, 67, 68, 100–105, 110, 113, 114, 115, 118, 278, 279. *See also* Fort San Carlos de Austria, archaeology at

Presidio Santa María de Galve, artifacts from: activity-related, 103, 111, 114, 297; arms, 103, 111, 114, 116; building and architecture, 102, 103, 104, 110, 111, 113–14, 226, 280, 297; ceramics, 45–48, 67–69, 102, 103, 104, 105, 110–13, 115, 116, 302, 304, 305–8, 309, 310, 311, 312, 313, 314, 330; clothing, 48, 103, 111, 115, 297, 301; distribution of, 101, 115; and ethnicity, 115; faunal, 48, 69, 70, 102, 103, 105, 111, 113, 115; French, 116; furniture, 70, 103, 111, 115, 297; and gender, 115; glass, 44, 69, 70, 102, 103, 104, 111, 113, 114, 115, 116, 299, 319; human remains, 43; kitchen-related, 48, 69, 102, 103, 104, 111, 113–14, 297; metal, 43, *44,* 48, 70, 103, 104, 111, 113, 115, 116, 298, 300, 319; numbers/weights of, 45–48, 67–69, 70, 102, 103, 104, 105, 110–14, 115, 294, 295, 296, 297, 310, 318; personal items, 44, 48, 70, 103, 104, 111, 113, 114–15, 297, 298, 300, 319; plant, 48, 69, 103, 111; and socioeconomic status, 48, 69–70, 101, 112, 113, 115; stone, 44, 70, 103, 111, 114, 115, 298; tobacco-related, 70, 103, 111, 115, 116, 297. *See also* Fort San Carlos de Austria, artifacts from

Presidio Santa María de Galve, population at: Apalachee Indians, 38, 45, 53, 100, 117, 142, 146, 258, 312; carpenters and woodworkers, 36; Chacato Indians, 45, 53, 117, 258; children, 33, 35, 37–38, 48, 53; civilians, 48; convicts, 23, 33, 34, 36, 38, 54, 55, 117; craftspeople, 33,

JUDITH A. BENSE is professor of anthropology/archaeology and president emerita of the University of West Florida in Pensacola, Florida. She is the editor and lead contributor of two research books, the *Archaeology of Colonial Pensacola* and *Presidio Santa María de Galve*. She is also the author of *Archaeology of the Southeastern United States: PaleoIndian to World War I*.

Ripley P. Bullen Series

FLORIDA MUSEUM OF NATURAL HISTORY

Tacachale: Essays on the Indians of Florida and Southeastern Georgia during the Historic Period, edited by Jerald T. Milanich and Samuel Proctor (1978)

Aboriginal Subsistence Technology on the Southeastern Coastal Plain during the Late Prehistoric Period, by Lewis H. Larson (1980)

Cemochechobee: Archaeology of a Mississippian Ceremonial Center on the Chattahoochee River, by Frank T. Schnell, Vernon J. Knight Jr., and Gail S. Schnell (1981)

Fort Center: An Archaeological Site in the Lake Okeechobee Basin, by William H. Sears, with contributions by Elsie O'R. Sears and Karl T. Steinen (1982)

Perspectives on Gulf Coast Prehistory, edited by Dave D. Davis (1984)

Archaeology of Aboriginal Culture Change in the Interior Southeast: Depopulation during the Early Historic Period, by Marvin T. Smith (1987)

Apalachee: The Land between the Rivers, by John H. Hann (1988)

Key Marco's Buried Treasure: Archaeology and Adventure in the Nineteenth Century, by Marion Spjut Gilliland (1989)

First Encounters: Spanish Explorations in the Caribbean and the United States, 1492–1570, edited by Jerald T. Milanich and Susan Milbrath (1989)

Missions to the Calusa, edited and translated by John H. Hann, with an introduction by William H. Marquardt (1991)

Excavations on the Franciscan Frontier: Archaeology at the Fig Springs Mission, by Brent Richards Weisman (1992)

The People Who Discovered Columbus: The Prehistory of the Bahamas, by William F. Keegan (1992)

Hernando de Soto and the Indians of Florida, by Jerald T. Milanich and Charles Hudson (1992)

Foraging and Farming in the Eastern Woodlands, edited by C. Margaret Scarry (1993)

Puerto Real: The Archaeology of a Sixteenth-Century Spanish Town in Hispaniola, edited by Kathleen Deagan (1995)

Political Structure and Change in the Prehistoric Southeastern United States, edited by John F. Scarry (1996)

Bioarchaeology of Native American Adaptation in the Spanish Borderlands, edited by Brenda J. Baker and Lisa Kealhofer (1996)

A History of the Timucua Indians and Missions, by John H. Hann (1996)

Archaeology of the Mid-Holocene Southeast, edited by Kenneth E. Sassaman and David G. Anderson (1996)

The Indigenous People of the Caribbean, edited by Samuel M. Wilson (1997; first paperback edition, 1999)

Hernando de Soto among the Apalachee: The Archaeology of the First Winter Encampment, by Charles R. Ewen and John H. Hann (1998)

The Timucuan Chiefdoms of Spanish Florida, by John E. Worth: vol. 1, *Assimilation*; vol. 2, *Resistance and Destruction* (1998; first paperback edition, 2020)

Ancient Earthen Enclosures of the Eastern Woodlands, edited by Robert C. Mainfort Jr. and Lynne P. Sullivan (1998)

An Environmental History of Northeast Florida, by James J. Miller (1998)

Precolumbian Architecture in Eastern North America, by William N. Morgan (1999)

Archaeology of Colonial Pensacola, edited by Judith A. Bense (1999)

Grit-Tempered: Early Women Archaeologists in the Southeastern United States, edited by Nancy Marie White, Lynne P. Sullivan, and Rochelle A. Marrinan (1999; first paperback edition, 2001)

Coosa: The Rise and Fall of a Southeastern Mississippian Chiefdom, by Marvin T. Smith (2000)

Religion, Power, and Politics in Colonial St. Augustine, by Robert L. Kapitzke (2001)

Bioarchaeology of Spanish Florida: The Impact of Colonialism, edited by Clark Spencer Larsen (2001)

Archaeological Studies of Gender in the Southeastern United States, edited by Jane M. Eastman and Christopher B. Rodning (2001)

The Archaeology of Traditions: Agency and History Before and After Columbus, edited by Timothy R. Pauketat (2001)

Foraging, Farming, and Coastal Biocultural Adaptation in Late Prehistoric North Carolina, by Dale L. Hutchinson (2002)

Windover: Multidisciplinary Investigations of an Early Archaic Florida Cemetery, edited by Glen H. Doran (2002)

Archaeology of the Everglades, by John W. Griffin (2002; first paperback edition, 2017)

Pioneer in Space and Time: John Mann Goggin and the Development of Florida Archaeology, by Brent Richards Weisman (2002)

Indians of Central and South Florida, 1513–1763, by John H. Hann (2003)

Presidio Santa María de Galve: A Struggle for Survival in Colonial Spanish Pensacola, edited by Judith A. Bense (2003)

Bioarchaeology of the Florida Gulf Coast: Adaptation, Conflict, and Change, by Dale L. Hutchinson (2004; first paperback edition, 2020)

The Myth of Syphilis: The Natural History of Treponematosis in North America, edited by Mary Lucas Powell and Della Collins Cook (2005)

The Florida Journals of Frank Hamilton Cushing, edited by Phyllis E. Kolianos and Brent R. Weisman (2005)

The Lost Florida Manuscript of Frank Hamilton Cushing, edited by Phyllis E. Kolianos and Brent R. Weisman (2005)

The Native American World Beyond Apalachee: West Florida and the Chattahoochee Valley, by John H. Hann (2006)

Tatham Mound and the Bioarchaeology of European Contact: Disease and Depopulation in Central Gulf Coast Florida, by Dale L. Hutchinson (2007)

Taíno Indian Myth and Practice: The Arrival of the Stranger King, by William F. Keegan (2007)

An Archaeology of Black Markets: Local Ceramics and Economies in Eighteenth-Century Jamaica, by Mark W. Hauser (2008; first paperback edition, 2013)

Mississippian Mortuary Practices: Beyond Hierarchy and the Representationist Perspective, edited by Lynne P. Sullivan and Robert C. Mainfort Jr. (2010; first paperback edition, 2012)

Bioarchaeology of Ethnogenesis in the Colonial Southeast, by Christopher M. Stojanowski (2010; first paperback edition, 2013)

French Colonial Archaeology in the Southeast and Caribbean, edited by Kenneth G. Kelly and Meredith D. Hardy (2011; first paperback edition, 2015)

Late Prehistoric Florida: Archaeology at the Edge of the Mississippian World, edited by Keith Ashley and Nancy Marie White (2012; first paperback edition, 2015)

Early and Middle Woodland Landscapes of the Southeast, edited by Alice P. Wright and Edward R. Henry (2013; first paperback edition, 2019)

Trends and Traditions in Southeastern Zooarchaeology, edited by Tanya M. Peres (2014)

New Histories of Pre-Columbian Florida, edited by Neill J. Wallis and Asa R. Randall (2014; first paperback edition, 2016)

Discovering Florida: First-Contact Narratives from Spanish Expeditions along the Lower Gulf Coast, edited and translated by John E. Worth (2014; first paperback edition, 2016)

Constructing Histories: Archaic Freshwater Shell Mounds and Social Landscapes of the St. Johns River, Florida, by Asa R. Randall (2015)

Archaeology of Early Colonial Interaction at El Chorro de Maíta, Cuba, by Roberto Valcárcel Rojas (2016)

Fort San Juan and the Limits of Empire: Colonialism and Household Practice at the Berry Site, edited by Robin A. Beck, Christopher B. Rodning, and David G. Moore (2016)

Rethinking Moundville and Its Hinterland, edited by Vincas P. Steponaitis and C. Margaret Scarry (2016; first paperback edition, 2019)

Gathering at Silver Glen: Community and History in Late Archaic Florida, by Zackary I. Gilmore (2016)

Paleoindian Societies of the Coastal Southeast, by James S. Dunbar (2016; first paperback edition, 2019)

Cuban Archaeology in the Caribbean, edited by Ivan Roksandic (2016)

Handbook of Ceramic Animal Symbols in the Ancient Lesser Antilles, by Lawrence Waldron (2016)

Archaeologies of Slavery and Freedom in the Caribbean: Exploring the Spaces in Between, edited by Lynsey A. Bates, John M. Chenoweth, and James A. Delle (2016; first paperback edition, 2018)

Setting the Table: Ceramics, Dining, and Cultural Exchange in Andalucía and La Florida, by Kathryn L. Ness (2017)

Simplicity, Equality, and Slavery: An Archaeology of Quakerism in the British Virgin Islands, 1740–1780, by John M. Chenoweth (2017)

Fit for War: Sustenance and Order in the Mid-Eighteenth-Century Catawba Nation, by Mary Elizabeth Fitts (2017)

Water from Stone: Archaeology and Conservation at Florida's Springs, by Jason O'Donoughue (2017)

Mississippian Beginnings, edited by Gregory D. Wilson (2017; first paperback edition, 2019)

Harney Flats: A Florida Paleoindian Site, by I. Randolph Daniel Jr. and Michael Wisenbaker (2017)

Honoring Ancestors in Sacred Space: The Archaeology of an Eighteenth-Century African-Bahamian Cemetery, by Grace Turner (2017)

Investigating the Ordinary: Everyday Matters in Southeast Archaeology, edited by Sarah E. Price and Philip J. Carr (2018)